"As both a producer and a journalist, I view Michael Wiese's original *Film and Video Budgets* as an essential reference work that has long been on my bookshelf. With so much having changed in the world of production, I'm thrilled to see it updated — especially by Maureen Ryan, who brings a realistic insider's point of view to film finances and budgets."

—Scott Macaulay, editor-in-chief, *Filmmaker Magazine*; producer, Forensic Films

"The best book on film budgeting for independent film bar none. I have used this book repeatedly in my classes and I constantly recommend it. Ryan knows this world inside and out. An essential resource."

—Jon Reiss, filmmaker; author; media strategist, Hybrid Cinema

"When you're first starting out as a producer you tend to have limited budgets and will often find it necessary to be something of a one-man-band production team: equal parts coordinator, manager, line producer, post supervisor, publicist, sales rep, and of course producer. I wish Ryan's book had been available to me when I was starting out in my career, as the information in here is comprehensive, all-inclusive, and invaluable. This book is a true nuts-and-bolts guide to production and should be a part of any producer's library, regardless of experience level."

—Jacob Jaffke, producer, *In a Valley of Violence, Sleepwalk with Me*

"Ryan has a knack for making budgets easy to understand. This book simplifies and educates you on creating your most powerful funding tool."

—Carole Dean, author, *The Art of Film Funding*; creator, Roy Dean Film Grants

"What every producer has always wanted, all in one place. Accessible and comprehensive, Ryan's book walks you through each budget, and with online templates that are easy to use, *Film and Video Budgets* is an essential tool for any production."

—Chandra C. Silver, producer, Silver Lining Film Group

"Sound budgeting is the foundation on which to build any film production, regardless of size and scope. It provides a framework to explore creative decisions with a production mindset. This book breaks down the fundamental components of building a realistic budget . . . essential to the skill set of today's producer."

—Veronica Nickel, producer, *Stand Clear of the Closing Doors* and *Dead Man's Burden*

"This is it! It's one of the few books anyone working in film production should have on their desk to quickly and constantly reference. This new edition, a budgeting bible, is as concise, complete, fun, and easy-to-read as ever. It's an updated version that answers many of the doubts that come up as a consequence of this always-changing industry. Make it your own!"

—Alvaro R. Valente, independent producer

"This new edition of *Film and Video Budgets* is a must-read for every independent filmmaker. Ryan's expertise and insight provide the first-time filmmaker with a wealth of knowledge far beyond what they could expect to learn on-set. Ryan's lifelong commitment to producing creative, on-time, and under-budget films informs her budgeting and writing. Her prose style matches her producing style: nothing superfluous, highly effective, and well-informed."

—Markus Kirschner, production designer

"Maureen Ryan is responsible for every production I have ever made, thanks to her indispensable *Producer to Producer*. Like her previous work, *Film and Video Budgets* pays for itself over and over again. This business changes every day, but one thing stays the same—you need money to make movies. *Film and Video Budgets* liberates the artist to focus on her or his creativity, knowing that the biggest hurdle to successful filmmaking has already been cleared."

—Jeff Pucillo, producer/video artist, *Top of the World, Roots in Water, Repairs,* and *Closure*

"An incredibly practical resource by the finest producer I have ever worked with."

—Paul Cotter, writer/director, *Bomber*

FILM + VIDEO BUDGETS

6th Edition

Maureen A. Ryan

MICHAEL WIESE PRODUCTIONS

Published by Michael Wiese Productions
12400 Ventura Blvd. #1111
Studio City, CA 91604
(818) 379-8799, (818) 986-3408 (FAX)
mw@mwp.com
www.mwp.com

Cover design: Johnny Ink. www.johnnyink.com
Interior design and layout: William Morosi
Copyeditor: David Wright
Printed by McNaughton & Gunn

Manufactured in the United States of America

Library of Congress Cataloging-in-Publication Data
Ryan, Maureen A.
Film & video budgets / Maureen A. Ryan. — 6th updated edition.
pages cm
Includes bibliographical references and index.
ISBN 978-1-61593-221-4
1. Motion picture industry—United States—Finance. 2. Video recordings industry—United States—Finance. I. Title. II. Title: Film and video budgets.
PN1993.5.U6W4915 2015
384'.83'0973—dc23

2014040591

Printed on Recycled Stock

Dedication

For Michael Wiese — who started it all.

TABLE OF CONTENTS

ACKNOWLEDGMENTS

Many professionals contributed time and advice to make the information in this new sixth edition of *Film and Video Budgets* as accurate as possible. My thanks to all of you!

Julie Buck, Producer, Hello Please, New York, NY
Carole Dean, Film Consultant, From the Heart Productions, Oxnard, CA
David Feldman, Sales, Company 3/Deluxe, New York, NY
Andrew Hauser, Post-Production Supervisor, New York, NY
Rosemary Lombard, Line Producer/UPM, New York, NY
Geoff Quan, Producer/Line Producer, Bay Area, CA
Mike Neal, Marine Coordinator, Bull River Cruises, Savannah, GA
Stuart Macphee, Post-Production Supervisor, New York, NY
Rick Siegel, Director of Photography/Lighting Designer, New York, NY
Pierson Silver, Libra Head Operator, Silver Lining Film Group, Brooklyn, NY
Alex Steyermark, New York, NY

I would also like to thank all the people at Michael Wiese Productions who gave invaluable assistance in making this book happen — Vice President Ken Lee, copyeditor David Wright, interior designer and layout artist Bill Morosi, and cover designer John Brenner. Special thanks to Carole Dean for her constant support and encouragement — this book would not have happened without her efforts. Much thanks to the folks at The Standard Grill in NYC — the daily morning breakfast rituals sustained me during the writing of this book.

Thanks to all the cast and crews I have had the pleasure to work with over the years. You have taught me much of what is in this book. Much appreciation to the students, faculty, and staff at Columbia University's Graduate Film Program — it's a great gift to teach what I love.

And last but not least — deep gratitude to my kind and steadfast supporter and partner in life, Rick Siegel. Thank you for our life together — I'm a very lucky woman.

INTRODUCTION TO THE 6TH EDITION

The book you hold in your hands may be one of the most powerful tools you will ever encounter to help you produce your films and videos. Understanding budgets is the key to production. Without a roadmap you'll never come in on time or on budget. This book is that roadmap.

This book was first written in 1984 by Michael Wiese to supplement his first book, *The Independent Film & Videomaker's Guide*, which is devoted to the financing and distribution of films and videos. In 1995, Michael asked his friend and producing partner Deke Simon to join the enterprise for the second and subsequent editions. This time around Michael asked me to do the sixth edition and I am honored.

These editions have sold more than 76,000 copies, probably because this book is one of the few places you can find hard information about budgeting for low-budget features, documentaries, industrials, student films, and other forms of programs. It is used as a textbook in production management courses throughout the world and by professionals who are producing projects with parameters different from their past work and want a helping hand.

Since production technologies are ever-changing, I have revised the book yet again, with updates to the free downloadable budget templates (mwp.com) that reflect the quickly evolving technologies of the last few years — from pre-production to post-production. Although most people no longer shoot film, I will often use the term "filming" and refer to all kinds of productions as "films."

This is not, however, a book about what things cost. The purpose of this book is to get you to seriously think about the production you are budgeting. This book is a friendly and easy-to-use guide, and will give you many ideas about how to approach budgeting, how to look for savings, how to negotiate, and so forth. Sorry, there is no magic formula. The budgets in this book are templates and the prices are examples only. **Actual rates and costs in the real world change annually, if not more often.** The numbers will get you in the ballpark, but in the end you're going to have to research the costs yourself.

The one who actually benefits the most from doing a budget is you — the producer or the producer *in* you. With low-budget productions, often the director or the writer will be the one to get the project off the ground and will need to create a budget during the development stage if a producer hasn't committed to the project yet. The process of figuring out what personnel, equipment, and services your project needs, and how long you will need each item makes you the expert. And you need to know your project inside out. But besides you, others will want to see a budget, like your supervisor, your investor, your client, a foundation, a government agency, or a department within your corporation.

The budget is normally Step 3 in a three-step process. Budgets are determined first by examining the script, storyboard, or breakdown in great detail. Then you do a schedule, and finally, a budget. Once the budget is defined, it becomes a blueprint for bringing your ideas into reality. Budgeting can excite you by this fact alone: You are moving closer and closer to making your ideas real.

Film and video projects do not allow for too many mistakes. Reputations are made and lost on the question "Did you come in on budget?" So it's best to prepare an accurate and detailed budget and know what you can and cannot afford.

For many people the idea of writing a budget brings on a cold sweat. But sooner or later, if you pursue the film or video production business, you will be called upon to account for costs, i.e., to prepare a budget. This book may ease your mind and give you confidence.

I love budgeting because it requires you to do all the steps that are necessary to be a *filmmaker*. You are conceptualizing, researching, scouting, studying, discussing, and deciding exactly *how* you plan to create a project. A line-by-line budget is the culmination of all of that work and becomes the plan for how to accomplish the concept, the script, the "dream" of what everyone wants to create. Although things will always change throughout the process of making a project, the budget reflects the proposed choices that have been made for each step and decision necessary to produce it. Once I have completed my final pass on a budget I can actually see all the facets of the production in front of me and can finally get my arms around how we will accomplish the almost impossible task ahead of us. Budgeting can be a deeply rewarding experience, one that is enriched by all that you put into the process of creating it.

For almost twenty-five years, I have been producing or overseeing the production of countless hours of film/video productions. It has been my responsibility to negotiate rates with agents, crews, actors, narrators, composers, film stages, equipment houses, and post-production facilities. I've produced feature films — both narrative and documentaries — television shows, commercials, live music events, corporate videos, music videos, and short films. Each and every project had a budget.

This book represents a lot of accumulated knowledge and experience. What I didn't know, I asked the experts in their fields. The budget formats in this book use the "standard" methods of production and equipment that most producers use. Study them, because besides being a list of necessary expenses, they also demonstrate a very well thoughout production process.

On some of my own projects I've saved tens of thousands of dollars. On a few occasions I've made some mistakes. What I will do in this book is share my insights so you can avoid costly errors and even find savings in your budgets.

Study this book. Challenge it. Make it your own. You may discover many items you would have otherwise overlooked, which may save you hundreds of times the price of this book. Hopefully, these budgets will spark your imagination so that you will find innovative ways to bring more value onto the screen.

When you've completed your budget, your anxiety will most likely be replaced with a calm confidence. You'll know what you can do and what you can't. You'll know how to make your budget go further and make a real contribution to the production. I sincerely hope that this book increases your ability to successfully complete all your productions. Enjoy.

Maureen A. Ryan
New York, NY
June 2015

Rates and Prices in This Book Are Examples Only!

The budgets and all rates and prices cited in this book are solely for purposes of illustration! It is critical that you search for the very latest rates and prices when calculating your own budget . . . then double check them further down the road so that you don't have any unpleasant (read *costly*) surprises when it's time to pay the invoices.

HOW TO USE THIS BOOK

Don't read the whole thing! (Feel better already?) However, you will need to understand every line item in your budget, and therefore I recommend that you first read the Line Items in Chapter 5 to familiarize yourself with the meanings of the budget items I use in these budgets.

Next, flip directly to the budget template that is closest to the project you are doing in cost and category. These budgets should get you 80% or more of the way to determining your own budgets.

If your type of production is not listed, then go through the Line Items, selecting those items you'll use in your production. Most producers exceed their budget because they forget something! That's where the information in this book will help. It is very thorough and should give you the confidence that you are covered.

Another thing: Do not take the numbers that I use as gospel. These numbers only approximate what things cost. You can't just take these numbers and plug them into your own budgets. Instead, research your own production costs. You may find that your line items may be lower. In addition, you must negotiate (more on this later) to get the best budget possible. **Do not copy the rates in these budget templates.** Sorry, but there are no shortcuts when it comes to budgeting. You may grumble now, but you'll thank me when you finish your production and still have some money left!

Finally, as the owner of this book, you have the privilege of downloading — free of charge — all these budget templates from the publisher's website at *www.mwp.com*. Adapt them for your own use. Make custom templates, add or take away line items, and most importantly, input your own numbers.

To download your free Excel Budget Templates:

1. Go to *www.mwp.com*
2. Click on "MW Film School."
3. Open the item "Sample Budgets/Forms."
4. Download the free Excel Budget Template most appropriate to your project.
5. Save it to your computer.
6. Remember that these budgets are sample templates. Make sure to create your own budget with figures based on your research on current rates and prices available to you.

I

SETTING UP A PRODUCTION COMPANY

Everyone has to begin at the beginning. If you carefully follow the advice in this book, these activities will help you get your own production company up and running. Think of that warm satisfaction that will come over you every morning when you read your company's name on the door as you enter your office. Hey, we did it! We're a real company!

For many, starting your own production company may seem daunting. This chapter will help dissolve that feeling of being overwhelmed. Take things one step at a time and you'll get there. Once it's done, you'll have a foundation to build on.

INCORPORATION

To incorporate . . . or not to incorporate? Most lawyers will suggest that you incorporate in order to protect your personal assets from liability.

If you are a United States resident and plan to have thirty-five or fewer stockholders (or maybe just one stockholder, you), most accountants will recommend an S Corporation or a Limited Liability Company (LLC). With an S Corporation or LLC, your company owes no federal income tax on profit. The profit passes through the company directly to stockholders (that includes you!). The company will still pay state income tax, which, if you pay out or reinvest all your profits at year-end, may only be the minimum.

How much does it cost to incorporate? It depends on the state and on the fees of the attorney or accountant in charge. There are also online websites that streamline the process. You'll probably want your attorney to look it over before you finalize the paperwork. If you already have an accountant, maybe he or she may be able to do it for you inexpensively.

If you choose not to incorporate, then it's probably a good idea to establish your company under a trade name other than your own, known as "d/b/a" (doing business as). Your accountant can help you with the application process.

FEDERAL ID

Whether you are incorporated or d/b/a, you still must apply for a federal ID (or EIN) number, which you need if you plan to pay the people who work on your projects. The ID number exists to help the IRS with its accounting. Go to *www.irs.gov* to apply for a number. Remember, if you are a sole owner, you are not on the payroll. You take your salary from company profit, and yes, you do owe federal tax on your salary.

Every payment you receive will now be written to the corporation and not to you personally.

BUSINESS LICENSE

Depending on the regulations for your city and state, you may need to get a business license for your company. Check online for the requirements if you start a company, a d/b/a, or an LLC.

BANK ACCOUNT

You cannot open a corporate bank account until you have your articles of incorporation (which you prepare before filing for corporation status), or your Operating Agreement if you're an LLC, and your federal ID number. The bank will require copies of these documents.

For smaller companies, one business checking account should suffice. Ask if it can be an interest-bearing account, which might help offset fees banks charge for business accounts.

If you have a sizable payroll, you may want to set up a separate payroll account and have a payroll service do the paperwork and actual payments. For small payrolls, most businesses do it themselves.

Be sure to go to the bank and introduce yourself to the bank manager, president, or vice president. Get to know them. The day will come when you'll want to borrow money, set up an escrow account, or employ other services. All this will come much easier if they feel they know you.

CORPORATE TAXES

Surprise — your new business owes the state! Your accountant prepares the state income tax return and calculates what you owe. Some business structures like S Corporations and some LLCs don't require you to pay federal corporate income tax.

ACCOUNTING SOFTWARE

In most small companies, people do their own bookkeeping, or hire a bookkeeper who may come in once a week or more. Production accountants sometimes use high-powered software such as Vista and Media Web.

ACCOUNTANT

Your accountant can help you incorporate, give business planning advice, project a business budget, supply you with W-2 and I-9 tax payroll forms, and file your corporate and personal tax returns.

Your accountant will become one of your greatest allies. First, he or she will help you set up your business, making sure you don't miss any filing or tax deadlines. This is their business. What may be hard for you is extremely easy for them. They will enjoy their relationship with a film or video producer because in the same way that numbers baffle you, movies baffle them!

ATTORNEY

Your attorney should be an *entertainment* attorney, distinct from, for example, a corporate or real estate attorney. Entertainment attorneys know things the rest of us don't but should — like production contracts, options and rights acquisition, licensing and releases of every stripe.

Your attorney should be someone whom you know and respect. Someone who can get things done in the entertainment community. Even if this costs more (on an hourly basis), you will be way ahead of the game when you want to do something, whether it's closing an investment deal or getting a distribution contract. In addition, as you work with your attorney you will gain a great deal of knowledge yourself that will be of immeasurable benefit over the years.

EMPLOYEES

Even in Hollywood, many incorporated production companies are made up of no more than one or two people. When you are in production you have many people on salary. When you are developing your projects you want to have few employees to keep your overhead costs down.

In the beginning you will probably hire a full-time assistant to help with the administrative chores, which will be many. As your business grows, others will be brought on. Here's where you want to hire the right people for the job. You want people that supplement — no, complement — your skills. If you are not extremely well organized, then look for this quality in those you hire. If you are well organized, then you may want more creative types for those aspects of your business. Do not hire someone just like you, because your aim is to balance your company.

Create a fun atmosphere for people to work in and your productivity will soar. Make sure they are free to make contributions to the projects and credit them appropriately. Giving credit is one of the easiest (and cheapest) things you can do. It's a way of saying thanks that goes a long way.

BECOMING A SIGNATORY TO GUILDS AND UNIONS

You may or may not have to deal with guilds, but in case you do, these are the main guilds (see Appendix for addresses): the Writers Guild of America (WGA), Directors Guild of America (DGA), and Screen Actors Guild-American Federation of Radio and Television Artists (SAG-AFTRA).

The prevailing wisdom is that by using guild members, you get more experienced actors, writers, and directors, and that's mainly true. On the other hand, it all boils down to who you want to work with. Guild membership doesn't instantly qualify anyone for anything. You have to meet your prospective collaborators and decide for yourself.

Technically, guild members are not supposed to work with a production company that has not signed an agreement with their guild. A writer, actor, or director may do it anyway, and sometimes use another name in the credits. Some work non-guild jobs happily, others do it grudgingly. Still others choose not to work with non-signatory companies at all. When guild members choose to work on a non-guild project, make it clear that they do so at their own risk, not the production company's.

You can be a signatory to one guild/union or many — it is up to the owner of a production company. One producer I know has three different companies: one a signatory to SAG-AFTRA, one a signatory to SAG-AFTRA and the DGA, and one that is not a signatory to anything. Why go through that paperwork nightmare? He wants to avoid dealing with residual payments for certain projects, and avoid paying the extra expense of pension and health (P&H) that guilds require — usually around 15% to 17% of the member's gross salary. (For really high salaries, like a star's, there is a cutoff beyond which the company does not have to pay P&H. Check with each guild for what it is.)

WGA (Writers Guild of America) — To become a signatory and hire WGA writers, your company must be legally structured, as in an S Corporation (not a d/b/a). Simply call and request the application forms. There is no fee to become a signatory. Your company cannot disengage from signatory status until the current WGA agreement expires, and these agreements run for about five-year terms. You can check out the current Minimum Basic Agreement (MBA) online, as well as other Agreements and Contracts, e.g., "Low-Budget" and "Standard Theatrical." www.wga.org

SAG-AFTRA (Screen Actors Guild-American Federation of Radio and Television Artists) — The company must be legally structured (not a d/b/a, although there may be exceptions). There are a number of contracts companies can sign, depending on what type of programming they produce (e.g., free TV, cable, public TV, new media, etc.). There is no fee, but a new company may have to provide a bond to cover payment of actors. Bonds can be in the form of a certified check, or a letter from a payroll service attesting that money is on account. Check the respective websites for contracts and/or digests of agreements. www.sag.org

DGA (Directors Guild of America) — The company could be a d/b/a or incorporated or a partnership. The application requests information about stockholders and ownership. It asks for documentation, like a copy of the fictitious name statement or articles of incorporation. In most cases, the company must have a project lined up in order to become a signatory. They want to know what the project is, what DGA member functions you'll be hiring, where the financing comes from, and if you have a distributor. Basically, they want to make sure members will be paid. If the financing looks shaky, they may ask you to put the DGA money in escrow. For TV movies and features, they may demand a security agreement that puts a lien on the film in case you go bankrupt. That way they can better collect any residuals. There is no fee to sign up. www.dga.org

IATSE — The crafts people and technicians who work in television and movies are represented by the International Alliance of Theatrical and Stage Employees (IATSE), and a host of other locals, including the Teamsters (the people who drive all the studio trucks and vans). Because it is so complicated, it can be difficult to get signatory information.

First of all, if you're a small production company doing very low-budget projects, you probably won't become a signatory to IATSE because your budget won't be able to support the salaries and benefits packages. But IATSE now has low-budget agreements so you should find out if they can work for your production before making a final decision.

Why become a signatory to IATSE? The theory goes that union crews (camera operators, sound mixers, grips, electrics, etc.) are more experienced, hence more efficient. This is usually true — although there are plenty of excellent people who are not union members.

When you hire union crews for scale (some feature productions are over-scale), there's no negotiating; you pay whatever the going rate is for that job, plus the usual payroll taxes. Plus you'll pay union fringes: Health/Retiree Health and Pension, and Vacation/Holiday. Check with your local to get all the current rates, rules, and regulations.

IATSE has local chapters in most major cities in the United States. To become a signatory, check out *www.iatse.net* and contact the office in your area. They will ask you to fill out a questionnaire. If you are approved, you're in. For production companies, there's no fee. If you can't find the right office, call a payroll service (a company that handles union and non-union payroll for production companies), since these people seem to know a lot about unions.

BON VOYAGE

It may take you a week or two or several months to complete all the paperwork required to set up your production company as a corporation and become a signatory to some or all of the unions. When you do set up your first corporation you'll find that it isn't as intimidating as you thought, and you'll feel empowered.

What follows are the nuts and bolts of budgeting; a potpourri of ideas that will help you think through and prepare your own production budgets.

The goal is always to come in under budget. This book is designed to help you become remembered for your remarkable foresight and ability to deliver a project on time and under budget. That's what clients, backers, and employees expect. By careful planning and researching you can create a very accurate budget before the cameras roll.

2

PRE-PRODUCTION

Ask any production veteran: Pre-Production is the key to a successful production. This is where you make the plans you live with in Production and Post. It's a grand scheme made up of a dizzying number of details. There's the production triangle — good, fast, and cheap — from which you can only get two out of three. If you want good and cheap (which we all do), it won't be fast, so make sure to give yourself enough time in Pre-Production.

There is a method to Pre-Production, but the method for fiction films is different than for non-fiction. There are whole books written about both, so let's just sketch out the two approaches.

PRE-PRODUCTION FOR FICTION FILMS

Once the script is "locked," meaning the major characters, major locations, stunts, effects, big scenes, and major sets are decided upon, you go through a process called "script breakdown." You need to comb through each scene of the script and highlight everything in that scene (every character, prop, vehicle, significant wardrobe, set dressing, extra, special effect, etc.) that will be needed to shoot it.

That information is carefully entered into a scheduling program, of which there are several that are very good. EP Scheduling and Showbiz Scheduling are good ones. When that process is complete, you create a shooting schedule that makes sense according to a number of factors. The usual ones are:

1. Location

Let's say there are nine scenes to shoot, three each in Canada, the United States, and Mexico. Obviously, you would not shoot one scene in Canada, hop a plane to the US location, shoot a scene, travel to Mexico and shoot a scene, then return to Canada and so on. You would "shoot out," as they say, all your Canada scenes, then move to the United States, then finish in Mexico. The same logic applies regionally. If possible, shoot all the scenes in "A" country or city, then move to "B" country or city. Try to order scenes by locations, so you keep your globe-trotting to a minimum.

2. Set

The same logic applies to sets. If you're shooting in a house or on a stage with multiple sets, when possible, try to "shoot out" each set to avoid shooting on the same set twice. Why be upstairs in a bedroom, go to the trouble of dressing it and lighting it, and then return to it two days later to repeat the whole process for another scene unless you absolutely have to?

3. Cast

The rule of thumb is, try to schedule actors so they work consecutive days.

For SAG-AFTRA shoots, in-between days are "Hold" days, and actors get paid. More than ten Hold days and you must do a "Drop/Pick-up," meaning the actor is dropped from his/her contract and picked up again. This can only happen once per film. For non-union actors these rules do not apply, but try to work them consecutively anyway. It's more efficient and cost effective.

4. Day/Night

Be aware of turnaround — the time between camera wrap and the next crew call. A 10-hour turnaround (or rest period) is customary for crew, 12 for SAG-AFTRA actors. Be sure to check local rules and any other union contracts you have signed for your production.

- You can't schedule an EXTERIOR (EXT) NIGHT that goes all night followed by an EXT DAY. There must a break of at least 10–12 hours in between.
- Try to schedule all EXT NIGHTS together so people are on the same biological clock. Allow a day off before resuming a day schedule.
- In an overall schedule, it's usually most efficient to schedule all the days first and then switch to nights.

5. Exterior/Interior

It's generally wise to shoot exteriors early in the schedule. That way, if there's bad weather, you can cover yourself with the option of shooting interiors (aka "cover sets"). If you wait until the end of the schedule to shoot exteriors, and bad weather hits, you won't be able to get your shots and will need to add days to your schedule, which will add money to your budget as well.

- Arrange all cover sets/locations with owners in advance so you can switch to one of them if you get rain or snow. The First Law of Production is "Never assume anything."

6. Children

SAG-AFTRA and each state's Department of Labor have special rules covering children under 18, including permits, working hours, rest breaks, meals, and school instruction. You may also need to budget for a teacher and a social worker on set, or maybe more than one depending on the number of children. Also find out the driving distance from the child's home to set. If the child lives outside certain pre-set geographic limits, you may have to count travel time toward his or her work day.

7. Time of Year/Climate

How much available light do you have this time of year?

- What's the prevailing weather in this season?
- Always check weather/wind forecasts before and during your shoot.

8. Special Effects/Stunts

Is a Stunt Coordinator on hand for run of show? If not, try to schedule all stunts and special effects (mechanical, aka physical) together. Major stunts/effects will need prep time.

9. Key Scenes

It's usually wise to make the first shoot day a light work day to allow for crew and talent to get up to speed.

- Highly emotional scenes need consideration about when they should be scheduled. Discuss with your actors and team.

Once you have a schedule, you know a lot more about your production, such as how many shoot days, how many actors and extras, what your props are, your locations and when you'll be using them, major sets and when you'll need them, key picture vehicles, prep time required for any special effects, and much more. Armed with this knowledge, you can now begin the next phase of pre-production — the budget. You'll find several budget templates for fiction projects later in this book.

Doing a budget is not the end of the pre-production process. Here's a checklist to help guide you through the process:

PRE-PRODUCTION CHECKLIST

Completed at Least Three Weeks before Production

SCRIPT REVISIONS ("final" draft script)

SCRIPT RESEARCH REPORT (send "final" draft to script research company for clearance)

A.D. BREAKDOWN PAGES COMPLETE

SHOOTING SCHEDULE

LOCKED BUDGET

COST REPORT ON DEVELOPMENT COSTS (or CLOSE OUT OF DEVELOPMENT COSTS)

PAYROLL SERVICE (make deal/prelim schedule)

HIRING CREW MEMBERS

CASTING — STARS AND SUPPORT CAST

CREW DEAL MEMOS
UNION NEGOTIATIONS (as needed)
CREW LIST (names/contact info)
CAST CONTRACTS
CAST LIST (names/contact info)
TRAVEL ARRANGEMENTS FOR CAST/CREW
STUDIO (sound stage)
LOCATIONS SCOUTING/SURVEYING
POST HOUSE (make selection/discuss workflow/negotiate deal/do tests/prelim schedule)
DIGITAL/FILM/AUDIO STOCK (place orders)
EQUIPMENT ORDERS (all departments — prelim orders)
INSURANCE (prod. insurance/general liability/workers' comp)
COMPLETION BOND (or COMPLETION GUARANTEE)
ISAN APPLICATION*
OTHER SUPPLIERS/VENDORS (place orders)
UNIT PUBLICITY PLAN (ONLINE & ON SET)
SET UP OFFICE, FTP SITE AND WEBSITE (if applicable)
CATERING CHOICE (make selection/negotiate/prelim schedule)

Two Weeks before Production

STUNT CONTRACTS
PRE-CALCULATE EXTRA DAY COSTS, EXTRA OVERTIME (OT) COSTS
REHEARSAL ROOM (book and schedule)
CHOOSE FORMS FOR CALL SHEET AND PRODUCTION REPORT
CATERING DEAL MEMO

---

* ISAN (International Standard Audiovisual Number) is a global identifier for audio-visual projects, a numerical version of your project title. The ISAN number is constant, so it's helpful, for example, for Producers tracking global revenue for their project even if the program was aired with a different title that the Producer didn't know about. The ISAN number is also useful for international distributors and festivals; they scan the visual bar code, and they have consistent descriptive data about the project. ISAN is a required deliverable for many outlets and distribution companies (see *www.isan.org*).

DIGITAL/FILM/AUDIO STOCK IN
CRAFT SERVICE (place orders)
BATTERY STOCK IN
EXPENDABLES ORDER
PRODUCTION AND DEPARTMENT MEETINGS
LOCATION/TECH SURVEYS

One Week before Production
FINAL PRODUCTION MEETING (all departments)
FINAL LOCATION/TECH SURVEYS
FIRST CALL SHEET
CAMERA TEST/EQUIPMENT PICKUP
CREW DEAL MEMOS COMPLETED AND SIGNED

The above Pre-Production Checklist is just a summary. It is edited from a more complete list courtesy of Deborah S. Patz and her fine book, *Film Production Management 101* (*www.mwp.com*). If you want to know more about how to line produce features, check it out.

Let's move on to Pre-Production for Non-Fiction.

PRE-PRODUCTION FOR NON-FICTION FILMS

I'm referring to "non-fiction" rather than "documentary" to be inclusive of all kinds of films that are not solely comprised of a script and actors. There are many types of non-fiction films and often different kinds of material are included in the same film, such as cinema vérité, interviews, archival material, re-creations (with actors and a script), and diary/confessional material. Non-fiction films include documentaries, industrials, biographies, plus training and instructional projects. Depending on which kind of non-fiction film you plan to produce, you'll have a different path through pre-production. Listed below, there are several steps that are generally necessary to produce a non-fiction film.

Research

Find out everything you can about the topic of your non-fiction project. If it's a documentary you'll need to research the topic, talk to people, read articles and books, look for archival material, etc. If it's a corporate industrial you'll need to get all the relevant material from the client, talk to the appropriate employees and managers and gather up the materials to come up with an outline for the program. If it is a training video you'll need to find out everything about the subject and break it down into the steps you want to discuss and illustrate.

Writing the Treatment

After you have done the "content" research you'll need to determine what elements will be used to create the visual aspects of the film. Archival photos, stock footage, interviews, cinema vérité, computer graphics, and historical re-creations are all possibilities and you'll need to create a very detailed treatment or "script" at the outset to map out exactly how you plan to create the film. Just like a narrative script, you need to create the film on paper before you shoot one minute of material. How else will you be able to create a schedule and budget?

When conceptualizing all of the above you'll also need to consider who the audience is for your film and what is the program's purpose. These factors are always important when making final decisions on what your film is and is not.

Archival Materials Budgeting/Strategy

For a non-fiction film, archival photos and stock footage will take up a larger percentage of your budget, so the need to research and budget properly for this line item is even more critical than for a fiction film. (See Archival Photos and Stock Footage below.) You may decide to "fair use" some or all of the archive material. If so, you'll need to hire an entertainment attorney who can research and give you a legal opinion during the pre-production process because it will have real consequences for your budget. (See Fair Use later in this chapter.)

Scheduling

The Production and Post-Production schedule for a non-fiction film is often longer — or more spread out — than for a fiction project. As opposed to a strict 25 consecutive day shooting schedule for an indie narrative feature, you may stop and start your filming over the course of several years for a non-fiction feature. This may be due to funding issues or availability of subjects and other elements. Additionally, the editorial period is often much longer for a non-fiction project so you will have to plan and budget accordingly.

Pre-Production Checklist

Refer to the Pre-Production Checklist above because you will still need to do many of those steps for your non-fiction project.

Important Information for Both Fiction and Non-Fiction Films

Following are all the issues you need to understand and consider before you can create your budget. Read them carefully and gather the information before you sit down to create your own budget.

LINE ITEMS CHECKLIST

Pre-Production for fiction or non-fiction is made easier by having a checklist that contains practically every personnel function, every service, and every piece of equipment you might use. For our purposes, that's the budget Line Items in Chapter 5 in this book. Use it to help you think through every phase of Pre-Production, Production, and Post. What you don't need from the list, discard.

It is incredibly helpful when creating a budget to actually visualize a shoot, day-by-day, hour-by-hour, imagining what everyone is doing at any given time. This kind of detailed thinking also helps to work out the daily schedules and avoid conflicts.

It's important to think about contingencies during this phase. What if the weather turns bad? Do we have an alternate location ready to go? Is there something else we can shoot so we don't waste the day? What if we need something we don't have? Where are the nearest hardware stores, gas stations, restaurants, groceries, rental cars, and so on? If a crew member calls in sick, do we have a list of people we can call?

While the budget Line Items are the ultimate Pre-Production checklist, here are some other goods and services you'll need during this stage.

LEGAL

If you don't have one, find an entertainment lawyer you can work with. Don't be afraid to call several. You can find them in or around the larger entertainment industry cities like New York, Los Angeles, Miami, Chicago, San Francisco, etc. Explain that you are interviewing prospective lawyers and you'd like to meet and talk about your project. Often attorneys will give potential new clients a 20–30 minute "gratis" call to talk about your project in the hope that you will hire them. If you're not familiar with things legal, don't be afraid to ask all the questions people are sometimes too afraid to ask, like "Are you charging us for this meeting?"

In the meeting, explain the project and ask about what services your lawyer will perform and how much they will cost. For budgeting, you'll need to know how much to allot for the entire project. Some lawyers charge by the hour, but many accept a flat fee for a project, or a percentage of the budget like 1–1.5%. Once you've interviewed a few attorneys, you'll have a good sense of the range of prices for your project.

Your lawyer will probably generate various deal memos, contracts, personal release forms/materials releases/location releases, rights options, and the like. Tons of carefully worded paper will cross your desk and he or she will help you to understand it so you can protect your project legally.

One way to save money in the future is to enter these documents into your computer. On your next project, you may need to merely alter some details. Discuss this with your lawyer first, because laws change, and you may waste time generating your own document only to have your lawyer recommend a new one. In any case, you'll still want him or her to review documents before they go out for signature. There are also a few books with sample legal documents written by entertainment lawyers that can be helpful to look over (see Resources section).

RIGHTS ACQUISITION

Is your project based on a book, article, stage play, screenplay, radio play, or someone's life story? If so, you'll need to get the rights to produce it. If it's published, call the publisher and ask who owns the copyright. You can go to the U.S. Copyright Office and search at www.copyright.gov. Additionally, you can contact a copyright search firm and hire them to find the rights holder. When you've tracked down who actually owns the rights you can negotiate to buy the rights or buy an option. You'll want your lawyer to advise you, since rights acquisition is a critical step for your film.

OPTION

An option gives you the exclusive right to later acquire the rights to a book or some other property. It allows you to tie up the property for a specified period of time (usually a year or two). This means no one else can take the project from you. During the option period, you will look for financing, write script drafts, and attract talent. The option agreement usually states that if the term ends with no production agreement, and if the option is not renewed, then the rights revert to the original owner. If, however, the project goes forward, the option will spell out the terms for actually buying the rights, including how much money and profit participation (if any) the owner will get. Option agreements can be simple or complex, depending on the property and who is involved. Options can be bought for a dollar. Other times, when it's clear the property has immediate value, you must pay for an option. If it's a celebrity's life story, you'll need to pay a fee upon signing the agreement.

STAFF CONTRACTS

If your company has become a signatory to one or more of the guilds, you may want to use standard deal-memo forms for personnel such as writers (WGA), directors, stage managers, associate directors, unit production managers (DGA), and actors, dancers, or narrators (SAG-AFTRA).

Go online (see Appendix) to view the various union/guild production agreements appropriate to your project (e.g., feature film, educational, music video, etc.). Have your lawyer review the forms in case they need to be customized.

The deal memos state that you agree not to pay less than the guild minimum scale. To find out how much that scale is, as well as basic guild rules, you need to refer to the appropriate rate cards and Basic Agreement books, which you get from the guilds. (Also see the Resources section for *The Showbiz Labor Guide*.) Make sure to read the guild materials, even though you may wind up calling back several times to confirm the rates, residuals, and other matters for your specific project. That's because contracts can be complex and you will need to understand them fully. We usually go back and forth a few times until it's finally settled. (Also see "Negotiating with Crews" later in this chapter.)

If you are doing a non-union project, your lawyer will create crew and cast deal memos that state the job title, work rate, and start/end dates for the project. These work contracts also state the employment expectations regarding confidentiality, approvals, and other work-related rules.

MUSIC CLEARANCE

If copyrighted music is an important part of your project, start the clearance process as soon as the script is "locked," that is, approved. Why start early? Some music may be too expensive, or perhaps the owner won't give permission for its use. Until you know what you can use, and how much it will cost, your budget — and your project — will be incomplete.

When you clear a piece of music, you pay a license fee to the copyright owner in exchange for the right to use that music in your project. The price depends on what medium you use (e.g., feature film, television, DVD, web, etc.), what territories you'll distribute to (United States, North American, European, etc.), and what term you want or can afford (three years, five years, in perpetuity).

Many producers use a Music Supervisor, music clearance person or service to track down copyright owners and negotiate prices. If your needs are at all complex, this is the way to go, since it is a specialized business. If clearances are not obtained correctly, and if you're caught, the copyright holder can send a "cease and desist" notice and you'll need to stop releasing the film and complete a licensing agreement or re-edit the film to remove the music from your film.

Music clearance services charge different fees for their work, so contact several to find out about rates. L.A. 411 at *www.LA411.com*, the NYPG (*New York Production Guide*) at *www.nypg.com*, *ProductionHub .com* and other sites are good places to research for this service.

It is prudent to contact a clearance service or your attorney, even if you believe your music to be in the public domain, or if you intend to claim "fair use." Public domain music must be verified as such, and "fair use," while it may apply to limited use of music in news, criticism, or scholarship, may or may not be appropriate for your project.

FAIR USE

As mentioned above in the Non-Fiction section, the concept of "fair use," whether you intend to apply it with music, clips, or what your own camera captures, requires your careful study. Under certain strict legal criteria you may be able to include audio or visual clips without paying a license fee. If you incorporate music or archival footage under fair use and later discover that you cannot use it, you may face a host of issues, including: a court battle, cutting out the footage, leaving in the footage but not being able get Errors and Omissions insurance and therefore not being able to get a Distributor. That said, fair use, properly applied, can be your good friend. For a great source of information on the topic, see American

University's Center for Media & Social Impact (*http://www.cmsimpact.org/fair-use/*). There are attorneys who specialize in fair use law who can help you decide what is right for your film.

FEATURE FILM CLIPS

If you want to use clips from Hollywood feature films in your project, you may be in for a trip on a long and winding road. With patience and perseverance you will prevail. The cost per clip depends on the rights you or your distributor need. So the first step is to call your distributor and find out. If you don't have one yet, then anticipate what rights you'll need by talking to a few producers of similar projects who have been through the distribution wars.

What rights are there to be had? The big banana is "worldwide" (or as they sometimes say, "throughout the universe"), "in all media, in perpetuity," which means you can use the clip in any territory (or on any planet), in films, television, DVD, web, and any future technology for all eternity. Ask for these rights first, because you never know, you just might get them. On the other hand, if you really don't need these rights (they will cost more), go for what you do need. Most major studios, for example, won't grant rights in perpetuity — the usual term is three years or so. (This is usually not long enough for DVD distribution, which generally requires seven years.)

Rights are broken down by territory and by media/distribution format. For example you could ask for:

- US & Territories TV rights
- North American TV rights
- World TV rights
- All Rights, which includes free TV/pay TV/cable TV/satellite-delivered TV/DVD/Airline/Non-Theatrical (educational)/Web, New Media, and so forth.

Be clear about what rights and clips you need from the outset; otherwise, the conversation gets confusing very fast. After you know what rights you want and what clips you want, how do you find out who owns the feature film so you can start negotiating?

First, try calling the studio directly. Remember that over the years many film libraries have been sold and you will need to find the current owner. If you've rented the DVD, check the front or tail credits for the distribution company's logo.

www.Bibnet.com is a website that compiles information about all films — TV films, series, specials, etc. — appearing on television. Distributor information is also provided. You can purchase information from their website.

There is also an international group called Focal (Federation of Commercial Audio Visual Libraries Ltd.) in London (*www.focalint.org*). Their website lists many sources for footage around the world.

The U.S. Copyright Office can do a search to determine ownership or whether a film is in the public domain (*www.copyright.gov*). There is a charge for this service.

Finally, you can hire a research and clearance service to locate the owners and negotiate the rights. Services charge by the hour, or anywhere from $1,500 to $2,500 per week, depending on the show, its length, the nature of the clips, etc. Even if you've used a service, have your own attorney review the license agreements from the studios before you sign.

So now you've located the owner and negotiated the rights for the license fee. Are you done? Nope. Many producers forget the next step and pay dearly when they go over budget.

The use of many clips requires the producer to get permission from, and pay residuals to, "third parties" like actors, writers, and directors. The copyright laws change every couple of years, so do your research to find out if you'll need to pay/obtain approval from third parties. Even if an actor has died, the rights often reside with his or her estate.

All actors *recognizable in a scene* must give their permission and be paid at least SAG-AFTRA scale (call the respective guild for clip rates). Stunt people get more money and may even ask for what they originally got for the stunt. You are excused from crowd scenes with extras, but crowd scenes with recognizable credited actors must be cleared. For the writers and directors of the film with your desired clip, call the respective guild for clip rates.

Somehow, producers can get the idea that since they worked so hard and paid so much to license a film clip, the musical score ought to be part of the deal. Sometimes it is, but most of the time it's not. If not, add that to the list for the music clearance (see above).

ARCHIVAL PHOTOS AND STOCK FOOTAGE

Need clips from newsreels, old cartoons, educational films, and nature footage? Need a stock photo of a New York City street from 1972? You need to search at stock footage libraries (see Resources). Go online and search by keyword, name, or topic. Usually you'll need to register as a customer and you'll be allowed to download a free, watermarked, "low-resolution" version of your clip that you can place in your editing timeline to see how it works. You can save a copy of it to put in your customer bin on the website. If you like the look of the clip, return to the website, pay the licensing fee by credit card, and download the high-resolution version. Prices are usually for a minimum of a certain number of seconds, like 30, so even if you only need 5 seconds, you still pay for 30. But check their terms; some companies offer "royalty free," meaning you pay a one-time fee for use in your project forever; some companies also offer "editorial use," which is a lower rate for documentary and educational projects. If in doubt, call them and negotiate.

If you are looking for very specific images, like photos from Black River Falls, WI, in 1885, you may need to contact local libraries that don't have online catalogs. Often these libraries can search for you (for a fee) and send you the low resolution images you are looking for. If you decide to license it, then you often pay for the photo or footage to be dubbed to an HD format for the highest resolution.

THE BUDGET

A "detailed" budget lists each and every line item. A multimillion-dollar feature budget could run a hundred pages. A student documentary film could run five pages. But both should be as detailed as possible. A "summary" budget, also called a "topsheet," is just that — a summary. It groups the line items into categories so that an investor or client need only look at one short page to see how the money is allocated. The categories of a "summary budget" or "topsheet" might be grouped like this:

01–00 Story & Rights
02–00 Producers Unit
03–00 Direction
04–00 Cast
05–00 Travel and Living — Producers/Director
06–00 Travel and Living — Cast
07–00 Residuals
08–00 Production Staff
09–00 Background Actors/Extras
10–00 Sound Stage
11–00 Production Design
12–00 Set Construction
13–00 Set Operations
14–00 Special Effects
15–00 Set Dressing
16–00 Property
17–00 Wardrobe
18–00 Makeup and Hair
19–00 Electrical
20–00 Camera
21–00 Production Sound
22–00 Transportation
23–00 Location Expenses
24–00 Picture Vehicles/Animals
25–00 Media

26–00 Travel and Living — Crew
27–00 Editorial
28–00 Music
29–00 Post-Production — Sound
30–00 Post-Production — Digital and Film
31–00 Digital Intermediate
32–00 Titling and Graphics
33–00 Deliverables
34–00 Digital Visual Effects/Animation
35–00 Insurance
36–00 General and Administrative Expenses
37–00 Publicity and Marketing

This sequence of categories is fairly standard, but different producers and studios often create their own versions. Once you have assessed all your categories and line items, feel free to group them in any way you (and your accountant) like. (You will be assigning each category code numbers [Chart of Accounts] for tracking purposes, as above, but more on that later.)

There are standardized budget formats, like those used by the AICP (Association of Independent Commercial Producers — see Appendix), which are used for commercial bidding. With this format, an ad agency or client can quickly review competitive bids from different producers and compare costs on a line-by-line basis before awarding a contract. Other producers who like the AICP format simply borrow it for their own use.

The budget templates in this book are arranged according to the Summary Budget above. Feel free to adapt them to your own needs. Use whatever format works for you. All the budget templates in this book are available for free from MWP as Excel documents.

NEGOTIATIONS

Negotiating is a fundamental skill in producing. Actually, it is just clear communication. If you are good at it, you can reduce your costs 10%, 20%, 30%, or more. Webster's definition of *negotiation* is "to confer, bargain, or discuss with a view of reaching agreement, to succeed in crossing, surmounting, moving through." For our purposes, it is when two or more people settle on the specific terms of the exchange. This could take the form of cash payment, deferred payment, title credits, profit sharing, or any number of other elements. (There should always be some form of an exchange even if you are getting something for free — such as a thank-you note or flowers.)

An agreement is only binding when both parties agree upon the terms of the exchange. Until that time, you are negotiating the deal. It gives you the opportunity to clearly define the exchange with the people with whom you'll work.

Too often, wages and prices are not fully discussed. Each person has only a partial understanding of the arrangement. Assumptions are made and it's not until the bill comes and all hell breaks loose that the differences are apparent. Then it's too late. Feelings are hurt. Trust and confidence are broken. Friends are lost. And to top it all off, more money is spent than planned — all because the terms of the agreement were not clear. This just cannot happen if you want to produce films. Life is too short. It's better to learn how to negotiate, come to an honorable agreement, and get on with it.

Negotiation is a big part of producing. The more you do it, the better you get at it. Here are some tips:

Question every price. Could the price be lower? Assume it can. Don't accept the first quote offered. Crew services, equipment rental rates, and post-production services are often flexible. You simply have to ask! It's not unusual to receive anywhere from 5% to 50% off the original or "list" rate.

Shop around. Check at least three sources for the same job or piece of equipment — prices can vary tremendously.

Give yourself time. Do the necessary research to find the best price and the best quality. If you are forced to do something right away (for example, creating titles on a Sunday), you will spend two or three times the normal price for "rush charges." Furthermore, with added pressure the job may not come out as well as you hoped. Rush shipping is usually an unnecessary waste, too. Leave enough time to do the job well. Plan ahead and save money.

Collect information. Give yourself time to collect information and you'll be ahead of the game. Most information is free. If you are too busy, hire a research assistant. The more you learn, the more options you'll discover. You'll find new technical processes, locate facilities, and be less willing to pay the first price quoted. The more "mystical" or complex a job seems to you, the more it will cost. Once understood, these things lose their mystique. With enough time and information, and the willingness to negotiate rates, you'll gain that necessary edge to make the best deal possible and save money. You'll also find better ways of doing the job.

NEGOTIATING WITH CREWS

Take time to talk with the person you want to hire. Describe the shoot, what you want to accomplish, the working conditions, who else will be in the crew and cast. Learning about the project will increase his or her interest in joining you. The person will get an image of what the shoot will be like and all its intangible benefits. Perhaps the shoot includes locations in Taiwan and he's always wanted to go there. Perhaps she'll be working with a favorite actor or personality. Maybe the cause of the film is close to his heart. Or maybe none of the above counts and it's strictly business, but you've entered into a dialogue.

CHECK REFERENCES

Just like when you are getting feedback about a particular vendor you are considering for your equipment rentals, you need to check at least two references for each person in consideration for each crew position. *Do not skip this step!* There are only two times in my career that I ignored my own advice and I regretted it terribly. Ask the person to send you the email and phone number for two references and then make sure that you contact them for a brief reference conversation. Ask what this person was like to work with. Fast/slow?

Respectful? Good collaborator? Were there any problems? Would you work with her again? If you had to name one weakness, what would it be?

What follows may get a little thick. For many readers, this is more information than you will need to know. For others, as your production budgets increase, your knowledge of negotiations will necessarily have to increase as well. I decided to lay out all the details here so you can refer to them easily. Hang in there, take it a chunk at a time, and you'll be able to digest it all.

Flat Rates vs. Hourly Rates

There is great confusion in the industry about hiring a crew member for a flat rate of, say, $300 for a day's work, a "day" being anything the producer says it is. Producers love this approach because they can work crews until they drop from exhaustion and not pay any overtime. Crew people hate these kinds of flats, for obvious reasons.

The fact is, except for some positions (see *Exceptions to the Overtime Rule* below), the labor law says people must be paid at regular, straight-time wages for the first 8 hours of work per day or for the first 40 hours of work per week. For non-union workers the wages are negotiable; for union workers they are set. Any hours worked over those must be paid at 1.5 times the regular rate (time and a half) up to 12 hours in a day. In some states, after 12 hours, the employer must pay double time. Other states do not have such a rule and the worker continues to be paid at time and a half. Call a payroll service to find out the rules that apply to the state in which you are shooting. (Do an Internet search for "payroll service entertainment," or a similar combination of key words, and your city, and you'll likely find some local payroll services familiar with the arcane rules and regulations of paying cast and crew.)

Exceptions to the Overtime Rule

Such key department head positions as Production Designer, Director of Photography, Art Director, Production Accountant, or a Costume Designer are "on call." These people are regarded as "management" of a sort, since they head their departments. This means that in non-union situations, the person can be hired by the week, at a flat rate, with no allowance for overtime. In union cases, there are limits and overtime pay that vary by the job and by state.

Here's an example of how the wage structure can work for regular employees:

Key Grip (non-union)
For non-union crew, you often do the salary based on two criteria — what the rate per day is and how long the day is. For the Key Grip on a low-budget non-union feature it could be $300/10-hr. day. The lunch would be "off the clock" and not computed as part of the work hours. If the day goes to 12 hours, then the 10th and 11th hours are computed as "time and a half" or 1.5× the hourly rate of $30/hr. ($300 divided by 10) which equals $45/hr: the total would be $390 for a 12-hr. day. Starting at the 12th hour, overtime is usually computed at "double time" or 2× the hourly rate: $60/hr. If he works for eleven and three quarter hours, you prorate the hourly wage to the nearest quarter hour. Because he is non-union, he gets no benefits for pension, health, vacation and holiday. You apply normal employer contributions for Social Security, etc., in the form of an approximately 21% payroll tax, also referred to as "fringes."

Key Grip (union)
With the union worker, in this case IATSE, the minimum straight-time wage is set. For Key Grips in California for the Basic agreement, it's $340.48 for the first 8 hours. If you are budgeting for a 12-hour day, that's $340.48 for 8 hours, and $63.84/hour (time and a half) for 4 hours, or $255.36. (After 12 hours, it's double time.) The total for 12 hours is $595.84.

Because he is an IATSE member, he also gets Pension and Health benefits to the tune of $5.99 for every hour worked ($5.99 × 12 = $71.88). Plus 7.72%, based on straight-time pay for Vacation and Holiday ($71.88 × 8 hours × .0772 = $44.39). The grand total (without payroll tax) is $595.84 + $71.88 + $44.39 = $712.11 for 12 hours of work.

The payroll tax is figured on the gross wages not including benefits, in this case $595.84.

Work Hours and Pay Rates

When you negotiate with your crew people, be straightforward and honest so everyone knows what the deal is. Explain how overtime works (in consultation with state labor laws) so everyone is on the same page.

If you are working under a union contract, overtime is usually calculated based on rounding up to the closest 10 minutes. For non-union, if you negotiate it in the deal memo, overtime can be rounded up to the closest 15 minutes.

Most people will not work for less than an 8-hour minimum (for unions, it's standard). The exceptions are when you are hiring someone for a longer project and they'll throw in a few half days. If it's a union shoot, review what the P&H and Vacation and Holiday rates are, and how they are applied.

Deal Memos

Finally, you or the Production Coordinator should prepare a deal memo for each crew member, reiterating the hourly wages, and the formula for paying them. The crew member signs it, then the Producer signs it. No confusion. Standard deal memo forms are available from your attorney or for download at various websites. If you obtain one from a website, make sure your lawyer approves it.

Budget for at least 12 hours of work per day, and try to allow an extra 10% of the person's gross wages for an "overtime" contingency.

Work out what you will offer for hourly rates in the budget before you make your calls to crew, and *be consistent in your rates across the various departments*. This is important, because if you are inconsistent you'll have unhappy people on the set, or spend valuable time renegotiating rates. For example, the Gaffer's rate should be the same as the Key Grip's rate. The Best Boy Electric and Best Boy Grip rates should be the same. All Grips and Electrics should get the same. And so on. This is called "most favored nations" and is a legal concept that stipulates that every person in the same category on the film will get the same rate. People know what the show is paying and they can take it or not.

What do you do if you really want a particular crew person, a Key Grip for example, but your hourly rate is too low? Try sweetening the deal with a little more money on the “kit rental” (the box of supplies she brings to the job). That way, you’ve kept her rate the same as those on a comparable level, but she’s making a bit more money for her tools and equipment. Do this only if this is someone you cannot live without, otherwise you’ll be making side deals on kit rentals all over the place and spending money for no good reason. Generally, if you can’t make suitable deals within your budget, you should look to hire someone else.

If you have negotiated your deals honestly and fairly with the above formula, you eliminate the jealousies that can occur when people in the same job level make different amounts of money. There are no secrets on the set. If there are inequities they’ll be exposed before the camera starts rolling.

Sometimes you’ll be doing a non-union shoot and calling union members to work on it. You need to say it’s non-union, because union crews are used to getting whatever the minimum rate is for that job, plus union fringes.

Union vs. Non-Union: Don’t “mix” crews

It’s problematic to hire non-union crew if your film is a signatory to a union contract or to hire union crew if you are doing a non-union film. Let’s say you’re doing a non-union show for a large production company, and it’s time to staff up. If you hire union people for your non-union show, and if the union discovers this, it can picket, and you can be pretty sure that union members will not cross the line. The union wants to become the bargaining agent for the crew, and if a certain percentage of the crew votes to have the union represent them, the producer has two choices: either sign a deal with the union, or do not sign. If the producer does not sign, all union members must leave the show (if they want to stay in the union). If you have hired union people in key positions (Gaffer, Key Grip, Sound, Camera, etc.), you'll probably be down for a day or so while you re-staff.

You should make a decision ahead of time if you plan to do a union film and sign the signatory paperwork or if you plan to do a non-union film and not sign a union agreement. Once you have decided, hire accordingly (all union or all non-union) and don't "mix" crews.

Your ability to negotiate rates that are affordable and fair have to do with your own relationships with crew members, the attraction of your project, and your production budget. If you have a multimillion-dollar budget, it's out of line to ask people to work long days for low pay. If you have a shoestring budget, you'll have to ask for favors.

Here's a checklist to have in front of you when negotiating crew rates.

1. Schedule. The number of prep and wrap days. The number of shoot days. Anticipated number of hours per day.
2. Hourly or weekly rates. Formula for overtime rates consistent with the same level jobs in other departments ("most favored nations"). No guaranteed minimum hours.
3. Kit rentals
4. Meals — provided on-set or a per diem
5. Pre-Production/technical survey day rates
6. Travel day rates
7. Per diems, lodging, etc.
8. Pay day(s)
9. Payroll taxes for non-union crew. Pension/health/vacation/holiday fringes for union members.
10. Screen credits
11. Profit sharing (if appropriate)
12. Deferments (if appropriate)

Let's take these points one by one:

Schedule
Discuss all "prep," "shoot," and "wrap" days as well as any holidays, breaks in the schedule, and time off. (Union crews are paid for holidays; non-union generally are not.)

Rates
Hourly or weekly rates as discussed above.

Kit Rentals
Kits contain special tools of the trade, and the production is better off renting them than buying them. Makeup, Hair, Key Grip, Gaffer, Construction Coordinator, and many other positions have kit rentals (also called "box" rentals). Most people have standard kit fees, but if you need to sweeten the pot for someone while keeping his or her daily wage on a par with others in the same position, upping the kit rental is a way to do it.

Meals
There is a standard practice when it comes to figuring meal time. If the producer caters lunch, the minimum time is one half-hour, and it's off the work clock. If you have a "walk-away" meal, meaning that people are on their own, you must allow one hour, and only a half-hour is off the clock. If you do walk-away lunches it can take a while to get the crew back working after they have wandered away for an hour. Generally, breakfasts are offered before the call time, or as "walking meals," meaning people munch as they work. "Second meals," meaning dinners, are counted as work time if people grab the food and keep working.

Catering is usually the best bet, since the crew is kept close at hand, and more focused on the shoot. For large crews, hire a catering service, and they can advise you about menus. For small crews of five to fifteen, pass around a menu from a local restaurant that delivers.

All union contracts require that the cast and crew must be fed *every six hours*. It is the producer's job to have a warm meal ready and waiting at that time of day in the schedule. If you have to do a second meal you will serve that six hours after the cast/crew resumes work after lunch. If you don't keep to the six-hour rule you are violating the union contract rules and automatic meal penalties will be charged. If you violate it on a non-union project you are disrespecting the crew and open yourself to acrimony and potential mutiny by your hard-working cast/crew members!

Pre-Production/Technical Survey Days
Pre-Production meetings and technical surveys (also called "tech scouts") can be anything from a minimum 8-hour call with overtime (union) to a negotiated half-day rate (non-union). These meetings and surveys prepare people for the job, and are usually well worth the expense.

Travel Days
Again, there are no set rules. Travel days can be 50% of the daily straight-time rate (non-union) to an 8-hour minimum with overtime (union). The producer pays for all transportation, including taxis, limousines, airfares, and extra baggage related to the show.

Lodging/Per Diem
Lodging is arranged and paid by the producer. On overnight trips, a per diem ($39 to $100+ per day) is usually paid to each crewmember to cover meals and incidentals. By choosing to eat inexpensive breakfasts and dinners, the crew will take home more cash. When lunches on the set are provided by the producer, you can either deduct the cost of lunch from the per diem, or let it slide and create some good will. On low-budget productions, the per diem may be miniscule or non-existent, as long as the producer provides all meals.

Pay Day
Be specific on the pay schedule and stick to it. Paying people on time will quickly gain you a favorable reputation. Slow or non-payment will also earn you a reputation!

Payroll Taxes—Pension and Health
(Also see Chapter 5, Fringes)

To hire union employees on an official union shoot, either the production company or the payroll service must be a signatory. Consult the union rate card or the payroll service for the appropriate fringes in your state.

As an employer, you'll be paying the usual FICA, FUI, SUI, and workers' compensation on any employee's payroll, union or not. Check with your accountant and your union local or payroll service for up-to-date figures.

If you hire non-union people, I suggest you deduct taxes per the IRS W-2 Form completed by the employee. You can only pay on a 1099 Form (and not withhold taxes) if the person is a true Independent Contractor, which is to say she has a company and a federal ID number, and meets the IRS criteria for Independent Contractors (search IRS websites for "Employees vs. Independent Contractors"). If you've hired someone as an independent contractor and she doesn't have a federal ID number and she doesn't pay her taxes, or the IRS audits you and decides that this person is really doing the work of an employee, the IRS can and will go after the production company for an employee's delinquent taxes, plus the employer's contributions, plus penalties. If in doubt, consult an accountant or attorney about your particular project. But be aware that in your budgeting, employer contributions will add about 21% of your wages to the bottom line. For a specific rundown of these costs, see Chapter 5, Fringes.

Screen Credits

Commercials, music videos, and sometimes industrials give no on-screen credit. Features and documentaries do. With above-the-line credits, and a few below-the-line, like Director of Photography, Production Designer, Composer, Production Manager, and Editor, discuss the size and placement of the credit. With crew, once the credit is determined and included in the deal memo, its size and placement is usually left to the producer's discretion. If credits are a puzzlement, rent a few DVDs that are like your project and write down the sequence and placement.

Profit Sharing
On most projects there probably will not be profit sharing, but if you feel someone has made a major contribution to the film, or worked for low or no wages, compensation can be enhanced by a percentage of the profits. (In order to give away percentages you must be sure your project is structured so that you can do so. Ask your lawyer.)

Deferments
Deferments are salaries that are paid later. Deferments are almost unheard of on large projects, but on smaller projects that are labors of love with very low budgets, it is done sometimes. If you are paying someone on deferment, you both should have a clear, written understanding of when the deferment is paid. Before the investors receive their money? Before the actors? After any over-budget expenses are paid first? Exactly when?

Anyone taking a deferment will appreciate this demonstration of integrity and responsibility. You should also be very clear if it is unlikely they will ever receive their deferred payment. Manage expectations so they don't count on ever getting paid and if they do, it will be a pleasant surprise.

That ends the checklist for negotiating with crews. I suggest completing your budget before you do your crew deals. This way, you know what you are paying for each position, you know how much leeway you have on kit rentals, and you've considered all the other items on the checklist. Now make your calls, and you'll find it's not really negotiating at all; it's more like staffing up with those who agree to the terms you offer. If your terms are fair, and your passion for your project high, you shouldn't have a problem getting a crew.

UNIONS

Why hire union crews? Sometimes there are certain people whom you know and whose work is first rate, and you just want them.

Whether you are producing a commercial, television show, or a feature, if your company is not a signatory to IATSE, you may be able to still work with union people by going through a production company or a payroll service that is a signatory (see Payroll Services below). Make sure to discuss with the union representative.

It's worth noting that IATSE and Teamsters both have special agreements for television shows and very low-budget projects. The easiest way to contact the appropriate local chapter of the union (there are tons of them) is through a payroll service. The DGA also has some special deals for low-budget projects that allow the production company to defer partial salaries.

For readers who wish to prepare a union budget and include all the additional rates and fringes, the names and addresses of the major unions and guilds are in the Appendix. You may also obtain current rates and the major rules and practices governing work by purchasing *The Showbiz Labor Guide* online (see Resources), which saves a lot of legwork by compiling it in one volume.

Taken as a group, the rules of the various guilds and unions are complex and overwhelming. Studied one at a time, they begin to make sense. You can understand the concerns, needs, philosophies, and restrictions inherent in each union.

For many producers, especially those with limited budgets, union rules and regulations make working with them prohibitively expensive. As mentioned above, there are low-budget agreements for most guilds/unions, so you can look into those possibilities. You can also hire a non-union crew and make your film that way.

PAYROLL SERVICES

A Payroll Service is a wonderful thing. The service takes your employee's completed and signed time card showing hours worked and hourly rate and calculates what is owed. Then they add on the requisite union fringes, if any, such as Current Health, Retirement Health, Pension, Vacation and Holiday. Finally, they issue the check, and you are free of the hassle!

Since the service also acts as the employer of record, workers' compensation and unemployment go through them, not you. Plus, they complete and send W-2 forms to all your employees at year's end. Fees are usually 1%–3% of your total employees' gross wages or on the entire invoice of gross wages plus fringes, depending on the company. If you can afford it, it's great headache relief.

Payroll services can act as your signatory to SAG-AFTRA for industrial/educational programs, but not for TV, features, commercials, home video, or interactive. That means if you're shooting an industrial/educational project, you can use the payroll service to pay SAG-AFTRA members without being a signatory company yourself. If you are shooting any of the other kinds of projects, your company must become signatory to legally hire those members. (For a further discussion of signatory status, see Chapter 1.)

To legally hire members of the DGA, WGA, and AFM (American Federation of Musicians), the production company must be a signatory. You can then hire a payroll service to handle the payroll chores, if you want.

For IATSE (which includes Teamsters) a payroll service can act as your signatory, and your non-signatory company can now use union crews. Call a payroll service for details, since there are many ifs, ands, and buts and you need to customize the service to your project and your company.

PRODUCTIONS FOR LARGE COMPANIES

Large companies have accounting departments with layers of approvals. And they like to hold on to their money as long as possible to earn interest.

This can add up to slow payments that drive people crazy.

It's bad business when a crew has to wait more than 10 or 15 days to get paid — especially if they were promised prompt payments. Additionally, many states have laws regarding how soon employees need to be paid after they have completed work. Try to make accounting departments stick to a pre-agreed schedule, and even make it a contractual point with the company.

BELOW-THE-LINE RATES

The below-the-line rates in this book are *non-union*. By definition then, there are no set rates, it's all open to negotiation and industry standards. That's why I usually cite a range rather than a specific figure. The rates are loosely based on a 10-hour day, which is average for most shoots. None of the rates take into account payroll taxes or union fringes (pension, health, vacation and holiday). If your production has different assumptions, make sure you budget accordingly.

NEGOTIATING FOR EQUIPMENT AND SERVICES

Equipment rental houses, video post houses, production stages, catering companies and the like are all open to negotiation. If you have a lot of work for them, if you contact them during one of their slow periods, if you can offer lots of future work, or even if none of the above applies, you can ask for discounts. It doesn't hurt to try, but do it nicely and respect their needs as a business. Vendors get frustrated if you ask for a deep discount on *every* job.

If you are not familiar with the service or equipment you seek, call around to several companies and ask for bids. Talk through the situation, and ask dumb questions — the good companies will be happy to answer them because they want your business, both now and in the future, when you know the ropes.

After you've been educated by several places and have their bids, you can compare apples to apples and start your negotiating. There's no harm in saying you have a bid for $21 per person from Brown Bag Catering and asking if the Tastee Treat Company can do better for the same menu.

Sometimes companies will say yes to your request, but only if you pay when service is completed. Try to establish a credit line wherever you go so that you don't have to pay bills for 30 to 60 days. This way you may be able to make a little interest on the money in your bank account, boosting your assets. Weigh the costs versus the benefits. Most vendors accept credit cards for payment which may be a good way for you to pay for many of your invoices.

PRODUCTION SCHEDULE

Studios or others who are financing your project will want to see a Production Schedule. Use the budget and breakdown to help forecast how long each phase will take.

CASH FLOW SCHEDULE

A Cash Flow Schedule projects expenses across the production schedule, and helps both the producer and the financing entity plan for the major cash transfers.

When you are producing a film or video or television show for a distributor or broadcaster, you generally receive your payments on a payment schedule, never all at once. This means that you will have to know exactly how much cash is needed when. You prepare a cash flow schedule so that you can meet your needs. This is an important step so make sure you have an accurate production/post schedule so you can receive payments to cover each step in the filmmaking process.

Here's a tip. The usual pattern for cash transfer is one third on signature of contract, one third on start of principal photography, and one third on delivery of the master. Try to get most of the last payment at the start of post-production. With cash on hand, you can cut a much better deal with your editing facility.

CASTING

To find great actors it is usually best to hire a Casting Director. These people have extensive contacts with agents and take your script and/or character descriptions and arrange for the appropriate actors.

Casting Directors cost, but they do everything for you except make the decision. You show up at the appointed day, take a seat, sip your coffee, and watch as actor after actor performs. You can direct the actor if you want, or leave it up to the Casting Director. They'll also videotape each actor for an extra charge. At the end of the session, they'll arrange for any callbacks. They also negotiate the agreements with actors and agents, and handle some of the SAG-AFTRA paperwork.

Casting Directors for movies and TV shows usually work by the project, and get a flat fee which is based on how much talent there is to cast, and how long it will take. Usually the producer has allotted a fixed amount in the budget — $20,000 to $40,000 is typical for a low- to mid-level feature.

For commercials, they usually hold the first session without you and upload a video on a password-protected website for you to watch. You view the tape and sit in for the callbacks only. Commercial Casting Directors charge anywhere from $500 to $800 per day. If a Casting Director is outside your budget, however, there are some other routes.

Many scripts are written with specific professional actors, hosts, or narrators in mind. If you know who you want, simply contact SAG-AFTRA to find the agency listings. From there you get the actor's agent, and you can make your offer. If you know you want a union actor, you can look through the *Academy Players Directory* (*www.playersdirectory.com*). They have an e-book you can purchase with over 120,000 actor listings. You can also find useful contact information at *www.pro.IMDb*.

If you plan to cast the film yourself, you can post your project on an online casting service like Breakdown Services (*www.breakdownservices.com*). You fill out the form for the required information (including if it is union or non-union) and pay your fee and your posting will go up on the website for all actors to check. They will then send in their headshot, résumé, and video (if requested) and you can look at everyone online and make your selections for your first auditions.

Creating good character descriptions for each role is important. Check out other descriptions online so you can write a concise and compelling few sentences to get actors interested in the role. State age, ethnicity, gender, and special skills that are required. If violence, nudity, or sexual situations are required, state that as well.

If you are handling the auditions yourself, you'll need to be prepared. Have a waiting area for actors where they can be greeted and sign in. Have "sides" on hand — a few pages of the script the actor prepares while waiting. In the audition room, which should be spacious enough to allow movement, have a video camera and an operator. Chances are, you'll want to review some of the actors' auditions on tape. For most parts, allow about 10 to 15 minutes for each actor, and try to stay on schedule. You'll probably get exhausted saying the same thing to each actor, but keep your energy up and remember that they are there to help you achieve your vision.

When you've made your choices, always keep track of the others you liked. You never know if your actors will get a better offer and beg off. Call the final few people who didn't get the role and thank them for their time and talent. You never know if you'll have to call them last minute if another actor drops out.

Finally, in dealing with any agent, know in advance whether it's a guild or non-guild shoot, what the tentative shoot dates are, and how much you are prepared to offer. Agents always get 10% of their client's gross salary, but you can try to fold the agent's fee into the gross, instead of adding it on top.

Actor Clearance

One final note on working with union actors. At least 12 hours before the start of shooting, you or the Casting Director must call SAG-AFTRA and verify that they are members in good standing. It's called "Station 12" in the union lingo. If they are not, you cannot employ them legally until the matter is straightened out.

POST-PRODUCTION

You haven't even started shooting yet and it's time to consider post. The reason is, there are several post-production options to use, and you have to budget for one of them.

First question: What format are you shooting on?
Second question: What system are you editing on?
Third question: What format will you deliver your final master on?

Let's outline the general path that any film goes through from shooting to mastering.

1. Capture your material on whatever format you are shooting on.
2. Process your capture format properly.
   a. If digital video, you'll have your digital files transferred onto at least two hard drives and/or a "cloud" backup system before you start editing.
   b. If film, you'll have the negative processed and telecined/transferred to digital files and then transferred onto at least two hard drives and/or a "cloud" backup system before you start editing.
3. The material will be edited on a digital editing system.
4. After the "picture is locked," the film will either be "finished" in the editing system or outputted to another system to create the Digital Intermediate (DI).
5. At the final finishing stages, an audio mix and color grading are done.
6. The final master is outputted to the final master format, e.g., Digital Cinema Print (DCP), Film Print, HD cam, and/or digital file.
7. The final master is duplicated.

Your distributor or broadcaster is clear about what format they require for distribution. So you need to be clear about what format the master should be created on and what the primary distribution or broadcast mode will be before budgeting. See the sections about Mastering in Chapter 6, Sample Budgets for Specific Projects.

BOOKING POST-PRODUCTION FACILITIES

A big part of your budget will be post-production, so if you're not familiar with this phase, talk to a post-production supervisor, an editor, and various post-production and audio post houses and get bids for your job.

Once you've identified the post houses that you like (video and audio) and you know your post schedule, put your estimated editing days on hold. Even though the editing schedule will slip and slide, at least you are on their schedule books and won't be forgotten. Keep them posted as your schedule changes.

COMPLETION BOND

Let's say you have what's known as a negative pickup deal for your proposed feature film (or less frequently TV or other project) where your distributor agrees to pay you an agreed sum when you deliver your competed film master. You take that contract to a bank or group of investors and you borrow the money you need for production against the contract. The only hitch is, the investing group wants to be sure you'll make the film you say you'll make, on time and on budget. So they demand a completion bond (or completion guarantee).

If this is the case you must go to a completion bond company that will vet you, your company, the project, and your partners. If they agree to provide the completion bond, it gives them certain contractual rights, among them the right to monitor your production closely, and to step in if you even look like you're going over budget. "Stepping in" can mean giving you strong advice, or it can mean taking over the reins of production (which rarely happens). Should the worst occur, and the project goes belly up, the completion bond company gets stuck with repaying the investors. To protect themselves against that, they put themselves in a position of recoupment, second to the investors, just in case they can finish the film and get it to market.

The cost is usually 3–6% of the total budget, above- and below-the-line. Plus, they insist that the budget contain a 10% contingency fee.

INSURANCE

Any project that's hiring people or renting gear needs to be insured. For one thing, most equipment vendors, film permit offices, locations, and others need proof of insurance, so it's next to impossible to produce anything without the proper insurance. Additionally, you want to make sure that your cast, crew, and equipment are all insured against any claims.

There are many insurance brokers that specialize in film and television production insurance. Make sure they are accessible to you day or night in case of emergency. And make sure you can obtain certificates of insurance (COI) to be provided to whomever needs one promptly, like within an hour or so if necessary. This is usually done online through a website set up by the insurance company.

The type of insurance depends on what you're doing. If you are setting up a production company, you may just need liability and clerical workers' compensation insurance. When you get into pre-production, send a script and a copy of the budget to the broker. Be sure and point out any stunts, special effects, animals, boats or aircraft, or hazardous shooting. You'll probably need some or all of the items in an "entertainment package" or "producer's blanket policy" such as:

Cast Insurance — covers delay due to death, injury, or sickness of principal cast members. The artist must pass a physical exam (paid for by the producer).

Negative Film and Videotape — covers loss or damage to raw and/or exposed or recorded stock.

Faulty Stock, Camera, Processing — covers loss or damage to stock/digital equipment caused by faulty materials or equipment.

Props, Sets, Wardrobe — covers loss or damage.

Extra Expense — covers delay due to damage of property or facilities.

Miscellaneous Equipment — covers loss or damage to equipment owned by or rented to the production company.

Third Property Damage Liability — covers damage to property of others (with conditions).

Comprehensive General and Automobile Liability — required for filming on city or state roads, or any location requiring permits.

Non-Owned/Hired Car Liability — covers rented personal cars or production vehicles.

Umbrella Liability — usually a $1–$2 million General Aggregate Limit.

Monies and Securities — covers loss of stolen cash.

Workers' Compensation — required by state law, this coverage applies to all permanent and temporary office and crew workers, and provides medical, disability, or death benefits to anyone injured in the course of employment.

Guild/Union Travel Accident — necessary for any guild or union member on location.

Errors and Omissions (E&O) — covers legal liability and defense against lawsuits alleging unauthorized use of ideas, plagiarism, libel, slander, and such. This coverage is usually required by distribution companies prior to release. Note that the insurance carrier (not the broker) must approve your application for this coverage. In order to do that, your attorney must have reviewed and approved the script. Allow at least a week for the insurance carrier to approve your E&O policy.

The cost of insurance depends on many factors, such as the budget of your show, whether there are stunts, travel, big stars, and so on. Many producers calculate 3% of the total budget as an allowance, but you can get an actual bid by calling an entertainment insurance broker and answering their questions about the show. It is usually charged as an annual premium and then renewed if your production goes longer.

LOCATIONS

Scouting. Are you hiring a Location Manager to help you find locations and plan your shoot? If so, get an estimate on how much time he or she thinks it will take to do the job and factor it into the budget. Be sure to ask about and include expenses like mileage, posting digital photos online, and video. They will upload the photos for you and your team to look at and decide on.

If you are scouting locations yourself, bring along someone familiar with production. There are lots of potential issues here, and you need to consider things like electrical power, weather, noise, neighborhood happenings (when school lets out), traffic, parking, rest rooms, eating places, light at various times of day, and so on. Here's a checklist:

Site Survey Report **Date:**

1. Location description:
2. Fee:
3. Contact:
4. Address/Phone/E-mail:
5. Room dimensions:
6. Walls/Surface/Colors:
7. Ceiling type/Flooring:
8. Windows: (number/size/direction/coverings)
9. Interiors: Existing lighting:
10. Interior noise: AC: Intercom: Appliances: Fluorescents: Machines: Other:
11. Exterior noise: Traffic: Airplanes: Construction: School: Fire/ Police: Other:
12. Power: Amperage: Breaker box location:
13. Equipment access: Stairs: Elevators: Ramps: Storage:
14. Facilities: Eating: Restrooms: Makeup: Wardrobe: Offices: Dressing rooms: Security: Parking: Actors holding area: Equipment staging area: Set dressing area: Water:
15. Neighbors' issues:
16. Permits/Fire/Police:
17. Trash disposal:
18. Traffic closure:

Once you have a location you think you like, show it to the Director, Assistant Director, the Sound Mixer, the Production Designer, and the Director of Photography so you can get everyone's approval. Later, you'll do a Tech Scout with all of the above, plus, depending on the complexity of the shoot at this location, the Production Manager, Transportation Coordinator, Gaffer, Key Grip, and perhaps Stunt Coordinator.

State and City Film Commissions. Many producers and location managers use a film commission's library to view photos of possible locations. They narrow down the list and visit those that look most promising. (Most commissions' libraries are accessible online.) Out-of-town producers can call and discuss their needs. The commission will then send them information about what's available. Film commissions want to be helpful because they know that film productions bring money and jobs to wherever they shoot. They may also have information about support services, such as housing, catering, transportation, and so forth.

Location Services. Most have listings of homes or other sites. You go online and review photos, find places you want to visit, and have a look for yourself. Most do not charge a service fee to the producer, since they get a percentage from the homeowner. The producer pays for use of the actual location they choose.

Location Fees. This is the money you pay to the owner of the place, and the price can be from one dollar to many thousands of dollars per day. You'll want to get a location release signed that details the fee, the hours for shooting, and if there are any overtime or additional charges. Remember to protect the location: Use "lay-out boards," — 4 × 8 sheets of thin cardboard — to cover carpets and floors. You'll bring your own food, drinks, and toilet paper, and leave the place spotless. You will also need to provide an insurance certificate for any location you use.

Location Permits. In many cities and counties, unless you are shooting in a bona fide studio, you need a permit. Call the local film commission to find out the rules for the area you plan to shoot in. If it's a small town, city hall may be the place to ask for all the rules and regulations. If you have to close streets, or have stunts or special effects to do, you may need police and fire personnel, which the permit office will tell you about. There may be additional charges for labor costs.

BUDGETS FROM ALL DEPARTMENT HEADS

For any production, ask all your department heads (Director of Photography, Key Grip, Gaffer, Art Director, Key Makeup, etc.) to prepare department budgets. This helps everyone think through their jobs and puts many heads together to troubleshoot. If their totals are too high, you've still got time to think up brilliant ways to do the same thing but cheaper. Some production companies insist on each department head signing off on the final department budgets.

ART DIRECTION/PRODUCTION AND SET DESIGN

This area covers anything from a stylist to help make your product shot look great to building huge sets. After you've done your script breakdown and know what you need, have conferences with your production designer to plan and budget everything from staff needs to materials and construction costs, to strike crew and cartage. As mentioned above, ask the production designer to prepare a department budget. If it's too high, you'll need to figure out ways to lower the budget.

CREDIT ACCOUNTS WITH VENDORS

Vendors require you to complete a credit application and provide proof of insurance. Having accounts around town also allows you the convenience of paying bills at the end of the month instead of C.O.D. Typical vendors include cameras, lighting and grip equipment, dollies, vans and trucks, props, sets and greens, wardrobe, labs, and post-production. Most vendors will allow you to pay on credit card as well.

PRODUCTION FORMS

You will need many forms to run the production — purchase orders, sample contracts, release forms, call sheets, etc. Usually your entertainment attorney will provide you with the legal documents. For the production-related paperwork, the production manager and coordinator usually have the computer documents that will be required.

PURCHASE ORDERS

Some vendors won't release equipment to be charged to an account without a Purchase Order, so it's a very good idea to use POs when booking jobs or ordering supplies. A PO corresponds to every invoice, and thus every expense is monitored. You should do this for any size job — it is very helpful for the actualization of your budget.

CHECK REQUESTS/TRACKING COSTS

When you have to pay cash and need a check, fill out a Check Request Form. This keeps a record of who wants what for how much. On larger productions that boast an Accountant or Auditor, the Unit Production Manager completes a Daily Production Report which records how many hours crew and cast worked, how much material was shot, how many people were fed, location fees, equipment used, and so on. The Accountant reviews the Production Report and calculates the expenses in each category.

How do you know if you're over or under budget? You already estimated how much overtime you've allowed for cast and crew. You can easily prorate that amount over the number of shoot days. If, after a number of days, you are consistently over on your daily allowance of overtime, you know you're getting into hot water. Unless you're saving comparable sums elsewhere, it's time to cut back, which may mean a heart-to-heart chat with the Director.

"Hot costs" refer to the labor costs (cast and crew) for a production. They are usually tracked in a weekly cost report that shows costs for each category in the budget. Some films — particularly those in production -— track hot costs on a daily basis to keep on top of the labor costs on a day-by-day basis.

Despite having a Production Accountant, as Producer you are responsible for tracking costs and making sure you are on or under budget. So check the checker, and carefully review the Accountant's calculations.

CONTACT SHEET

As you begin to build your personnel for your project, start and maintain a Contact Sheet. Most producers like to organize it by Department. The list should have each and every person's name, address, e-mail address, phone numbers, cell phones, and so forth. The idea is to be able to reach anyone on the show at a moment's notice. This list (or a shortened version of it) can be circulated among all production people.

CONCLUSION

The time and energy you put into Pre-Production will help to insure you have the best experience possible during Principal Photography. Make sure you put in the effort during this phase so you can support and create the best project possible.

3

DEVELOPMENT/MARKETING

Being a producer isn't just knowing how to make the movie, it's also knowing how to put all the pieces together so the movie gets made. That's the front end. Then it's knowing how to market and promote the project before, during, and after it's made, so that it finds its audience. That is, after all, the whole point. Finally, you need to sell the project. This chapter is therefore a brief introduction to development and marketing, something that too many producers ignore altogether. Sales and distribution is a huge topic unto itself, but we'll also talk a bit about self-distribution.

DEVELOPMENT

Much of a producer's time is spent pulling a would-be project together: script rewrites, attracting actors, getting financing, etc. In the studio world, it's called development. Producers tend to call it "development hell." During this long and arduous process, many hours, weeks, months, and years can accrue. A great deal of money may also be spent (whether or not the movie actually gets made). In the independent world this money comes from the filmmakers, their friends and family, or investors' pockets. In the studio or network/cable world, it comes from their development department.

Filmmakers often make the mistake of leaving these development costs off their budgets, probably because it's painful to think that they may have to raise this money or pay these expenses themselves. Consider them now, figure out what you need to spend, double or triple it, and add it to your budget. These dollars can be recouped once the film is financed.

Of course, for small projects, shorts, and videos, these expenses may be limited to phone calls and a few presentations.

For features or big documentary projects they can be rather extensive and run into the thousands, hundreds of thousands, or even millions of dollars.

Script Development
Script analysis and evaluation (by others)
Rewrites (by one or more writers)
Research Trips (location trips, research, investor presentations)
Fees to writers, cowriters, script doctors, and consultants
Photocopying
Postage, messengers, etc.

Casting Agent hire
"Pay or play" fees for actors

Presentations
Storyboards or presentation art
Key art/poster design
Still photo sessions
Trailer shoot and expenses (a mini-budget in itself)
Travel
Actors and crew fees, etc.

Preparation of breakdown and shooting schedule
Preparation of budget
Projections
Cash flow analysis
Business plan

Legal documents
Initial agreements for principals
Contracts, agreements with actors, producers, co-producers, director, etc.

Travel to markets (Cannes, American Film Market, European Film Market) and festivals
Airfare, hotel, and per diem
Meetings in Los Angeles, New York, etc.

It is not unusual for a producer to spend $50,000 to $100,000 or more developing a small, multi-million dollar budget. (The studios spend millions and sometimes never make the project.) The higher the budget, the more "names" have to be attached. This is a time-consuming process and may involve months or years of work, rewrites, etc. It could even include "pay or play" offers to the actors where they are guaranteed a fee whether or not the financing is ever fully raised, just to be "attached" to the project.

These are not only hard costs (as per the line items above), but also a vast amount of the producer's time for which he or she should be compensated in fees in the final budget. If a filmmaker is serious about making his or her livelihood from making films, they cannot self-finance the development and not get reimbursed. Otherwise they end up making the film for a fee that may be less than what they spent developing it.

MARKETING/PUBLICITY

It may seem crass for us as *artists* to think this, but independent features, shorts, and documentaries are products, and like any other product, they need to be marketed and sold. Products succeed in finding their "audience" because of successful marketing and promotional campaigns. Entertainment products are no different. We must find and satisfy an audience.

There is a huge arsenal of tools available to market and promote our films and videos — from direct mail and personal sales to custom websites and trade magazine advertising. And there are many ways to get the attention of potential viewers' or buyers' eyes and ears with your film's "hooks." How, and when, do you start this whole process and decide which techniques are necessary?

The answer to the question of "when?" is now. It's possible to begin marketing and promoting your project the day you decide to make it. How do you promote something you don't have? You market your *idea* until a tangible object can take its place.

That's what the studios do with billboards, websites, previews, and magazine and newspaper articles. Why shouldn't you?

Let's look at what's included in the marketing/promotion section of an independent film budget. It really depends on what you can afford. It's great to hope that at the end of production you'll still have that little pot of money that you set aside to hire a distributor's rep, but if you really need it to pay your editor for another month or you won't finish, nobody will blame you for being a filmmaker first and a promoter second. Just keep in mind that when you do finish, those roles will be reversed, and you may as well be cheerful about spending some money on the marketing, because done right, it can get your project seen. And that might help you get your next role as a filmmaker.

Consider the Initial Steps a list of "must-dos." It is the least you can do to create awareness for your project with the right buyers or viewers. Consider the Additional Steps category as a guide describing how much time and funding the process of independent film marketing can consume. To cover all these items in detail is beyond the scope of this chapter, but to give you an idea of what some of these things cost, please see the list of Costs below.

Initial Steps:

- Create a promotional website.
- Create social media accounts and engage your audience through social media outlets.
- Provide an electronic media kit with downloadable photos, clips, and releases on the website.
- Solicit distributors/buyers directly with a screener and cover letter.
- Send press releases to pertinent media outlets.
- Pursue film festival screenings.
- Stage a premiere.

Additional Steps:

- Create a full presentation package to accompany distributor solicitations.
- Arrange distributor screenings.
- Set up an e-commerce section on the website to sell copies of the film as well as branded film merchandise (T-shirts, hats, coffee mugs, etc.).
- Hire a professional on-set photographer.
- Hire a publicist.
- Hire a distribution representative.
- Create and place print ads.
- Create and place online ads.
- Create and distribute marketing materials (posters, postcards, etc.) to appropriate audiences before you complete the film.
- Stage publicity events.
- Obtain sponsors for events and screenings.
- Solicit a wide range of media for interviews and coverage.
- Self-distribution: four-walling, fulfillment, advertising, sales percentages, UPC codes, etc.

FILM MARKETING/PUBLICITY LINE ITEMS COSTS

- Promotional Website

a. Domain Name Registration	$10 annually
b. Site design	$500+
c. Hosting	$150+ annually
d. E-commerce store	$30+ monthly

- Film Festival Screenings

a. Entry fees for festival	$25–$75 each
b. Travel (if selected to screen)	$0–$3,000 or more depending on festival location
c. Handouts (postcards, invites)	$200

- Premiere — staging a premiere can be done on the cheap if you are a good negotiator and can barter services (such as the rental of a theater). Some costs to consider include:
    a. Theater rental $750 and up
    b. Digital projector rental $200 and up
    c. Advertising in local media $500 and up
    d. Posters, handouts $200 and up
- Presentation Package
    a. Key Art $500+
  If you're on a budget, seek out illustrators/graphic artists at local art schools. Call the department chair and ask for referrals.
    b. Photography/Prints $200+
- Stationery Package
    a. Logo design $100+
    b. Letterhead/envelopes $150+
    c. Business cards/labels $50+
- Advertising/Promotion
  This will depend on who/what/where/how long
- Professional Services, e.g., Photographer, Publicist
  This will depend on who/what/where/how long
- Self-Distribution
  There are theatrical on-demand services online like *www.Tugg.com* where you can create your own theater events across the country. Additionally, you can "four wall" your film at various theaters — you rent the theater by the day or week, sell tickets through their box office, and split the proceeds. Research your options by contacting the specific theater directly.
- Marketing Materials (depending on quantities)
    a. Posters $200+
    b. Postcards $100+

Don't forget that sometimes "invisible" costs can break the bank. Keep a close eye on the copying and paper usage, postage, and mailing supplies (envelopes, padding, etc.).

SELF-DISTRIBUTION

If you sell or license your film to a broadcast or cable entity, there may be restrictions on whether or not you can self-distribute it. If you think you can carve out self-distribution in certain markets, ask your lawyer to negotiate the terms in your contract. If you license your film exclusively to one distribution company for all markets, it will be a lot simpler. But if you plan to self-distribute your film, whether it's a narrative or documentary feature, you'll need to make it your full-time job for many, many months. This is a business and it will require your full attention.

One of the pioneers of self-distribution, Peter Broderick (*www.peterbroderick.com*), elucidates several key ideas that filmmakers can use that distinguish self-distribution from the old model. To paraphrase just a few of the items on his list:

- Control — The filmmaker controls the distribution process, choosing which rights to give to distribution partners and which rights to hold on to.
- Hybrid model — Filmmakers can split up rights, for example, licensing to a distribution company but retaining the right to make direct sales. Or retain the right to make TV/cable, VOD, airline, or educational deals.
- Core audiences — The filmmaker targets the core audience for the project and markets to that group. If successful, crossover to a wider audience may be possible. There are specific strategies for marketing to core audiences, including establishing relationships with organizations, cross-promotions, e-mailing lists, websites, attendance/screenings at conferences, articles in publications, etc.

- Reducing costs — Spend less on print, TV, and radio ads and use the Internet, social media, cross-promotion, e-mail with permission, publicity.
- Direct sales — The model for self-distribution is to make profit margins as high as possible. Direct sales to customers via their own or partner websites achieve this.

Self-distribution is not easy. Like the settlers who braved the Oregon Trail, self-distributors may see danger lurking by the wagon tracks, but the brave ones will continue on to find success. If you are contemplating it, thoroughly research the latest opportunities including fulfillment houses, streaming from your own website, and four walling your film in various cities and communities. Contact filmmakers who self-distributed successfully to learn what they did as a case study.

4

HIGH DEFINITION

Special thanks to Director of Photography/Lighting Designer Rick Siegel (www.ricksiegel.net) for his technical expertise, which was a great help to me in writing this section.

High definition video is today's primary acquisition format. Technology changes at a very fast rate these days but it is helpful for a producer to have a basic understanding of many of the terms and tech specs included in this format.

As you consider your project during pre-production, make your plan "soup to nuts," that is, beginning to end, script to delivery. Research various acquisition formats, do camera tests, and then test the format through the post-production workflow so you know everything works properly, looks good, and is the right answer for your project. So ask the experts *before* you shoot a frame. This cannot be overemphasized.

Before we get to the plan, let's consider some attributes of High Definition formats that are key to understanding it:

Sensors and Pixels
Frame Size
Aspect Ratios
Frame Rate
Recording Method
Codecs/Compression
Bit Depth
Camera Sensor and Dynamic Range
Look Up Table (LUT)
Color Sampling

SENSORS AND PIXELS

If we peek inside a video camera, somewhere behind the lens we'll find one or three sensors, called either CCDs (charged coupled devices) or CMOS (complementary metal oxide semiconductors). On the flat surface of these sensors is a grid of tiny sensors, (picture elements — pix-els, get it?). One sensor less than an inch in size may have millions of pixels. When light strikes these pixels, each one reads the brightness and color information in its own tiny spot in that moment in time, and creates and stores an electrical charge. The more light, the more charge. In an instant, all the charges from the pixels are read and processed into a digital video signal that is then recorded (oversimplifying here).

Different video formats have different numbers of pixels. Too few for your filming situation and the image looks fuzzy or blocky. A sufficient number of pixels for the end use of the project — say projection in a theater — and our eyes won't even see that there are pixels. That's why we filmmakers need to know this stuff. It's not enough to just pick up a video camera and start shooting. Where will this project be shown? In theaters? Only on the Web? Under what conditions? Who is it for? What is its purpose? These questions have as much to do with your technical approach as they do with creativity and content.

FRAME SIZE

The Advanced Television Systems Committee (ATSC) is the entity responsible for defining standards like video formats. There are many formats for digital TV broadcast and digital theatrical projection, but don't worry, we're not going through every format here (search the Web for "ATSC video formats" for the whole table). Frame size is one aspect of format. Let's start with pixels, the building blocks of the digital video image. Every image consists of rows and rows of individual pixels, square or rectangular in shape, all stacked on top of each other in a grid. These horizontal rows, or lines, are called scan lines. Look closely at your TV screen and you may be able to see them. All the pixels taken together — or you could say all the scan lines taken together — form what we call the raster image (from the Latin *rastrum*, a rake, from *radere*, to scrape; see the grid pattern?). The number of pixels and scan lines determines the frame size.

When we say "definition," we're talking about the amount of detail in the image. Definition is measured by the number of scan lines in a frame. High definition has two basic sizes, both in 16:9 aspect ratio, 720 and 1,080. 720 is also known as 1,280 × 720, meaning there are 720 lines of 1,280 pixels per line. 1,080 is also known as 1,920 × 1,080 — 1,080 lines with 1,920 pixels per line.

Additionally there's 2K, 4K, 5K (and more Ks in the future), because their scan lines exceed 2,000, 4,000 and 5,000 horizontal lines respectively. The 4K image is 4,096 × 2,160 pixels, or four times the resolution of 2K (2,048 lines with 1,080 pixels per line).

From this point forward in the book I will be defining "digital video" as any format that includes high definition, 2K, 4K and 5K (and beyond).

As an aside, there are "legacy" television formats — NTSC, PAL, and SECAM — still used in some countries. In NTSC territories (most of the Americas, Japan, South Korea, Taiwan, the Philippines, Burma, and some Pacific island nations and territories), the standard definition frame size is referred to as 720 by 480 (720 × 480), meaning it has 480 horizontal scan lines and each line is 720 pixels wide. Interestingly, the pixel count is the same whether it's shot or displayed in 16:9 widescreen aspect ratio or 4:3, the old TV standard aspect ratio — the pixels themselves adjust to be shorter and fatter for 16:9, and taller and thinner for 4:3. In PAL countries (much of Europe), there are 576 scan lines, also 720 pixels wide (720 × 576). SECAM is mostly in Russia, many African nations, and some Middle East and Far East countries and there are 625 scan lines.

ASPECT RATIOS

We've just talked about one property of the frame, its size. The other property is its shape. Video and film frames are generally rectangular, but the proportions of width and height vary. The ratio of the width to the height of a picture is called the *aspect ratio*. For digital video the common aspect ratio is 16:9, or 1.77:1, (which equals 16 divided by 9). Theatrical films use 1.85:1, and widescreen films go up to 2.35:1. For legacy standard video the aspect ratio is 4:3, meaning that the standard video frame has a width of 4 units and a height of 3 units. This is also expressed as 1.33:1 (which equals 4 divided by 3).

FRAME RATE

Frame rate refers to the number of images that are recorded or displayed per second. (This is not to be confused with shutter speed, which is the amount of time that light gets to the sensor as each frame is captured.) Discuss with the Cinematographer to decide what frame rate and shutter speed is right for your overall project and individual shots within your project.

PULL DOWN

Understanding the concept of "pull down" is necessary when converting your digital material from one frame rate to another. What pull down will be required is determined by the difference between your current frame and the one you need to convert to. Let's say we shot in 24 fps and you need to convert to 29.97 fps. The pull down will be 3:2. Every interlaced video frame has two fields for each frame. The 3:2 pull down is where the digital transfer process adds a third video field to every second video frame. This way the mathematics work to "stretch" the video to conform to the 29.97 format.

In the following diagram, the top row represents four frames shot at 24 fps. When we do the 3:2 pull down process (aka 3:2 pull·down, or normal pull down), we'll end up at the bottom row in 29.97 fps. Here's what happens.

The group of four 24 fps frames (and *every* group of four 24 fps frames in the entire stream) gets converted to five frames (which is 10 fields — count all the little boxes in the bottom row) in the video stream. Frame A from the top row gets converted to Frames A1 and A2. Frame C also gets converted to two frames: C1 and C2. But Frames B and D get converted to three frames each: B1, B2, B3, and D1, D2, and D3 respectively. See the pattern? It goes 2:3:2:3, which is how the pull down got its name.

4 frames of original film @ 24 fps

A	B	C	D

A1	A2	B1	B2	B3	C1	C2	D1	D2	D3

5 frames (10 fields) of interlaced video pull down to 29.97

As another example — if post-production needs to be finished at 23.976 fps and the original camera materials were captured at 24 fps, then there will be a pull down for that conversion (slowing down by 0.1%). The sound is also slowed down by 0.1%. This slowing down, or speed variance, is the first part of pull down. Please note that it results in a sound pitch difference that your post-production technician will need to adjust.

DO A TEST, PLEASE

Workflow and deliverables are vitally important to your film from a budget and technical perspective. You'll need to talk with your DP and your Editor, in the same room at the same time, to work out the complexities of your workflow and do a test with your camera of choice. Shoot some shots that closely resemble what you really expect to shoot. Edit in your format of choice and output to your format of choice. Know in advance what your deliverables are, like what formats are required, at what timings, at what frame rates, etc. The more tech specs you have up front the better.

CODECS/COMPRESSION

Compression schemes are called *codecs* (*co*mpressor/*dec*ompressor), and while the topic is pretty complex (more than we'll get into here), the basic idea is simple. Video and audio signals are compressed during storage and transmission. Usually the signals are decompressed when you master your project. Codecs come into play when you transcode your material. For instance, you may shoot your project in a very high resolution codec but you need to transcode to a lower resolution file to import to your editing system. Later on you will go back to your high res camera original for your OnLine conform before you master your film. Two common codecs in use today are Apple ProRes (currently a family of five codecs: Proxy, LT, 422, 422HQ, and 4444) and DNxHD.

Compression can happen at every point in the process from camera capture to editing to release. For example, one of the first places compression may occur in some formats is with Color Sampling (more on this later), wherein the video camera tosses out half of the color pixels, thus reducing the color data by half compared to the luminance, or brightness, data. Most of us can't see the difference. Technically, if color sampling has taken place, the video has now been compressed.

Some cameras will allow you to record "RAW" which is uncompressed video. That means that the image comes into the camera, hits the image sensor and does not go through any compression or processing and is recorded on an off-board digital device — thus called RAW. It allows you to record the full dynamic range of the camera's sensor. This means there has been no interpretation of the data in camera and/or the recording device and you will need to do this in the post-production process. This will give you more options in finishing your film but will require more time, money, and much more digital storage space. It may or may not be the right choice for your project. Always remember to *test* the workflow!

BIT DEPTH

Bit depth in video is a measure of light sample size or shades of gray, or you could say color representation (audio uses bit depth too — same basic idea, but measuring voltage in an audio sample). It's always expressed as a number, usually as either 8 bit or 10 bit, but it can go higher, and since it's a binary number (we're in computer land, remember) it's a power of 2, so 8 bit = 2 to the 8th power or 256 steps. 10 bit = 2 to the 10th power or 1,024 steps. Steps of what? Steps between black and white, also known as "shades of gray" or "color." Or we could measure steps of no red to maximum red, or no green to maximum green, and so on. Remember that what's being measured, say black to white, does not change. What's changing is the tool doing the measuring. To use an analogy, with 8 bit, we're using a ruler with 256 markers between every foot. With 10 bit, there are 1,024 markers between every foot. 10 bit gives us more precision. Practically speaking, if we have more markers, we can measure more precisely, and then we can render and manipulate with more detail. If we can't measure it, we can't get to it.

Here's an example. If I'm shooting a movie in black and white with an 8-bit video camera, chances are I'll have few problems. Why? Because it turns out that the gray scale from black to white, at least as represented in video, can be accommodated quite well within the 256 steps of 8-bit depth. But as soon as I switch over to color, and cue my redheaded actress with the sun catching the burnished highlights in her hair, the wind fluttering the folds of her many-colored dress as she stands in dappled shade with her bouquet of daffodils and pink geraniums, there are just too many colors and shades of gray here to be measured accurately by an 8-bit camera, at least if I expect more from my picture than a small image, like on TV or the Web. If I'm projecting on a big screen, or doing any effects work with my images, or color correction, perhaps I should re-think my choice of camera and go with a format that includes 10 bit.

This doesn't mean that you should avoid 8-bit formats, just that you need to know what your goals are and whether you have the tools you need. Discuss and test with the Director of Photography and Editor prior to choosing a camera and capture format for your film.

CAMERA SENSOR AND DYNAMIC RANGE

Cameras today have 12–14 exposure stops of dynamic range, which is a tremendous amount of exposure latitude (almost exactly the same as 35mm film). Unfortunately, our best television monitors and theatrical projectors only allow our eyes to see approximately 5 exposure stops of dynamic range. Many camera manufacturers have created logarithmic formulas that process the 12–14 exposure stops to allow us to maximize that full dynamic range on a 5-exposure stop display device. The camera manufacturers do this to try to replicate what the human eye sees when looking at the world directly and not through a camera lens. A few of these formulas have names — for instance, Sony engineers have created S-Log, Arri has created C-Log, and RED has their own logarithmic formula.

LOOK UP TABLE (LUT)

When shooting with a digital camera that is capturing images at the full dynamic range, the image that you will see on the set monitor will look rather flat and washed out. That is the visual result of what we just discussed above. Consequently it is helpful to apply a Look Up Table (LUT) to the camera so that the digital material on-set looks closer to what the image could look like after it has been graded in post-production.

To do this, the Digital Imaging Technician (DIT) creates the LUT through a computer application and then loads it into the camera, which then affects the look of the material (i.e., adding more color and contrast) when viewing via on-set monitors. The LUT is "non-destructive" and does not actually change the raw footage logarithmically to the off-board recorder. If you wish to capture the LUT-applied material for editing purposes, you will need to record that separately to on-board digital media and send that to the Assistant Editor for use in the edit room. By the way, LUTs can be applied at every stage in the workflow. You may decide to apply the LUT only in the edit room.

The default LUT is "Rec 709" which was created to conform to the 5 exposure stops of dynamic range that display devices can show. This is a common and much used LUT and should work for most on-set requirements. If you are shooting a film with a very specific look, your DP/DIT may create a different LUT. Period films, projects with extreme contrast situations (e.g., snow scenes or night shooting) may require customized LUTs.

COLOR SAMPLING

Human vision is better at perceiving fine details of brightness than of color. Praise the rods and blame the cones, I guess. We have cones sensitive to red, green, and blue, the primary colors that form the basis for all colors. The original video signal back in the 1930s was black and white, and it was, and still is, called *luminance*, since it was all about brightness. When color came along in the 1950s, a new signal was introduced, called *chrominance* — it describes color.

Video engineers, big brains that they are, figured out that a video image still looks pretty darned good even when they throw away a bunch of the color information used to make it. Anytime we can maintain quality while reducing the quantity of data to transmit through the system, that's a good thing. When the video signal from the sensor in the camera is processed, some of the color data is thus thrown out. How much depends on the video format.

To explain all this, engineers decided on a form of color called YUV, where Y = the black and white (luminance) of the image and U and V = the color parts of the image (chrominance). (Later, when digital video appeared, to delineate digital color space from analog they called the digital color Y Cb Cr.)

Imagine four pixels in a row. In its purest or highest quality form, each pixel has a unique Y value (luminance), as well as a unique Cb and Cr value (color). Each pixel is fully loaded.

Y Cb Cr	Y Cb Cr	Y Cb Cr	Y Cb Cr

This is called 4:4:4 ("four-four-four") because there are four pixels each of Y, Cb and Cr. This is full color resolution: high-end 4:4:4 component color.

Now let's knock it down a notch. Let's throw away some color. Let's compress a little. What happens if we average a pair of neighbor Cb pixels and we do the same with a pair of neighbor Cr pixels? Then we get this:

Y Cb Cr	Y	Y Cb Cr	Y

This is called 4:2:2 ("four-two-two") because there are four pixels of Y, and two pixels each of Cb and Cr. This is also called *Chroma sub-sampling*. Now we have half as much color resolution as brightness resolution. Is this a terrible thing? No. There are many high-quality component digital formats in 4:2:2.

Let's go down one more, to 4:1:1, in which we have four luminance samples for every one Cb and Cr, and we have one-quarter the color resolution.

Y Cb Cr	Y	Y	Y

This is the Chroma sub-sampling used in DV (NTSC). It's not recommended for compositing (matte work) or titles and effects where color resolution is more critical, but it may be perfectly fine for your project. Again, know your end use.

There are other Chroma sub-sampling scenarios as well, such as 4:2:0.

CONCLUSION

There isn't any such thing as the "best" video format. It all goes back to your project and its unique needs and deliverables. Will you use green screen? Do you need a fast turnaround? Will you be doing a lot of compositing or effects work? Are you headed for projection in a movie theater or will it only be viewed on television monitors and computer screens? The technical information presented above comes into play when you are weighing all these considerations. Chroma sub-sampling and bit depth determine how accurately you can measure color value and how well you can composite images and make effects. Knowing about workflow from camera capture to recording (codecs) can help you understand transcoding and method of output for your deliverables. All of this technical knowledge helps you pick the best camera, equipment, and workflow to support the creative choices and the look for your project.

Here's a formula for a relatively hassle-free workflow: Work backwards. For each project, start by carefully considering what formats you must deliver, where it's going to be played. Consider what special elements you'll be working with (green screen, color correction, visual effects, etc.). Then, in consultation and testing with your DP and Editor, identify what format you'll be editing in. Finally, test and choose a capture format and *stick with it*. Try very hard not to change formats with different frame rates and frame sizes during that project. It's a fascinating, ever-changing world — do your research and enjoy!

5

A MASTER BUDGET, LINE BY LINE

First there are the budget *categories*, then the *line items* — the nitty-gritty details without which we would have no budget at all. This chapter shakes the budget so that all the line items fall out into the daylight where we can study them. You'll find a Master Budget Template in Excel which corresponds to this chapter's discussion at www.mwp.com. It has all the formulas and line items you'll need: You can build any budget for any of your projects from this one template.

To download your free Excel Master Budget Template:

1. Go to *www.mwp.com*
2. Click on "MW Film School."
3. Open the item "Sample Budgets/Forms."
4. Download the free Excel Master Budget Template.
5. Save it to your computer.

Two things to keep in mind:

1) Do not put any numbers on Page 1, known as the Top Sheet — this is where all the subtotals from all the other pages get transferred over so they can be totaled. If you start putting in "hard" numbers on any of these lines you will destroy the formulas that allow the Excel spreadsheet to do its math magic!

2) Keep all the line items in the master budget template in your own budget: Don't delete any of them until you have completely locked your budget and you are going into production. The template is lengthy but until you lock your budget, you don't know if you may need another line item that is already included in the master

budget template: It is an automatic, built-in checklist that provides you with all the possibilities that you may encounter throughout the pre-production phase. Keep this in mind before you start deleting various categories and line items.

Remember: Rates and Prices Are Examples Only!

The budgets and all rates and prices cited in this book are solely for purposes of illustration! It is critical that you search for the very latest rates and prices when calculating your own budget . . . then double check them further down the road so that you don't have any unpleasant (read *costly*) surprises when it's time to pay the invoices.

Later, in Chapter 6, you'll find specific examples — each with a free downloadable budget template available — of a variety of feature and documentary film templates.

The Master Budget discussion that follows outlines all of the line items that can be used in film production. I'll go line by line and give you an explanation of each line and some general costs so you have an understanding for each one.

ABOVE-THE-LINE AND BELOW-THE-LINE

Feature film budgets distinguish between "above-the-line" and "below-the-line." "Above-the-line" refers to the producer, director, actors, script and writers, the so-called creative elements. These are also divided because "above-the-line" could vary tremendously since it is a function of expensive creative talent, where "below-the-line" figures are more stable and predictable. In many ways the word "creative" is a misnomer, since jobs below-the-line call for creativity as well. Everything else — crew and equipment, and everything editorial — is "below-the-line." Often you'll see a third division, "Other," covering categories like insurance, general/administrative costs, publicity, festival expenses, etc.

The separation is made because above-the-line people often get salaries based on their current standing in the industry and may also get "points" (percentages) in the film's profit. This above-the-line figure is therefore based more on market conditions and what it costs to get a certain person than on the hard rock reality of the below-the-line, which reflects what the actual production may cost. Executives or investors can therefore readily see the differences in cost between above-the-line (talent) and below-the-line (production) costs and determine if they are getting their money's worth.

ABOVE-THE-LINE

01–00 Story & Rights
Rights Purchases
Options
Writer Salaries/Screenplay Purchase
Research/Clearances
Title Registration
Script Timing
Storyboards/Pre-Viz
WGA Publication Fee
Development

02–00 Producers Unit
Executive Producer
Producer
Associate Producer
Assistant to Producer(s)
Consultants
Miscellaneous Expenses

03–00 Direction
Director
Assistant to Director

04–00 Cast
Lead Actors
Supporting Cast
Day Players
Casting Director/Staff

Casting Expenses
Choreographer
Assistant(s) to Choreographer
Dialect Coach
Narrator/Voiceover Artist
Stunt Coordinator
Stunt Players
Stunt Costs/Adjustments
Stunt Equipment
ADR (Actors' Fees)
Cast Overtime

05–00 Travel and Living — Producers/Director
Airfares
Hotel
Taxi/Limo
Auto
Train
Excess Baggage
Phone
Gratuities
Per Diem

06–00 Travel and Living — Cast
Airfares
Hotel
Taxi/Limo
Auto
Train
Excess Baggage
Phone
Gratuities
Per Diem

07–00 Residuals (e.g., 2nd Run)
Writer
Director
Actors

Fringes
Note: In the sample budget templates, all fringes, both above- and below-the-line, are calculated within each category and indicated as Payroll, DGA, WGA, SAG-AFTRA, etc. I present the following laundry list so you can see all the Fringes in one place.

Payroll Taxes:
FICA-SS (Social Security)
FICA-HI (Medicare)
FUTA (Federal Unemployment Insurance)
SUTA (State Unemployment Insurance)
CREW WKCOMP (Workers' Compensation)
OFFICE WKCOMP
HANDLING FEE (Payroll Service)

Guilds/Unions:
DGA DIRECTOR
SAG-AFTRA
WGA WRITER
SAG-AFTRA/DGA WKCOMP
VACATION/HOLIDAY (Union)
AFM (American Federation of Musicians)

BELOW-THE-LINE

08–00 Production Staff

UPM/Line Producer
1st Assistant Director
2nd Assistant Directors
Stage Manager
Production Coordinator
Script Supervisor
Production Accountant/Auditor
Technical Advisors
Production Assistants
Studio Teacher/Tutor

09–00 Background Actors/Extras

Stand-Ins
Extras
Extras Casting Fee
Extras Transportation

10–00 Sound Stage

Stage Rental
Stage Lighting Rental
Stage Grip Rental
Phones/Internet
Garbage Removal
Green Room
Makeup Room
Office Rental
Parking

11–00 Production Design

Production Designer
Art Director
Art Assistants
Set Designer

Model Makers/Miniatures
Draftsperson
Research/Materials
Vehicle Expenses
Purchases/Rentals

12–00 Set Construction
Construction Coordinator
Foreman
Scenic Painters
Greensman
Construction Materials — Purchases
Construction Materials — Rentals
Construction Equipment
Set Strike

13–00 Set Operations
Key Grip
Best Boy Grip
Grips
Dolly/Crane Grips
Grip Rentals
Expendables
Kit Rentals
Craft Service
Air Conditioning/Heating

14–00 Special Effects (SFX)
Special Effects Person
SFX Assistant(s)
Manufacturing Labor
Fabrication
Rentals

15–00 Set Dressing
Set Decorator

Lead Person
Swing Gang/Set Dressers
Additional Labor
Expendables
Purchases
Rentals
Loss & Damage
Kit Rentals
Vehicle Expenses

16–00 Property
Property Master
Prop Assistants
Purchases
Rentals
Loss & Damage
Kit Rentals
Vehicle Expenses

17–00 Wardrobe
Costume Designer
Costumer
Additional Costumer(s)
Expendables
Purchases
Rentals
Alteration & Repairs
Cleaning & Dyeing
Loss & Damage
Kit Rentals
Vehicle Expenses

18–00 Makeup and Hair
Key Makeup Artist
Additional Makeup Artist(s)
Key Hair Stylist

Additional Hair Stylist(s)
Special Effects Makeup
Purchases
Rentals
Kit Rentals

19–00 Electrical
Gaffer
Best Boy Electric
Electrics
Additional Labor
Equipment Purchases
Lighting Package Rentals
Additional Rentals
Electrical Generator/Driver
Loss & Damage
Kit Rentals

20–00 Camera
Director of Photography
Camera Operator or B Camera
1st Assistant Camera
2nd Assistant Camera
Digital Imaging Technician (DIT)
Still Photographer
Camera Package Rentals
Camera Package Purchase
Steadicam Operator & Equipment
Teleprompter/Operator
Video Assist/Operator
Aerial Photography
Underwater and Topside Photography
Drones/GoPros
Maintenance/Loss & Damage
Motion Control

Expendables
Video Truck
Video Truck Crew
Kit Rentals

21–00 Production Sound
Mixer
Boom Operator
Expendables/Batteries
Sound Package
Walkie-Talkies
Sound Truck
Misc. plus Loss & Damage

22–00 Transportation
Transportation Coordinator
Drivers
Vehicle Rentals
Parking/Tolls/Gas
Repairs & Maintenance
Honeywagon Pumping
Miscellaneous Expenses

23–00 Location Expenses
Location Manager
Location Assistants
First Aid/Medic
Fire Officers
Security
Police
Permits
Parking
Catering Service
  Crew Meals
  Extras
  Ice/Propane

- 2nd Meals
- Sales Tax
- Tent/Tables/Chairs

Location Office Space Rental
Location Office Supplies
Location Office Equipment
Location Office Telephone/Fax
Location Site Rental Fees
Location Scout
Auto Rentals
Miscellaneous Expenses

24–00 Picture Vehicles/Animals
Animal Trainers

- Boss Wrangler
- Assistant Wrangler
- Wranglers
- Riders/Handlers, etc.

Animals

- Rentals
- Veterinary Expenses
- Feed/Shelter
- Transportation

Picture Cars

25–00 Media
Digital Media
Raw Film Stock
Film Lab—Negative Prep & Process
Telecine/Film to Digital Transfer
Videotape Stock

26–00 Travel and Living — Crew
Airfares
Hotels
Taxi

Auto
Train
Excess Baggage
Per Diem
Gratuities

Below-the-Line Fringes
Payroll Taxes:
  FICA-SS (Social Security)
  FICA-HI (Medicare)
  FUTA (Federal Unemployment Insurance)
  SUTA (State Unemployment Insurance)
  CREW WKCOMP (Workers' Compensation)
  OFFICE WKCOMP
  HANDLING FEE (Payroll Service)

Guilds/Unions:
  DGA (Assistant Directors, Stage Managers, UPMs)
  SAG-AFTRA
  SAG-AFTRA/DGA WKCOMP
  VACATION/HOLIDAY (Union)
  IATSE/Teamsters

27–00 Editorial
Editor — Shoot/Post
Assistant Editor — Shoot/Post
Post-Production Supervisor
Editing Room Rental
Edit System Rental
Online Editing/Conform

28–00 Music
Composer Fee
Musicians
Music Prep
Studio Costs

Music Scoring Stage
Cartage & Rentals
Music Mix Room
Singers
Payroll Service
Miscellaneous
Music Licensing
Music Supervisor/Clearance

29–00 Post-Production Sound
Sound Editor
Assistant Sound Editor
Music Editor
Dialogue Editor
Spotting (Music & FX)
ADR (Studio/Editor)
Foley Stage/Editor
Foley Artists
Narration Recording
Audio Laydown
Audio Mix
Dolby License
Miscellaneous Expenses

30–00 Post-Production — Digital and Film
Stock Footage
Archive Supplies
Archival Researcher
Clearance Supervisor
Screeners
Film Prints
Miscellaneous Expenses

31–00 Digital Intermediate
Digital Intermediate
Hard Drive Purchases

32–00 Titling and Graphics
Titling
Graphic Designer
Special Graphic Effects
Motion Control
Closed Captioning
Subtitling

33–00 Deliverables
Masters/Clones
Transfers and Dubs
Screening Copies

34–00 Digital Visual Effects/Animation
VFX
Animation

35–00 Insurance
Producer's Entertainment Package
Media/Negative
Faulty Stock
Equipment
Props/Sets
Extra Expense
3rd-Party Property Damage
Office Contents
General Liability
Hired Auto
Cast Insurance
Workers' Compensation
Errors and Omissions

36–00 General and Administrative Expenses
Business License/Taxes
Legal
Accounting Fees

Telephone/Fax
Copying/Scanning
Postage & Freight
Office Space Rental
Office Furniture
Office Equipment & Supplies
Computer Rental
Software/Apps/FTP
Transcription
Messenger/Overnight
Parking
Storage
Publicity
Wrap Party
Working Meals
Overhead (Production Fee)
Completion Bond

37–00 Publicity and Marketing
Publicity
Marketing

These are the basic costs which may be incurred in every budget in this book. They should cover 95% of all the items in your own budgets, so study this list to be sure you've included everything your project will require.

The next section provides a detailed description of these line items and associated costs.

These numbers are guidelines! **Your actual costs will vary depending on your geographic location, your skill in acquiring goods and services, and your inventiveness in solving production problems. Check with unions, guilds, and payroll services to get current rates and percentages as they usually change each year.**

ABOVE-THE-LINE

01–00 Story and Rights

This category covers the costs to develop the project.

01–01 Rights Purchases

If you base your project on copyrighted material like a novel, a song, or a magazine article, you not only need the owner's permission, but you'll also have to pay the owner for the right to make the film version. The same applies if you are telling someone's life story, unless you are gathering material from public domain sources like court transcripts and newspaper stories, and even then, you must be careful about defamation of character.

To track down the owner of the copyright, call the publisher. If that doesn't work, and if copyright registration, renewal, or transfer of ownership was after 1978, try an online search through the US Copyright Office (www.copyright.gov). If prior to 1978 it requires a manual search. There's no charge if you go there yourself (in the Library of Congress, Washington, DC), or you can hire their staff to do the search for you at an hourly rate. You can also determine whether or not a title is or has fallen into the public domain.

Once you know who the owner is, negotiate to buy the rights or buy an option. You may want your lawyer to advise you — rights deals can be complex, and you'll need to protect yourself and the project by negotiating the proper deal.

A cost effective way to hire a lawyer is to contact Volunteer Lawyers for the Arts (www.vlany.org), an organization that can provide lower-cost attorneys to assist filmmakers on their projects. There are also several good books with sample contracts (see Appendix: Cost-Saving Ideas) to help you learn about the general agreements before you hire an attorney to do the final deal.

01–02 Options

An *option* gives you the exclusive right to hold the property for a specified term (usually a year or two) while you look for financing, or write script drafts, and attract stars and a director. The option agreement usually states that if the term ends with no production agreement, and if the option is not renewed, then the rights revert to the original owner. The option payment (if any) is non-refundable. That's why a renewal clause is important. You don't want to have the project on the verge of a "green light" somewhere and then have the option expire with no renewal.

If the project goes forward, the option spells out how much money the copyright owner then gets for the rights. These agreements can be simple or complex, depending on the property and who is involved.

A TV movie option for someone's life story might cost the producer anywhere from $500 on the low end to $10,000+ on the high end or more if it's a famous person. When the project is made, the rights payment may be anywhere from $50,000 to $75,000 for an average TV movie (unless you're dealing with a blockbuster personality, when the sky's the limit). Having said that, often producers can obtain an option for $1 to $100 if the person is very interested in you having the opportunity to develop the project.

01–03 Writer Salaries/Screenplay Purchase

For budgeting, the script is the most important element in the entire production. The more work put into a detailed script, preferably a "shooting script," the more complete the budget and the greater the savings.

Before you hire a writer, check out her past work and get references to make sure she will be a good creative collaborator and make her deadlines. Develop the script with the writer concentrating on what is best for the project creatively. Once you are happy with it, start to look at the script from a budget point of view. Can that night scene be just as effective if shot in daylight? (Saving extra lights.) Can those two scenes in the two bedrooms be shot in one bedroom? (Saving a camera setup.) Can the car chase become a foot race? Save money but don't gut the story.

The writer's fee will vary depending on the scale of the project and the overall budget. I give some figures below from the Writers

Guild of America rate card, but don't use them without going through the WGA rate card yourself, as there are numerous ifs, ands, and buts that make every project unique.

$$$

Low-Budget Original Theatrical Screenplay including Treatment
$67,805
High-Budget Original Theatrical Screenplay including Treatment
$127, 295

Network Prime Time, Program 60 minutes or less
Writer's Fee: Story $14,547
Teleplay $23,984

Not Network Prime Time (high budget), 60 minutes or less
Story $10,118
Teleplay $17,523

Documentary Program (low budget), 60 minutes or less
Story $5,338

For a short, a documentary, an industrial, or an independent feature using non-WGA writing talent, these are not necessarily the figures to use. You'll need to see how much you can afford for the script and how much the writer is willing to take.

Treatments are more affordable. It will depend on your ability as a negotiator, the perceived value of the writer, and the timeliness of the subject matter.

When a writer (non-WGA) is eager to get his or her property produced, or just get some work, you can strike a "spec" deal. This means the writer:

a) becomes your partner and gets paid an agreed sum, plus a percentage of the "back end."
b) gets paid an agreed sum at an agreed time but no percentage.

Or some combination of the above.

What about the WGA? If a guild member chooses to work non-guild, that is the writer's choice and she will need to deal with the union about any consequences. It could become an issue for you if the project goes into production.

01–04 Research/Clearances (Additional Legal Fees are included in 36–00 General and Administrative Expenses.)

After the screenplay has been approved on the creative side, you'll need to pass it through a legal clearance procedure to make sure you haven't inadvertently named the maniacal serial killer after the chairman of an international conglomerate. The clearance people also check on other things, like titles and place names. Consult your attorney on this or contact a clearance company.

01–05 Title Registration

You'll need to register the screenplay with the US Copyright Office once you receive the first draft. Check with your attorney to find out if you need to register it again when you have the final draft.

01–06 Script Timing

For features and TV movies, the Script Supervisor reads the script and estimates the time it will play on screen. This is done once the script is approved for shooting.

01–07 Storyboards/Pre-Viz

These can be anything from a director scrawling a succession of shots on a napkin to a full-blown presentation by a professional storyboard artist to time spent with pre-visualization software, in which you can input certain camera specs, build your set, pop in your actors, and then experiment with the look of your shots in 3D so you have a pretty usable shot list. For complicated scenes, a storyboard or pre-viz program can really help visualize what action you want to happen when, and where to place the camera. Many experienced directors use storyboards or pre-viz for stunts, special effects, or any potential difficulty with continuity.

Producers also use boards in pitch meetings and written proposals. The pictures help convey action and feelings and may help you get financing.

$$$

Storyboard artists usually get $50–$75 per hour or $400–$600 per day or $2,000–$3,000 per week.

01–08 WGA Publication Fee

Some low-budget WGA agreements require a $10,000 publication fee paid to the writer on the first day of Principal Photography. Check with the guild to find out if your agreement has this requirement.

01–10 Development

This line item is for the costs accrued in the years you spent developing the project. Keep all your receipts so you can get reimbursed for these costs like travel expenses for meetings.

02–00 Producer's Unit

This section covers the fees and expenses for all the Producers on the project.

02–01 Executive Producer

Executive producers are people who get the financing and/or talent attachments for any given project. Depending on the project, they may have to find several thousand dollars or several million dollars. Depending on the size of the project you may have more than one executive producer.

Make sure to refer to the Producers Guild of America (www.producersguild.org) for a clear definition of each producer credit. There is a lot of confusion and sometimes "credit inflation" with producer screen credits. This organization has been working hard to clarify the titles and make sure people are credited properly. Remember this simple rule: You do the work, you get the credit.

$$$

The executive producer receives a flat fee or percentage of profits or both. For a feature in the $3.5 million budget range, he or she could earn from $100,000 to $150,000. For a $150,000 budget, the executive producer can get from $10,000 to $20,000.

02–02 Producer

The producer is the one person responsible for the entire production from soup to nuts. He or she is on the project longest and oversees all elements of the production, including preparing the budget, breaking down the script, hiring the director, camera operator, crew, and actors.

$$$

Producers can be paid a flat fee and often participate in profit sharing. Or they may prefer a weekly salary. The rates are negotiable and vary widely. A producer on a student film will either work for free to build his portfolio or get a flat fee like $1,000 to $2,000. For a non-union film project, a producer might get $2,000 to $2,500 a week.

If there is no executive producer, the producer packages the project (script, director, major actors). The producer handles the financing and the allotment of budget monies, negotiates the major contracts, and approves all expenditures. If a producer is hired for only one phase of the project such as production, he might get a co-producer credit.

A Line Producer, for example, oversees the pre-production and principal photography. The job ends after the production is wrapped out — usually a week or two after shooting ends.

Sometimes producers will make a deal for some fees up front and other fees on the "back-end" after the film has made a profit. It can work for "below-the-line" people as well, but they are usually accustomed to being paid at the end of the day. Every person and situation is different.

Co-Producer would also be in this line item. Some films have Co-Producers and some don't. Sometimes the Line Producer also receives a Co-Producer credit — these decisions are made by the Producer on a project-by-project basis.

02–03 Associate Producer

Unfortunately, there is a lot of confusion around the title and job description of associate producer (and producer, for that matter). The title loses some of its credibility when it is indiscriminately given to relatives, girl and boy friends, and investors.

The title can be as fictitious as a fairy tale, or it can be real. When it's real, it's often a title given to the Production Manager as a perk (see Production Staff 08–00). It's also real on TV series productions, where the AP can also be the Post-Production Supervisor, shepherding the project through the labyrinth of post. In the documentary world, the associate producer credit is usually given to the person doing all the research on the film.

02–04 Assistant to Producer(s)

This is an entry-level position for someone to help the Producer(s) do their jobs on the film. It can entail errands, sitting in on meetings, script coverage, etc.

$$$

This position usually has a rate of $750–$1,000 per week.

02–06 Consultants

Consultants is a line item that covers a great number of possible contributors to the project: financial consultants, distribution consultants, historians, scientists, police experts, and medical advisors. He or she usually receives a flat fee or retainer. The consultant can be called upon at various times throughout scripting or production should the need arise.

02–07 Miscellaneous Expenses

This line may contain costs like union signatory fees.

03–00 Direction

This section covers the fees for all the Directors of the project.

03–01 Director

The director is the person responsible for bringing the script into reality, the person with an artistic vision — an ability to work with people and images and bring a story, concept, or idea to fruition. The director's ideas usually alter the script and its development, so if you know who the director will be, get his or her input early on in the development process.

The director is also involved in casting and usually the selection of a Director of Photography, a Production Designer and Editor. The director is hired for artistic taste, ability to get the job done on budget, and to help determine the logistical approach to shooting the film or tape. He or she is a multitalented person who can manage a wide range of responsibilities. Usually the director's work continues through the editing of the film.

On smaller projects and documentaries, the director can also be the camera operator, or the writer, or even a producer. You may be able to make a flat deal with a director, or bring the director on for a specific number of days and pay on a daily basis.

Depending on the project, the director may agree to a deferred (or partially deferred) salary until money comes in for the budget. If a DGA director wants to work non-guild, she will need to deal with any consequences, and it may impact your budget/production as well.

$$$

Just for purposes of ballparking, the Directors Guild gives the following minimum rates in a few selected categories, or see *www.dga.org*.

Freelance Television

Free TV — Network Prime Time, 60 minutes
$41,457 15 days max shooting

Free TV — Non-network, Non-prime time
$21,085 guaranteed 6 days, max 3 shooting

Film Basic Agreement — Theatrical Motion Pictures

Low-Budget Films (up to $500,000)

Weekly salary $10,740 (discounts may apply, check DGA contract)
Guaranteed Prep period 2 weeks
Guaranteed Shoot days 10 weeks
Guaranteed Cutting days 1 week

High-Budget Films (over $11 million)
Weekly salary $17,604
Guaranteed Prep period 2 weeks
Guaranteed Shoot days 10 weeks
Guaranteed Cutting days 1 week

Shorts/Documentaries
Weekly salary $12,573
Guaranteed Prep period 2 days
Guaranteed Shoot days 1 week + 1 day
Guaranteed Cutting days 0

Non-Union Projects
It will depend on the budget and schedule. It could be a percentage of the budget, like 10%, or partially deferred with points on the back end for profit participation. It could be a weekly rate of $2,500–$5,000. Everything is open to negotiation.

If the DGA director is incorporated, with federal ID number, etc., he or she may want to do a "loan out" agreement, in which you pay his or her company directly, but not make his or her FICA, FUI, and SUI payments. Generally, however, you will pay DGA Pension and Health (currently 15.75%). If the director is not incorporated, then he or she becomes your employee, and you must pay payroll tax and DGA Pension and Health.

03–02 Assistant to Director
This is an entry-level position for someone to help the Director do her job on the film. It can entail errands, sitting in on meetings, script coverage, etc.

$$$
This position usually has a rate of $750–$1,000 per week.

04–00 Cast

This category covers the fees, overtime, and expenses for the cast members, including choreographers and stunt people.

04–01 Lead Actors and 04–02 Supporting Cast and 04–03 Day Players

Leading Actors and Supporting Cast are as important to the success of a film as a good script. To cast actors, refer to the section on Casting in Chapter 2. Rates can vary tremendously based on the name, experience, and perceived value of the actor. For union rates contact SAG-AFTRA to find out about salaries based on your type of project.

$$$

These are some samples of the minimum SAG-AFTRA rates for Performers:
Theatrical and Television (Basic)
Daily $859
Weekly $2,979

Standard Low-Budget Theatrical Film (total budget $625,000–$2.5 million)
Daily $504
Weekly $1,752

Modified Low-Budget Theatrical Film (total budget $200,000–$625,000)
Daily $268
Weekly $933

Ultra Low-Budget Theatrical Film (total budget less than $200,000)
Daily $125

These are only a few of the various rates. Contact SAG-AFTRA regarding other fees including meals, overtime, travel, night work, looping, rerun compensation, and so forth. Also check *www.sagindie.org* for the details on the various low-budget agreements mentioned above. Just allow plenty of time (weeks) to submit all the paperwork, get SAG-AFTRA approval, and set up your escrow account.

The better known an actor, the higher the rate. This could be double scale (two times the minimum) or much, much more. The more an agent can get for a client, the more he or she will try to charge each time, so it's worth negotiating. Because there are so many actors competing for the same jobs, you'll find prices may drop as the competition escalates.

Day Players are the actors that "play for only one or two days." You'll calculate their rate per day as opposed to per week.

Some agents take 10% of their actors' fees. If an actor is paid $1,000, the agent will get $100, the actor $900. But most agents will prefer to add 10% on top of the fee, so it will cost you $1,000 plus 10%, or a total of $1,100 (plus payroll taxes, and if it's a union job, then approximately 17.3% for Pension and Health). Be sure you understand this distinction when negotiating with agents.

The guilds also make pay distinctions for what an actor does in a scene. If an actor speaks, it's one rate; if she speaks five lines or less, it's a cheaper rate; if she walks through a scene, it's another. Be sure you understand your needs when hiring guild actors, as it will affect the rates you will be charged.

Remember that the SAG-AFTRA rates are based on an 8-hour day. From 9–10 hours there will be an overtime charge of 1.5× the hourly rate. For hour 11 and beyond it is 2× the hourly rate.

If an actor is a "loan out," follow the same procedures as for Director, but apply the appropriate SAG-AFTRA Pension and Health.

For student films, short films and new media projects, SAG-AFTRA has a deferred deal which allows filmmakers to pay the actors only *after* the film makes any money. If a film obtains any sales/licensing fees, the filmmaker must contact SAG-AFTRA for approval of the deal and the actors are in "first position" to receive their deferred compensation. On other non-guild low-budget projects you can also hire non-union talent and pay them whatever you can negotiate.

04–04 Casting Director/Staff

A Casting Director is very helpful when putting together your actor talent. If you can't afford the fee you can put up notices online and do the casting sessions yourself. (See the Casting section in Chapter 2.)

04–05 Casting Expenses

Casting requires a room to hold auditions, a waiting room for actors, copying of the "sides" (the script pages they'll audition with) and a video camera with operator.

04–06 Choreographer

If you have any dancing scenes in your film, you'll need to hire a choreographer.

Some directors really want help when staging actors, either to music or not. Some situation comedy directors even hire choreographers to help them block the action in imaginative ways. Sometimes a script will call for a character to do a "spontaneous dance," and the director may want a choreographer to make it special. Or you may have a beauty pageant that needs to be staged. So think of choreographers as more than dance designers — they can be movement designers, too.

Look into dance schools to find young talent if you can't afford an established choreographer. Remember that it's not only about dancing/movement, it is also about camera placement and the understanding of film as a medium.

$$$

Choreographers are not in any union. A reasonable pay range is $300 to $600 per 12-hour day, depending on experience. A major feature might pay $1,000 per day, and famous choreographers may command even more.

04–07 Assistant(s) to Choreographer

This person will assist the Choreographer in prep, rehearsal, and on shoot days. They may rehearse certain dancers separately from the Choreographer as well.

$$$

Assistant rates will be $750–$1,000 per week.

04–08 Dialect Coach

When an actor needs extra help with the spoken word, a dialect coach is hired. Maybe the actor speaks English with a heavy Chinese accent and needs to sound native-born. Perhaps the actor needs to acquire a Spanish accent for a role and requires help to achieve it. The dialect coach is the fixer.

04–09 Narrator/Voiceover Artist

The narrator is the voiceover used in documentaries, industrials, commercials, and sometimes features. Depending on the prominence of the personality, the rates vary greatly from below scale to whatever the market will bear for well-known voices. Commercial rates vary depending on whether the commercial is for local, regional, or national usage. Usually you must negotiate with the narrator's agent. When the commercial is aired, the narrator also receives additional money through residuals (check with SAG-AFTRA for rates).

$$$

SAG-AFTRA rate card for an Industrial/Educational program Category II
1st hour $446.50
Each additional half hour $117.50

There are several agencies that represent actors for voiceover only. Many agencies have their talent listings online with demo reels that you can listen to from their website.

Narration for experimental films or "cause" projects has a caché to it. Actors often do it for love and recognition. If your project has that kind of appeal, go to the biggest actor you can think of and ask if he or she will do it for minimum scale. You may be pleasantly surprised.

04–10 Stunt Coordinator

Use top professionals to do stunts for the best, safest stunts. Your number one responsibility here is the safety of your cast and crew.

The Coordinator is your source for everything stunt related: costs, personnel, equipment, safety. He or she breaks the script down into stunts and provides cost estimates. Stunt wisdom says to budget for at least two takes per stunt.

On the set, the Coordinator helps place cameras and generally runs the set when cameras roll.

$$$

SAG-AFTRA scale for Stunt Coordinators (flat deal) is currently $5,392.52 per week, but good ones (don't use any other kind) often get paid more. When the Coordinator actually directs the 2nd unit, he stops being paid as the Coordinator and starts getting paid as a 2nd Unit Director, a DGA position that garners a higher weekly rate. For a 2nd Unit Director, the DGA rate card lists a minimum of $1,500/day for movies with budgets greater than $2,600,000 but equal to or less than $3,750,000.

04–11 Stunt Players

These are the foot soldiers of the stunt world: the men and women who drive a car at high speeds down an urban street or jump out of a helicopter to the roof of a building to catch a "thief."

$$$

They are covered under a SAG-AFTRA agreement that pays a minimum rate of $880 per day, plus what is called an *adjustment*. The adjustment is based on the degree of difficulty and danger in the stunt. For $300–$500, a stunt player could take a fall as she runs along a rocky road. Budget a $900 adjustment for a fall out of a window. Budget $3,000–$7,000 or so if she'll turn over a flaming car or plunge from a high rise. A fully enveloped fire burn, running, will cost you even more.

Defer to the stunt coordinator for the adjustment rates. (If you are licensing a stunt clip from a feature film, you must negotiate with the stunt person. You may have to pay what he or she got for the original stunt.)

04–12 Stunt Costs/Adjustments

These are completely determined by the script. If you've got serious stunts, the only way to budget them is to ask a Stunt Coordinator to break it down. Just for example, let's say you want a guy to drive a car into a telephone pole. The player gets his daily 8-hour rate of $880. His adjustment might be $3,000. The two cars (remember, two takes) will run about $1,000 each (include overtime because stunts always take longer than you think.) And the cost of the phone pole, its installation, and dressing with wires could easily run $1,200 or more.

04–13 Stunt Equipment

This covers the costs for the equipment necessary to do the stunt(s).

04–14 ADR (Automatic Dialogue Replacement)

SAG-AFTRA day players (actors hired by the day for original production) receive 100% of their day rate for ADR sessions.

SAG-AFTRA weekly players receive 50% of the pro rata day rate for a 4-hour session. After 4 hours, they get 100% of the pro rata day rate.

05–00 Travel and Living — Producers/Director

If you are shooting the film out of town, you need to transport the Producers and/or Director and house them.

05–01 Airfares

Since union actors, writers, directors, and certain crew (Directors of Photography, Production Designers) must travel first class, the Executive Producer and Producer will naturally want to travel first class as well. If you're doing a non-union show, then it's negotiable, but try and make the same deal for everyone — the "most favored nations" concept, in which every person on the same level earns the same rate.

05–02 thru 05–08 Hotel, Taxi-Limo, Auto, Train, Excess Baggage, Phone, Gratuities

These are the travel costs associated with transporting the Producers and Directors from their home city to set. Gratuities are for tips to bell captains, porters, valets, etc.

05–09 Per Diem

Per Diem for Producers and Directors on features is in the $100+ a day range and can't be less than what SAG-AFTRA requires for their members. On low-budget, non-union projects, if everyone is fed three square meals a day, transported and sheltered, there may be no per diem at all.

06–00 Travel and Living — Cast

If you are shooting your film out of town, you need to transport your cast and house them.

06–01 Airfares

As we said above, all actors working a union show must travel first class, unless it isn't available.

06–02 thru 06–08 Hotel, Taxi-Limo, Auto, Train, Excess Baggage, Phone, Gratuities

These are the travel costs associated with transporting the Cast from their home city to set. Gratuities are for tips to bell captains, porters, valets, etc.

06–09 Per Diem

Per Diem for a SAG actor on an overnight location is $60 per day for three meals. Anything above that amount is subject to negotiation. The breakdown is as follows:

Breakfast:	$12.00
Lunch:	$18.00
Dinner:	$30.00
Total:	$60.00

If the Producer provides lunch, you can deduct $18.00. If the Producer provides breakfast, you can deduct $12.00. Or you can be nice and not deduct anything. You can decide — depending on your budget.

07–00 Residuals

When commercials play, or when TV programs air after their initial run or are syndicated, or when a program enters a "Supplemental Market" (e.g., DVD, Video on Demand [VOD], or New Media) or a film goes to TV (Pay, Broadcast, or Cable), extra monies — called residuals — may be owed to actors, directors, writers, and musicians. Residuals can either be factored into a production budget (as TV movies often do for their second run), or not. Check with the distributor or studio ahead of time. If included, check with the guilds for residual rates, or consult *The Showbiz Labor Guide* or Entertainment Partners' *The Paymaster*. They are updated annually.

Fringes

Anyone who works for you (i.e., is not a "loan out" from his or her own corporation) is an official "employee" in the eyes of the law. "Fringes" are what your company must contribute to appropriate government agencies and union pension/health funds on behalf of your employees. The package is also called "payroll taxes." These include:

- Social Security and Medicare (FICA-SS and FICA-HI) 6.2% up to $7,000 in salary.
- State Unemployment Insurance (SUTA) adjustable by state. In California it's 6.2% on the first $7,000 in salary.
- Federal Unemployment Insurance (FUTA) 6% of first $7,000 in salary. Please note that you can take a credit for your SUTA up to 5.4% so you may only pay .6% of FUTA.
- Workers' Compensation rate is set annually by state and differs with each industry. Workers' Comp is less expensive for office people than for grips. Call your state agency or payroll service to ask how much to average for your project budget.
- Some states have additional taxes. In California there is an Employment Training Tax of 0.1% on the first $7,000 of salary and a State Disability Insurance tax of 1% on the first $101,636 of salary.

The sum total of these adds up to 19%–23% of a person's gross salary. Your accountant or your payroll service can keep you abreast of any changes in the individual percentages and can handle actual payments from your company to the respective government agencies and union funds.

In addition to the payroll taxes, union employees receive pension and health benefits. These are some current rates as examples. Call each guild, or your payroll service, to get accurate rates for your project and your geographical area.

WGA 17%
SAG-AFTRA 17.3%
DGA 15.75%

For example, adding together all of the above fringes, if an Associate Producer earns $1,850 per week, add another 23% ($425.50) in payroll taxes to get the actual cost to your company — $2,275.50. If you are producing a short documentary and paying someone from a guild, say a Director (and the person is not on a loan out from his or her own company), then you owe his or her salary, say $12,207 for eight days of work, plus the payroll taxes at 23% ($2,807.61), plus the DGA Pension/Health at 15.75% of the salary ($1,922.60), for a grand total cost to you of $16,937.21.

If the person is on a loan out, then you pay the base salary of $12,207 plus the DGA Pension/Health ($1,922.60) — but no payroll taxes — for a total cost to you of $14,129.60.

Note: In the sample budgets in this book, all fringes are calculated as part of each category.

BELOW-THE-LINE

PRODUCTION

08–00 Production Staff

This section covers all the fees and expenses for the Production personnel, from the Unit Production Manager to the Production Assistants.

08–01 Unit Production Manager/Line Producer

A good Unit Production Manager, or UPM, is the glue between all facets of the production and the Producer/Production Company. In many cases she creates the original budget, and then spends the next weeks or months sweating bullets so that the production sticks to it. She schedules the main blocks of production, books the crew, supervises location scouts and contracts, organizes the casting process, and works with the Director and Producer to keep everything running smoothly, on schedule, and on budget. Some UPMs are released after shooting, while others stay on through editing, right up to delivery of the final master. On really small productions, the Producer may have to take on the work of the UPM, but if that's the case, be aware that it's difficult to split your mind between the creative parts of your shoot and the logistical nuts and bolts that hold it together. One part or the other will probably suffer. Depending on how you staff the Production Department, you may hire a Line Producer and/or a UPM. If you have both they will be put on this line. Line Producers are not covered by any union or guild contracts.

$$$

The pay scale for Production Managers varies, like everything else. For non-DGA, it would depend on the budget. For a non-union film with a $500,000 budget, the Production Manager can earn $1,200 to $1,600 per week. On a million dollar film the UPM could get $1,500–$2,000. On a $3 million film it could be $2,500–$3,000.

A UPM can also join the DGA. For the DGA Basic TV rate, the UPM weekly rate is $4,878 plus a production fee of $1,057 per week, plus a severance allowance of one week's pay which is called a Completion of Assignment. Check the DGA rate card for appropriate minimums and production fees for your show (www.dga.org).

08–02 Assistant Directors

The 1st AD keeps the set running smoothly and efficiently — always one step ahead of the next shot. He or she coordinates with all the department heads to make sure everything is ready and safe before each shot. The 1st AD also creates a shooting schedule for each day's work, coordinating cast and crew so that makeup, wardrobe, and rehearsal with the Director can go on while the crew is busy setting up. Every possible moment must be used to accomplish something.

It helps to have a 1st AD with a strong voice and a commanding presence who utilizes respect and good rapport across departments to get the job done. All productions — no matter what budget level — should have a 1st AD on set to coordinate departments and keep everyone on schedule.

In television, with multi-camera shoots, the Assistant Director is usually called the Associate Director, and often sits with the Director in the control room, assisting with show timing and getting camera people ready for upcoming shots.

On larger productions, there is also a 2nd Assistant Director, and even 2nd 2nd ADs. Since the 1st AD should not leave the set, the 2nd AD helps the 1st AD by carrying out orders off the set, like coordinating the talent and escorting them to and from set. The 2nd AD also handles the call sheets for the next day's cast and crew and various other production reports. The 2nd 2nd ADs are hired when there is a very large production with lots of background actors and more elements to organize.

$$$

First ADs in the DGA Basic Agreement are paid $4,639 per week (plus a production fee of $860/week).

The DGA scale for Key 2nd ADs is $3,109 per week in studio (plus a production fee of $655/week).

Non-union rates for a 1st AD are $1,200–$2,500 per week.

08–03 Stage Manager

In multi-camera television, when the Director and Associate Director are in the control room, someone has to keep order on the set, cue performers to speak, get makeup in for touch-up, make sure everything is ready for shooting, and so forth. That's the Stage Manager's job.

$$$

DGA scale for Stage Managers is $3,597 per 40-hour week for Dramatic Prime Time programs with a weekly production fee of $754.

08–04 Production Coordinator
The Coordinator runs the production office. The good ones are geniuses at knowing whom to call for anything from scenic backdrops of the Swiss Alps to iced cappuccino. They must be "buttoned up" people — very reliable, detail oriented, trustworthy, and calm under fire.

$$$
Production Coordinators are paid anywhere from $900–$1,700 per week depending on the budget.

08–05 Script Supervisor
On movies, the Script Supervisor handles timing, which is the estimation of how long a script will play on screen. If a script is long or short, it's best to know well before shooting begins, so you can make changes inexpensively. The Script Supervisor stays close to the Director on set, marking the takes the Director wants to keep, keeping notes on what goes wrong in a take, and watching for continuity. If an actor wears an eye patch on his right eye before lunch and on his left eye after lunch, you've got a break in continuity and an unintentionally funny scene . . . which must be reshot at further expense.

$$$
Script Supervisors make $1,200 to $2,500 per week on non-union films, depending on the budget.

08–06 Production Accountant/Auditor
This person keeps track of your expenses and produces daily and weekly cost reports. For movies, they are paid anywhere from $1,200 to $2,500 per week. Feature projects may have an Assistant Accountant. If you are producing a low-budget project, it is a good idea to hire a bookkeeper familiar with film production to come in once a week or so to pay bills, keep accounts straight, and reconcile bank statements. If you are organized and adept at Quicken software you can consider doing it yourself.

08–07 Technical Advisors

When you need a true expert on the set, bring in a Technical Advisor. If you're shooting a cop movie, hire a police officer who really knows the ins and outs of cop reality. Technical Advisors can also be brought on for safety expertise (when, for example, the script calls for underwater scenes or scenes with airplanes). Rates vary, of course, on who it is, but figure anywhere from $800 to $1,500 per week.

08–08 Production Assistants

All minor tasks not specifically assigned to other crew members are handled by the Production Assistants. They make petty cash purchases, are the primary "runners" on shoots, and work on the shoot's logistical elements. This is the entry-level position on any production. Top-flight PAs are cheerful, think on their feet, and are self-motivated problem-solvers who are worth their weight in gold. Larger productions need several PAs who report to the 1st Assistant Director, Production Manager, and/or Producer as either Set PAs or Office PAs.

$$$

Figure $150–$200 per flat day for an experienced PA, plus mileage or gas reimbursement if they drive their own cars. On low-budget productions, you can often find free PAs from local colleges with a film or television program who are looking for experience on a professional film.

08–09 Studio Teacher/Tutor

If you have minors on your set (under age 18), and if they are being paid, state law dictates certain rules. Depending on the state's law, you may have to hire a Teacher/Welfare Worker "to care and attend to the health, safety, and morals of all minors." This is usually one person who wears the two hats of teacher and welfare worker.

There are various regulations that vary by state, but the general idea is that children of various ages can only work specified hours, must have specific rest and recreation periods and mealtimes, must be with a parent or guardian, and, on school days, must spend specified hours being schooled.

Two other points about employing children: permits and permits.

- The production company needs a permit to employ minors. In California it is obtained through the Department of Industrial Relations (*www.dir.ca.gov*). It is usually free, and they'll want proof that you have workers' compensation insurance. Another helpful resource while filming with minors in California is www.studioteachers.com. This website has excellent information links and info about available teachers for on-set learning. For other states, contact the state film commission and they will give you the website with the relevant state regulations and permit application information.
- The child also needs a permit. The parent needs to obtain one from the state Labor Commission. Most states have an online application from which you can obtain the proper permit.

Finally, when you are using kids in certain circumstances, in certain ways on non-school days, or after-school hours and they are unpaid, you may be able to avoid hiring a teacher. Check with a Studio Teaching agency to find out if your project qualifies. Be warned, however, that should an accident happen, your liability is probably less if there is a Teacher/Welfare Worker on the set.

$$$
Typical rates:
Non-union — $250 to $350 per 10-hour day.
Union (IATSE) — approximately $372 per day for 8 hours. (Book through the local.)

09–00 Background Actors/Extras
This section includes fees and expenses to cast, feed, and transport the Background Actors.

09–01 Stand-Ins
Stand-Ins are actors who generally look like a lead actor in the project. They will be the same height and weight and have the same type of skin color and complexion. When the Director of Photography

and Gaffer are lighting the scene the Stand-In will be there so they can set the lights, etc. The Lead actor will be prepping with Hair/Makeup/Wardrobe simultaneously so more work can be done faster.

$$$

SAG-AFTRA Rates

Stand-Ins	$163 per day

09–02 Extras, SAG-AFTRA

Background Actors or Extras are the people who work in the background of a scene and lend authenticity to the film.

$$$

SAG-AFTRA Rates

General Extras	$148 per day (8 hours)
Special Ability Photo Double	$158 per day
Choreographed Skaters & Swimmers	$342 per day

There is additional compensation when the extra also supplies an extra change of clothes ($9), period wardrobe ($18), hairpiece ($18), pets ($23), camera or luggage ($5.50), car ($35), motorcycle ($35), and so forth. See the SAG-AFTRA rate card or *The Showbiz Labor Guide*.

09–05 Extras Casting Fee

When you need a lot of background atmosphere, like hundreds of pedestrians in an intersection, or an angry mob, or a stadium full of feverish fans, it may be time to delegate the task of casting all those people to an Extras Casting Service. There are many online. Contact an Extras Casting person and describe your unique needs and they'll fill you in on their rates and services.

09–10 Extras Transportation

If you need to move your extras from location to location be sure to have the proper transportation at hand so you can keep to your schedule. Hiring passenger vans with drivers is one solution.

10–00 Sound Stage

Prices of studios and sound stages vary depending on the size, location, and equipment provided. They can be rented for months, days, or hours. When you do rent a stage, be sure to ask about the ancillary charges, such as overtime, power usage (some stages have no power, and you'll have to provide a generator; see 19–00 Electrical), office space, dressing, hair and makeup rooms, wardrobe room, green room, school room, eating area, tables and chairs, prop and set storage, prop and set assembly area, dumpster usage, parking, telephone, Wi-Fi, security, keys, rehearsal stage, first aid, stage manager, heating and air conditioning.

$$$

Prices for Sound Stages vary depending on the setup.

- A fully equipped 2,400-square-foot stage with video control room, three cameras, two digital recording machines, and full crew can cost from $10,000 to $15,000 for one day of shooting, depending on how many lights you use, and how much time you spend loading in your set (the day before), and striking it (the day after).
- A four-wall 4,700-square-foot stage with a three-wall hard cyc (a clean, painted background), air-conditioned, soundproofed, with limited parking, some production offices, makeup and dressing rooms, and lounge can cost $1,000–$4,000 per 10-hour prep and strike day, and $1,500–$4,500 per 10-hour shoot day, plus power at $20 per hour, and other charges for phones, kitchen, stage manager, and whatever lights are used.
- Larger stages with more equipment and requirements will cost more money. It's best to search online, call, and visit various places before committing to a certain stage. You'll want to find out about all the little charges (such as for Wi-Fi and parking) to make sure you have budgeted for the full amount.

10–01 Stage Rental
For any charges to rent a stage on a daily, weekly or monthly basis. Often there is a more expensive rate for shoot days vs. prep, build or wrap days.

$$$
See above. It all depends on the size of the stage rental. It can cost as little as $1,000 for a small insert stage to $5,000 for a large sound stage.

10–02 thru 10–09 Stage Lighting & Grip Rental, Phones, Internet, Garbage Removal, Green Room and Makeup Room, Office Rental and Parking
These are all the potential additional charges you may incur when renting a stage. Make sure to ask for the rate sheet on *all* of these charges before you book the space. Sometimes the day rate is really inexpensive but when you add in all these other charges and overtime it's not a very good deal.

11–00 Production Design
The "look" of your show is the domain of the Production Designer or Art Director. Big projects have both functions, the Art Director reporting to/working with the Production Designer. Smaller ones have one or the other — usually Production Designer for a film and Art Director for a commercial or music video.

11–01 Production Designer
He or she takes a script and, with the Director, interprets it visually, giving the set concrete detail, authenticity, and inspiration. On low-budget projects, a Production Designer can be employed for a wide range of jobs during pre-production and production. He or she can illustrate perspectives, scenes, set designs, and create scale models, attend to color schemes and textures, and is in charge of all sets and the way they are dressed. On bigger projects, the Production Designer's job is more conceptual, and tasks are handed to the Art Director to supervise, to the Set Designer to actually draft blueprints, to Model Makers and Estimators, and so on.

The Production Designer usually works on set every day, assuring that the look of the show has the greatest visual impact. He or she is that "third" eye only concerned with how things look.

$$$
For non-union, small projects, figure $1,000–$1,500 per week for someone starting out and $2,500 per week and up for masters on larger projects. For union projects the rates will be higher and negotiated based on the Production Designer's past work and the budget level for the film. Assistants' pay may range from $750 to $1,400 per week non-union, and about $1,615 per week union. Also allow for research and car allowance, depending on the project.

11–02 Art Director
Depending on the size and budget of the production, you may hire an Art Director in addition to the Production Designer. The Art Director will execute the designs and plans and oversee the Art crew. If working on a commercial, the lead Art person is usually referred to as the Art Director.

$$$
Union scale for Art Directors is about $2,437+ per week depending on experience. For non-union, small projects, figure $1,000–$1,500 per week for someone starting out and $2,500 per week and up for masters on larger projects. Assistants' pay may range from $750 to $1,400 per week non-union, and about $1,615 per week union. Also allow for research and car allowance, depending on the project.

11–03 Art Assistants
Sometimes called Art PAs, this is the entry-level position in the Art Department. Work consists of errands, set/props pickups and returns, painting (on non-union projects), etc.

$$$
Rates are $100–$200 per day.

11–04 Set Designer

This person is a draftsman familiar not only with sets and the requirements of cinematography and lighting but also with the language of architects and skilled builders and craftsmen. His or her plans will be used by the Construction Coordinator and his or her team to build the sets.

$$$

For non-union, small projects, figure $800–$1,200 per week for someone starting out and $2,000 per week and up for masters on larger projects. Union scale for Set Designer is about $1,700–$2,000 per week depending on the type of production and budget. Assistants' pay may range from $750 to $1,000 per week non-union, and about $1,615 per week union. Also allow for research and car allowance, depending on the project.

11–05 Model Makers/Miniatures

Sometimes it helps everyone, especially the Director, to see a miniature of a set to visualize where to place actors and how best to shoot it. These are called Design/Study Models, they're made of foam core, and they can cost as little as $500 or as much as thousands. If your script calls for futuristic space vehicles or submarines, or the destruction of Manhattan by a tidal wave, miniatures are one way to do it. Cost is by the project, as little as $150 for a single item or $350,000 for a space fleet.

11–06 Draftsperson

Used by Directors and Art Directors to help visualize scenes and place cameras. Allow $1,000 to $1,500 per week. Pre-viz software can be a cost-effective alternative.

11–08 thru 11–10 Research, Vehicles, and Purchases/Rentals

These lines items are for the costs to create the designs and materials necessary for the Production Design.

12–00 Set Construction

There are two ways to go about Set Construction:

- Hire a Construction Coordinator who will supervise crew, purchases, rentals, equipment, cartage, strike, and disposal. Everyone will therefore be on your payroll.
- Retain a set construction company that will do it all for you, at a markup, but save you the trouble and expense of putting more people through payroll.

12–01 Construction Coordinator

This person plans, budgets, and schedules all the Set Construction. Allow $1,500 to $1,800 per week; plus tool rental ($750–$850 week), and truck rental ($200–$300 per week).

12–02 thru 12–05 Foremen, Carpenters, Scenic Painters, and Greensmen

Foremen, Carpenters, and Painters are key areas for labor. Greensmen are the people who procure and tend anything "green" such as plants, flowers, grass, vines, and any other landscaping. Some sample weekly rates:

Foreman $1,700–$2,000
Painters $1,200–$1,700
Scenic Painters $1,000–$1,800
Carpenters $1,000–$1,700
Greensmen $1,200–$1,700

12–06 thru 12–07 Construction Materials—Purchases and Rentals

These line items are for the costs to purchase or rent construction materials.

12–08 Construction Equipment

Often special equipment needs to be purchased or rented to build sets and other design elements.

12–09 Set Strike

Sometimes another separate, well-rested crew is brought in after Wrap is called so the set and other design elements can be taken down. If you have to vacate the location before the next morning, this crew will come in at night and have it all gone by sunrise.

13–00 Set Operations

This category is for the Grip Department which handles all other rigging and setting up necessary for a shoot — like hanging scenic backdrops, setting up dolly track, blacking out a window, and so on. They work in tandem with the Electrical Department. (Electricians are in 19–00 Electrical.)

13–01 Key or First Grip

The Key Grip is the head of the Grip Department.

$$$

Key Grips (non-union) get $250 to $550 per 10-hour day. Union scale rates go from $1,300–$2,700 per week.

13–02 Best Boy Grip

The 2nd Grip makes $25 less per day than the Gaffer. The 3rd Grip would make $25 less per day than the 2nd Grip. $225–$525 per 10-hr. day non-union.

13–03 Grips

$200 to $500 per 10-hour day non-union.

13–04 Dolly/Crane/Drone Grips

The person who sets up booms, dollies, cranes, and drones and works them smoothly. $200 to $550 per 10-hour day non-union.

13–06 Grip Rentals

This line covers the miscellaneous grip equipment that may be needed — stands, scrims, apple boxes, tape, and other expendables, and lots more. It is often included in the grip truck/lighting package (see 19–00 Electrical).

Dolly Rentals (included under "Grip Rentals"). A dolly is a four-wheeled moving camera platform. Not all shoots require moving camera shots, but for that extra bit of production value, movement can bring life to an otherwise static shot. Using a dolly will take more time to set up than tripod or hand-held shots, especially if plywood or tracks need to be laid for a smooth ride.

Cranes are in this category also. Another device called a jib, in which the camera but no operator is mounted on the end of a camera boom, can deliver certain crane-like effects for less money. Ask your DP.

There are different kinds of jibs, cranes, and dollies from a few companies. Consult with the Director and the Director of Photography and agree on type of equipment, how much track, and whether you need any of the extras that come with them. Don't forget about cartage (if you do it) or delivery charge (if they do it).

$$$

Depending on what you rent, prices can go from $75 per day for a Western Dolly to $150 a day for a Doorway Dolly. A Fisher studio dolly without the head would be $700 per day. Jib cranes go from $500–$650 per day. Local pickup/delivery can be $125 to $200. Techno cranes are about $3,000 per day including trucking.

13–07 Expendables

This line item consists of materials to be used by the Grip Department like clothes pins, wedges, gaffers' tape, rope, paper tape, etc.

13–08 Kit Rentals

Lots of craftspeople have boxes or kits that they will rent to you. Key Grips may have all sorts of goodies that may be cheaper to rent than put in the Grip Package. Makeup people have makeup supplies. Gaffers have lighting equipment.

Kit Rentals can also serve another useful purpose. Say you really want a certain Key Grip, but his or her daily rate is higher than you can pay for other Key people. (As discussed earlier, it's important to keep rates equal between the same levels of personnel in each department — the "most favored nations" rule.) Pay him or her the same daily rate as other Keys, but up his or her pay on the Kit Rental. That way you can keep everyone on the same day rate.

13–10 Craft Service

The "Craft" refers to the working people on a set — all the grips and electrics, camera people, props people, etc., who get real hungry and thirsty between meals and need a quick pick-me-up. So Craft Service means those who service the crafts people by providing hot coffee, cold drinks, and munchies of all sorts.

The job usually goes to a person or company for one package price that includes labor and food. Sometimes a "kit rental fee" is added to cover the overhead on all the food gear like hotplates and coffee urns. For low-budget productions it is often done by PAs purchasing food and putting it out on a table.

$$$

Figure $750 to $1,500 per week for the person (non-union), plus a $25–$50/day kit rental fee. Additionally you'll need to budget for whatever food costs are needed.

13–15 Air Conditioning/Heating

On hot summer days you'll need air conditioning. Air Conditioning/ Heating companies size the unit to suit the need. Rarely will they be asked to cool a stage higher than 8 feet above the floor (although some big stars insist on cooling the whole building so everyone is comfortable).

These companies help out in other ways too. For example, if you need to see real breath for winter scenes, they'll regulate the temperature and humidity for you. Temperature can be as high as the fifties and still get "breath" with proper lighting and humidity.

Air conditioning comes by the unit ton. Figure 100 sq. ft. per ton as a starting point, than add lighting load and the number of people. The company will get you an estimate of tonnage needed.

$$$

Prices are based on the size of units plus time and labor. A 10-ton rents for $700 per week. Trucking would be an additional $400 each way.

Depending on size, heaters can rent for $550–$1,600 per week. These prices do not include power and fuel.

14–00 Special Effects

These effects are mechanical or pyrotechnic, not computer-created — anything from a shot in which a baby pulls a car door off its hinges to small gags, like squeezing a sneaker and having green slime ooze out of its heel.

Obviously costs depend on whether you're blowing up an obsolete Las Vegas hotel or doing something simple like the shoe gag.

14–01 Special Effects Person

The Key Special Effects Person works closely with the Stunt Coordinator to make the effects as terrific as possible, and safe for cast and crew.

$$$

Rates vary from $1,750 to $2,500 per week.

14–02 SFX Assistants(s)

The Assistants will help the SFX Person with any tasks necessary to make it all work.

$$$

Allow for $750–$1,000 per week.

14–03 Additional Labor

If there's rigging to do before a special effect can be shot, you'll save time and money bringing in a rigging crew so all is ready by the time the rest of the company gets to the shot.

$$$

Allow $1,000 to $1,500 per week per person.

14–06 Manufacturing Labor

Sometimes outside labor is needed to make a particular element for the Special Effect. The SFX person will design and consult with the manufacturer.

14–07 Fabrication
If you need just the right "gizmo for your flotchet," and you're in the Mojave Desert, you'll be glad your Key Special Effects Person brought along his or her mobile workshop. In town or out, give your Special Effects people enough time to fabricate what you need. Fabrication costs depend on script.

14–09 Rentals
For any rentals needed to do the Special Effect for the project.

15–00 Set Dressing or Set Decoration
This section covers the labor and expenses for the materials that will fill up all the sets during production.

15–01 Set Decorator
The Set Decorator works with the Production Designer and/or Art Director to create a look for all the sets that matches the Director's and Production Designer's vision for the movie and all its characters, their tastes, personalities, quirks, and conflicts. It's all the things that characters use to furnish their various worlds. Set Decs furnish the sets with all the stuff that makes a home a home, or an office, or a warehouse.

$$$
Non-union rates go from $1,500 to $2,300 per week. Union scale rates go from $1,700–$2,600 per week.

15–02 Lead Person
He or she is the person in charge of the Swing Gang (see below). Rates go from $1,300 to $1,600 per week.

15–03 Swing Gang/Set Dressers
Movers of furniture or whatever accoutrements are needed on the set. Rates are usually $750 to $1,600 per week.

15–04 thru 15–07 Additional Labor, Expendables, Purchases, Rentals
For all the costs needed to set dress the project.

15–08 Loss & Damage
This line item occurs in many of the departments that rent equipment or design elements. It's important to anticipate possible loss or damage and budget for some charges to pay for losses or damage.

15–09 Kit Rentals
For kit rentals for the use of the Set Decorator's tools and materials.

15–10 Vehicle Expenses
This department utilizes many vehicles for pickups, deliveries, and returns. Make sure to budget for possible expenses.

16–00 Property
Props (property) are things actors pick up and use, as distinct from Set Dressing, which is not touched or held by the actors.

16–01 Property Master
The Property Master purchases and rents all necessary props. On smaller shoots, he or she may also handle the special effects props and design special riggings.

$$$
IATSE lists numerous classifications of "prop people," such as Prop Maker Foreman, Prop Maker Gang Boss, Special Effects Foreman, Upholsterer, Draper Foreman, Greens Foreman, and many others. See IATSE rate card for the various costs and work rules involved.

Figure from $250–$550 per day for a non-union Prop Master. Kit Rental might fetch $250 per week.

If you use firearms or explosives you need what's called a Licensed Powder Person, who gets a 10% bonus if the explosive explodes . . . deliberately that is.

16–02 Prop Assistant
The prop assistant works for the props master to help with any purchases, rentals, and picking up and returning props.

16–03 thru 16–07 Purchases, Rentals, Loss & Damage, Kit Rentals, and Vehicle Expenses

See above in the Set Dressing department.

16–08 Armorer

The armorer is in charge of all prop weapons on set. He or she coordinates the transportation and control of all weapons on set and trains any actors or personnel on how to safely use them.

17–00 Wardrobe

The wardrobe department is in charge of acquiring — through rentals and purchases and construction — the costumes for all actors on screen.

17–01 Costume Designer

Sometimes these people are called upon to actually design clothing; other times they supervise the purchase and rental of wardrobe, and the assembly of custom clothing. In any case, you are relying on their aesthetic sense to work well with that of the Director and Production Designer. The clothes, after all, must fit the overall look of the show.

The Costume Designer/Wardrobe Supervisor are similar to the Production Designer — they help create the overall look of the film and its characters and create a budget to make it all work.

$$$

Rates go from $1,250 to $2,500 per week non-union, depending on the budget and their experience. Union scale rates go from $1,700 to $4,100 per week.

17–02 thru 17–03 Costumer and Extras Costumers

On shows with no Designer per se, the Costumer might head the department. When there are lots of costumes, you might have a men's and a women's Costumer, each of whom would head their own divisions, hire other wardrobe people, and so forth.

$$$
Rates go from $800 to $2,300 per week.

17–04 thru 17–11 Expendables, Purchases, Rentals, Alterations & Repairs, Cleaning & Dyeing, Loss & Damage, Kit Rentals, Vehicle Expenses
These are really separate line items, but need to be budgeted for. If, for example, you are shooting a fistfight and the actors tear up some clothing, you may need all of the above, plus duplicates for Take 2 and 3. You always need to clean any garments you rent before returning them to the rental house.

18–00 Makeup and Hair
Whether you've got actors who have to look gorgeous, or monsters with blood oozing from eye sockets, the Makeup Artists and Hair Stylists are the folks who do the job. They purchase, prepare, and apply all facial and body makeup, special effect transformations, prosthetics, wigs, and hairpieces.

Since makeup is the first chore of the day for actors, hire cheerful makeup artists who will send the actors out in a good mood. Seriously.

Also allow enough time. Men usually take about 15 minutes to a half hour. Women can take an hour or more. It all depends.

When you have a big star, he or she may insist on a personal makeup/hair person, who usually charges twice what your regular person charges. If that is the case, there's not much you can do about it.

18–01 Key Makeup Artist
Allow from $250 to $550 per day non-union, plus Kit Rental of $25–$50/day. Union scale rates go from $1,000 to $2,400 per week.

18–02 Additional Makeup Artist(s)
If you have scenes with lots of actors you'll need to hire additional makeup artists to get everyone ready on time.

18–03 Key Hair Stylist

Allow from $250 to $550 per day non-union, plus Kit rental of $25–$50 per day. Union scale rates go from $1,000 to $2,400 per week.

18–04 Additional Hair Stylist(s)

Same as above.

18–05 SFX (Special Effects) Makeup Artist

This line item covers everything from prosthetics (fake body parts), appliances (extra body parts, like heads that fit over an actor's head), gaping wounds, blood, scraped faces or knees, extra long finger nails, and so on. You need to budget for purchases, design, and manufacture, and the time to apply them.

18–06 thru 18–08 Makeup/Hair Purchases, Rentals and Kit Rentals

Consult your key people and budget for them.

19–00 Electrical

You'll decide what you need for lighting with your Director, Director of Photography, and Gaffer. They will discuss the creative approach, ordering every light they may need. Then you call the lighting company and make your deal for your grip truck and lighting package.

Equipment houses can recommend gaffers and grips for your production, which may eliminate hiring additional people from the rental house to watch over equipment or drive the truck. It's worth asking for these things when shopping for your equipment needs. Generally, however, the Director of Photography will have a list of favorite Gaffers and Key Grips.

19–01 Gaffer

This person heads the Electric Department, translating the requests of the Director of Photography into specific orders for renting lighting equipment and setting up lights, light rigging, and all electrical functions for the set.

Consult regularly with the Gaffer (and indeed with all department heads) to troubleshoot for upcoming situations. They can alert you to potential delays, as well as the need for more or less labor or equipment. In fact, it's helpful to have one or more small, informal production meetings in the course of a day, in which a few department heads gather for a few minutes to hash things out for the next few hours or the next day.

$$$

Rates for Gaffers are $250 to $550 per 10-hour day non-union. Union scale rates go from $1,300–$2,700 per week.

19–02 Best Boy Electric

The Gaffer's first assistant. The Best Boy can also keep track of what instruments are used from a truck, so that when she returns the truck to the lighting equipment company, she makes sure you are not charged for instruments not used (if that was your deal), and not charged for any damage you did not cause. It may cost you an extra day to have her do a checkout before the shoot begins, but on large lighting orders it's worth it.

$$$

Rates go from $225 to $525 per 10-hour day.

19–03 Electrics

They rig, place, operate, and strike all the lighting and electrical gear. Rates go from $200 to $500 per day.

19–04 Additional Labor

If you have a complicated electrical setup, consider bringing in a separate crew of electricians ahead of your shoot crew. That way you virtually plug in and shoot when the time comes. The cost will more than offset what you'll pay your regular company to sit around for a few hours waiting — and losing momentum.

19–05 Equipment Purchases

Consult the Gaffer to determine if any equipment needs to be purchased for the Lighting Department.

19–06 Lighting Package Rental

Your lighting package may be a portable lighting kit for talking heads (usually comes with the camera package), a medium-size 2-ton grip truck with a full complement of small to large lights and grip gear, or a 40-foot trailer with enough candlepower to light a square dance in a cornfield.

Often you can strike a deal where a certain minimum is paid for the basic grip truck and lighting package. You are then charged an additional rate for any other equipment that you use. This way you are assured of having all the equipment you need, but you don't have to pay for it unless you use it. This does not apply to large items, like HMI lights, because an equipment house won't want to tie these up on spec. HMIs are usually charged out by the day.

You will be asked for a certificate of insurance, which you get from your insurance broker.

$$$

For a 1-ton grip truck figure $250, a 3-ton is $450 per day (plus mileage outside a given radius); larger trucks go up to $850 or more. Then you add a per-instrument charge for bigger lights. A complete lighting package for a TV movie can easily run up a $35,000–$50,000 bill for three to four weeks of rentals.

19–07 Additional Rentals

You may find that even though you rent a fully equipped studio there will still be some lights that your gaffer wants to rent. Use this line item for any miscellaneous lighting expenditures.

Additional equipment could include special riggings, dimmers, or light tents. Sometimes the camera operator will own lights that can be rented as part of his or her package at good rates.

19–08 Electrical Generator/Driver

Whenever the power needs of your lights (or other equipment, like power tools) exceed what's available, you rent a generator. The Gaffer or Best Boy will tell you what kind and size to get, and how long it will have to operate. Some are self-contained in vans, others are small or large monsters that are towed in and parked, or included in a 40-foot trailer/production truck. You will need a Driver/Operator, which on small shoots may be your Best Boy. On big shoots it will be a separate person. You'll also need fuel to feed the generators, based on how many hours they need to be running per day.

$$$

- The smallest generators are in the 250 amps range. They can be hitched to a tow, and either delivered by the company or picked up by someone on the production team. Average price is $250/day, plus about $50 in fuel for 10 hours of shooting.
- Mid-range units are 500 amps at $550/day, plus fuel at $100/day.
- Larger units are 1,000 amps at $1,000 day, plus fuel at $150/day.
- For generator trucks, they will be driven to set by the operator and you'll need to pay $400–$650/day for the genny operator in addition to mileage and fuel.

19–09 Loss & Damage
As stated in other sections, you should budget for potential additional costs.

19–10 Kit Rentals
As discussed in other sections.

20–00 Camera
You'll do research and discuss with the Director and Director of Photography before you decide which camera you will purchase or rent for the production. There are so many options and each project will have different creative, production and financial criteria that will factor into choosing specific equipment for the project.

20–01 Director of Photography
The Director of Photography translates the Director's vision into "paintings of light and shadow." DPs must know cameras, lenses, lights, acquisition formats and tech specs, basic editing and must match lighting and camera direction scene to scene.

The DP's job encompasses both the physical and creative aspects of production. Vision and ability to work quickly and smoothly with others is key to the success of a production.

There are general areas of specialization for DPs but many work in different genres. Here is a list of those general areas:

- Dramatic (TV episodic, TV movies, features, commercials, music videos)
- Documentary/Industrial (operates the camera, works with small crew)
- Aerial (in charge of air-to-air and air-to-ground photography)
- Underwater (working alone or with full crew)

In all of the above, the DP orders the type of camera — digital or film — and is involved with the selection of the lighting/grip package, and checks the actors (hair, makeup, costumes), sets, props, etc., for photographic consistency. The DP supervises the camera crews, lighting, sets the camera positions (with the Director), orders any special mounts (for boats, cars, planes, helicopters), and orders dollies and cranes. After shooting, the DP supervises the color correction and telecine (film/tape to tape transfer), and screens dailies for quality control.

In pre-production, especially for narrative projects, it's wise for the Director to spend enough time with the DP to work out not only a general creative approach, a camera test (plus post-production workflow), and location surveys, but also shot lists for each scene. The shot lists should be prioritized into "must haves" and "expendables." This list must be shared with the 1st AD before he or she makes up the daily schedules.

$$$

DPs earn about $1,000–$2,000 per day for TV movies and most features. Union scale rates start at around $800 per 8-hr. day. For commercials and music videos the rate can vary from $750 to $5,000 per day, with $2,000 being average. For documentary work, a DP might also operate the camera for a day rate of $600 to $1,200 per day, which may or may not include the camera package.

DPs usually charge for any prep, scout, or travel days. Try to negotiate half-day rates for travel, which is pretty standard.

20–02 Camera Operator or B Camera

This person operates the camera and is the one who looks through the camera during the shot, carrying out what the DP wants in composition, movement, and focus. He or she has many other duties — making sure that the media is on the drive or checking the film gate for dust after each take. They will make sure the F-stop, white balance, and focus are correct as well. They work in tandem with the 1st Assistant Camera and/or the Digital Imaging Technician (DIT). In studio situations, with the big cameras on moving pedestals, the Camera Operator follows the orders of the Director in the Control Room to change position, frame shots, and focus.

$$$

Rates for Camera Operators go from $500 to $800 per 10-hour day. Union scale rates range from $500 to $600 per 8-hr. day.

20–03 1st Assistant Camera

The 1st Assistant Camera is also called the Focus Puller (mostly in England). In addition to following focus on shots that require it, the 1st AC also maintains camera reports of takes and footage/gigabytes used, makes sure the right film stock is in the camera and coordinates media cards/hard drives with the DIT. The 1st AC also troubleshoots if there is a mechanical/technical issue with the camera equipment. The 1st AC will also need to be hired for a full day on each side of principal photography to check the camera package, make sure that all the parts are there and that they work, and transport the equipment.

$$$

Figure $250 to $550 per 10-hour day. Union scale rates range from $250–$750 per 10-hr day.

20–04 2nd Assistant Camera
This person is yet another attending to the camera's every need. If shooting film, he or she loads film magazines, logs and labels film cans, and often works the slate or clapper.

$$$
Figure $225 to $525 per 10-hour day.

20–05 Digital Imaging Technician (DIT)
The DIT supervises setup, operation, troubleshooting and maintenance of digital cameras, in-camera recording, waveform monitors, television monitors, recording devices, driver software, and related equipment. The DIT must also understand digital audio acquisition, timecode, and how they integrate into post environments. They are in charge of backing up the media on set immediately and maintaining the technical specifications that are required by the production for media acquisition.

$$$
The DIT is an IATSE designation, currently $486/day for 8 hours.

20–06 Still Photographer
Production stills (sets, makeup, wardrobe, continuity) are different from publicity shots. The production stills are usually shot by the respective department person. So this category is really about publicity stills.

There is a difference between shooting "documents" of the production and taking shots that can be used on posters. The former case involves a photographer who roams the set and shoots during rehearsals. For the latter case, the photographer usually sets up in a professional studio.

Make sure to negotiate who owns what rights to the publicity stills. Some photographers will offer a lower day rate in exchange for some rights to license their photos themselves. This will need to be approved by the actors as well, who may require approvals on which photos may be used.

Professional still photographers have rates as varied as those of cinematographers and are based on experience and reputation.

$$$
To get high-quality, original work you can expect to pay $250 to $545 per 10-hour day or more for a top-notch documenting photographer, and $500 to $2,000 for a studio shoot, just for the photographer. The studio itself may be $500 to $1,000 per day. Your photographer will prepare a budget for you to include fees, studio and equipment, makeup and hair, lights, backdrops, props, film, processing, prints, and so on. You should also consider budgeting one additional day for the photographer to catalog all the photos so they can be utilized for publicity purposes.

20–07 Camera Package Rental
Digital Video Cameras
Digital Video Cameras record images onto digital file-based media, such as a memory card, disc, hard drive or solid-state drive. Some older digital cameras still record to videotape.

Since the explosion of digital video there are literally hundreds of different video cameras, everything from cell phones to pro-sumer camcorders to HDSLRs and high-end Arri, Sony, Panasonic and RED cameras. Purchase prices range from $200 to $125,000 depending on the camera and format.

HD Camera Formats
HD digital cameras come in different formats, resolutions, and price points.

Sensor size
Sensor size is one of the tech specs to study when deciding on which camera(s) to use for your project. Sensors are divided into "small" sensors (2/3 inch or less) and "large" sensors (larger than 2/3 inch). Sensor size affects your camera's depth of field. The larger the sensor, the shallower depth of field. Discuss with the DP what sensor size is best for the cinemagraphic look you are going for in your film.

Frame Size: 2K-5K+
For a discussion of Frame Size see Chapter 4.

Lens choices
With HD digital cameras, lens choices are more important than ever. In some ways, the HD camera body has become a digital "box" and thus the lens choices are a much more important decision regarding the look and feel of your captured images. Lenses have almost become like filters as to how they affect the look of your imagery.

Lens Kit
DPs will require a lens package for whatever camera you choose for your project. Prime lenses have a fixed focal length and zoom lenses focus in a range between two different focal lengths. You may also think of a zoom lens as a "variable" prime lens. Aperture (or iris, f-stop, or t-stop) is another factor when choosing lenses. This is referred to as the "speed" of the lens. Prime lenses are usually "faster." This may become critical when working with shallow depth of field for your project.

Zoom lens rental prices fetch from $100 to $550 per day in 35mm, and from $75 to $150 per day in 16mm. Prime lenses can go from $60 to $300 per day in 35mm, and from $40 to $300 per day in 16mm.

To Buy or Rent
Because the cost to purchase certain HD cameras has become much more affordable, often it makes sense for a production to purchase a camera and/or lenses and accessories. The longer the production period, the more it becomes financially possible/preferable to purchase equipment. Additionally, there is a robust resale market for film equipment and with eBay and other online sales websites you can sell your equipment after you have completed your reshoots and make back some of your original investment. Do the math on the buy vs. rent options once you have decided on your equipment needs.

Producers and Directors agonize over camera formats and that's OK. I suggest watching projects similar to yours that you like. Contact the production company and find out what camera and lenses they used.

Common HD camera formats in increasing price order

DSLR (Digital Single Lens Reflex)
Canon 5D Mark III
Sony Alpha
Please note: HDSLR cameras usually require that the audio be recorded on a separate device and then synced up in post-production.

Large sensor cameras
BlackMagic
Sony
RED
Arri
Panasonic

$$$
As stated above, retail prices for digital cameras run the gamut, from $200 to $125,000. Check out retailers on the Web, like *www.bhphotovideo.com*.

Camera equipment houses usually rent a few cameras in each expense category. Depending on the length of your shooting period, you can get a "3-day week" — 3× the daily rental rate for a weekly rate. Or, for short shoots, you can rent the camera on a Friday afternoon and return it Monday morning for a 1-day rate. Many rental houses will give a discount of 10% to 35% or more, especially if your camera operator or DP is a preferred or repeat customer. Always ask for the biggest discount; even if you don't get it, they'll still often give you something off the original bid.

A few example rates:
Arri Alexa camera $2,000-$2,500 per week
RED Epic camera $2,000–$2,500 per week
Canon 5D Mark III camera $250 per week

Film Cameras
Some projects may decide to shoot in film. Are you shooting in 35mm or 16mm? The Producer, Director, DP, and especially your budget

will make that decision. Here are some rates for various cameras, just to give you some idea of prices. For larger shoots, you may want a second camera body, both as a reserve for distant location work and for simultaneous shooting with your first camera. In the latter instance, hire a second camera operator and 1st AC to run it.

35mm film
Arri 35 BL4–$400/day

Super 16mm film
Arri 16R3 Advanced — $325/day
Aaton Etera Super 16 — $325/day
Aaton XTR Super 16 — $225/day

$$$
The rates given are by the day, but as discussed above you can get a big discount based on how long you plan to rent the package.

Camera Supplies
The camera will also require expendables like camera tape, filters, canned air, packing foam, and marking pens. Figure $200 to $400 for the first day and $100+ for subsequent days. Sometimes this equipment can be rented from the 1st AC or Camera Operator for greater savings, since you pay only for what is used.

Many DP/Operators own their own equipment and may rent it to you cheaper than an equipment house. The advantage of going through a house, however, is that it will take care of maintenance or camera replacement if something goes down on set.

20–10 Camera Package Purchase
Depending on the camera or lenses you decide to use for your project, it may make sense for the production to purchase some of the equipment. After the film is over, the production company can sell it or decide to keep it for their next production.

20–11 Steadicam Operator and Equipment
The Steadicam is an ingenious piece of technology with springs, counterweights, and shock absorbers worn by a Steadicam Operator.

The camera is attached to it, and then the whole rig can walk, walk fast, run, climb or descend stairs, and generally move around all the while delivering a steady, jerk-free image.

$$$

There's a real knack to it, so Steadicam Operators get paid a bit more than an average Camera Operator — about $750–$1,000 per 10-hour day or more for real athletes of the genre.

Most Operators own and maintain their own Steadicam rig and charge around $500 to $750 per day for the equipment.

20–12 Teleprompter/Operator

Direct-to-camera performers (such as news anchors) aren't able to memorize lines since reports are edited and changed right up to air time, so they rely on a teleprompter. They are standard equipment at most TV studios and can be fitted to any studio or field camera (digital or film). When attached to the camera, you have a through-the-lens effect, meaning the actor or reporter reads the lines looking right at you.

When you want the talent to look at another person and pretend to be eloquent, the Operator places a monitor with the words just over the other person's shoulder and out of camera range.

$$$

Rates for Operator with Teleprompter run about $350 to $650 per 10-hour day. Some companies offer half-day rates as well.

20–13 Video Assist/Operator

A video tap is a piece of equipment that attaches to the camera allowing you to see a video image on a separate monitor. This is good for the Director, the DP, other crew members, and executives to see what's being shot. If you want, you can add digital video assist to the package, so you can play back what you've shot at variable-speed frame rates. Picture and sound are usually recorded on a hard drive.

$$$

Tap and assist systems vary on the camera type and record capability. The camera portion is supplied by the camera rental house. There are companies that specialize in video assist. They supply playback services and other support equipment such as accurate slow-motion video playback from a high-speed film camera.

Prices average around $350–$650 for the package and $450–$600 for the technician for a 10-hour day.

20–14 Aerial Photography

Shooting from airplanes and helicopters requires some specialized personnel and equipment. Pilots not experienced in the precision flying needed for this job can waste your time. The pilot is also the person who will set up the aircraft and walk you through the process, so for safety as well as professionalism, go with someone experienced in aerial photography.

You'll hear talk of the "Tyler mount" as an indispensable piece of equipment. It is a camera mount, usually rented from the camera rental house, that stabilizes the camera and reduces vibration. Tyler is one system. Wescam is another.

$$$

Expenses for aerial shooting vary on the camera package, the type of aircraft (jet helicopter, Cessna, etc.), the experience of the pilot, and how long you shoot. Cities like New York and Los Angeles will be more expensive than other places. This is the breakdown for doing an aerial shoot in New York City:

NYC-based Pilot $2,000 per 8-hr. day
Twin engine helicopter $2,000 per flight hour (with a 3-hr. minimum)
Director of Photography $1,000–$2,000 per 8-hr. day
Cineflex camera system w/ Alexa camera $4,950 per day
Landing fee at NYC Westside heliport $300
Parking at NYC Westside heliport $150 per hour

20–15 Underwater and Topside Water Photography

Here's another specialty area for professionals only. Some underwater filming experts (Marine Coordinators) own and maintain their own film and video cameras, packages, housings, and some lights, as well as boats and dive equipment. Others are more freelance.

For topside work, Coordinators know boat behavior and can make it work the way you want for your shots. They also coordinate the water scene for safety and look. They know the various insurance rates and Coast Guard regulations.

This special area has changed a lot now that many people can purchase their own underwater housing for a DSLR camera. Look into the costs to purchase your own housing if you have a small camera and plan to shoot for multiple days. You still need to have a Safety Person and Lifeguard to make sure you are filming in the safest way possible.

$$$

You can spend tens of thousands of dollars for an underwater shoot. Your budget will be based on very specific factors pertaining to your film, but here are some sample prices:

Marine Coordinator $50–$60 per hour
Safety Divers and Boat Operators $35–$45 per hour
Underwater camera operators $700 to $1,250 per 10-hour day
Underwater camera housing for a RED Epic $1,300 per day
Underwater camera housing for a DSLR camera $300–$400 per day

20–16 Drones/GoPros

This is a new area of technology for obtaining certain kinds of shots for your film.

Drones allow you to attach a small camera to the device which then takes it up into the air for aerial shots that are remote-controlled by an operator from the ground. As the technology advances, drones will be able to support bigger and heavier cameras for remote operation. Please note that legal regulations may prevent drone technology in certain cities and regions of the country. You'll need to research what the rules are for the location you plan to use for your scene.

GoPros allow you to attach very small and lightweight high-resolution cameras to a person's body, inside small spaces and other places that were impossible to reach just a few years ago. It allows for immersive POV, follow-cam, and "selfie" shots through various mounts that can be purchased or rented.

$$$
Professional quality drone, DSLR camera, wireless focus, and wireless video rig can rent for $2,000 per day

Camera operator $715–$1,000 per 10-hour day
Tech/pilot $715–$1,000 per 10-hour day
GoPros $200–$500 to purchase depending on which model you buy
Helmet mounts, suction cups, 3-way mounts, etc. $15–$70 to purchase

There are pro-sumer drones and non-union operators and technicians that will be able to do the job for less money. Insurance and liability issues are a big concern with this technology so you need to do your research to make sure you are getting professional and experienced personnel and have the proper insurance to cover whatever shots you plan to execute.

20–17 Maintenance/Loss & Damage
As stated in other sections, you should budget for potential additional costs.

20–18 Motion Control
Motion Control is utilized for some visual effects. If you require precise repetitive camera moves, you can use a camera that records the moves via computer programming. "MoCo" is often used for composite work, stop-motion cinematography, or high dynamic range cinematography. You may decide to put this line item into category 34–00 Digital Visual Effects/Animation.

$$$

This is rather expensive technology that requires experienced technicians. Cost will be determined by what you are planning to shoot on set. Contact a Motion Control company in your area to discuss the storyboards and get an estimate. A sample rate for a studio with equipment:

Motion Control studio, MoCo rig, HD camera, and camera operator $4,000 per 10-hour day

20–19 Expendables

As stated above in other sections.

20–20 Video Truck

When your show needs multiple cameras and you can't shoot in a studio with a complete camera setup, you call a video truck company. They send complete video studios on wheels to sports events, concerts, even situation comedies set up in converted warehouses. If you are shooting a concert and need multitrack audio, ask if they have a sound truck, or if they can recommend a source.

Once you have a bid from a company you like, ask them to send someone over to the location with you for a technical survey. They'll help you work out how much cable to lay out, best places to load in equipment, where to put the generator, possible camera positions, and so forth.

Fly Pack

If you can't or don't wish to bring in a video truck for some reason (e.g., size of the venue), you can also rent a "fly pack" which is a compartmentalized version of the truck — cameras, recording devices, paint boxes, and a switcher; everything is in cases and gets rolled into the venue.

$$$

Video trucks come in different sizes, so prices will vary. And the equipment menu is à la carte, so if you're shooting a sit-com with four cameras and a fly pack, it'll be a lot less than shooting at Dodger

Stadium with nine cameras. For average situations, expect to pay between $15,000 and $25,000 for a day's work.

20-25 Video Studio or Truck Crew

Whether you're in a video studio or video truck, you'll need the same crew (Director, DP, Grip, and Electric crew are in their respective categories elsewhere). Here's the rundown with day rates for a 10-hour day:

Camera Operators $500–$750
Utilities (people who pull cable and set up cameras) $450–$650
Audio $450–$650
Audio Assist (A-2) $400–$625
Boom Operator (Audio) $400–$625
Technical Director (crew chief and camera switcher) $500–$850
Video Control (quality control of video picture) $500–$850
Video Tape Operator (runs record machines) $400–$625

A few other crew people unique to video stage or video truck production:

Lighting Designer/Director $1,000–$5,000 (reports to DP or, lacking same, creates the lighting)
Associate Director (DGA rate for "Other than Prime Time" projects) $633 for 8 hours (in Control Room, with Director, readies shots for Director)
Stage Manager (DGA rate for "Other than Prime Time" projects) (readies and cues all talent) $577 for 8 hours

20-26 Kit Rentals

As discussed previously.

21–00 Production Sound

If the sound you record in the field is the sound you'll use in the master, it had better be good. Audiences tolerate lousy picture quality if the story is gripping, but they quickly become annoyed with bad sound. Feature films do a lot of ADR work (Automatic Dialogue Replacement) in audio post to correct problems with recordings in the field. Sometimes those problems are unavoidable, but a good mixer will help prevent those that are avoidable. ADR is expensive and time consuming, so save money and headaches now by heeding the advice of your Sound Mixer.

21–01 Mixer

Good ones have an uncanny ability to hear what the rest of us ignore. Background sounds like air conditioning (especially when it cuts on and off, causing havoc in editing), dripping faucets, chattering squirrels, or distant school children all land on the Mixer's sensitive eardrums. Even camera noise can sometimes cause a problem. And when your Mixer says she needs to get "room tone" for every setup, back her up and get it. Why? Because even though it means everyone on the whole set has to stand there in *complete silence* for 30 seconds, if you don't get it, guess who will be paying a sound editor to build it frame by frame at $75/hour?

$$$

Rates for Mixers average $250 to $550 per 10-hour day.

21–02 Boom Operator

These people develop amazing triceps from holding aloft a microphone attached to a "fish pole" for hours at a time. They are also good (hopefully) at keeping the mike out of the frame, yet as close as possible to the talent and properly pointed. While the job may look easy, it requires skill and constant attention. A weak link here between the speaker's voice and the microphone can put you in a tight spot in post: Hire a good Boom Operator.

On sound stages, the Boom Ops handle the mechanical Microphone Booms.

$$$

Rates average $225 to $500 per 10-hour day.

21–03 Expendables/Batteries

Some of the sound equipment requires professional batteries. Consult with the Sound Mixer for an estimate.

21–04 Sound Package

The Sound Package is normally a digital recorder plus assorted microphones (including wireless radio mics or lavaliers), a stereo mixing panel, mic boom poles, batteries, and baffles. Timecode-based systems are used so you can sync up your sound with your digital or film media. When recording on set, timecode is displayed on a "smart slate," a clapper slate with a timecode window display.

The mixer unit and other equipment can be rented through the camera house and included in the camera package, although most Mixers prefer to bring their own gear because they know they can rely on it.

Some productions will have the Mixer record directly into the camera and then you don't need to rent a digital recorder. If shooting on lower end digital/video cameras, make sure the camera has XLR audio inputs or get a Mini-to-XLR adapter.

When pressed for money, many documentary filmmakers opt to put a shotgun mic on the camera and skip the Sound Mixer/Boom Op altogether — or worse, just use the mic that comes with the camera. Whenever possible, do not use the camera mic. Learn about the different kinds of microphones and hire a Mixer who can also function as a Boom Operator. Good sound will actually take you further than bad sound and good picture.

$$$

Sound Packages go for around $200 to $500 per day, depending on the microphones and accessories.

21–05 Walkie-Talkies

Walkie-talkies are an essential part of any production when you need to communicate to several people over long distances. They allow you to lock up a location, hold traffic, and talk to other members of your department without yelling.

$$$

Basic walkies with a headset go for about $14 a day, weekly at $42. Make sure to ask for a discount — this is a piece of equipment where the price can be flexible.

21–06 Sound Truck

If you need to produce a music show for television, you'll want to find an audio services company that rents sound trucks. If the music is to be remixed later, you want multitrack recording capability — probably up to 48 tracks for this gig. The Mixer will mix the band, orchestra, chorus, and whatever else is a part of the show. When the concert is over, you'll remix at a recording studio or post-production sound facility.

If the sound is going out live and you have no time for a remix (now or later), then you can save money because you won't need multitrack recording — only a good audio board to send the mixed stereo sound over to the video truck where it is added to the picture and beamed out on the satellite feed.

$$$

Basic rate (with no travel) for a truck plus crew will be in the $5,000 per day range.

21–08–09 Miscellaneous/Loss & Damage

As discussed previously.

22–00 Transportation

Getting there is half the expense. Moving everything and everyone from location to location is a formidable job. What follows is for TV/cable series and movies and features. For smaller, non-union shoots, your drivers will probably be your crew and PAs.

If you are using Teamsters on your shoot, consult the IATSE rate card job categories, work rules, and rates.

22–01 Transportation Coordinator

This person coordinates the whole enchilada, and hires the Captains and Drivers, and administrates the operation. The Captains report to him, and handle the parking, the moving of vehicles, and so forth.

$$$

Rates: $2,200 to $2,500 per 5-day week.

22–02 Drivers

Captains

$2,000 to $2,300 per 5-day week.

Drivers

Rates vary on the type of vehicle driven. Some samples by the five-day week:

Auto/Station Wagons/Small Vans (non-union) $200–$300 per 12-hr day
Honeywagon/Makeup Trailer (non-union) $350–$400 per 12-hr. day
Camera Car Driver $400–$500 per 12-hr. day

22–03 Transportation Equipment Rental

The Transportation Coordinator will make the truck rental deals according to your budget. If you're on your own, consult the local production guides for vehicle rental companies.

Star Dressing Room

A mobile home or trailer is often part of the contract negotiations handled by the Casting Director. How big it is reflects the status of the star. Dressing rooms therefore range in size from huge to a shared room in the three-room Cast Trailer.

$$$

A luxury mobile home with two makeup stations rents for $2,500–$3,000 per week, plus towing or driving costs. A two-room Star 40-ft. trailer with slideout costs $900–$1,100 per week.

$$$

Here are some typical rates of other vehicles (not including delivery, driving costs, fuel, or auto insurance):

40-ft. Production Trailer (including copier/printer/Internet) $700 per day or $3,000 per week
Makeup/Wardrobe Combo 42-ft. Trailer $350 per day or $800 per week
6-Room 43-ft. Honeywagon $350–$450 per day, $1,200–$1,400 per week
2-Unit Portable Toilets $175–$225 per week plus $25 delivery charge (a service call will be extra)
Production Cargo Van $80 per day, $400 per week
15-passenger Van $119 per day, $605 per week
Prop 20-ft. Truck with lift gate $139 per day, $839 per week
Camera Car $650–$800 per day
Process Trailer $350 per day

22–04 thru 22–07 — Parking/Tolls/Gas, Repairs & Maintenance, Honeywagon Pumping, and Miscellaneous
These costs can *really* add up so make sure you budget for enough money to pay for the additional costs for all of your transportation vehicles.

23–00 Location Expenses (see Chapter 2 for more on Locations)

23–01 Location Manager
A good Location Manager, after finding the perfect places, makes the deals for the locations, gets permits, police, parking, fire, and approvals for same including those from the neighborhood. She also troubleshoots the location during production. The Location Manager may also need an assistant to handle the troubleshooting, while she works ahead of the shooting company to set up the next place.

$$$
Rates are $350 to $650 per 10-hour day, or $1,600 per week for low-budget projects.

23–02 Location Assistants
Depending on the number and difficulty in finding locations, the Manager will need Assistants to help with scouting, mapping, directions, and prepping locations.

$$$
Rates can be $150–$300 per day depending on experience.

23–03 First Aid/Medic
A location nurse or other qualified medical person with kit will run around $250–$350 per 10-hour day.

23–04 Fire Officers
Local regulations may require Fire Officers on the set whenever you use any electric lights, but especially if you're using open flame or pyrotechnics. Check with the local permit office for details and rates. A Fire Marshal or Set Firefighter can run $500 per 10-hour day.

23–05 Security
A Security person will cost about $150 per 12-hour day, but you and/or your sets and equipment may need 24-hour protection. On a feature, this figure can run into the thousands.

23–06 Police
Depending on local regulations, you may need police. In some cities they charge you, in others they don't. Check locally with the film commission or permit department. Big city rates can hover around $400 per 10-hour day. Sometimes there is a requirement for a minimum number of officers and number of hours.

23–07 Permits
Every big city and many small ones have permit departments. Since there can be many twists and turns to getting the right permit for your shoot, call them and get the local rules and regulations while you're budgeting.

23–08 Parking

During the scouting period, the Location Manager may have parking expenses.

23–09 Catering Services

Most caterers are sensitive to the variety of palates and diets on a movie set, and do a good job of designing a menu. A good menu, therefore, has a meat dish, a vegetarian dish, salad, veggies, dessert, and beverages.

Most services stock tables and chairs, although there may be a setup charge. You may also need tents, and even heaters if you're shooting a winter scene.

$$$

Caterers charge by the head, with average prices for a two-entrée meal being from $20 to $30 per person, with a minimum of 20 or 30 people. They may also charge a setup fee, server fee, and transportation costs, so you need to inquire.

Don't forget to budget for second meals on those days you expect to go long.

On low-budget shows, if you don't have enough people to warrant hiring a caterer, pass around the menu from a good local restaurant and have a Production Assistant take orders.

High budget or low, don't overlook where you serve the food. People use meals as a break from the job, and an opportunity for a little fellowship, so keep them warm or cool, as required, and away from unpleasant distractions like traffic exhaust, barking dogs, or gawking humans. Sometimes, a little quiet background music helps set the mood.

23–11 Location Office Space Rental

If you are all staying at a hotel, it may be convenient to rent an office or an extra room and have office furniture brought in, or make it part of the overall hotel deal and get the office for free. Another way is to rent a motor home or trailer equipped with desks, office gear, and a generator to run lights, computers, copiers, etc. Main occupants are the Production Coordinator and the Production Accountant, with room for the Producer, the UPM and Production Assistants. A meeting space for the Director is also a good idea.

$$$
A fancy motor home or trailer decked out as an office rents for about $3,000 per week.

23–12 thru 23–14 Office Supplies, Equipment, Telephone/Fax
These costs can really add up so make sure you estimate properly for paper, pens, location copier, phones, etc.

23–17 Location Site Rental Fees
Whether you're shooting the Brooklyn Bridge or your aunt's backyard, allow whatever is appropriate for both fees and permits. If you are going through a location service or using a Location Manager, they'll apprise you of the likely costs. On private property, the fee might be negotiated for less on prep and wrap days than on shoot days, saving a few dollars.

The price can be anything from a barter agreement (a free DVD of the film in exchange for a few days in someone's apple orchard) to thousands of dollars. In many cities, some homeowners are well used to movie companies and actually design their homes to attract the lucrative fees. Some fees are flat and some are for a certain number of hours.

$$$
Location fees can be anywhere from $0 to $25,000/day.

23–18 Location Scout
You may need to hire Scouts in addition to the Location Manager when you are prepping the film.

$$$
$300–$600 per day depending on experience and budget.

23–19 Auto Rentals
You may pay the Location Scout a rental fee for their own vehicle during the scout period.

23-20 Miscellaneous Expenses
Sometimes you will reimburse for mileage to use a Scout's vehicle. Ask before you hire the Scout.

24–00 Picture Vehicles/Animals
The vehicles we see in the show — from vintage automobiles to pickup trucks— are the Picture Vehicles. Animals are animals.

24–01 Animal Trainers

Boss Animal Wrangler
He works with the Stunt Coordinator and Director to map out stunts and otherwise handles the animal's care, feeding, transportation, shelter, tack, and working conditions. He'll prepare a budget including all of the above. Sometimes the animal needs training sessions ahead of the shoot day as well.

$$$
Boss Animal Wranglers earn $450–$500 per 10-hour day and more in special situations.
Assistant Wranglers earn from $200–$300 per 10-hour day.

24–02 Animals
The cost for the critters themselves varies, as you might expect, on their level of expertise. If you want a chimp to sharpen a pencil, and he doesn't know how, you'll need to pay to have the trainer teach him. See below some sample rates that include the animal and trainer for 4- or 8-hr. days

$$$
Dog $750 4-hr. day, $1,050 8-hr. day
Snake $950 4-hr.day, $1,250 8-hr. day
Horse $1,550 4-hr.day, $1,750 8-hr. day. Add $250 for round trip travel in a horse trailer.

24–03 Picture Vehicles

If you need a yellow taxi, armored truck, pink Ferrari, bus, cop car, limousine, or hearse, then you need a picture vehicle rental company. Costs depend on the scarcity and value of the vehicle and whether it will have to be painted, towed, driven by one of their drivers (a "non-performing driver"), and so forth.

$$$

Some sample day rates for 10-hr. days:
Contemporary police car $450–$550, Contemporary taxi $450–$550
Vintage London cab $650
Armored car $850
Shelby Cobra $650

Please note that you'll be paying "portal to portal" — from the time the car leaves the location where it is housed and back again after the shoot is over. With overtime, it often works out to $1,000 per day per vehicle.

25–00 Media

This category is for the production period only (see 30–00 for Post-Production-Digital and Film), and therefore includes:

- For digital media: Solid state recording media/hard drives/computer cards
- For film: Raw stock, lab processing, telecine (transfer of film to digital)
- For video: Various videotape stocks.

The prices quoted here are *rate card* and tend to be high. As you establish relationships with post facilities, you will be able to negotiate better rates or a flat-rate deal for various processes.

25–01 Digital Media

Based on the camera, resolution, and other technical decisions (e.g., compressed or uncompressed digital media), you will need to compute how much recording media and backup computer drives you will need to purchase for the production period of your film.

$$$
Prices change constantly for various size hard drives and other digital storage options.

25–02 Raw Film Stock
Most projects shoot in digital media but if you decide to shoot some or all of your project in film you'll want to have the DP do some tests before deciding on the film stock(s). When you order your film, it's best to ask the company to set aside stock with the same batch and emulsion numbers in case you have to purchase additional cans later in your production.

Film stock companies sometimes keep "short ends," and "re-canned" film stock. Short ends are leftover reels with less than the original amount of film per reel. Re-canned stock means they may have put the film in the magazine and changed their minds. Long ends and re-cans are used by productions big and small, but there are some possible snags.

Insist that the film be tested or do your own test, processing a strip from each can at a lab to check for density levels, scratches, fogging, and edge damage. Testing is also the only way to verify what kind of film is in the can, since cans are often mislabeled or de-labeled in the field.

$$$
These are some fairly typical prices for popular film stocks:

35mm
Kodak 500 ASA Color Negative $700 per 1000-ft. can
Super 16mm 500 ASA Color Negative (perforated one edge)
Kodak #7205 $160 per 400 ft.-can

25–03 Film Lab — Negative Prep and Processing
Same story as raw stock — prices vary with labor and stock increases, so get quotes. These prices may go higher as more and more film labs close and it becomes more expensive to get film processed. In choosing a lab, whether a big one or a small one, go for impeccable credentials. You really don't want to reshoot hard-earned scenes.

$$$
Typical processing costs:
35mm $0.18 per foot
Super 16mm $0.18 per foot

25–04 Telecine/Film to Digital Transfer
As the name implies, Telecine is the process of transferring production-acquired material (usually only film) to digital media so you can edit in your digital editing system. Once you have "locked picture" and you are ready to finish your project, you can go back to the camera original material and retransfer if you wish to or do a color grading in the On-Line (see *Post-Production* section).

Telecine is done on expensive machines by highly trained people called "Colorists," who "color correct" your images to make them look the way you want. A good colorist can do amazing work with your film originals. Telecine is an expensive process usually billed at an hourly rate so you want to use it wisely. There are a number of approaches:

(1) "supervised," meaning you'll have the colorist work on every shot, getting every scene just right.

(2) "one light," meaning you run the film through telecine without any stopping for color correction. Why? Because all you want at this stage is material you can edit with. Later, you'll do the real color grading on your finished film.

(3) "best light," a cross between the two.

(4) "scanned dailies," the newest way to handle this conversion process from film to digital. In this process, the negative is scanned to 2K resolution and archived to an LTO tape. The film negative is never touched again and the digital file is the "digital negative" for any color correction that is done after you lock picture.

Which one you choose depends on how much material you have to transfer, how much time you have, how much money you have, and what your editing process is. You should review all this with your editing facility and decide on a plan.

For sound, the digital audio is usually synced to picture as part of the telecine process.

For other discussions of post-production, see Chapter 2 under the subheading "Post-Production." In this chapter see Editorial (27–00), Post-Production — Digital and Film (30–00), and Digital Intermediate (31–00).

$$$

Scanned dailies: Super 16mm to 2K digital files — $.50 per foot
1 hour of digital content archived to LTO tape — $200 (includes time and stock)
Supervised Telecine:
35mm or 16mm to Digital media — $500–$700 per facility hour

How much time do you allow for telecine? A one-light transfer will be faster than a supervised transfer. For a supervised session, budget for 3–5 times the length of the material you are transferring. If you are using archival materials from different sources it may take a lot longer to color correct because of many variables in the disparate footage.

25–05 Videotape Stock

You may need to purchase videotape stock for production and transfers. These are some common videotape stocks used for production. (You can usually purchase these stocks from the post facility but the prices will be higher.)

HDCAM

This format comes in small and large format sizes depending on the length of the tape. Some cameras only accept the small size so be sure to check with your DP.
Small — 40 min. $32
Large — 94 min. $62

HDCAM-SR

Small — 40 min. $60
Large — 94 min. $180

LTO 5
This format is used for archiving digital material — it is not an acquisition format.
Sony LTO 5 — Compressed Capacity 3.0 TB/Native Capacity 1.5 TB
$23

26–00 Travel and Living — Crew

26–01 Airfares
Economy fare is sufficient for most non-union crew. The exceptions are Directors of Photography and Production Designers who are sometimes open to negotiation. Also, some contracts may demand flight insurance.

This is less common these days, but sometimes flight packages may be negotiated with airlines and a promotional deal may be worked out. Explore promotional tie-ins for savings on air travel.

Don't forget that humans are only one half of your travel expense. Equipment has to fly too, so allow for extra baggage and/or shipping.

26–02 Hotels
By multiplying the number of crew times the hotel day rate times the number of days, you come up with the hotel line budget. Sometimes promotions or package deals can be arranged for long stays.

If you're going to be on location for a long time, say a month or more, check out renting apartments. It's probably cheaper and more like home. Online rental websites are very helpful in finding local homes or apartments.

26–03 thru 26–06 Taxi, Auto, Train, Excessive Baggage
Costs associated with travel for the Crew.

26–08 Per Diem
Meals on the set have been accounted for in Catering (23–00 Location Expenses), but what about breakfast and dinner when you're all in London? The producer can either pay all meal expenses as they occur or more frequently distribute the per diem ($50 to $75 per day per person depending on local prices) and let each person take care

of his or her own meals. This way, the more frugal members of the cast and crew will go home with some pocket money and the producer will know, before the shoot, what to allot for meals.

If the producer provides all meals through catered breakfasts, lunches, and dinners, no per diem is needed, although you may want to give $10 per day for incidentals. In any case, when the producer serves a lunch, you can either deduct it from the per diem or make for a happy crew and not deduct it. Serving good healthy food on film sets is essential to maintaining a focused, hardworking production.

26–09 Gratuities

Gratuities are sometimes added to the budget. Especially when working in large cities, where you'll need to tip the car valet, the concierge, and other personnel who help you.

Below-the-Line Fringe

Always check the new taxation laws and the union/guild contracts for the latest information about these costs because they usually change from year to year. Fringes are usually computed by a payroll company who will be current on the most recent rules and tax changes. Remember in this budget each section computes the fringe for the Labor in that department.

These folks are mostly employees (although you may have a few "loan outs" among your Line Producer, Production Designer, etc.). Once again, these are the employer contributions:

- Social Security and Medicare (FICA-SS and FICA-HI) 6.2% up to $7,000 in salary.
- State Unemployment Insurance (SUTA) adjustable by state. In California it's 6.2% on the first $7,000 in salary.
- Federal Unemployment Insurance (FUTA) 6% of the first $7,000 in salary. Please note that you can take a credit for your SUTA up to 5.4% so you may only pay .6% of FUTA.
- Workers' Compensation rate is set annually by state and differs with each industry. Workers' Compensation is less expensive

for office people than for Grips. Call your state agency or payroll service to ask how much to average for your project.

- Some states have additional taxes. In California there is an Employment Training Tax of 0.1% on the first $7,000 of salary and a State Disability Insurance tax of 1% on the first $101,636 of salary.

The sum total of these adds up to 19%–23% of a person's gross salary. Your accountant or your payroll service can keep you abreast of any changes in the individual percentages and can handle actual payments from your company to the respective government agencies and union funds.

In addition to the payroll taxes, union employees receive pension and health benefits. These are some current rates as examples. Call each guild or your payroll service to get accurate rates for your project and your geographical area.

For Guild members, add:
WGA 17%
SAG-AFTRA 17.3%
DGA 15.75%

For IATSE members add:
Pension and Health $5.99 per hour (based on straight-time rate for any OT hours worked)
Vacation and Holiday 7.72% on day rates based on straight time

POST-PRODUCTION

27–00 Editorial

These are the costs for labor and equipment to edit the film to completion.

27–01 Editor

The Editor's creative decisions, under the Director's supervision, contribute tremendously to the success of the film. The Editor (usually with an assistant) screens dailies, edits the material (usually while shooting continues) into an assembly cut, then continues editing to a rough cut and then to a fine cut. Additionally, the editor edits the audio tracks, prepares digital files for Automatic Dialogue Replacement (ADR, also called "looping"), and checks the sync accuracy for all tracks (voice, music, and sound effects). Materials will also be prepped for the Composer, Sound Editor, Music Editor, SFX person, and Colorist, and they will screen the final master for quality control.

When no Sound Effects Editor is on the film, the Editor may also select sound effects, build the sound effects tracks, check sync, and prepare cue sheets for sound effects dubbing.

If no Music Editor is on board, the Editor may also build the music track to conform with the work print, check sync, and prepare music cue sheets for dubbing.

On large projects there will be an entire editing team with a Music Editor, Sound Effects Editors, and perhaps others. A big-budget blockbuster film requires a veritable army of editors. On small projects an Editor with possibly an Assistant Editor can manage.

How long will editing take? For a feature, the Editor starts assembly when principal photography begins and continues through production. There may be a finished assembly or Editor's cut within a week of completion of photography. If it's a DGA feature, the Director has a minimum of ten weeks to complete the Director's cut. For low-budget features (under $1.5 million), the Director usually has final cut so they stay on till the "picture is locked" — approximately 10–12 weeks.

For scripted television the complexity and length of the show will dictate how long it will take to edit the program.

Commercials and music videos are usually edited in a few days or weeks. It all hangs on the quantity of material shot, the quality of the Script Supervisor's notes, the speed of the Editor, and the ability of the Director and Editor to communicate.

A 90-minute documentary, on the other hand, can take 20 to 40 weeks to edit. For documentaries, often the acquired materials are transcribed and then a "paper cut" is created and select reels are put together by the Assistant Editor for the Editor and Director to work with. This process helps to manage the large quantity of material that is often acquired for a documentary.

If the prerequisites for editing are carefully orchestrated so the Editor isn't waiting around for sound or picture elements, the process will be cheaper and more efficient.

$$$
There's a big range. $300–$800 per 10-hour day. It will depend on the budget, the experience, and desirability of the editor.

27–02 Assistant Editor
Editors usually hire their own assistants, who sync and ingest camera originals; book screenings, editing rooms and equipment; order editing supplies, backup computer drives, and maintain a clean and orderly editing room and a cheerful attitude.

$$$
Rates go from $200 to $300 per 10-hour day.

27–04 Post Production Supervisor
The Post Production Supervisor is the "producer" of the Post-Production period. It may be the same person who produced the Production period or it may be a different person brought onto the project when you are getting close to "locking picture" and finishing your film. It's a fairly specialized world of technology which is why some producers work solely in the post side of the filmmaking.

$$$
Depending on the film's budget, the rate will be $1,700–$3,000 per week.

27–05 Editing Room Rental
This is the space(s) used by the Editor and Assistant Editor.

$$$
Edit Room space — $500–$800 per week for the space.
If the Ass't Editor needs a separate space, that will be an additional charge.

Post-Production Overview

Start with the deliverables — the masters. What formats are required? What are the tech specs? All broadcasters and festivals have tech specs. Where will your film be seen — only on the Web and video-on-demand or will it have a theatrical run? If you don't have a buyer or a festival destination yet, at least ask your post house to prepare for those kinds of tech specs. Now work backwards. What edit system will best suit your project's needs? Does it have many special effects or is it straightforward live action? What are the effects? Analyze them one by one to see how much time they'll take to create. You'll work backwards to build your entire plan and your budget. This will include your selection of camera, format, frame rate, editing platform, codec(s), and master format.

And then it should include a test run. You should shoot a camera test and then ingest it into your editing system and then finish to your master format so you know how it looks and all the technical steps you need to do from start to finish. It's essential if you wish to stay on schedule and on budget.

Workflow

The workflow steps are usually the following:

1) Shoot digital media or film during production.

2A) If shooting digital, the DIT on set will transcode and backup the digital media to storage drives. They will probably create a lower resolution digital copy by compressing the camera originals which will be added to the storage drives and it will all be sent to the Edit Room.

2B) If shooting film negative it will be sent to the Film Lab where it will be processed, telecined/transferred to digital files (with lower resolution digital copies), and then sent on storage drives to the Edit Room.

3) The Assistant Editor will usually ingest the lower resolution digital files into the computer digital editing system. The highest resolution digital files (camera originals) will be stored safely (in a "cloud" system or some other backup system) for use later in the finishing process.

4) The Editor will edit on the system and keep an Edit Decision List (EDL) that will be used while finishing the project during the On-Line/Confirm Edit. The EDL shows the time and edit code for every cut, fade, and dissolve. For the On-Line you will re-assemble the film per the EDL from the highest resolution materials that you acquired on set or transferred from film in your telecine. If you have archival materials you order/license the highest resolution copy of the photos or moving images from the library that holds the master.

27–06 Edit System Rental

There are three ways to go. You can edit at a post-production house; you can hire a freelance editor, rent a system, and set it up somewhere; or find an editor with his or her own equipment. The first is usually more expensive, because you are also buying the overhead (the fancy bathrooms, free snacks, and instant maintenance). On the other hand, if you do all the editing and finishing at the same house, they may cut you an all-in deal that's worth it. Also, if you are a first-timer delivering for a broadcaster or even a festival, an experienced post house can guide you through the post-production process. It will save you headaches. The second way, renting a system and hiring an Editor, can also work, but if it's a long edit, compare the cost of rental with the cost of purchase. The third option, finding an editor with his or her own equipment, is increasingly popular. These days, there are many editors with their own systems, so that can be very cost-effective. Remember you will need to purchase a copy of a computer editing software program for each computer system you utilize. Additionally there may be some computer "plug-ins" you need to purchase as well to maximize the system for your editorial needs. Make sure to do your homework before making the rental/purchase decision.

$$$

Edit System — $500+ per week for each edit system

Digital storage space to sync between multiple systems — $500 per week

If the Ass't Editor needs an edit system, that will be an additional charge.

27–10 On-Line Editing/Conform

Depending on your budget, master requirements, and workflow you may decide to finish your project on your computer editing system. You can output the master and do any of the finishing work like audio mix, titling, and color grading on that same computer editing system and then output so you can master to a DCP or videotape format like HDCAM SR. The technical tools available to an Editor through today's computer editing systems are impressive but they are not as technically sophisticated as what you will find at a Post facility where you can do a separate audio mix and On-Line/Conform of your film.

Most often, after you have "locked picture" you will then go into an On-Line Edit where you will do a Conform as the next step in your post-production process. For the Conform, you take the EDL, project file, and reference cut and replace all of the low resolution (low res) materials with the exact same frames from the high res (uncompressed) materials from your camera originals (or telecined masters) that you had kept in digital storage. During this process, your visual effects and stock footage will also be integrated. The Conform is usually a combination of automated reassembling and the hands-on work of the On-Line Editor and his or her Assistant. After the Conform, there will be Color Grading and then an output to a Digital Intermediate (DI). Often the final step includes the creation of a DCP master with an LTO videotape as an archival backup.

On-Line Editing/Conform is billed by the hour and the rate depends on how many "machines" and personnel you utilize for each step. Work out what services you'll need, how many hours you expect to use (ask your sales person), what effects you'll use, how much titling time you'll need (show your credits list and other on-screen verbiage to the sales person). Also budget for Mastering and Dubs, which includes master coded stock, and any duplicate masters (based on your deliverables list). Call a few Post facilities and get bids. Try to get the rates down lower. Say you'll work nights and weekends. But always insist on a fully qualified On-Line Editor — no apprentices.

This step is one of the most expensive steps in the whole post-production process. If the DIT (during production) and the Assistant Editor did an excellent job transcoding your camera original materials you will have straightforward and cost-effective Conform. If they were sloppy or not experienced enough to know what to do, you will spend lots of money in the Conform tracking down technical mistakes and correcting them in a very expensive On-Line suite. This is why creating a good workflow and sticking to it every step of the way is so critical on any project.

$$$
Here are some average On-Line and Effects Rates. Editor is included.

Online/Conform
$350–$450/hr.

Mastering — HDCAM SR
$400/hr. plus tape stock. For a 90-min. film, you'll be charged 2 hrs.

Finishing Effects Editing Cleanup work. $350-$450/hr.

28–00 Music
This category covers the buying, licensing, or creating of music, and the hiring of a Music Supervisor. The technical methods of recording and editing it are in 29–00 Post-Production Sound. There are three common ways to get music for your project:

(1) Have it composed.

(2) License pre-recorded music from a music library.

(3) License pre-recorded music from an individual musical artist's recording.

28–01 Composer Fee
A composer (preferably one with experience scoring visual media) screens your final cut and composes music directly to picture. If you

get a good composer, this is the best way to go because it has been created specifically for your project.

Costs depend on the composer's reputation, the number of musicians used, recording studio time, and total number of minutes of music needed. Many composers create the score and play all the music parts on a synthesizer. That's usually the cheapest method. If the resulting sound is too synthesized for you, composers can lay down a synthesized foundation, then bring in some musicians to sweeten the sound. A few real violins or French horns over the electronic ones can make a world of difference.

If you don't know any composers and don't really know what you can get for your budget, watch some programs, documentaries, or movies whose music you like and contact the composer or production company, or call some agents who handle composers, and tell them how much you want to spend. They'll refer you to some of their clients appropriate for your project.

If you know or have been referred to some composers, ask them to bid on the music package, which may include composing, arranging, and producing all necessary music, studio time, musicians, and equipment. It's called an "all-in" or a "package" deal. The composer ultimately presents you with a finished tape ready for audio post.

$$$

Some sample package budgets:

- A composer for a feature film might receive $40,000 to $60,000+ as a package deal.
- A half-hour TV show might pay as little as $3,000 to $5,000.
- A 3-minute promotional might pay $1,500 to $2,500.

When you do a package deal with a composer, you avoid having to deal directly with the musician's union, the American Federation of Musicians (AFM). Not that they are bad people, but if you are unfamiliar with the complexities of union wages and extras, you have a steep learning curve ahead. That's why many producers like packages.

Other producers go one of two other routes:

(1) If the composer is a signatory company to the AFM, she can hire union people and take care of the union payrolls herself.

(2) If the composer is not a signatory, he or she can use a payroll service that is a signatory, and administrate the union payrolls through the service.

Music Line Items

If for whatever reason you decide to hire the composer for creative talents only and put the rest of the music package together yourself, there are hard costs to contend with.

Composer's Fee (creative only)

Composers are outside the jurisdiction of the AFM. Fees are a negotiable amount that can be as little as $2,000 for an episode of a half-hour weekly prime time series to $100,000 for a feature if you're dealing with an established master.

28–02 Musicians

If you are working with non-union musicians, fees are negotiable, although you can get some clues by reading the American Federation of Musicians basic agreements (or see *The Showbiz Labor Guide* in the Resources section). The union work rules are complex. There are different fees for features, trailers, shorts, commercials, industrial/documentary, television, home video, and so on. Length of the program is important. Musicians who "double" (play more than one instrument) get more money (50% more). (Since it is possible to produce very different sounds by changing instruments, this is a very cost-effective way of broadening the soundscape of the musical score.) The AFM has low-budget production union agreements now, so make sure to research what agreement is appropriate for your music composition budget.

Figuring a union music budget requires an experienced hand. Additional costs must be taken into consideration, such as leader fees, rehearsals, meal penalties, overtime, and instrument rental and cartage.

Other contractual considerations will be the publishing and auxiliary rights to the music produced (soundtrack and songs), which may affect the composer's and musicians' fees. A music rights lawyer should be consulted on these issues. The union commitment does not stop after the musicians walk out the door. There is a "back end" payment for musicians if the music is released as a soundtrack, or in foreign or other supplementary markets, and for commercials there are residual fees. Contact the music payroll service about these issues.

$$$

Some sample rates from the AFM agreement:

Theatrical Films

Musician, minimum of 3 hours, $265.97 per first 3-hr. session (35 players or more), includes 4% vacation pay

$305.90 per first 3-hr. session (23 players or less), includes 4% vacation pay

TV Film

Musician minimum of 3 hours, $284.92 per first 3-hr. session (4 players or less), includes 4% vacation pay

AFM Low Budget

Recording Musician, minimum of 3 hours, $198.52 per first 3-hr. session, does not include vacation pay

Again, these are just sample rates. They don't include cartage, rental, pension, health, and other fringes. If you are putting together your own package, consult the agreement and work with someone who knows how the agreement applies to your show. Discuss it with a music payroll service.

28–03 Music Prep

Once the harmonic, rhythmic, and melodic structure has been established by the Composer, either the Composer or an Orchestrator/Arranger assigns the various voices (including instruments) in the form of a music score. Then a Copyist produces a finished score for each musician.

$$$

Music Prep people get paid by the page, but at the beginning of a project you won't know how many pages there will be or how many musicians, so here's a rule of thumb. For an orchestra of 12–15 people, plan on four 3-hour sessions and budget an extra 50% of the musicians' gross wages for the Music Prep folks. Adjust it later when you know what you've got.

28–04 Recording Studio Costs

Studio costs often include the room rate, the setup, piano tuning, outboard gear, digital media, and a 2nd Engineer. (The 1st Engineer is either a staff person or a freelancer whom you will pay separately.)

$$$

Costs are $50 to $100 per hour. Try to get a flat package deal with the studio. Typically you can rent a small studio that will accommodate 12–15 musicians for $175/day or $800/week (may include an assistant engineer). You'll need to hire a 1st Engineer at $400–$800 per 10-hr. day.

28–05 Music Scoring Stage

This is a recording studio with projection capability, so the Composer/Conductor can record the music in sync to picture. The music is recorded digitally.

$$$

Scoring stages cost $175 to $700 per hour, depending on your budget and how elaborate you want your recording to be. The Engineer will be a separate hire. A low-budget feature composition could take three days of two sessions per day to record the score.

If you can't record at a scoring stage, find a soundproofed room and rig video projection that you can sync to your recording machine. If you already have a synthesizer music foundation and have transferred the music to a multitrack digital media with timecode, you are already synced to picture and your combo can record along to the synth. On the other hand your musicians lose the opportunity to put in "stings," which are musical accents that illuminate visual action.

28–06 Cartage and Rentals
Depending on the instrument there may be cartage fees. This is to cover the cost to have the instrument transported to and from the studio. You may have to rent certain instruments and additional equipment, too.

$$$
Cello players, for example, get $12, but percussionists with a van full of congas, bullroarers, and slit gongs can get up to $400, as do synth players. Guitar amps and grand pianos have cartage fees as well.

Even working non-union, musicians who play more than one instrument will expect an additional rental and playing fee, but that is small compared to what it would cost to hire additional musicians. It's called "doubling" and you will need to budget for how many instruments you expect each musician to play.

Depending on the size of the project, budget for at least $1,000 for instrument rentals and $1,000 for equipment rentals.

Synthesizer Programming
If your composer is laying down a synth foundation, the machine needs to be programmed. This is also a handy place to hide additional creative fees to the composer (assuming he or she is actually playing the synth).

28–07 Music Mix Room
After the recording is completed, the Music Editor will mix the music and correctly place the mix tracks to picture in a process called *prelay*. These files are then sent to the Sound Editor for the Final Mix.

$$$
The rate for the Mix Down room is $175 to $400 per hour, depending on how "high-end" you are. If the Music Editor has her own home studio, some of this work can be done there more cheaply.

28–08 Singers

Singers are covered by the SAG-AFTRA union agreement, and are paid according to a complicated formula based on what the show is, whether they are on camera or off, whether they over-dub, if they "step out" from a group and sing solo up to 16 bars, and so on. Consult the SAG-AFTRA agreement or *The Showbiz Labor Guide* (see Resources) for rates.

$$$

Theatrical or TV Standard agreement
Solo/Duo Singer, on or off camera $929/8-hr. day

Standard Low Budget ($625,000–$2.5 million)
$544/8-hr. day

Modified Low Budget ($200,000–$625,000)
$285/8-hr. day

Ultra Low Budget (under $200,000)
$125/8-hr. day

28–09 Payroll Service

Because music is so complicated to budget and track paperwork and residuals, there are payroll services that specialize in it. Their fees may be the same as for a production payroll service or higher if they become a signatory to the AFM for you. Still, it's probably well worth it. A good service will really work with you to help get the best deals on the union contracts and keep you straight with the paperwork. Typically, the fringes are around 30–32% on top of any salary.

28–10 Miscellaneous

Music hard costs suffer the same slings and arrows as production hard costs, so allow for office expenses, phones, shipping, messenger, and other expenses (see 36–00 General and Administrative Expenses for a master checklist).

A cost-effective way to hire a talented composer and musicians is to go to music schools and find people there. Yet another way is to ask the composer for any unreleased recordings or "back catalog" you can license directly, provided the composer owns 100% of the publishing rights (sync and master rights).

28–11 Music Licensing

If you wish to include pre-recorded music in your film you'll need to license it from various entities — music labels, music libraries, online websites, and unsigned bands/musicians. You'll need to obtain two licenses — the synchronization license and the master use license. Generally, the sync license is obtained from the music publisher and the master use license resides with the music label. If you are purchasing a license from a music library or online website, they may have both licenses available under one payment agreement which makes it easier/faster for the producer.

Music license rates are determined by several factors — the length of the clip from a music recording, how many clips are used from one piece of music, how the clip is used (e.g., under the opening title sequence or in a brief edited scene in the film), what rights you require — worldwide, all media, in perpetuity for a national car commercial or only film festival rights for three years. If you are requesting a license from a music label or publisher you will need to put this information in a request letter and follow up with your request many times. Give yourself at least two months to negotiate the licensing agreement — it takes a long time. There may also be re-usage fees to the musicians who performed on the original recording — this is where a Music Clearance person can be most helpful (see 28-12).

Online music libraries are a great place to find and license music. You can download music and purchase the rights you need from the websites. Remember to obtain both the synchronization license and the master use license. Before you sign and purchase music, read the agreements to make sure the license covers all the rights you need.

Do not pay music license fees until after you've completed your film and know for sure what cuts you'll use. Many filmmakers mistakenly purchase music rights and then do not use the music.

$$$

Music Libraries/Online Websites/Music Labels will charge anywhere from $100–$5,000+ for use of a piece of music in a low-budget feature film. If a musical composition requires both the synchronization license (i.e., publishing) and the master use license (i.e., record label), usually each license will cost the same amount. You negotiate the license that you think you can get the best deal on and then go to the other license holder for the same composition and they will often accept the same amount for the fee.

28–12 Music Supervisor/Clearance

The Music Supervisor or clearance service negotiates the licensing of any music used for a project that is not originally composed. So if you want any pre-recorded music, or if you want someone to do a cover of someone else's music, or if you need to ascertain if a piece of music or its arrangement is in the public domain, you'll want help: Enter the music supervisor. She may also handle record contracts for a soundtrack album, negotiate publishing deals for a film's music, and generally work with all parties in creating or supplying music for a project.

Do you have a scene in a club that requires pre-recorded dance music? The music supervisor works with you creatively to select the right music and then negotiates the deal. Music clearance and negotiation is a complex end of the business that requires expertise and time. Do not leave it to the last minute. If music figures prominently in your project, you must get a Music Supervisor on board early in order to create a realistic schedule and budget.

$$$

Independent feature films may budget anywhere from $5,000 to $15,000 to pay a Music Supervisor, depending on the number of songs that need to be cleared, whether these songs are major artist or indie songs, the caliber of the song above and beyond who wrote or recorded it, the publishers and record labels involved, whether the job requires both creative (selecting songs) or just the administrative side (clearance, licensing, cue sheets, dealing with all the politics and any other administrative tasks), and the individual Music Supervisor's experience.

29–00 Post-Production Sound

Because audio post is the last step in the process before mastering, some producers give it less respect, or less money, or maybe they've run out of money. In any case, it deserves full attention, and its fair share of the budget, because an inadequate soundtrack can ruin your project, and conversely, an inspired one can elevate your storytelling to another level.

There are two sides to this coin: creative and technical. On the creative side, consult with the Sound Designer, aka Supervising Sound Editor, early in pre-production. Get his ideas about how sound can help tell the story. Why? Because it may change the way you shoot certain scenes. On the technical side, make sure there is a conversation between the Editor and the Sound Editor about how the Editor should prepare dialogue and other sound elements during the picture edit. Obviously, this little talk should occur before the picture edit begins. Good communication at this stage will save you time and money during audio post!

Audio Post for Film

On a large production, there will be a Supervising Sound Editor to ride herd on all the post sound editors, artists and elements. On a small project, there may be just one Sound Editor. When the project is ready for audio post, there are lots of sounds to prepare: music, dialogue, automated dialogue replacement (ADR), Foley (sound effects), and possibly narration. Let's take each item one at a time, starting with the main positions.

29–01 Sound Editor

The supervising Sound Editor, aka Sound Designer, works with the Director and other team members to design the overall creative and technical approach to the sound of the project. This process begins in pre-production and should coordinate with the picture editor. The

Sound Editor may also do much of the actual editing, that is, laying out all the separate tracks, placing effects in their proper places, and preparing for the mix.

$$$
Supervising Sound Editors earn $300 to $700 per 10-hour day.

29–02 Assistant Sound Editor
The Assistant will work on laying out the tracks and prep for the Sound Designer.

$$$
Assistant Sound Editor rates are about $1,200–$1,500 per week.

29–03 Music Editor
The Music Editor works with the Composer before the scoring session. She also assists during the recording session and then mixes the music tracks down in preparation for the final sound mix. She will also do the *pre-lay* where she lays out the music in the proper placement before the Final Audio Mix. She builds the music track to conform with the edited master, checks sync, and prepares music cue sheets for dubbing, and checks sync and the music cue sheets again when dubbing is finished to make sure everything is accurate.

$$$
Rates are $1,500 to $2,500 per week.

29–04 Dialogue Editor
The dialogue editor assembles, synchronizes, edits, cleans up and smooths out all the dialogue in a project. If he can use the production tracks, he will, but if any of them are unusable he will replace them with alternate production tracks recorded on set or with automated dialogue replacement (ADR). ADR is recorded in post as the actors watch their performances in a sound studio and re-record their lines. Often the dialogue editor needs to fill a track with *room tone*, which is usually a 30-second recording of the sound of the actual place — crew and actors and equipment and all — just after a given

camera setup. Room tone is the dialogue editor's lifeblood. A good Sound Mixer on set will always ask for room tone. A good Director will always get it and demand silence on set during the 30-second recording. Don't leave your camera setup without it.

$$$
Rates are $1,500 to $2,500 per week.

29–05 Spotting (Music and Effects)
The Supervising Sound Editor, Music Editor, the Composer, the Director, and sometimes the Producer watch the finished picture edit of the film in what is called a "spotting session." They all talk about where music should be, and what kinds of feelings it should evoke. The Composer writes the music and plays it for the Director, Producer, and Editor in "listening sessions." Once the creative aspects of the score are approved, it is ready to be recorded on a Music Scoring Stage.

The Director and the Supervising Sound Editor also have a long session in which they spot for sound effects. Where should effects be and what should they sound like? What emotions are intended? The aural dimension is rich with possibilities to enhance the story.

After spotting for effects, the Sound Editor pulls the effects from an effects library, and/or supervises and engineers the Foley effects sessions, and syncs the effects to picture in the pre-lay.

If you can't afford to score with real musicians, then the composer writes the score and records it from synthesizer to a digital format.

29–08 ADR Studio/Editor
Now that the music is underway, it's time to consider Automatic Dialogue Replacement. Prior to booking your ADR Stage, you had a "spotting" session at your audio post house, in which you confirmed which sections of the dialogue need to be replaced. Your ADR Editor prepares actors' lines and cue sheets for the ADR Mixer. You now bring your actors to the ADR stage, project the film, and have them do their best to lip sync to the picture as they listen to their original lines through headphones.

If an actor is in a different city from the director, you can hook up the actor through a local studio using a phone patch or ISDN line. This will require you to hire two studios — one for the actor and one for the director, plus the ISDN line.

If you can't afford a studio, a quiet room with a microphone, headphones and a digital recording device can work as long as you can screen the scenes for the actor and sync it with the recorded audio.

For crowd scenes you may need to hire several background actors to create the overall sound you would hear on a street or in a restaurant. This is called a Loop Group and the head person is called the Loop Group Leader. If you need something specific — the crowd is on the street in Lebanon — then you will need to specify what language the actors must speak.

$$$

ADR rates vary from $175 to $400 per hour for one Mixer. The Loop Group actors will be paid the SAG-AFTRA rate for ADR recording or approximately $200–$300 per day if non-union.

29–09 Foley Stage/Foley Editor

A Foley Stage is a specially designed soundproof room in which Foley Artists watch a projection of the project and create on-screen sounds that sync up with the picture. The Artists are masters at finding ingenious ways to make sounds, and include footsteps, horses walking, body punches, and a zillion other effects in their repertoire. Most films Foley every footstep in the show. But you can save money by selecting only the sections that really need it. You may also use library sound effects, but be careful — the editor may spend so much time trying to make the library effect work that you would have spent the same money or less in Foley.

$$$

Foley Stages (including the Foley Artist) go for about $250 to $350 per hour. Typically, a low-budget feature would require 40 hours of Foley. A Foley Editor costs $1,500–$2,000 per week.

29–10 Foley Artists

These are the people who create the customized sounds out of all different kinds of materials and tools.

$$$

Foley Artists earn $350 to $425 per day.

29–12 Narration Recording

Some producers like to record a rough, or "scratch" narration track while editing, using themselves as unpaid talent. This gives you freedom to make script changes as you go, and tailor the script to scenes as they change.

When the cut is approved, a professional Narrator is called into the recording studio to record the final track. Some like to record to a running picture; others find this a distraction and prefer to just record it to the producer's cues for length of each speech.

Depending on the complexity of the script and the ability of the Narrator, figure one to three hours for a 30-minute documentary. Take the time necessary to do the job right.

For long documentaries, calculate additional time to return to the studio to record "pickup" lines, should re-editing become necessary. Use the same studio so the sound quality and microphones will match. If non-union be sure your rate for a Narrator includes these pickup sessions whenever possible.

$$$

Off-Camera Narrators/announcers work under the SAG-AFTRA agreement. The rate for a one-hour documentary is a flat rate of $645.

An ADR recording stage, with Recordist and Engineer, costs $300–$400/hour.

29–13 Audio Laydown

After all the different sound elements have been prepared, they are ready to be synced to the picture in the Pre-Lay (see Music Pre-Lay above, and Sound Editor below). The audio post house takes the approved Master file and does a *laydown*, wherein the production sound is stripped from the picture, and laid down to one track on a multitrack media file. Timecode goes to another track for reference. All the other sound elements, music, ADR, Foley, and so forth are Pre-Layed — synced to picture — on different tracks of this multi-track media file.

$$$

Laydown rates are in the neighborhood of $160 to $275 per hour.

29–15 Audio Mix

In the final mix session, all your sound elements, including production dialogue and sound, ADR dialogue, narration, Foley, music, and sound effects are combined into a stereo two-track, four-track (left, center, right, and surround), or six-track (5.1-left , center, right, left surround, right surround, and sub) configuration on a final multi-track digital file.

$$$

Mixing can cost anywhere from $400 to $550 per hour, depending on what equipment you use, where you mix, and how many Mixers are in the session (big or complicated projects can require up to three Mixers).

29–17 Dolby License

Depending on your deliverables you may need to purchase a Dolby or other theatrical sound license. This digital technology encodes the soundtrack into four channels: left, center, and right (which play back on speakers located behind the screen), and surround, which is heard over speakers at the sides and rear of the theater for ambient sound and special effects. These are usually needed for a theatrical 35mm print but not for a DCP master. Check online for the license regulations and prices and check with the audio post facility about any extra expense for adding on a Dolby product (*www.dolby.com*).

29–18 Miscellaneous Expenses

Any costs that are not covered by the above like tape stock or equipment rentals.

Audio Post Budgeting

Since audio post is often budgeted as a package "all-in" deal, first figure out exactly what you'll need and about how much you can afford, then call two or three audio post houses and get bids. Give them as much information as possible. This will help to avoid surprises. Negotiate the best deal you can and remember that you get what you pay for and going with the lowest rate is not necessarily in your best interest.

The established audio post facility is where you'll most likely find the most qualified people, but nowadays you can find many sound editors hard at work in their soundproofed garages with Pro Tools or similar software. You may not get the same range of services as you would in a facility, but you can get almost everything done you need to get done. The key is finding competent talent by checking references before you make the hire.

30–00 Post-Production — Digital and Film

This comprises the stock footage and archival costs for projects that require that kind of material.

30–01 Stock Footage

Need a shot of the Colorado State Capitol's golden dome in fresh snow? How about archival footage from a civil rights march in the 1960s? Or World War I footage of life in the trenches? A stock footage house somewhere has your shot. If they don't, you might find one that will go out and shoot it for you, and only charge you the regular stock footage rate.

If you need to license archival footage and/or still images you'll need to budget for the licensing fees. You'll need to know what territories, distribution outlets, and length of time you need to purchase for: all media, worldwide, in perpetuity? US VOD only? Internet only? Remember, stock footage companies often have minimum orders (usually 30 seconds) so even if you only need 15 seconds you'll be charged the minimum order amount.

$$$

Stock footage libraries and archive houses usually charge by the second ($75 per second is average) with a 30-second minimum. They may charge you a research fee of $50 to $150 average for putting together and shipping a screening reel. If you use 90–120 seconds from one library you can negotiate for lower rates. There will be different prices based on the kinds of rights you need to acquire. All rights, worldwide, and in perpetuity will be the most expensive. If you need less rights than that the price will decrease.

30–02

Archive Film/Television Clips

Studios and television networks have stock footage departments as well. If it's contemporary sports footage you want, you'll have to go through the professional sports leagues like the NFL, NBA, NHL or MLB. Direct your request to their clip licensing departments. Some film clips will require you to get clearance from the actors or the news anchor talent that is in the footage. That may require a talent payment as well. (See the discussion of feature film clip clearance and stock footage in Chapter 2.)

$$$

The rates are generally $75–$120 per second for all rights, worldwide, in perpetuity.

30–04 Archival Researcher

This person knows where to go to find the shots you need for your film. He has worked with all the stock footage libraries and has a strong background in researching the best place to find what you are looking for. He may also "clear" the stills/moving footage at the end of your edit after you lock picture or you can hire a different clearance supervisor to do the job.

$$$

Archival Researchers usually charge $2,000–$2,500 per week.

30–06 Clearance Supervisor

If the Archival Researcher is not going to clear the rights, you'll need to hire a Clearance person to license the stock photos/footage you need for your project. Meet with this person early in your planning to discuss budget, because depending on what you have in mind, clips can really add up. Some movie clips, for example, cannot be used without permission from and fees paid to the current owner of the film, the major actors in the clip, the director and writer, any stunt people, plus the composer and musicians for any music performed and the owner of the music rights. You need to make sure you are getting all the permissions and paying the fees.

Clearance Supervisors can also advise you about:

Moving Image Clips Licensing
Stills Rights
Artwork Rights

$$$

Clearance Supervisors usually make $2,000-$2,500 per week.

30–09 Screeners

These are low-resolution, watermarked versions of the stock footage/archival materials you may want to edit into your film. You'll need to pay for the dub, the stock, and shipping costs. Sometimes you can get them as digital files but there is often a price for the file as well.

$$$

Anywhere from $50–$250 per footage request depending of who, what, and how.

30–11 Film Prints

The need for a film print is rare these days but if you need to create one you will make it from your Digital Intermediate by recording that file to film. You can record it onto Intermediate Negative (IN) stock, which has a finer grain structure than camera negative stock (OCN) that DPs use during production. From there you would create an Answer Print. You could also take the DI and create an

Intermediate Positive Print and project that print without having to make an Answer Print.

$$$
Film Interpositive runs $1.65 per foot
Film Internegative runs $1.65 per foot
Film Answer Print runs $0.69 per foot
Optical Soundtrack Negative runs $1,400 per Reel for Quad Audio (features are usually at least five reels long)

Release Prints
After you create an Answer Print you will make your 35mm Release Print(s) that will be distributed to cinemas for projection.

30–12 Miscellaneous Expenses

Lab Rush Charges
Labs are always asked to produce miracles and meet impossible deadlines. They'll do it but it costs. Rush charges can amount to 100%–300% above standard rates. Avoid rush charges (including shipping) with proper planning.

Negative Cutter
As outlined above, 99.9% of the time, the film negative (OCN) is telecined/film-to-digital transfer and then never touched again. If it is ever needed to be physically cut, you would hire a Negative Cutter to do the job.

31–00 Digital Intermediate
The definition of the term "digital intermediate" or DI has been going through a bit of a transition lately. It was originally used to describe the scanning and recording of film into a digital format. It is now used to describe the color correction or color grading and final mastering in the digital workflow.

31–01 DI
The digital intermediate (DI) is where the final edited images of the project (digital and/or film originals) are manipulated: Dead pixels

can be corrected and color grading is done with superb precision. The DI process must be well planned and executed carefully. There are four main stages to the process: scanning, grading, mastering, and color management.

Scanning means translating the information from film negative into the digital domain. If you've captured your project on a digital cinema camera you won't need to do this step.

If you have camera-original materials from film negative, you will go back to the negative and scan the sections that are in the final master. Your goal is to get as much of the detail from the original negative as possible for what you can afford. This will translate into whether you get a "2K scan" or a "4K scan." 4k means a bit over 4,000 pixels of horizontal resolution. 2k has a bit over 2,000 pixels. But the vertical makes the difference. Simply put, a 4k image has four times the number of pixels that a 2k image has. Should you scan at 4k or higher? The decision will be based on your budget and your technical requirements and deliverables. Talk this all out with your DP, Director, and Post house.

Color grading refers to the changes made to your images in the digital realm by the Colorist and others. The high-tech computers used by a colorist allow for the adjustment/manipulation of every visual aspect of your high res camera originals — a huge palate of colors, tints, hues, and shades with which to treat all or just part of the frame. You can also do "digital lighting" — create the appearance of light or the diminution of light in an area of the frame in a scene.

The next step is usually the creation of a Digital Cinema Package (DCP) from your digitally color-corrected files and final audio mix. These rates run $20–$40 per minute or it can be a flat fee like $900 per reel. If you do not have digitally color-corrected files, you may need to first create a Digital Cinema Distribution Master (DCDM). The DCDM files are an interim step to get to the DCP. If you want to keep the DCDM files though, the Post facility will charge you approximately the same fees as for the DCP.

DCPs can be encrypted and non-encrypted. Encrypted means that the DCP needs a digital key, or KDM, anytime it needs to be played. They run around $20–$40 per key to create, but it means the film will be harder to copy. DKDM is the key that allows you to create more keys and is delivered to the distributor.

Since almost all US cinemas converted to Digital Projection systems in 2013, it is much less common to create Film Prints for theatrical release. If you do need to create film prints, then all the DI information must be transferred back onto film negative and then film prints will be created.

The final step is Color Management/Quality Control. You'll need to watch all created masters to make sure they pass all the technical specifications for where you plan to deliver the film — e.g., television broadcaster or international distributor. Another aspect of color management is determining what color space to use. There are many different color spaces, e.g., Rec 709 or P-3. Look at your deliverables list to see if you need to conform to a specific color space standard. If you have to deliver in more than one color space then you will have more than one master file.

One more note: If you plan to have a theatrical release for your film, as part of the Quality Control process you'll want to screen the DCP on a very good digital projector, rather than a monitor, to show and test the work in an environment as close to a theatrical experience as possible.

$$$

Let's assume the feature film has a 90-minute total running time.
Digital conform prices are $350–$450 per hour.
Color grading runs $500–$700 per hour. Allow 50–70 hours. Top colorists cost more, so there is a range in the prices.
DCDM costs $20–$40 per minute or $900 per reel.
DCP costs $20–$40 per minute or $900 per reel.

31–02 Hard Drive Purchases

You purchased many digital storage drives for the production phase. You will need to purchase more for the post-production phase — for "shuttle" drives and other hard drives for when you transfer materials, acquire archival or reshoot materials, additional backups, etc.

32–00 Titling and Graphics

The film will require opening and closing titles and may also need graphics to complete all the elements in the script.

32–01 Titling

Usually you can get a package deal from a Post Facility to create simple graphics for the opening credits and film title, lower third titles, and end credit titles. The minimum is usually $3,000–$5,000 for white letters on a black background. There are online websites that can do end credit crawls much cheaper than many graphics facilities.

32–02 Graphic Designer

If you need a more complicated opening title sequence or other graphic elements created for your film you'll need to hire a graphic designer to create the work. You should write up your notes and ideas for all graphic treatments that your film will require and then contact a few designers and look at their reels. Meet with two or three and discuss your needs and then go with the one who understands what you want to accomplish and can do it for the money you have to spend.

Good communication from the start really helps. The designer should feed back how he understood the concept. Sketches and storyboards help. The producer and director can react to that. Then the designer goes away and does the work, returning with the finished files — give or take a few minor changes.

At the other end of the spectrum are the high-end graphics houses that do opening titles for features and TV programs, animation effects for features and commercials, and special computer generated (CG) effects for features.

32–05 Special Graphic Effects

Designers can also create or find special effects. If your script calls for Santa to wave his hand, producing a shower of magic dust that reveals a fully decorated Christmas tree, go to a graphics designer. But go before you shoot, because you'll need to work out exactly how to integrate your live action with your special effects.

There are cheap ways and expensive ways to achieve effects. Some computer software like After Effects can do many special effects for less money. Whether you go custom or plug-in, ask the designer to show you an example of the effects in the discussion stage, so you can all agree on the look.

$$$

It will depend on what you need, how much time and what kind of technical/computer/live action is needed to accomplish the look and running time for the graphic elements or sequences.

32–06 Motion Control (See Motion Control in 20–18.)

A really fun (and potentially cheap) way to make title graphics is to build or use actual 3D pieces and shoot them under a motion control camera. You can use a snorkel lens, which gets you right down among the pieces. The overall effect gives a lot of texture and 3D reality (because it is!) compared to the high cost of high-end 3D computer graphics.

Motion control is sometimes used to do camera moves on still photographs or other flat archival materials. Today, this is done almost entirely in the digital realm by scanning the material into a computer and doing "digital camera moves" on the material.

If your film has voiceover narration, time each section of the film that requires stills so you will be able to plan the speed of the move and what parts of the still to focus on as you move.

32–08 Closed Captioning

Closed captioning is the text that is seen on the bottom of a television screen when the monitor is switched to that mode. It allows a viewer to read what is being said on the soundtrack by the actors, news anchor, or commentator. This is used by hearing impaired viewers or in situations where the audio can't be heard, like a bar or large airport lounge.

$$$
Rates are determined by what kind of captions you require and the master's running time.

Roll-Up Captions — captions continually roll up the screen — like live event captions.
$3 per minute

Center Pop-On Captions — captions appear one at a time, at the bottom center of the screen.
$4 per minute

Placed Pop-On Captions — captions appear one at a time and are placed appropriately on screen by a technician.
$5 per minute

32–09 Subtitling
Subtitling is text on screen that is a translation of the audio to another language. If your film is in English but there is a scene where one of the characters speaks Spanish, you will need to translate the audio and place the English words on the bottom of the screen. Remember that some languages may "take more time" than the original language. Placement is key so the viewer can have enough time to read the translation to understand it and enjoy the film.

$$$
Depending on the language, it can cost $8 per minute or more.

33–00 Deliverables
Broadcasting entities and distribution companies will provide the deliverables list with all the tech and paper elements they require for the Producer to "deliver the film" and get final payment.

33–01 Masters/Clones

What format(s) you deliver as your master will be dictated by your deliverables list(s). If you are delivering to a broadcaster, they will require digital and maybe a tape format. If you are delivering for a theatrical distributor, they usually require a DCP and sometimes a 35mm print master. If you are delivering for Video on Demand (VOD) or DVD, they will require digital formats only. And don't forget to add a Duplicate Master, plus check your deliverables list for other possible masters, such as M&E (Music and Effects — for foreign language versions), textless, closed captions, etc. Your total deliverables bill can be quite high, so tally it up at the start of the project to avoid costly surprises. Additionally, the producer needs to submit many paper deliverables like copies of the release forms, licensing agreements, cast and crew lists, copyright registration, etc.

Television Standards

When an edited videotape master is shipped to a foreign country, it needs to be converted into a different standard so their machines and televisions can read it. PAL, NTSC and SECAM are the most common standards used around the world for recording and playing back video. Different countries use different standards, and wouldn't you know it, none is compatible with any other. NTSC is used in the United Sates, and in some other countries.

PAL, used in the United Kingdom and much of Europe, displays 25 frames of video per second, compared to NTSC's 30 fps, and has 625 lines of video information per frame, compared to NTSC's 525. SECAM is used in France and in the countries of the former Soviet Union. This is also changing because digital delivery isn't tied to PAL/NTSC/SECAM as much as before.

Here's a brief rundown of some of the most common stocks for mastering.

HDCAM

$$$
A 94-minute load of HDCAM stock is about $62. If you purchase the stock at a Post facility it will probably cost $100.

HDCAM SR

$$$
A 94-minute load of HDCAM SR stock is about $180. If you purchase the stock at a Post facility it will probably cost $300.

Digital Betacam

$$$
94 minutes of DigiBeta stock is around $40. If you purchase the stock at a Post facility it will probably cost $55.

33–03 Transfers and Dubs
This is a catch-all line item in which to put an allowance for the cost of dubs and transfers.

33–05 Screening Copies
These are not final DVD duplications or replications (see 37–00 Publicity and Marketing), but rather quick and dirty dubs from the editing process to be used as approval copies.

34–00 Digital Visual Effects/Animation
Many post houses and boutique effects companies provide digital visual effects. They can create computer generated images (CGI), main title design, traveling mattes, blue/green screen composites, high-end 3D animation, and live-action effects and digital compositing.

34–01 Digital Visual Effects
Let's say you have an actor playing an android and he has to unbutton his shirt, open up his rib cage, and pull a damaged chip from where the liver usually lives. That's 3D special effects. If you are planning anything like this, or any series of digital visual effects, it's

imperative that you meet with the Director and the Artist and Visual Effects Supervisor doing the effect(s) during pre-production — first to see if you can afford it, and second to prepare for the shoot and for the post-production process. Visual Effects people are fond of saying that a one-hour conversation before shooting the scene can save tens of thousands of dollars in post. It's true.

The Visual Effects Supervisor will walk you through the team you'll need and the steps the team will take to get what you want and put it into a schedule and a budget. Usually a member of the VFX team will be on set during the shooting of the scene(s) so everyone is on the same page and getting the correct technical specs on set so it will go smoothly in post-production.

A Visual Effects person will also be able to clean up any unwanted architectural elements or phone poles from any of your exterior camera original materials. Years ago I produced a period film that took place in 1899. One of our scenes was shot outside in the snow and we didn't notice that a contemporary Ford Mustang drove by in the background. The Ford Model T wasn't even invented until 1908, so we had to digitally erase the automobile out of the background!

$$$

Usually you will bid out the storyboards to several visual effects companies and then compare the bids. The companies usually charge by the shot. It could cost anywhere from $200–$1,100 per shot, depending on complexity.

34–07 Animation

This is such a specialized area, it's really outside our scope for this book. Suffice it to say that if you want animation in your show, either standing alone or composited over live action, there are many excellent animation houses and independent artists who can work for you. 3D Graphics are more expensive than 2D Graphics, but depending on what you are going for it may be the right answer.

$$$

Costs are all over the map. Animators will ask: How smooth must your images move? How many backgrounds? Do the backgrounds move? Do you want shadows and reflections? Flash animation programs are plentiful and relatively cheap to produce.

Remember, there are many film schools with excellent animation programs. Contacting a school about their most talented students and alumni is a great way to find talented animators when you are on a budget. Discuss the project and your concept, tell them your budget, and ask for a proposal for what they can create for that figure.

GENERAL

35–00 Insurance

35–01 thru 35–06 Producer's Entertainment Package (General Liability, Hired Auto, Cast Insurance, Other Coverage) plus Workers' Compensation, Errors & Omissions

Because you are hiring many people; renting equipment, vehicles and property; and signing many contracts, you'll need to insure your production company with a standard Producer's Entertainment Package. To insure against anyone on your cast or crew injuring anyone from the general public during the course of your production, you'll need General Liability. To insure against any of your cast and crew getting injured, you'll need Workers' Compensation. Your distributor will probably insist on an Errors and Omissions policy as well to insure against anyone suing you or her for defamation or libel. If you have a star whose sudden disappearance or indisposition on shoot day sinks your project, you'll want Cast insurance as well. (See discussion of insurance in Chapter 2.)

$$$

Some producers allow 3% of the total budget for insurance. The safer route is to call an entertainment insurance broker and get a precise quote for your project. For an annual policy for a low-budget feature film it will be between $12–$25,000. E&O insurance will cost $5,000–$10,000.

36–00 General and Administrative Expenses
Inexperienced producers always seem to get stung on this one because they forget or underestimate what it costs to set up an office and do business. (See the discussion of Setting Up in Chapter 1, and many parallel references in Chapter 2.)

36–01 Business License/Taxes
Depending on your city and state, you may need a business license for your company. Go online to research the regulations for the location of your company. (See Chapter 1.) You will also need to file city, state, and federal taxes depending on your company's business structure and the tax laws for the city and state where your company is registered. Contact your accountant to budget properly for these charges. Remember that it may take several years for you to complete and sell your film so you may have to pay and file multiple annual tax returns.

36–02 Legal Fees
Have a heart-to-heart with your entertainment attorney about each project and what he or she estimates in fees. Some producers allow anywhere from 1% all the way up to 10% of the budget. With that kind of spread, it's better to talk it out with your lawyer. (See Chapter 1, "Attorney," and Chapter 2, "Legal.")

36–03 Accounting Fees
Hopefully, you have hired a Production Accountant or Bookkeeper as part of your Production Staff (budget category 08–00) to keep track of the books during and immediately after production. If you are using a Payroll Service (see Chapter 2, "Payroll Services"), you are already factoring in accounting costs for personnel into your Payroll Tax percentage. Even so, you may have accounting costs beyond those mentioned, and this is the place to put them. Many producers

allow about 1% of the budget here. (See Chapter 1, "Accountant," and Chapter 2, "Tracking Costs.")

36–05 Telephone & Fax

Estimate monthly phone and Internet charges and multiply by the number of months you'll be working on the project. Think about other charges like SKYPE (Internet video calling) or Vimeo (website to upload password-protected videos) that may also bill monthly. Two or more lines in an office may be needed, especially during production and to accommodate other staff members.

36–06 Copying/Scanning

Copies of treatments, scripts, legal contracts, releases, invoices, correspondence, and news clippings are entered here. You'll want to make sure your copier has a scanner feature as well.

36–07 Postage & Freight

Include postage for research, promotion, mailing DVD screening copies, and distribution activities. Freight and shipping costs will be incurred if there are shoots on distant locations. Shipping for hard drives, masters, equipment, promotional materials, and a host of other unknown expenses will be included here.

36–08 Office Space Rental

Allow for Pre-Production, Production, and Post-Production, but keep track of your needs for space. In Pre-Production, for example, if your writer and researchers are working out of their homes and billing you for telephone and other expenses, you may not even need an office for a month or more, or at most, only one room. In Production, if it's local, you may need to add a room or two or three for meetings, and additional staff, like Production Coordinator, Production Manager, and Production Assistants. In Post-Production, your needs will shrink again, probably back to one office, or two if you are setting up your Editing system there as well.

36–09 Office Furniture

Some office buildings offer a furniture package, or you can rent from a rental company or visit Goodwill, the Salvation Army, and other thrift stores. Handy items are desks, chairs, filing cabinets, shelves, and 8-foot tables for meetings and plenty of spread-it-out room for artwork, and so forth.

36–10 Office Equipment and Supplies

Include printer purchases/rentals, computer programs, calculators, monitors, and hard drives. Office supplies (pens, papers, staplers, envelopes, etc.) usually add up pretty fast. Make sure you add those costs to this line item.

36–11 Computer Rental

If you have to rent computers from a rental house, do the math and see if it's cheaper to buy. Sometimes your producer or coordinator or production assistants bring in their own computers. On a low-budget show, they may do it as a favor. On bigger budgets, pay them a weekly rental fee that is less than the fee you would pay to a rental house. If you are going to use the computer for a long period of time it might make more sense to purchase it.

36–12 Software/Apps/FTP Sites

There is some excellent production software out there. Entertainment Partners and Showbiz both have Budgeting and Scheduling programs. Then there are numerous script formatting, script collaborating, and storyboarding programs, plus others to make your life simpler.

Apps are also very useful to our industry. Call sheets, sunrise/sunset calendars, releases, etc., are all available as apps. Some are free and others charge a one-time fee.

36–13 Transcription

Whenever you have long interviews you need to cut into pieces and edit into a show, get them transcribed — it will save your sanity many times over.

Be sure to specify whether you want the interviewer's questions transcribed or not, and whether you want a verbatim copy. Verbatim gives you all the "uh's" and "ahh's" and coughs and laughs.

Find out from the transcriber what is the best way to get the material sent. Often the audio recordist on set can do a simultaneous recording to a "smaller" file format and can upload to the transcriber via uploading software (like Dropbox) to a URL. They can include timecode as well so the transcriber can add those numbers throughout the document.

$$$

Rates are in the range of $100 to $140 per hour of recorded audio.

36–14 Messenger/Overnight Shipping

This is for the charges to a messenger or courier service for the city you are working in.

36–15 Parking

Depending on the city, there may be charges for parking vehicles for your office personnel.

36–16 Storage

Any project will generate countless boxes of scripts, receipts, tax statements, income statements, bank statements, financial journals, records, hard drives, mixed music masters, narration tracks, sound effects, etc. Film or tape will need to be stored in a dust-free, safe, temperature-controlled environment. Years later, you may choose to destroy stuff you no longer need, but for the two or three years after production, keep and file everything — you'll be surprised at what you may need to retrieve.

36–18 Publicity

This expense may be covered by the distributor, but if you want to send DVDs to your own list, or throw a screening party, this is the line item.

36–19 Wrap Party

If you can afford it, it is nice to either bring in some food and drink or go to a local restaurant on the last day of production, or the day after.

36-20 Working Meals

When your investors or distributors come to visit you'll want to take them to a nice restaurant.

36-21 Overhead (Production Fee)

In preparing a bid for a commercial or a client-sponsored industrial, many producers add overhead (also called the Production Fee) to represent the company's profit on the project. The fee is usually 15%–30% of the budget. If regular production expenses can be held down, then profits will be increased. If there are cost overruns, profits will be reduced — or, in the worst of situations, it will cost the production company out-of-pocket money, that is, your salary.

36-22 Completion Bond

Please see Chapter 2, "Completion Bond."

37–00 Publicity and Marketing

Please see Chapter 3, Development and Marketing.

37–01 Publicity

As outlined earlier in this book, this line item is for costs associated with Publicity (see Chapter 3).

37–02 Marketing

As outlined earlier in this book, this line item is for costs associated with Marketing (see Chapter 3).

Contingency

There are hundreds, if not thousands of variables involved in any project. The ability to foresee all these expenses is beyond that of most soothsayers, but that is exactly what a producer must do. It's easy to forget something. By carefully studying the script, breaking it down, and preparing the budget, and by maintaining strong control during production, a producer will come close to the estimated budget.

But when the terrain is unknown, or the script has not been fully developed, an experienced producer will add a "contingency" to the budget. How much depends on what's available: 5% is helpful, 10% is a good average, 20% is high but may be necessary if you're wading into a swamp.

Weather, changes in the script, music, recasting, reshooting, change of location, ad infinitum, conspire to push budgets upward. There will always be unforeseen expenses and a contingency comes to the rescue.

Clients and grant foundations, on the other hand, may not want to see a contingency line in the budget. They may think it is unprofessional, that it's simply the producer's way of saying, "I don't know, so I'll slop in some more money here."

If a client or investor doesn't want a contingency line in the budget, then the producer needs to make sure that each section of the budget has enough money for omissions, errors, and the surprises that are a part of any production.

The Bottom Line

This is the estimated total cost of the project. It's the first place a client's eye will go. If the total exceeds an acceptable bid, a grant application, or the amount of money a producer can raise, the production must be re-planned and the budget reduced.

What things can be eliminated? Now begins the delicate dance of deletion. But be careful here. In your zeal to get the job or the film funded, you may cut too much. There is a point beyond which the show cannot be produced, at least without revising the concept (and the script). The budget cannot be too high (or the bid won't be accepted) or too low (to allow actually doing the work).

SUMMARY

The figures quoted in this chapter and in the next, "Sample Budgets for Specific Projects," are based on average "book" rates in Los Angeles and New York, the two biggest production centers in the United States. Some cities will offer lower rates, others will be higher. **It is absolutely essential that you research costs with the**

people and facilities where production will actually take place, and negotiate your own good deals.

These figures are only meant to guide and assist you in the preparation of your own budgets. Hopefully, by studying the budgets that follow, you'll be able to construct your own to include all your necessary line items. If this book does nothing more than identify one oversight in one line item in your own planning, it will have been worth many times the price of this book.

CONCLUSION

Filmmaking is an amazing experience from start to finish. It begins with only an idea, a story. And then bit by bit, step by step, with the help of many dedicated and talented people, hours and hours of hard work, and a certain amount of money, it becomes a film. It isn't easy, it isn't glamorous, but when done thoughtfully and well it is a phenomenal experience to be a part of.

There are certain things you MUST have to make a film. A script. A cast. A crew. A script breakdown and schedule. Some (or a lot of) money. And a BUDGET. The budget is not just a bunch of numbers on a page with many columns and rows. It's the concrete, well-researched, well-considered PLAN that will steer your production to a successful finish. Based on creative conversations, vendor bids, location scouting, casting, negotiations — a gazillion factors — it becomes the bedrock that you build the whole production on. If you haven't factored in all of the aspects of a production discussed in this book, the budget will not be bulletproof, and when the first (of many) problems arise, your production will be in serious trouble. The budget is your way of protecting the creative vision, the cast and crew, the financiers, and the vendors: Everything has been considered and budgeted for so you can accomplish the miracle that is making a film.

Use this book — and the Budget Templates in Excel which you can download at *mwp.com* — as an important tool to guide and inform your envisioning of your film. Knowledge is power and this book's information can be an invaluable asset when employed in the creation of your next project.

6

SAMPLE BUDGETS FOR SPECIFIC PROJECTS

First there are the budget *categories* — the big picture. Then there are the *line items* — the nitty-gritty details without which we have no budget at all. The preceding chapter illuminated every category and line item. In this chapter we can study them in situations that resemble a real production.

Let's be clear that this chapter is for illustrative purposes only. These budgets show examples of how producers plan and budget for real world situations, albeit hypothetical ones. Please do not fall into the trap of taking a sample budget and applying it to your project without doing the proper research that will be necessary for any film you produce. Every project is different and requires its own creative thinking and budgeting.

The sample budget templates that follow are designed to cover the most common forms of production that most independent producers will encounter across fiction and non-fiction projects. After each budget template there will be a Budget Assumptions paragraph that outlines the context for that particular budget's creation. Then there is a succinct line-by-line explanation in each category. Refer to the Master Budget Template in Chapter 5 for an in-depth description and examples of dollar estimates for each line item as well.

$1.8 MILLION NARRATIVE FEATURE FILM BUDGET

To download your free Excel budget template:

- Go to *www.mwp.com*.
- Click on "MW Film School."
- Open the item "Sample Budgets/Forms."
- Download the corresponding free Excel Budget Template.
- Save it to your computer.
- Last, this budget is a sample template. Make sure to create your budget with figures based on your research on current rates and prices available to you.

Budget Assumptions

The film will be shot in the greater Philadelphia area for 23 days. They will shoot 5-day weeks so it will be a 4.6-week production for the filming phase. They are working under the SAG-AFTRA Low-Budget agreement and the IATSE Low-Budget agreement (which IATSE calls "Tier 0" because the budget limits are below the Tier 1 agreement). The IATSE Pension Fund (IAP) is 6% of the salary costs and the Motion Picture Industry Pension Fund (MPIP) is $88/person per day worked. At this budget level the producers don't anticipate working under a Teamsters contract for transportation labor but that will need to be confirmed during Pre-Production.

The director is not DGA so the Assistant Directors and UPM will not be from that guild. The writer is a WGA member so the scale purchase price applies. Everyone will be paid through a payroll service so the fringes are generally set at 22%. The day rates are fairly low but the added Pension and Health costs contribute to the overall gross salary costs. The producers plan to sell the indie feature after its premiere at a top film festival.

$1.8 Million Narrative Feature Budget

SUMMARY BUDGET			
Fringe assumptions:		Production:	$1.8 Million Narrative
Payroll Tax	22.0%	Shoot Days:	23 (4.6 5-day weeks)
WGA	17.0%	Location:	Philadelphia, PA
DGA-No	0.0%	Unions:	SAG-AFTRA Low Budget, IA Tier 0
SAG-AFTRA	17.3%	Shooting Format: Digital HD	
Overtime	10%	Delivery format: HDCam SR	
Contingency	10%		
IAP	6%		
MPIP (per day)	$88		

Account		Subtotal	Total
01-00 Story & Rights		$79,098	
02-00 Producers Unit		$50,000	
03-00 Direction		$25,000	
04-00 Cast		$137,970	
05-00 Travel & Living – Producers/Director		$12,850	
06-00 Travel & Living- Cast		$7,560	
07-00 Residuals		$0	
	TOTAL ABOVE-THE-LINE		$312,478
08-00 Production Staff		$151,857	
09-00 Background Actors/Extras		$59,541	
10-00 Sound Stage		$0	
11-00 Production Design		$50,607	
12-00 Set Construction		$0	
13-00 Set Operations		$63,985	
14-00 Special Effects		$6,742	
15-00 Set Dressing		$63,379	
16-00 Property		$39,514	
17-00 Wardrobe		$53,550	
18-00 Make-Up and Hair		$29,506	
19-00 Electrical		$54,701	
20-00 Camera		$118,960	
21-00 Production Sound		$27,125	
22-00 Transportation		$114,298	
23-00 Location Expenses		$183,126	
24-00 Picture Vehicles/Animals		$6,600	
25-00 Media		$9,000	
26-00 Travel and Living-Crew		$0	
	TOTAL PRODUCTION		$1,032,489
27-00 Editorial		$42,292	
28-00 Music		$53,000	
29-00 Post-Production Sound		$35,000	
30-00 Post-Production - Digital and Film		$1,500	
31-00 Digital Intermediate		$24,750	
32-00 Titling and Graphics		$5,000	
33-00 Deliverables		$14,700	
34-00 Digital Visual Effects/Animation		$42,250	
	TOTAL POST-PRODUCTION		$218,492
35-00 Insurance		$32,500	
36-00 General & Administrative Expenses		$40,900	
37-00 Publicity and Marketing		$0	
	TOTAL GENERAL		$73,400
Total Above-the-Line			$312,478
Total Below-the-Line			$1,324,381
Total Above and Below-the-Line			$1,636,859
Contingency			$163,686
	GRAND TOTAL		$1,800,545

$1.8 Million Narrative Feature Budget

ABOVE-THE-LINE								
		Amt.	*Units*	*x*	*Rate*	*Sub-Total*	*Total*	
01-00 Story & Rights								
01-01 Rights Purchases			Allow	1		0	0	
01-02 Options			Allow	1		0	0	
01-03 Writer Salaries/Screenplay Purchase		1	Allow	1	45,556	45,556	45,556	
01-04 Research/Clearances		1	Allow	1	1,875	1,875	1,875	
01-05 Title Registration			Allow	1		0	0	
01-06 Script Timing			Allow	1		0	0	
01-07 Storyboards/Pre-Viz			Allow	1		0	0	
01-08 WGA Publication fee		1	Allow	1	10,000	10,000	10,000	
01-10 Development			Allow	1		0	0	
	Payroll					55,556	12,222	
	WGA					55,556	9,445	
					Total for 01-00			79,098
02-00 Producers Unit								
02-01 Executive Producer			Allow	1		0	0	
02-02 Producer		1	Allow	2	20,000	40,000	40,000	
02-03 Associate Producer			Allow	1		0	0	
02-04 Assistant to Producer(s)			Week(s)	1		0	0	
02-06 Consultants			Allow	1		0	0	
02-07 Misc. Expenses - IA Signatory Fee		1	Allow	1	10,000	10,000	10,000	
	Payroll - Assumes All in Fee					40,000	0	
					Total for 02-00			50,000
03-00 Direction								
03-01 Director		1	Allow	1	25,000	25,000	25,000	
03-02 Assistant to Director		1	Weeks	1		0	0	
	Payroll - Assumes All in Fee					25,000	0	
	DGA					25,000	0	
					Total for 03-00			25,000
04-00 Cast								
04-01 Lead Actors								
Actor #1	Rehearsal	1	Week(s)	1	1,752	1,752		
	Weekly Scale	4.6	Week(s)	1	1,752	8,059		
	Overtime (40%)		Allow	1	9,811	3,924		
Actor #2	Rehearsal	1	Week(s)	1	1,752	1,752		
	Weekly Scale	4.6	Week(s)	1	1,752	8,059		
	Overtime (40%)		Allow	1	9,811	3,924		
Actor #3	Rehearsal	1	Week(s)	1	1,752	1,752		
	Weekly Scale	4.6	Week(s)	1	1,752	8,059		
	Overtime (40%)		Allow	1	9,811	3,924	41,207	
04-02 Supporting Cast								
Actor #1	Weekly Scale	2	Week(s)	1	1,752	3,504		
Actor #1	Overtime (40%)		Allow	1	3,504	1,402		
Actor #2	Shoot (includes OT 4 hrs.)	7	Days	1	882	6,174		
Actor #3	Shoot (includes OT 4 hrs.)	6	Days	1	882	5,292		
Actor #4	Shoot (includes OT 4 hrs.)	5	Days	1	882	4,410		
Actor #5	Shoot (includes OT 4 hrs.)	5	Days	1	882	4,410		
Actor #6	Shoot (includes OT 4 hrs.)	3	Days	1	882	2,646		
Actor #7	Shoot (includes OT 4 hrs.)	2	Days	1	882	1,764		
Actor #8	Weekly Scale	1	Week	1	1,752	1,752		
							31,354	
04-03 Day Players								
Actor #9	Shoot - 8 hrs.	1	Day(s)	1	504	504		
Actor #10	Shoot - 8 hrs.	1	Day(s)	1	504	504		
Actor #11	Shoot - 8 hrs.	1	Day(s)	1	504	504		
Actor #12	Shoot - 8 hrs.	1	Day(s)	1	504	504		
Actor #13	Shoot - 8 hrs.	1	Day(s)	1	504	504		
Actor #14	Shoot - 8 hrs.	1	Day(s)	1	504	504		
Actor #15	Shoot - 8 hrs.	1	Day(s)	1	504	504		

$1.8 Million Narrative Feature Budget

		Amt.	Units	x	Rate	Sub-Total	Total	
Overtime Allowance (40%)			Allow	1	3,528	1,411	4,939	
04-04 Casting Director/Staff		1	Allow	1	7,500	7,500	7,500	
04-05 Casting Expenses		1	Allow	1	500	500	500	
04-06 Choreographer			Weeks	1		0	0	
04-07 Assistant(s) to Choreographer			Weeks	1		0	0	
04-08 Dialect Coach			Weeks	1		0	0	
04-09 Narrator/Voiceover Artist			Weeks	1		0	0	
04-10 Stunt Coordinator		2	Weeks	1	3,200	6,400	6,400	
04-11 Stunt Players (12 hr.)		2	Days	2	504	2,016	2,016	
	Stunt Drivers (12 hr.)	3	Days	2	504	3,024	3,024	
04-12 Stunt Costs/Adjustments		6	Allow	1	200	1,200	1,200	
04-13 Stunt Equipment		1	Allow	1	1,000	1,000	1,000	
04-14 ADR (Actors' fees) (4 hrs.)		1	Days	5	252	1,260	1,260	
	Payroll					98,900	21,758	
	SAG-AFTRA					91,400	15,812	
					Total for 04-00			137,970
05-00 Travel & Living – Producers/Director								
05-01 Airfares		1	RT	2	1,000	2,000	2,000	
05-02 Hotel		2.5	Month	1	3,500	8,750	8,750	
05-03 Taxi/Limo			Allow	1		0	0	
05-04 Auto		3	Months	1	700	2,100	2,100	
05-05 Train			Allow	1		0	0	
05-06 Excess Baggage			Allow	1		0	0	
05-07 Phone			Allow	1		0	0	
05-08 Gratuities			Allow	1		0	0	
05-09 Per Diem			Days	1		0	0	
					Total for 05-00			12,850
06-00 Travel & Living- Cast								
06-01 Airfares		1	RT	2	500	1,000	1,000	
06-02 Hotels		26	Nights	1	150	3,900	3,900	
06-03 Taxi/Limo		2	RT	2	100	400	400	
06-04 Auto		2	Weeks	1	500	1,000	1,000	
06-05 Train			Allow	1		0	0	
06-06 Excess Baggage			Allow	1		0	0	
06-07 Phone			Allow	1		0	0	
06-08 Gratuities			Allow	1		0	0	
06-09 Per Diem		3	Weeks	1	420	1,260	1,260	
					Total for 06-00			7,560
07-00 Residuals			Allow	1		0	0	
					Total for 07-00			0
TOTAL ABOVE-THE -LINE								312,478

$1.8 Million Narrative Feature Budget

		Amt.	Units	x	Rate	Sub-Total	Total
BELOW-THE-LINE							
08-00 Production Staff							
08-01 Line Producer							
	Prep/Travel	6	Weeks	1	1,250	7,500	
	Shoot	4.6	Weeks	1	1,250	5,750	
	Wrap	2	Weeks	1	1,250	2,500	
	Severance		Allow	1		0	15,750
08-02 Assistant Directors							
First AD							
	Prep/Travel	4	Weeks	1	1,000	4,000	
	Shoot	4.6	Weeks	1	1,000	4,600	
	Prod. Fee (shoot days)		Days	1		0	
	Severance		Allow	1		0	
	Overtime Allow		Days	1		0	8,600
2nd AD							
	Prep/Travel	5	Days	1	150	750	
	Shoot	23	Days	1	175	4,025	
	Overtime Allow		Days	1		0	4,775
2nd 2nd AD							
	Prep	2	Days	1	140	280	
	Shoot	23	Days	1	160	3,680	3,960
08-03 Production Supervisor							
	Prep/Travel	4	Weeks	1	1,000	4,000	
	Shoot	4.6	Weeks	1	1,000	4,600	
	Wrap	2	Weeks	1	1,000	2,000	
	Overtime Allow		Days	1		0	10,600
08-04 Production Coordinator							
	Prep/Travel	15	Days	1	150	2,250	
	Shoot	23	Days	1	150	3,450	
	Wrap	3	Days	1	150	450	6,150
Ass't Coord.							
	Prep	10	Days	1	140	1,400	
	Shoot	23	Days	1	140	3,220	
	Wrap		Day	1	140	0	4,620
08-05 Script Supervisor							
	Prep	2	Days	1	175	350	
	Shoot	23	Days	1	175	4,025	
	2 -Camera bump	15	Days	1	40	600	
	Wrap	1	Days	1	175	175	
	2nd Camera Days		Days	1		0	
	Overtime		Allow		5,150	515	5,665
08-06 Production Accountant							
	Prep/Travel	4	Weeks	1	1,000	4,000	
	Shoot	4.6	Weeks	1	1,000	4,600	
	Wrap	2	Weeks	1	1,000	2,000	
	Post-Production(1 day/wk)	12	Weeks	1	250	3,000	13,600
Assistant Accountant							
	Prep/Travel		Weeks	1		0	
	Shoot		Weeks	1		0	
	Wrap		Weeks	1		0	0
08-07 Technical Advisors			Flat	1		0	0
08-08 Production Assistants							
Office Prod. Assistant(s)							
	Prep	10	Days	1	125	1,250	
	Shoot	23	Days	1	125	2,875	
	Wrap		Days	1		0	
Set Prod. Assistant(s)							
	Prep	2	Days	2	125	500	
	Shoot	23	Days	5	125	14,375	19,000
08-09 Studio Teacher/Tutor		10	Days	1	200	2,000	2,000
	Payroll					94,720	20,838
	DGA					43,685	0
	IAP					30,035	1,802

$1.8 Million Narrative Feature Budget

		Amt.	Units	x	Rate	Sub-Total	Total	
	MPIP	392	Days	1	88		34,496	
					Total for 08-00			151,857
09-00 Background Actors/Extras								
09-01 Stand-ins			Days	1		0	0	
09-02 Extras-SAG-AFTRA		165	Extras	1	205	33,825	33,825	
09-03 Extras-Non-Union		50	Extras	1	100	5,000	5,000	
09-04 Casting Director		1	Allow	1	2,000	2,000	2,000	
09-05 Extras Agency Fee @ 10%		1	Allow	1	38,825	3,883	3,883	
	Payroll					40,825	8,982	
	SAG-AFTRA P&H					33,825	5,852	
					Total for 09-00			59,541
10-00 Sound Stage								
10-01 Stage Rental			Allow	1		0	0	
	Prep		Allow	1		0	0	
	Pre-Light		Allow	1		0	0	
	Shoot		Allow	1		0	0	
	Wrap		Allow	1		0	0	
	Overtime		Allow	1		0	0	
10-02 Stage Lighting Rental			Allow	1		0	0	
10-03 Stage Grip Rental			Allow	1		0	0	
10-04 Phones/ Internet			Allow	1		0	0	
10-05 Garbage removal			Allow	1		0	0	
10-06 Green Room			Allow	1		0	0	
10-07 Make Up Room			Allow	1		0	0	
10-08 Office Rental			Allow	1		0	0	
10-09 Parking			Allow	1		0	0	
					Total for 10-00			0
11-00 Production Design								
11-01 Production Designer								
	Prep	4	Weeks	1	1,000	4,000		
	Shoot	4.6	Weeks	1	1,000	4,600		
	Wrap	1	Weeks	1	1,000	1,000		
	Travel	0.4	Weeks	1	1,000	400	10,000	
11-02 Art Director/Set Designer								
	Prep	4	Weeks	1	875	3,500		
	Shoot	4.6	Weeks	1	875	4,025		
	Wrap	0.6	Weeks	1	875	525	8,050	
11-03 Art Assistants								
	Prep		Days	1		0		
	Shoot		Days	1		0	0	
	Wrap		Weeks	1		0	0	
11-04 Art Coordinator								
	Prep	15	Days	1	140	2,100		
	Shoot	23	Days	1	140	3,220		
	Wrap	3	Days	1	140	420	5,740	
11-07 Signage & Graphics		1	Allow	1	1,000	1,000	1,000	
11-08 Storage		4	Months	1	150	600	600	
11-09 Product Placement/Clearance Allowance		1	Allow	1	5,000	5,000	5,000	
11-10 Purchases/Rentals		1	Allow	1	1,500	1,500	1,500	
	Payroll					23,790	5,234	
	IAP					23,790	1,427	
	MPIP	137	Days	1	88		12,056	
					Total for 11-00			50,607
12-00 Set Construction								
12-01 Construction Coordinator								
	Prep		Days	1		0		
12-02 Foreman								
	Prep		Days	1		0		
	Shoot		Days	1		0		
Carpenters			Allow	1		0	0	
12-03 Scenic Painters								

$1.8 Million Narrative Feature Budget

		Amt.	Units	x	Rate	Sub-Total	Total	
Lead Scenic Painter								
	Prep		Days	1		0		
	Shoot		Days	1		0		
Painters			Allow	1		0	0	
12-05 Greensmen			Allow	1		0	0	
12-06 Construction materials - Purchases			Allow	1		0	0	
12-07 Construction materials - Rentals			Allow	1		0	0	
12-08 Construction Equipment			Allow	1		0	0	
12-09 Set Strike			Allow	1		0	0	
	Payroll					0	0	
					Total for 12-00			0
13-00 Set Operations								
13-01 Key Grip								
	Prep/Scout	3	Days	1	200	600		
	Shoot	23	Days	1	225	5,175		
	Wrap	1	Days	1	200	200		
	Overtime		Allow	1	5,975	598	6,573	
13-02 Best Boy Grip/Dolly Grip								
	Prep	1	Days	1	175	175		
	Shoot	23	Days	1	200	4,600		
	Wrap	1	Days	1	175	175		
	Overtime		Allow	1	4,950	495	5,445	
13-03 Grips								
3rd Grip								
	Prep	1	Days	1	125	125		
	Shoot	23	Days	1	150	3,450		
	Wrap		Days	1		0		
	Overtime		Allow	1	3,575	358	3,933	
4th Grip								
	Prep		Days	1		0		
	Shoot	23	Days	1	125	2,875		
	Wrap		Days	1		0		
	Overtime		Allow	1	2,875	288	3,163	
Additional Grips			Days	1		0		
	Overtime		Allow	1		0	0	
13-04 Dolly/Crane Grips								
	Prep		Days	1		0		
	Shoot		Days	1		0		
	Overtime		Allow	1	0	0	0	
13-06 Grip Rentals								
	Package	4.6	Weeks	1	1,500	6,900		
	Dollies	4.6	Weeks	1	900	4,140		
	Cranes (incl. Driver)		Days	1		0		
	Add'l Equip.	1	Allow	1	5,000	5,000	16,040	
13-07 Expendables		4.6	Allow	1	500	2,300	2,300	
13-08 Kit Rentals								
	Key Grip		Weeks	1		0	0	
	Craft Service	23	Days	1	25	575	575	
13-10 Craft Service								
	Prep	1	Days	1	150	150		
	Shoot	23	Days	1	150	3,450		
	Wrap		Days	1		0		
	Overtime		Allow	1	3,600	360	3,960	
Purchases		23	Days	1	275	6,325	6,325	
Extras		1	Allow	1	500	500	500	
13-15 Air Conditioning/Heating			Days	1		0	0	
	Payroll					23,073	5,076	
	IAP					23,073	1,384	
	MPIP	99	Days	1	88		8,712	
					Total for 13-00			63,985
14-00 Special Effects								
14-01 Special Effects Person								

$1.8 Million Narrative Feature Budget

		Amt.	Units	x	Rate	Sub-Total	Total	
	Prep	1	Days	1	200	200		
	Shoot	5	Days	1	225	1,125		
	Overtime		Allow	1	1,325	133	1,458	
14-02 SFX Assistant(s)								
	Shoot	5	Days	1	200	1,000		
	Overtime		Allow	1	1,000	100	1,100	
14-03 Additional Labor								
	Shoot		Days	1		0		
	Overtime		Allow	1	0	0	0	
14-06 Manufacturing Labor			Allow	1		0	0	
14-07 Fabrication			Allow	1		0	0	
14-09 Rentals & Purchases		1	Allow	1	2,500	2,500	2,500	
	Payroll				2,558	563	563	
	IAP				2,558	153	153	
	MPIP	11	Days	1	88	968	968	
					Total for 14-00			6,742
15-00 Set Dressing								
15-01 Set Decorator								
	Prep	15	Days	1	175	2,625		
	Shoot	23	Days	1	200	4,600		
	Wrap	2	Days	1	175	350		
	Overtime				7,575	758	8,333	
15-02 Lead Person								
	Prep/Travel	10	Days	1	150	1,500		
	Shoot	23	Days	1	175	4,025		
	Wrap	3	Days	1	150	450		
	Overtime				5,975	598	6,573	
15-03 Swing Gang/Set Dressers								
Set Dresser #1								
	Prep	10	Days	1	140	1,400		
	Shoot	23	Days	1	140	3,220		
	Wrap	3	Days	1	140	420		
	Overtime				5,040	504	5,544	
Set Dresser #2								
	Prep	10	Days	1	140	1,400		
	Shoot		Days	1		0		
	Wrap		Days	1		0		
	Overtime				1,400	140	1,540	
Set Dresser #3								
	Prep		Days	1		0		
	Shoot		Days	1		0		
	Wrap		Days	1		0		
	Overtime				0	0	0	
15-04 Additional Labor								
On-Set Dresser (Shoot)		23	Days	1	150	3,450		
	Overtime				3,450	345	3,795	
15-05 Expendables		1	Allow	1	1,500	1,500	1,500	
15-06 Purchases		1	Allow	1	8,000	8,000	8,000	
15-07 Rentals		1	Allow	1	8,000	8,000	8,000	
15-08 Loss & Damage			Allow	1		0	0	
15-09 Kit Rentals						0	0	
	Set Decorator	4.6	Weeks	1	25	115	115	
	Lead Person		Weeks	1		0	0	
15-10 Vehicle Expenses								
	Set Decorator		Weeks	1		0	0	
	Lead Person		Weeks	1		0	0	
	Payroll				25,784	5,672	5,672	
	IAP				25,784	1,547	1,547	
	MPIP	145	Days	1	88		12,760	
					Total for 15-00			63,379
16-00 Property								
16-01 Property Master								

$1.8 Million Narrative Feature Budget

		Amt.	*Units*	*x*	*Rate*	*Sub-Total*	*Total*	
	Prep	15	Days	1	200	3,000		
	Shoot	23	Days	1	225	5,175		
	Wrap	2	Days	1	200	400		
	Overtime				8,575	858	9,433	
16-02 Prop Assistant								
	Prep	10	Days	1	175	1,750		
	Shoot	23	Days	1	200	4,600		
	Wrap	2	Days	1	175	350		
	Overtime				6,700	670	7,370	
16-03 Purchases		1	Allow	1	6,000	6,000	6,000	
16-04 Rentals		1	Allow	1	6,000	6,000	6,000	
16-05 Loss & Damage		1	Allow	1	500	500	500	
16-06 Kit Rentals								
	Prop Master	4.6	Weeks	1	25	115	115	
16-08 Armorer		6	Days	1	175	1,050	1,050	
	Payroll				17,853	3,928	3,928	
	IAP				17,853	1,071	1,071	
	MPIP	46	Days	1	88		4,048	
					Total for 16-00			39,514
17-00 Wardrobe								
17-01 Costume Designer								
	Prep/Travel	15	Days	1	200	3,000		
	Shoot	23	Days	1	225	5,175		
	Wrap	5	Days	1	200	1,000	9,175	
17-02 Costumer								
	Prep/Travel	12	Days	1	150	1,800		
	Shoot	23	Days	1	150	3,450		
	Wrap	2	Days	1	150	300		
	Overtime		Allow	1	5,550	555	6,105	
17-03 Extras Costumer								
	Shoot	6	Days	1	140	840		
	Wrap		Days	1		0		
	Overtime		Allow	1	840	84	924	
17-04 Expendables		1	Allow	1	1,000	1,000	1,000	
17-05 Purchases		1	Allow	1	4,500	4,500	4,500	
17-06 Rentals		1	Allow	1	4,500	4,500	4,500	
17-07 Alteration & Repairs		1	Allow	1	750	750	750	
17-08 Cleaning & Dyeing		1	Allow	1	1,000	1,000	1,000	
17-09 Kit Rentals								
	Costume Designer	4.6	Weeks	1	25	115	115	
17-12 Costume Prod. Assistants								
	Prep	10	Days	2	125	2,500		
	Shoot	23	Days	2	125	5,750		
	Wrap	5	Days	2	125	1,250		
	Overtime		Allow	1	9,500	950	10,450	
	Payroll				26,654	5,864	5,864	
	IAP				26,654	1,599	1,599	
	MPIP	86	Days	1	88		7,568	
					Total for 17-00			53,550
18-00 Make-Up and Hair								
18-01 Key Make-Up Artist								
	Prep	1	Days	1	200	200		
	Shoot	23	Days	1	225	5,175		
	Overtime		Allow	1	5,375	538	5,913	
18-02 Additional Make-Up Artist(s)			Days	1		0		
	Shoot	13	Days	1	150	1,950		
	Overtime		Allow	1	1,950	195	2,145	
18-03 Key Hair Stylist								
	Prep/Travel	1	Days	1	200	200		
	Shoot	23	Days	1	225	5,175		
	Overtime		Allow	1	5,375	538	5,913	
18-04 Additional Hair Stylist(s)			Days	1		0		
	Shoot		Days	1		0		

$1.8 Million Narrative Feature Budget

		Amt.	Units	x	Rate	Sub-Total	Total	
	Overtime		Allow	1	0	0	0	
18-05 SFX Makeup Artist								
	Prep	1	Days	1	175	175		
	Shoot	5	Days	1	175	875		
	Overtime		Allow	1	1,050	105	1,155	
18-06 Purchases (includes SFX)		1	Allow	1	1,100	1,100	1,100	
18-07 Rentals (includes SFX)		1	Allow	1	1,100	1,100	1,100	
18-08 Kit Rentals								
	Key Make-Up	23	Days	1	25	575	575	
	Add'l Make-Up	13	Days	1	25	325	325	
	Hair Stylist	23	Days	1	25	575	575	
	SFX Makeup	23	Days	1	25	575	575	
	Payroll				15,125	3,328	3,328	
	IAP				15,125	908	908	
	MPIP	67	Days	1	88		5,896	
					Total for 18-00			29,506
19-00 Electrical								
19-01 Gaffer								
	Prep/Scout	3	Days	1	200	600		
	Shoot	23	Days	1	200	4,600		
	Wrap/Travel	1	Days	1	225	225		
	Overtime		Allow	1	5,425	543	5,968	
19-02 Best Boy Electric/Genny Operator								
	Prep	1	Days	1	175	175		
	Shoot	23	Days	1	200	4,600		
	Wrap	1	Days	1	175	175		
	Overtime		Allow	1	4,950	495	5,445	
19-03 Electrics								
3rd Electric								
	Prep	1	Days	1	150	150		
	Shoot	23	Days	1	175	4,025		
	Wrap		Days	1		0		
	Overtime		Allow	1	4,175	418	4,593	
4th Electric								
	Prep		Days	1		0		
	Shoot	23	Days	1	175	4,025		
	Wrap		Days	1		0		
	Overtime		Allow	1	4,025	403	4,428	
19-04 Additional Labor								
	Shoot		Days	1		0		
	Overtime		Allow	1	0	0	0	
19-05 Expendables/Purchases		4.6	Weeks	1	400	1,840	1,840	
19-06 Lighting Package Rental		4.6	Weeks	1	2,800	12,880	12,880	
	Add'l Equip(night shooting)	1	Allow	1	5,000	5,000	5,000	
	Condors		Allow	1		0	0	
	Additional Generator		Allow	1		0	0	
19-07 Additional Rentals			Allow	1		0	0	
19-08 Electrical Generator/Driver			Days	1		0	0	
19-09 Loss & Damage			Allow	1		0	0	
19-10 Kit Rentals								
	Gaffer	4.6	Weeks	1	25	115	115	
	Payroll				20,433	4,495	4,495	
	IAP				20,433	1,226	1,226	
	MPIP	99	Days	1	88		8,712	
					Total for 19-00			54,701
20-00 Camera								
20-01 Director of Photography								
	Prep/Travel	22	Days	1	200	4,400		
	Shoot	23	Days	1	225	5,175		
	Post (DI)	5	Days	1	200	1,000	10,575	
20-02 B Camera/Steadicam Operator								
	Prep	1	Days	1	175	175		
	Shoot	15	Days	1	200	3,000		

$1.8 Million Narrative Feature Budget

		Amt.	Units	x	Rate	Sub-Total	Total	
	Overtime		Allow	1	3,175	318	3,493	
20-03 1st Assistant Camera (A&B Cameras)								
	Prep/Travel	1	Days	2	175	350		
	Shoot	23	Days	2	200	9,200		
	Wrap	1	Days	2	175	350		
	Overtime		Allow	1	9,900	990	10,890	
20-04 2nd Ass't Camera (A&B Cameras)								
	Prep	1	Days	2	150	300		
	Shoot	23	Days	2	175	8,050		
	Wrap	1	Days	2	150	300		
	Overtime		Allow	1	8,650	865	9,515	
20-05 Digital Imaging Technician (DIT)			Week	1		0	0	
	Prep	1	Days	1	175	175		
	Shoot	23	Days	1	175	4,025		
	Wrap	1	Days	1	175	175		
	Overtime		Allow	1	4,375	438	4,813	
20-06 Still Photographer		16	Days	1	175	2,800	2,800	
20-07 Camera Package Rental (A&B)		1	Allow	1	40,000	40,000	40,000	
20-11 Steadicam Rig Rental		5	Weeks	1	1,250	6,250	6,250	
20-12 Teleprompter/Operator			Days	1		0	0	
20-13 Video Assist/Operator			Days	1		0	0	
20-14 Aerial Photography			Days	1		0	0	
20-15 Underwater and Topside Photography			Days	1		0	0	
20-16 Drones/GoPros			Days	1		0	0	
20-17 Loss & Damage		1	Allow	1	1,000	1,000	1,000	
20-18 Motion Control			Allow	1		0	0	
20-19 Expendables		4.6	Weeks	1	250	1,150	1,150	
20-20 Video Truck			Weeks	1		0	0	
20-25 Video Truck Crew			Weeks	1		0	0	
20-26 Kit Rentals								
	1st Ass't Cam (A&B) + DIT	23	Days	5	25	2,875	2,875	
	Payroll				42,085	9,259	9,259	
	IAP				42,085	2,525	2,525	
		157	Days	1	88		13,816	
					Total for 20-00			118,960
21-00 Production Sound								
21-01 Mixer								
	Prep	3	Days	1	200	600		
	Shoot	23	Days	1	225	5,175		
	Overtime		Allow	1	5,775	578	6,353	
21-02 Boom Operator								
	Shoot	23	Days	1	175	4,025		
	Overtime		Allow	1	4,025	403	4,428	
21-03 Expendables/Batteries		23	Days	1	25	575	575	
21-04 Sound Package		23	Days	1	200	4,600	4,600	
21-05 Walkie-Talkies		4.6	Weeks	50	8	1,840	1,840	
21-06 Sound Truck			Weeks	1		0	0	
21-08 Misc.Rentals/Loss & Damage		1	Allow	1	2,000	2,000	2,000	
	Payroll				10,780	2,372	2,372	
	IAP				10,780	647	647	
	MPIP	49	days	1	88		4,312	
					Total for 21-00			27,125
22-00 Transportation								
22-01 Transportation Coord.(drives Trailer)								
	Prep	10	Days	1	200	2,000		
	Shoot	23	Days	1	200	4,600		
	Wrap	3	Days	1	200	600		
	Overtime (20%)		Allow	1	7,200	1,440	8,640	
22-02 Drivers								
Driver #1								
	Prep	5	Day	1	150	750		
	Shoot	23	Days	1	150	3,450		
	Wrap	1	Day	1	150	150		

$1.8 Million Narrative Feature Budget

		Amt.	Units	x	Rate	Sub-Total	Total	
	Overtime (20%)		Allow	1	4,350	870	5,220	
Driver #2								
	Prep	1	Day	1	150	150		
	Shoot	23	Days	1	150	3,450		
	Wrap		Day	1	150	0		
	Overtime (20%)		Allow	1	3,600	720	4,320	
Driver #3								
	Prep	1	Days	1	150	150		
	Shoot	23	Days	1	150	3,450		
	Wrap	1	Days	1	150	150		
	Overtime (20%)		Allow	1	3,750	750	4,500	
Add'l Driver								
	Prep		Days	1		0		
	Shoot	23	Days	4	150	13,800		
	Wrap		Days	1		0		
	Overtime (20%)		Allow	1	13,800	2,760	16,560	
Insert Car (car to car cam platform)			Days	1		0	0	
Water Truck Driver			Days	1		0	0	
Caterer	Shoot		Days	1		0	0	
Caterer Ass't	Shoot		Days	1		0	0	
Additional Drivers			Allow	1		0	0	
22-03 Transportation Vehicle Rental								
Production Trailer (includes H/MU/Wardrobe)		4.6	Weeks	1	2,000	9,200	9,200	
Camera Cube Truck		4.6	Weeks	1	600	2,760	2,760	
G&E 10-Ton Truck		4.6	Weeks	1	600	2,760	2,760	
600A Tow Generator		3	Weeks	1	775	2,325	2,325	
Set Dressing Cube Truck		7.6	Weeks	1	600	4,560	4,560	
Props Van		6.6	Weeks	1	500	3,300	3,300	
Production Cube Truck		5.6	Weeks	1	600	3,360	3,360	
15-passenger Van		5.6	Weeks	1	500	2,800	2,800	
Miscellaneous Trucks/Vans		1	Allow	1	1,250	1,250	1,250	
Portable Toilets		1	Allow	1	1,000	1,000	1,000	
Production Van		5.6	Weeks	1	400	2,240	2,240	
22-04 Parking/Tolls/Gas				1				
Truck Parking		4.6	Weeks	1	600	2,760	2,760	
Miscellaneous Parking		1	Allow	1	750	750	750	
Prep Gas Allowance		1	Allow	1	1,250	1,250	1,250	
Shoot Allowance		4.6	Weeks	1	5,000	23,000	23,000	
22-05 Repairs & Maintenance		1	Allow	1	1,000	1,000	1,000	
22-06 Honeywagon Pumping		4.6	Weeks	1	350	1,610	1,610	
22-07 Miscellaneous		1	Allow	1	500	500	500	
	Payroll				39,240	8,633	8,633	
					Total for 22-00			114,298
23-00 Location Expenses								
23-01 Location Manager								
	Prep	4	Weeks	1	1,000	4,000	4,000	
	Shoot	4.6	Weeks	1	1,000	4,600	4,600	
23-02 Assistant Location Manager								
	Prep	3	Weeks	1	750	2,250	2,250	
	Shoot	4.6	Weeks	1	750	3,450	3,450	
23-03 First Aid/Medic		23	Days	1	175	4,025	4,025	
Kit Rental		23	Days	1	175	4,025	4,025	
23-04 Fire Officers								
	Shoot		Days	1		0	0	
23-05 Security								
	Prep Nights - 12 hr.	4	Nights	1	200	800	800	
	Shoot Nights - 12hr.	23	Nights	1	200	4,600	4,600	
	Idle Days - 12 hr.	12	Days	1	200	2,400	2,400	
	Idle Nights - 12 hr.	12	Nights	1	200	2,400	2,400	
23-06 Police		10	Days	2	1,100	22,000	22,000	
23-07 Permits		1	Allow	1	5,000	5,000	5,000	
23-08 Parking						0	0	
	Crew & Base Camp Parking	23	Days	1	650	14,950	14,950	
	BG Parking	200	Extras	1	10	2,000	2,000	

$1.8 Million Narrative Feature Budget

		Amt.	Units	x	Rate	Sub-Total	Total	
23-09 Catering Services								
Crew Meals		23	Days	70	23	37,030	37,030	
SAG Extras		165	Meals	1	23	3,795	3,795	
Misc Extras		50	Allow	1	13	650	650	
Working Meals		25	Days	5	15	1,875	1,875	
Walking Wrap Meals		11.5	Days	1	350	4,025	4,025	
Prep/Wrap meals		1	Allow	1	1,500	1,500	1,500	
23-11 Location Office Space Rental			Months	1		0	0	
23-12 Location Office Supplies			Allow	1		0	0	
23-13 Location Equipment		4.6	Weeks	1	1,250	5,750	5,750	
23-14 Location Office Telephone/Fax			Allow	1		0	0	
23-15 Site Cleaning/Trash Removal								
	Dumpsters	1	Allow	1	1,000	1,000	1,000	
		10	Allow	1	150	1,500	1,500	
23-17 Location Site Rental Fees								
	Shoot	1	Allow	1	36,000	36,000	36,000	
23-18 Location Scout Working Meals		1	Allow	1	500	500	500	
23-19 Auto Rentals								
Location Manager			Weeks	1		0	0	
Assistants			Weeks	1		0	0	
23-20 Miscellaneous Expenses		1	Allow	1	1,000	1,000	1,000	
	Mileage/DGA/SAG-AFTRA/Crew		Allow	1		0	0	
	Payroll				54,550	12,001	12,001	
					Total for 23-00			183,126
24-00 Picture Vehicles/Animals								
24-01 Animal Trainers								
Boss Wrangler			Weeks	1		0	0	
Assistant Wrangler			Weeks	1		0	0	
Wranglers			Week	1		0	0	
Riders/Handlers, etc			Day	1		0	0	
24-02 Animals								
	Horses		Allow	1		0	0	
Veterinary Expenses			Allow	1		0	0	
Feed/Shelter			Allow	1		0	0	
Transportation			Allow	1		0	0	
24-03 Picture Cars								
	Cars	3	Days	3	300	2,700	2,700	
	Van	1	Days	1	300	300	300	
	Police Car/Ambulance	1	Days	2	450	900	900	
	Stunt Cars	3	Days	3	300	2,700	2,700	
	Payroll				0	0	0	
					Total for 24-00			6,600
25-00 Media								
25-01 Digital Media - Hard drives		1	Allow	1	9,000	9,000	9,000	
25-02 Raw Film Stock			Feet	1		0	0	
25-03 Film Lab-Negative Prep & Process			Feet	1		0	0	
25-04 Telecine/Film to Digital transfer			Allow	1		0	0	
25-05 Videotape stock			Each	1		0	0	
					Total for 25-00			9,000
26-00 Travel and Living - Crew								
26-01 Airfares			Fares	1		0	0	
26-02 Hotels			Nites	1		0	0	
26-03 Taxi			Allow	1		0	0	
26-04 Auto		1	Weeks	1	0	0	0	
26-05 Train			RT	1		0	0	
26-06 Excess Baggage			Allow	1		0	0	
26-08 Per Diem			Days	1		0	0	
26-09 Gratuities			Days	1		0	0	
					Total for 26-00			0
TOTAL PRODUCTION								1,032,489

$1.8 Million Narrative Feature Budget

		Amt.	Units	x	Rate	Sub-Total	Total	
27-00 Editorial								
27-01 Editor - Shoot/Post								
	Shoot	4.6	Weeks	1	1,000	4,600	4,600	
	Post	12	Weeks	1	1,000	12,000	12,000	
27-02 Assistant Editor - Shoot/Post				1				
	Shoot	4.6	Weeks	1	750	3,450	3,450	
	Post	5	Weeks	1	750	3,750	3,750	
27-04 Post-Production Supervisor			Weeks	1		0	0	
27-05 Editing Room Rental - In Home			Weeks	1		0	0	
27-06 Edit System Rental			Weeks	1		0	0	
27-07 Online Screening Accounts		1	Allow	1	300	300	300	
27-10 On-Line Editing/Conform			Days	1		0	0	
	Payroll				23,800	5,236	5,236	
	IAP				23,800	1,428	1,428	
	MPIP	131	Days		88		11,528	
					Total for 27-00			**42,292**
28-00 Music								
28-01 Composer Fee		1	Allow	1	15,000	15,000	15,000	
28-02 Musicians			Allow	1		0	0	
28-03 Music Prep			Allow	1		0	0	
28-04 Studio Costs			Allow	1		0	0	
28-05 Music Scoring Stage			Allow	1		0	0	
28-06 Cartage and Rentals			Allow	1		0	0	
28-07 Music Mix Room			Allow	1		0	0	
28-08 Singers			Allow	1		0	0	
28-09 Payroll Service			Allow	1		0	0	
28-10 Miscellaneous			Allow	1		0	0	
28-11 Music Licensing		1	Allow	1	30,000	30,000	30,000	
28-12 Music Supervisor/Clearance		1	Allow	1	8,000	8,000	8,000	
					Total for 28-00			**53,000**
29-00 Post-Production Sound								
29-01 Sound Editor			Weeks	1		0	0	
29-02 Assistant Sound Editor			Weeks	1		0	0	
29-03 Music Editor			Weeks	1		0	0	
29-04 Dialogue Editor			Weeks	1		0	0	
29-05 Spotting (Music & FX)			Hours	1		0	0	
29-08 ADR (Studio/Editor)			Days	1		0	0	
29-09 Foley Stage/Editor			Days	1		0	0	
29-10 Foley Artists			Days	1		0	0	
29-12 Narration Recording			Hours	1		0	0	
29-13 Audio Laydown			Hours	1		0	0	
29-15 Audio Mix		1	Allow	1	35,000	35,000	35,000	
29-17 Dolby License			Allow	1		0	0	
29-18 Miscellaneous Expenses			Allow	1		0	0	
					Total for 29-00			**35,000**
30-00 Post-Producton - Digital and Film								
30-01 Stock Footage		1	Allow	1	1,500	1,500	1,500	
30-02 Archive Film/Television Clips			Allow	1		0	0	
30-04 Archival Researcher			Weeks	1		0	0	
30-06 Clearance Supervisor			Weeks	1		0	0	
30-09 Screeners			Allow	1		0	0	
30-11 Film Prints			Allow	1		0	0	
30-12 Miscellaneous Expenses			Allow	1		0	0	
					Total for 30-00			**1,500**
31-00 Digital Intermediate								
31-01 Digital Intermediate								
	DI (includes QT ProRes)	1	Allow	1	22,500	22,500	22,500	
	Archive Export	5	Reels	1	350	1,750	1,750	
31-02 Hard Drive Purchases		1	Allow	1	500	500	500	
					Total for 31-00			**24,750**
32-00 Titling and Graphics								
32-01 Titling - Opening & End Credits		1	Allow	1	5,000	5,000	5,000	

$1.8 Million Narrative Feature Budget

		Amt.	Units	x	Rate	Sub-Total	Total	
32-02 Graphic Designer			Allow	1		0	0	
32-05 Special Graphic Effects			Allow	1		0	0	
32-06 Motion Control			Allow	1		0	0	
32-08 Closed Captioning			Allow	1		0	0	
32-09 Subtitling			Allow	1		0	0	
					Total for 32-00			5,000
33-00 Deliverables								
33-01 Masters/Clones								
	DCP 2K	1	Allow	1	5,600	5,600	5,600	
	HDCam SR Master OAR	2	Hours	1	400	800	800	
	HDCam SR Master 1.78	2	Hours	1	400	800	800	
	HDCam SR Master(Pan&Scan)	2	Hours	1	400	800	800	
	HDCam Audio Layback	4	Hours	1	225	900	900	
	Pan&Scan Editorial	10	Hours	1	350	3,500	3,500	
	HDCam SR Tape Stock	2	Allow	1	250	500	500	
	DBeta NTSC	1	Allow	1	500	500	500	
	DBeta PAL	1	Allow	1	600	600	600	
	DVD Master Creation	4	Hours	1	150	600	600	
33-03 Transfers and Dubs			Allow	1		0	0	
33-05 Screening Copies		10	Allow	1	10	100	100	
					Total for 33-00			14,700
34-00 Digital Visual Effects/Animation								
34-01 VFX								
	VFX Supervisor	9	Days	1	250	2,250	2,250	
	CGI Enhancement/VFX	1	Allow	1	40,000	40,000	40,000	
34-07 Animation			Allow	1		0	0	
					Total for 34-00			42,250
POST-PRODUCTION TOTAL								218,492
35-00 Insurance								
35-01 Producers Entertainment Pckg.								
Media/Negative		1	Allow	1	27,000	27,000	27,000	
Faulty Stock			Allow	1		0	0	
Equipment			Allow	1		0	0	
Props/Sets			Allow	1		0	0	
Extra Expense			Allow	1		0	0	
3rd Party Property Damage			Allow	1		0	0	
Office Contents			Allow	1		0	0	
35-02 General Liability			Allow	1		0	0	
35-03 Hired Auto			Allow	1		0	0	
35-04 Cast Insurance			Allow	1		0	0	
35-05 Workers Compensation			Allow	1		0	0	
35-06 Errors & Omissions		1	Allow	1	5,500	5,500	5,500	
					Total for 35-00			32,500
36-00 General & Administrative Expenses								
36-01 Business License/Taxes								
	LLC Set Up Costs	1	Allow	1	650	650	650	
	CA State Filing Fee	1	Allow	1	800	800	800	
	Annual State tax fee	1	Allow	1	2,000	2,000	2,000	
36-02 Legal		1	Allow	1	25,000	25,000	25,000	
36-03 Accounting fees			Allow	1		0	0	
36-05 Telephone/Fax			Allow	1		0	0	
36-06 Copying/Scanning			Allow	1		0	0	
36-07 Office Craft Services		4	Weeks	1	200	800	800	
36-08 Office Space Rental			Allow	1		0	0	
	Prep	4	Weeks	1	500	2,000	2,000	
	Shoot	4.6	Weeks	1	500	2,300	2,300	
	Wrap	2	Months	1	500	1,000	1,000	
36-09 Office Furniture		1	Allow	1	1,000	1,000	1,000	
36-10 Office Equipment & Supplies		1	Allow	1	3,000	3,000	3,000	
36-11 Computer Printers								
	Office Printer	1	Allow	1	450	450	450	
	Accounting Printer	1	Allow	1	150	150	150	

$1.8 Million Narrative Feature Budget

	Amt.	Units	x	Rate	Sub-Total	Total	
36-12 Software/Apps/FTP		Allow	1		0	0	
36-13 Transcription		Hours	1		0	0	
36-14 Messenger/Overnight Shipping	25	Days	1	30	750	750	
36-15 Bank fees	1	Allow	1	500	500	500	
36-16 Storage		Allow	1		0	0	
36-17 Office Cleaning	1	Allow	1	500	500	500	
36-18 Publicity		Allow	1		0	0	
36-19 Wrap Party		Allow	1		0	0	
36-20 Working Meals		Allow	1		0	0	
36-21 Overhead (Production fee)		Allow	1		0	0	
36-22 Completion Bond		Allow	1		0	0	
				Total for 36-00			40,900
37-00 Publicity and Marketing							
37-01 Publicity		Allow	1		0	0	
37-02 Marketing		Allow	1		0	0	
				Total for 37-00			0
Total Above-the-Line							312,478
Total Below-the-Line							1,324,381
Total Above and Below-the-Line							1,636,859
Contingency							163,686
GRAND TOTAL							$1,800,545

01–03 Writer Salaries/Screenplay Purchase
The salary is set by the WGA contract.

01–04 Research/Clearances
Fees to clear the title and any other miscellaneous expenses.

01–08 WGA Publication Fee
For lower budget projects there is a WGA Publication fee.

02–02 Producer
There are two producers with the same flat fee.

02–07 Misc. Expenses — IATSE Signatory Fee
This fee is charged by IATSE when the "Tier 0" agreement gets signed.

03–01 Director
The director is hired after several of her short films win awards. The director is paid a low flat rate to direct her first feature film.

04–01 Lead Actors
These rates are scale payments for Lead Actors for rehearsal time, shoot time, and overtime for the 4.6-week shooting schedule.

04–02 Supporting Cast
These rates are scale payments for the Supporting Cast for shoot time and overtime for the 4.6-week shooting schedule.

04–03 Day Players
These rates are scale payments for Day Players for shoot time and overtime for the 4.6-week shooting schedule.

04–04 Casting Director/Staff
For casting the film's lead and supporting roles and day players.

04–05 Casting Expenses
For miscellaneous casting expenses.

04–10 Stunt Coordinator

There is one car crash that will take three days to set up and shoot. The Coordinator will plan out the stunt and hire the Drivers. This is the SAG-AFTRA scale payment.

04–11 Stunt Players

This is the SAG-AFTRA scale payment for players and drivers.

04–12 Stunt Costs/Adjustments

Depending on the complexity of the stunt, the players and drivers will get additional fees.

04–13 Stunt Equipment

For any costs for safety equipment, etc.

04–14 ADR (Actors' fees)

To have actors do ADR recording during post-production.

05–01, 05–02, and 05–04 Airfares, Hotel, and Auto

One of the producers lives in Los Angeles. These costs are for him to fly and stay in Philadelphia for the duration of prep, shoot, and wrap. He'll rent a house that he can work out of as well. No per diem — he'll pay for his own food costs.

06–01 thru 06–04 Airfares, Hotels, Taxi, and Auto

One actor is starring in a TV show in Los Angeles and will need to fly in twice during the filming and stay at a hotel.

06–09 Per Diem

The actor will be paid the SAG-AFTRA per diem rate for every day away from her home city.

08–01 Line Producer

The Line Producer will come onto the project six weeks before the start of principal photography and stay for two weeks to wrap out the job.

08–02 Assistant Directors

The 1st Assistant Director will prep for four weeks and bring on the 2nd AD one week before filming begins. Some films/budgets are big enough to require a 2nd 2nd Assistant Director who works with the 2nd AD to help in whatever work needs to be done. Usually it entails supporting the cast members.

08–03 Production Supervisor
This person will work in tandem with the Line Producer and hire all crew, coordinate schedules, and work with Department Heads.

08–04 Production Coordinator
This person assists the Supervisor with scheduling, coordinating paperwork, and other production-related work. The Assistant Production Coordinator will come in for the final two weeks of prep and stay for production.

08–05 Script Supervisor
This person will have two days to prep and will receive a "bump" up in pay on the days they plan to have two cameras rolling.

08–06 Production Accountant
The accountant will cut all checks, run cost reports, and meet with the Producers and Line Producers on a daily basis to stay on top of the budget and accounting.

08–08 Production Assistants
There will be one Office Production Assistant for prep, shoot, and wrap and five Set Production Assistants for the shooting period.

08–09 Studio Teacher/Tutor
There is one minor-age actor for two weeks of the shooting period. The Tutor will do educational work with the actor in between setups during the weekday filming days.

09–02 Extras, SAG-AFTRA
The SAG-AFTRA contract allows for a mixing of union and non-union Background Actors.

09–03 Extras, Non-Union
The rate for non-union Background Actors is lower than the guild rate.

09–04 Extras Casting Director

This fee will go to the Casting Director in charge of the Background Actors.

09–05 Extras Agency Fee

The 10% fee goes to the agents for any Background Actors that are cast in the film.

11–01 Production Designer

Fees for prep, shoot, and wrap for this key department head.

11–02 Art Director/Set Designer

This person will work in tandem with the Production Designer.

11–04 Art Coordinator

The Coordinator will come on three weeks before principal photography to coordinate orders, purchases, budgeting, and shipping for the art department.

11–07 Signage & Graphics

One of the stores needs a custom-built sign, so this will pay for design and printing.

11–08 Storage

They will need to store lots of props, set decorating, and online art purchases during prep and filming.

11–09 Production Placement/Clearance Allowance

There are two key branded props that may require a payment to the copyright owner.

11–10 Purchases/Rentals

For Art Department purchases and rentals.

13–01 thru 13–03 Key Grip, Best Boy Grip/Dolly Grip, plus 3rd and 4th Grips

For labor costs for the Grip department.

13–06 Grip Rentals
For Grip package rentals including a dolly.

13–07 Expendables
For gaffers tape, gels, clothespins, etc.

13–07 Kit Rentals
This charge is for the coffee maker, hot water server, serving trays, tables, utensils, etc., that the craft service person will rent to the production.

13–10 Craft Service
For labor and food costs for crew/cast craft service needs.

14–01 and 14–02 Special Effects Person and Assistant
This film will have to shoot a few "plates" (images that will be used as the background in a special effect) and do some special effects on set for use in post-production.

14–09 Rentals & Purchases
For SFX equipment rentals and purchases.

15–01 thru 15–07 Set Decorator, Lead Person, Set Dressers, Additional Labor, Expendables, Purchases and Rentals
This film will be shot entirely on location so Set Dressing will be key to the sets. These line items are for Set Decorating Labor, Rentals and Purchases.

15–09 Kit Rentals
For the Set Decorator's kit.

16–01 thru 16–06 Property Master, Assistant, Purchases, Rentals, Loss & Damage and Kit Rentals
For the Labor and Purchases/Rentals for the Props Department.

16–08 Armorer
For five filming days and one prep day, there will be an armorer on set when one of the actors works with a gun.

17–01 thru 17–08 Costume Designer, Costumer, Extras Costumer, Expendables, Purchases, Rentals, Alterations & Repairs, Cleaning & Dyeing, Kit Rentals
For Costume Department labor and cost — all contemporary clothing, no period pieces.

17–09 Kit Rentals
To rent the Costume Designer's kit.

17–12 Costume Production Assistants
For additional production assistants to help this department.

18–01 thru 18–03 Key Makeup Artist, Additional Makeup Artists, and Key Hair Stylist
For Labor costs for the Makeup and Hair Department.

18–05 SFX Makeup Artist
There will be a fight and a gun shot wound that will need to be created.

18–06 thru 18–08 Purchases, Rentals (including SFX), and Kit Rentals
For Makeup and Hair Departments costs.

19–01 thru 19–03 Gaffer, Best Boy Electric, and Electrics
For Labor costs in the Lighting Department.

19–05 and 19–06 Expendables and Lighting Package Rental
For Equipment and Expendables for the Lighting Department.

19–10 Kit Rentals
For the Gaffer's kit rental.

20–01 Director of Photography
A flat rate for the prep, shoot, and post work of the DP.

20–02 B Camera/Steadicam Operator
The B Camera operator will also operate the Steadicam rig on certain days.

20–03 thru 20–06 1st & 2nd Assistant Camera (A&B Cameras), DIT, and Still Photographer
For the Labor costs for the Camera Department.

20–07 Camera Package Rental (A&B Cameras)
For the Camera equipment rentals for the production period.

20–11 Steadicam Rig Rental
For the Steadicam rig during production.

20–17 Loss & Damage
For damage to equipment.

20–19 Expendables
For camera tape, sharpies, etc.

20-26 Kit Rentals
For kit rentals for the two 1st ACs and DIT.

21–01 thru 21–05 Mixer, Boom Operator, Batteries, Sound Package, and Walkie-Talkies
For the Labor and Equipment costs for the Sound Department.

21–08 Miscellaneous Rentals/Loss & Damage
For Sound Department's loss and damage and additional rentals.

22–01 and 22–02 Transportation Coordinator and Drivers
The Labor costs for the non-union Transportation Coordinator and Drivers.

22–03 thru 22–07 Transportation Vehicle Rental, Parking/Tolls/Gas, Repairs & Maintenance, Honeywagon Pumping, and Miscellaneous
This production will rent eight Production Vehicles — these amounts cover the rentals and costs to keep them on the road.

23–01 thru 23–03 Location Manager, Assistant Manager, and First Aid/Medic
For the labor costs during scout and production. There are no plans to shoot in a studio so everything will be shot in real locations.

23–05 thru 23–08 Security, Police, Permits, and Parking
For any Security, Police, and costs for Permits and Parking for all vehicles.

23–09 Catering Services
For all lunches and wrap meals for Cast, Crew, and Extras during production.

23–13 Location Equipment
For equipment during scout and shooting period for the Location Department.

23–15 Site Cleaning/Trash Removal/Dumpsters
A few locations will need to be professionally cleaned or require a dumpster rental.

23–17 Location Site Rental Fees
This flat fee will cover all location site rentals. Some of the locations will be free.

23–18 Location Scout Working Meals
For working meals while scouting for the film.

23-20 Miscellaneous Expenses
For expenses incurred by the Locations Department.

24–03 Picture Cars
For the gun fight scene and a few others, they will need to rent picture vehicles including a police car.

25–01 Digital Media
For all hard drives and backups for A and B cameras.

27–01 Editor — Shoot/Post
The Editor will cut while shooting and work with the Director through picture lock.

27–02 Assistant Editor — Shoot/Post
The Assistant Editor will work during production and then come back to finish the film toward the end of the editing period.

27–07 Online Screening Accounts
During post-production the Editor will share materials through an FTP site that is password-protected.

28–01 Composer Fee
For the composition and recording of the composer's music.

28–11 Music Licensing
For sync and master use licenses for "all rights, all media, in perpetuity" for several songs for the soundtrack.

28–12 Music Supervisor/Clearance
The Supervisor will recommend and clear all the music licenses.

29–15 Audio Mix
A flat rate for the Sound Editor's work, ADR recording, Foley work, and the Audio Mix.

30–01 Stock Footage
There is one scene that requires a short clip seen on a television. This is for the licensing costs.

31–01 Digital Intermediate
A flat rate for the DI including Color Grading.

31–02 Hard Drive Purchases
For additional hard drives in post-production.

32–01 Titling—Opening & End Credits
Fee to create the graphics for any opening and end credits. These can be simple or very elaborate based on the Director's vision and the project's budget allowance. End credits are often a combination of "cards" which usually scroll to accommodate the names of all the talented cast and crew necessary to make the film.

33–01 Masters/Clones
The costs to create the deliverables listed.

33–05 Screening Copies
For DVD copies.

34–01 VFX
This film has several scenes that require CGI/Visual Effects work. This bid is from the graphics company based on a very specific storyboard for each effect.

35–01 Producers Entertainment Package
For production, general liability, auto, workers' comp, and insurance coverage for the stunt/gun fight.

35–06 Errors & Omissions
For E&O insurance for the film.

36–01 Business License/Taxes
The producers set up an LLC in Los Angeles for this production.

36–02 Legal
This is a flat rate for all legal fees including licensing agreements.

36–07 thru 36–11 Office Craft Services, Space Rental, Furniture, Equipment, Supplies, and Printers
For all office space and equipment costs.

36–14 Messenger/Overnight Shipping
For Messenger and Overnight Shipping costs.

36–15 Bank Fees
For the bank charges for the business checking account.

36–17 Office Cleaning
This is part of the office space rental agreement.

Contingency
The contingency fee is set at 10%.

$1 MILLION DOCUMENTARY FEATURE FILM BUDGET

- Go to *www.mwp.com.*
- Click on "MW Film School."
- Open the item "Sample Budgets/Forms."
- Download the corresponding free Excel Budget Template.
- Save it to your computer.
- Last, this budget is a sample template. Make sure to create your budget with figures based on your research on current rates and prices available to you.

Budget Assumptions

This film will be shot mostly cinema-vérité style for 28 days over the course of six months. The director is also a professional Cinematographer and plans to shoot 10 days by himself if necessary and loan his camera to the production for free. The production will hire a second camera operator for the remaining 18 days and rent an HD digital camera for those days. Some crew members will be paid through their own loan-out companies so there will be no payroll taxes. For the rest of the crew, the payroll rate is 22%.

The producer plans to shoot in a few different cities in the United States and make two overseas trips — one to the UK and one to Japan. The producer made a pre-sale for the US television rights and the rest of the money will come from a crowdfunding campaign, a few foundation grants, and some of the director's savings. Once the film premieres at various film festivals, the plan is to sell the international rights and pay back the director's out-of-pocket money and the partially deferred fees for him and the producer.

$1 Million Documentary Budget

Fringe assumptions:		SUMMARY BUDGET	
Payroll Tax	22.00%	Production:	$1 Million Documentary Budget
WGA	0.00%	Shoot Days:	28 days-1 camera; 18 days with 2 cameras
DGA	0.00%	Location:	US and Int'l
SAG-AFTRA	0.00%	Unions:	No
Overtime	0%	Edit Weeks:	27
Contingency	10%	Exec. Producer:	
DP provides own A camera		Producer:	
		Director:	
Payroll tax for Employees only		Delivery format: HD Cam SR	

Account		Subtotal	Total
01-00 Story & Rights		$0	
02-00 Producers Unit		$70,000	
03-00 Direction		$70,000	
04-00 Cast		$0	
05-00 Travel & Living – Producers/Director		$0	
06-00 Travel & Living- Cast		$0	
07-00 Residuals		$0	
	TOTAL ABOVE-THE-LINE		$140,000
08-00 Production Staff		$81,086	
09-00 Background Actors/Extras		$0	
10-00 Sound Stage		$0	
11-00 Production Design		$0	
12-00 Set Construction		$0	
13-00 Set Operations		$15,300	
14-00 Special Effects		$0	
15-00 Set Dressing		$0	
16-00 Property		$0	
17-00 Wardrobe		$0	
18-00 Make-Up and Hair		$0	
19-00 Electrical		$19,980	
20-00 Camera		$119,900	
21-00 Production Sound		$53,000	
22-00 Transportation		$18,750	
23-00 Location Expenses		$4,480	
24-00 Picture Vehicle/Animals		$0	
25-00 Media		$3,000	
26-00 Travel and Living-Crew		$53,875	
	TOTAL PRODUCTION		$369,371
27-00 Editorial		$200,475	
28-00 Music		$38,000	
29-00 Post-Production Sound		$50,400	
30-00 Post-Production - Digital and Film		$4,500	
31-00 Digital Intermediate		$27,600	
32-00 Titling and Graphics		$3,000	
33-00 Deliverables		$19,300	
34-00 Digital Visual Effects/Animation		$0	
	TOTAL POST-PRODUCTION		$343,275
35-00 Insurance		$17,000	
36-00 General & Administrative Expenses		$36,290	
37-00 Publicity and Marketing		$3,500	
	TOTAL GENERAL		$56,790
Total Above-the-Line			$140,000
Total Below-the-Line			$769,436
Total Above and Below-the-Line			$909,436
Contingency			$90,944
GRAND TOTAL			$1,000,380

$1 Million Documentary Budget

ABOVE-THE-LINE							
	Amt.	*Units*	*x*	*Rate*	*Sub-Total*	*Total*	
01-00 Story & Rights							
01-01 Rights Purchases		Allow	1		0	0	
01-02 Options		Allow	1		0	0	
01-03 Writer Salaries/Screenplay Purchase		Allow	1		0	0	
01-04 Research/Clearances		Allow	1		0	0	
01-05 Title Registration		Allow	1		0	0	
01-06 Script Timing		Allow	1		0	0	
01-07 Storyboards/Pre-Viz		Allow	1		0	0	
01-08 WGA Publication fee		Allow	1		0	0	
01-10 Development		Allow	1		0	0	
Payroll					0	0	
WGA					0	0	
				Total for 01-00			0
02-00 Producers Unit							
02-01 Executive Producer		Allow	1		0	0	
02-02 Producer	1	Allow	1	70,000	70,000	70,000	
02-03 Associate Producer		Allow	1		0	0	
02-04 Assistant to Producer(s)		Week(s)	1		0	0	
02-06 Consultants		Allow	1		0	0	
02-07 Miscellaneous Expenses		Allow	1		0	0	
Payroll					70,000	0	
				Total for 02-00			70,000
03-00 Direction							
03-01 Director	1	Allow	1	70,000	70,000	70,000	
03-02 Assistant to Director	1	Weeks	1		0	0	
Payroll					70,000	0	
DGA					70,000	0	
				Total for 03-00			70,000
04-00 Cast							
04-01 Lead Actors							
		Allow	1		0		
		Allow	1		0		
Overtime Allowance		Allow	1		0	0	
04-02 Supporting Cast							
		Week(s)	1		0		
		Week(s)	1		0		
		Week(s)	1		0		
		Week(s)	1		0		
Overtime Allowance		Allow	1		0	0	
04-03 Day Players							
		Day(s)	1		0		
		Day(s)	1		0		
		Day(s)	1		0		
		Day(s)	1		0		
		Day(s)	1		0		
		Day(s)	1		0		
		Day(s)	1		0		
		Day(s)	1		0		
		Day(s)	1		0		
		Day(s)	1		0		
		Day(s)	1		0		
Overtime Allowance		Allow	1		0	0	
04-04 Casting Director/Staff		Allow	1		0	0	
04-05 Casting Expenses		Allow	1		0	0	
04-06 Choreographer		Weeks	1		0	0	
04-07 Assistant(s) to Choreographer		Weeks	1		0	0	
04-08 Dialect Coach		Weeks	1		0	0	
04-09 Narrator/Voiceover Artist		Weeks	1		0	0	

$1 Million Documentary Budget

		Amt.	Units	x	Rate	Sub-Total	Total	
04-10 Stunt Coordinator			Weeks	1		0	0	
04-11 Stunt Players (6 day weeks)			Weeks	1		0	0	
04-12 Stunt Costs/Adjustments			Allow	1		0	0	
04-13 Stunt Equipment			Allow	1		0	0	
04-14 ADR (Actors' fees)			Allow	1		0	0	
	Payroll					0	0	
	SAG-AFTRA					0	0	
					Total for 04-00			0
05-00 Travel & Living – Producers/Director								
05-01 Airfares			RT	1		0	0	
05-02 Hotel			Nights	1		0	0	
05-03 Taxi/Limo			Allow	1		0	0	
05-04 Auto			Allow	1		0	0	
05-05 Train			Allow	1		0	0	
05-06 Excess Baggage			Allow	1		0	0	
05-07 Phone			Allow	1		0	0	
05-08 Gratuities			Allow	1		0	0	
05-09 Airport Transfers			Allow	1		0	0	
05-09 Per Diem			Days	1		0	0	
					Total for 05-00			0
06-00 Travel & Living- Cast								
06-01 Airfares			RT	1		0	0	
06-02 Hotels			Nights	1		0	0	
06-03 Taxi/Limo			Allow	1		0	0	
06-04 Auto			Allow	1		0	0	
06-05 Train			Allow	1		0	0	
06-06 Excess Baggage			Allow	1		0	0	
06-07 Phone			Allow	1		0	0	
06-08 Gratuities			Allow	1		0	0	
06-09 Per Diem			Days	1		0	0	
					Total for 06-00			0
07-00 Residuals			Allow	1		0	0	
					Total for 07-00			0
TOTAL ABOVE-THE -LINE								140,000

$1 Million Documentary Budget

		Amt.	Units	x	Rate	Sub-Total	Total	
BELOW-THE-LINE								
08-00 Production Staff								
08-01 Field Producer								
	Prep/Travel	9	Weeks	1	2,000	18,000		
	Shoot	28	Days	1	500	14,000		
	Wrap		Weeks	1		0		
	Severance		Allow	1		0	32,000	
08-02 Assistant Directors								
First AD								
	Prep/Travel		Weeks	1		0		
	Shoot		Weeks	1		0		
	Prod. Fee (shoot days)		Days	1		0		
	Severance		Allow	1		0		
	Overtime Allow		Days	1		0	0	
2nd AD								
	Prep/Travel		Weeks	1		0		
	Shoot		Weeks	1		0		
	Prod. Fee		Days	1		0		
	Severance		Allow	1		0		
	Overtime Allow		Days	1		0	0	
08-03 International Fixer								
	Prep/Travel	4	Weeks	1	2,500	10,000		
	Shoot	14	Days	1	500	7,000		
	Prod. Fee		Days	1		0		
	Severance		Allow	1		0		
	Overtime Allow		Days	1		0	17,000	
08-04 Production Coordinator								
	Prep/Travel		Weeks	1		0		
	Shoot		Weeks	1		0		
	Wrap		Weeks	1		0	0	
Ass't Coord.								
	Prep		Weeks	1		0		
	Shoot		Weeks	1		0		
	Wrap		Weeks	1		0	0	
08-05 Script Supervisor								
	Prep		Days	1		0		
	Shoot		Days	1		0		
	Saturdays Worked		Days	1		0		
	Wrap		Days	1		0		
	2nd Camera Days		Days	1		0		
	Overtime		Allow		0	0	0	
08-06 Production Accountant/Auditor								
		12	Months	1	500	6,000		
	Shoot		Weeks	1		0		
	Wrap		Weeks	1		0		
	Post-Production		Weeks	1		0	6,000	
Assistant Accountant								
	Prep/Travel		Weeks	1		0		
	Shoot		Weeks	1		0		
	Wrap		Weeks	1		0	0	
08-07 Technical Advisors			Flat	1		0	0	
08-08 Production Assistants								
Office Prod. Assistant(s)								
	Prep	60	Days	1	175	10,500		
	Shoot	28	Days	2	175	9,800		
	Wrap		Days	1		0		
Set Prod. Assistant(s)								
	Prep		Days	1		0		
	Shoot		Days	1		0	20,300	
08-09 Studio Teacher/Tutor			Weeks	1		0	0	
	Payroll					26,300	5,786	
	DGA					0	0	
					Total for 08-00			**81,086**

$1 Million Documentary Budget

		Amt.	Units	x	Rate	Sub-Total	Total	
09-00 Background Actors/Extras								
09-01 Stand-ins			Days	1		0	0	
09-02 Extras			Extras	1		0	0	
09-05 Extras Casting Fee @ 10%			Allow	1		0	0	
09-10 Extras Transportation			Allow	1		0	0	
	Payroll					0	0	
	P&H					0	0	
					Total for 09-00			0
10-00 Sound Stage								
10-01 Stage Rental			Allow	1		0	0	
	Prep		Allow	1		0	0	
	Pre-Light		Allow	1		0	0	
	Shoot		Allow	1		0	0	
	Wrap		Allow	1		0	0	
	Overtime		Allow	1		0	0	
10-02 Stage Lighting Rental			Allow	1		0	0	
10-03 Stage Grip Rental			Allow	1		0	0	
10-04 Phones/ Internet			Allow	1		0	0	
10-05 Garbage removal			Allow	1		0	0	
10-06 Green Room			Allow	1		0	0	
10-07 Make Up Room			Allow	1		0	0	
10-08 Office Rental			Allow	1		0	0	
10-09 Parking			Allow	1		0	0	
					Total for 10-00			0
11-00 Production Design								
11-01 Production Designer								
	Prep/Travel		Weeks	1		0		
	Shoot		Weeks	1		0	0	
11-02 Art Director								
	Prep/Travel		Weeks	1		0		
	Shoot		Weeks	1		0	0	
11-03 Art Assistants								
	Prep/Travel		Days	1		0		
	Shoot		Days	1		0	0	
11-04 Set Designer								
	Prep/Travel		Weeks	1		0		
	Shoot		Weeks	1		0	0	
11-05 Model Makers/Miniatures			Allow	1		0	0	
11-06 Draftsperson			Allow	1		0	0	
11-08 Research/Materials			Allow	1		0	0	
11-09 Vehicle Expenses			Weeks	1		0	0	
11-10 Purchases/Rentals			Allow	1		0	0	
	Payroll					0	0	
					Total for 11-00			0
12-00 Set Construction								
12-01 Construction Coordinator								
	Prep		Days	1		0		
	Shoot		Days	1		0		
	Overtime		Allow	1	0	0	0	
12-02 Foreman								
	Prep		Days	1		0		
	Shoot		Days	1		0		
	Overtime		Allow	1	0	0	0	
Carpenters			Allow	1		0	0	
12-03 Scenic Painters								
Lead Scenic Painter								
	Prep		Days	1		0		
	Shoot		Days	1		0		
	Overtime		Allow	1	0	0	0	
Painters			Allow	1		0	0	
12-05 Greensmen			Allow	1		0	0	

$1 Million Documentary Budget

		Amt.	Units	x	Rate	Sub-Total	Total	
12-06 Construction materials - Purchases			Allow	1		0	0	
12-07 Construction materials - Rentals			Allow	1		0	0	
12-08 Construction Equipment			Allow	1		0	0	
12-09 Set Strike			Allow	1		0	0	
	Payroll					0	0	
					Total for 12-00			0
13-00 Set Operations								
13-01 Key Grip								
	Prep/Travel		Days	1		0		
	Shoot		Days	1		0		
	Wrap		Days	1		0		
	Overtime		Allow	1	0	0	0	
13-02 Best Boy Grip								
	Prep		Days	1		0		
	Shoot		Days	1		0		
	Wrap		Days	1		0		
	Overtime		Allow	1	0	0	0	
13-03 Grips								
3rd Grip								
	Prep		Days	1		0		
	Shoot		Days	1		0		
	Wrap		Days	1		0		
	Overtime		Allow	1	0	0	0	
4th Grip								
	Prep		Days	1		0		
	Shoot		Days	1		0		
	Wrap		Days	1		0		
	Overtime		Allow	1	0	0	0	
Additional Grips			Days	1		0		
	Overtime		Allow	1		0	0	
13-04 Dolly/Crane Grips								
	Prep		Days	1		0		
	Shoot		Days	1		0		
	Overtime		Allow	1	0	0	0	
13-06 Grip Rentals								
	Package	18	Days	1	500	9,000		
	Dollies		Weeks	1		0		
	Cranes (incl. Driver)		Days	1		0		
	Add'l Equip.		Allow	1		0	9,000	
15-07 Expendables		28	Allow	1	100	2,800	2,800	
15-08 Kit Rentals								
	Key Grip		Weeks	1		0	0	
	Craft Service		Weeks	1		0	0	
13-10 Craft Service								
	Prep		Days	1		0		
	Shoot	28	Days	1	125	3,500		
	Wrap		Days	1		0		
	Overtime		Allow	1	3,500	0	3,500	
Purchases			Days	1		0	0	
Rentals			Allow	1		0	0	
13-15 Air Conditioning/Heating			Days	1		0	0	
	Payroll					0	0	
					Total for 13-00			15,300
14-00 Special Effects								
14-01 Special Effects Person								
	Prep/Travel		Days	1		0		
	Shoot		Days	1		0		
	Overtime		Allow	1	0	0	0	
14-02 SFX Assistant(s)								
	Shoot		Days	1		0		
	Overtime		Allow	1	0	0	0	
14-03 Additional Labor								

$1 Million Documentary Budget

		Amt.	Units	x	Rate	Sub-Total	Total	
	Shoot		Days	1		0		
	Overtime		Allow	1	0	0	0	
14-06 Manufacturing Labor			Allow	1		0	0	
14-07 Fabrication			Allow	1		0	0	
14-09 Rentals			Allow	1		0	0	
	Payroll				0	0	0	
					Total for 14-00			0
15-00 Set Dressing								
15-01 Set Decorator								
	Prep/Travel		Days	1		0		
	Shoot		Days	1		0		
	Wrap		Days	1		0		
	Overtime				0	0	0	
15-02 Lead Person								
	Prep/Travel		Days	1		0		
	Shoot		Days	1		0		
	Wrap		Days	1		0		
	Overtime				0	0	0	
15-03 Swing Gang/Set Dressers								
Set Dresser #1								
	Prep		Days	1		0		
	Shoot		Days	1		0		
	Wrap		Days	1		0		
	Overtime				0	0	0	
Set Dresser #2								
	Prep		Days	1		0		
	Shoot		Days	1		0		
	Wrap		Days	1		0		
	Overtime				0	0	0	
Set Dresser #3								
	Prep		Days	1		0		
	Shoot		Days	1		0		
	Wrap		Days	1		0		
	Overtime				0	0	0	
15-04 Additional Labor								
On-Set Dresser (Shoot)			Days	1		0		
	Overtime				0	0	0	
15-05 Expendables			Allow	1		0	0	
15-06 Purchases			Allow	1		0	0	
15-07 Rentals			Allow	1		0	0	
15-08 Loss & Damage			Allow	1		0	0	
15-09 Kit Rentals						0	0	
	Set Decorator		Weeks	1		0	0	
	Lead Person		Weeks	1		0	0	
15-10 Vehicle Expenses								
	Set Decorator		Weeks	1		0	0	
	Lead Person		Weeks	1		0	0	
	Payroll				0	0	0	
					Total for 15-00			0
16-00 Property								
16-01 Property Master								
	Prep/Travel		Days	1		0		
	Shoot		Days	1		0		
	Wrap		Days	1		0		
	Overtime				0	0	0	
16-02 Prop Assistant								
	Prep		Days	1		0		
	Shoot		Days	1		0		
	Wrap		Days	1		0		
	Overtime				0	0	0	
16-03 Purchases			Allow	1		0	0	

$1 Million Documentary Budget

		Amt.	Units	x	Rate	Sub-Total	Total	
16-04 Rentals			Allow	1		0	0	
16-05 Loss & Damage			Allow	1		0	0	
16-06 Kit Rentals								
	Prop Master		Weeks	1		0	0	
16-07 Vehicle Expenses								
	Prop Master		Weeks	1		0	0	
	Assistant		Weeks	1		0	0	
	Payroll				0	0	0	
					Total for 16-00			0
17-00 Wardrobe								
17-01 Costume Designer								
	Prep/Travel		Weeks	1		0		
	Shoot		Weeks	1		0		
	Wrap		Week	1		0	0	
17-02 Costumer								
	Prep/Travel		Days	1		0		
	Shoot		Days	1		0		
	Wrap		Days	1		0		
	Overtime		Allow	1	0	0	0	
17-03 Additional Costumer(s)								
	Prep		Days	1		0		
	Shoot		Days	1		0		
	Wrap		Days	1		0		
	Overtime		Allow	1	0	0	0	
17-04 Expendables			Allow	1		0	0	
17-05 Purchases			Allow	1		0	0	
17-06 Rentals			Allow	1		0	0	
17-07 Alteration & Repairs			Allow	1		0	0	
17-08 Cleaning & Dyeing			Allow	1		0	0	
17-09 Loss & Damage			Allow	1		0	0	
17-10 Kit Rentals								
	Costume Designer		Weeks	1		0	0	
17-11 Vehicle Expenses								
	Costume Designer		Weeks	1		0	0	
	Payroll				0	0	0	
					Total for 17-00			0
18-00 Make-Up and Hair								
18-01 Key Make-Up Artist								
	Prep/Travel		Days	1		0		
	Shoot		Days	1		0		
	Wrap		Days	1		0		
	Overtime		Allow	1	0	0	0	
18-02 Additional Make-Up Artist(s)			Days	1		0		
	Shoot		Days	1		0		
	Overtime		Allow	1	0	0	0	
18-03 Key Hair Stylist								
	Prep/Travel		Days	1		0		
	Shoot		Days	1		0		
	Wrap		Days	1		0		
	Overtime		Allow	1	0	0	0	
18-04 Additional Hair Stylist(s)			Days	1		0		
	Shoot		Days	1		0		
	Overtime		Allow	1	0	0	0	
18-05 Special Effects Makeup Effects			Allow	1		0	0	
18-06 Purchases			Allow	1		0	0	
18-07 Rentals			Weeks	1		0	0	
18-08 Kit Rentals								
	Key Make-Up		Days	1		0	0	
	Add'l Make-Up		Days	1		0	0	
	Hair Stylist		Days	1		0	0	
	Add'l Hair		Days	1		0	0	
	Payroll				0	0	0	
					Total for 18-00			0

$1 Million Documentary Budget

		Amt.	Units	x	Rate	Sub-Total	Total	
19-00 Electrical								
19-01 Gaffer								
	Prep/Travel		Days	1		0		
	Shoot	18	Days	1	500	9,000		
	Wrap/Travel		Days	1		0		
	Overtime		Allow	1	9,000	0	9,000	
19-02 Best Boy Electric								
	Prep		Days	1		0		
	Shoot		Days	1		0		
	Wrap		Days	1		0		
	Overtime		Allow	1	0	0	0	
19-03 Electrics								
3rd Electric								
	Prep		Days	1		0		
	Shoot		Days	1		0		
	Wrap		Days	1		0		
	Overtime		Allow	1	0	0	0	
4th Electric								
	Prep		Days	1		0		
	Shoot		Days	1		0		
	Wrap		Days	1		0		
	Overtime		Allow	1	0	0	0	
19-04 Additional Labor								
	Shoot		Days	1		0		
	Overtime		Allow	1	0	0	0	
19-05 Equipment Purchases			Allow	1		0	0	
19-06 Lighting Package Rental		18	Days	1	500	9,000	9,000	
	Add'l Equip.		Allow	1		0	0	
	Condors		Allow	1		0	0	
	Additional Generator		Allow	1		0	0	
19-07 Additional Rentals			Allow	1		0	0	
19-08 Electrical Generator/Driver			Days	1		0	0	
19-09 Loss & Damage			Allow	1		0	0	
19-10 Kit Rentals								
	Gaffer		Weeks	1		0	0	
	Payroll				9,000	1,980	1,980	
					Total for 19-00			19,980
20-00 Camera								
20-01 Director of Photography								
	Prep/Travel	14	Days	1	1,250	17,500		
	Shoot	28	Days	1	1,250	35,000	52,500	
20-02 Camera Operator or B Camera								
	Prep/Travel		Days	1		0		
	Shoot	18	Days	1	750	13,500		
	Overtime		Allow	1	13,500	0	13,500	
20-03 1st Assistant Camera								
	Prep/Travel		Days	1		0		
	Shoot		Days	1		0		
	Wrap		Days	1		0		
	Overtime		Allow	1	0	0		
	B Cam 1st Ass't		Days	1		0	0	
	Overtime		Allow	1	0	0	0	
20-04 2nd Ass't Camera								
	Prep		Days	1		0		
	Shoot		Days	1		0		
	Wrap		Days	1		0		
	Overtime		Allow	1	0	0	0	
	B Cam 2nd Ass't		Days	1		0		
	Overtime		Allow	1	0	0	0	
20-05 Digital Imaging Technician (DIT)		28	Days	1	500	14,000	14,000	
20-06 Still Photographer		2	Days	1	500	1,000	1,000	
20-07 Camera Package Rental		18	Days	1	500	9,000	9,000	

$1 Million Documentary Budget

		Amt.	Units	x	Rate	Sub-Total	Total	
Camera Lens Rental-B Camera		18	Days	1	350	6,300	6,300	
Phantom camera rental(high speed)		1	Days	1	3,000	3,000	3,000	
20-08 Camera Package Purchase			Allow	1		0	0	
20-10 DIT Rental		28	Days	1	500	14,000	14,000	
20-11 Steadicam Operator & Equip.			Days	1		0	0	
20-12 Teleprompter/Operator			Days	1		0	0	
20-13 Video Assist/Operator			Days	1		0	0	
20-14 Aerial Photography			Days	1		0	0	
20-15 Underwater and Topside Photography			Days	1		0	0	
20-16 Drones/GoPros			Days	1		0	0	
22-17 Maintenance/Loss & Damage		1	Allow	1	500	500	500	
20-18 Motion Control			Allow	1		0	0	
20-19 Expendables		28	Days	1	100	2,800	2,800	
20-20 Video Truck			Weeks	1		0	0	
20-25 Video Truck Crew			Weeks	1		0	0	
20-26 Kit Rentals								
	1st Ass't Camera		Days	1		0	0	
	Payroll				15,000	3,300	3,300	
					Total for 20-00			119,900
21-00 Production Sound								
21-01 Sound Mixer								
	Prep/Travel	14	Days	1	500	7,000		
	Shoot	28	Days	1	500	14,000		
	Wrap/Travel		Days	1		0		
	Overtime		Allow	1	21,000	0	21,000	
21-02 2nd Mixer								
	Shoot	18	Days	1	500	9,000		
	Overtime		Allow	1	9,000	0	9,000	
21-03 Expendables/Batteries			Allow	1		0	0	
21-04 Sound Package		46	Days	1	500	23,000	23,000	
21-05 Walkie-Talkies			Weeks	1		0	0	
21-06 Sound Truck			Weeks	1		0	0	
21-08 Misc. / Loss & Damage			Allow	1		0	0	
	Payroll					0	0	
					Total for 21-00			53,000
22-00 Transportation								
22-01 Transportation Coordinator								
			Weeks	1		0	0	
22-02 Drivers								
Captain								
	Prep		Days	1		0		
	Shoot		Days	1		0		
	Wrap		Days	1		0	0	
Star Trailer Drivers								
Driver #1								
	Prep		Day	1		0		
	Shoot		Days	1		0		
	Wrap		Day	1		0	0	
Driver #2								
	Prep		Day	1		0		
	Shoot		Days	1		0		
	Wrap		Day	1		0	0	
Production Van Driver								
	Prep		Days	1		0		
	Shoot		Days	1		0		
	Wrap		Days	1		0	0	
Camera Truck Driver								
	Prep		Days	1		0		
	Shoot		Days	1		0		
	Wrap		Days	1		0	0	
Stakebed Driver (Construction)								
	Shoot		Days	1		0	0	
Set Dressing Driver								

$1 Million Documentary Budget

		Amt.	Units	x	Rate	Sub-Total	Total	
	Prep		Days	1		0		
	Shoot		Days	1		0		
	Wrap		Days	1		0	0	
Second Set Dressing 5 Ton			Days	1		0	0	
Props Driver								
	Prep		Days	1		0		
	Shoot		Days	1		0		
	Wrap		Days	1		0	0	
Make-Up/Wardrobe Driver								
	Prep		Days	1		0		
	Shoot		Days	1		0		
	Wrap		Days	1		0	0	
Prod. Office Trailer Driver								
	Prep		Days	1		0		
	Shoot		Days	1		0		
	Wrap		Days	1		0	0	
Honeywagon Driver								
	Shoot		Days	1		0		
	Wrap		Days	1		0	0	
15-Passenger Van #1 Driver								
	Prep		Days	1		0		
	Shoot		Days	1		0	0	
15-Passenger Van #2 Driver								
	Prep		Days	1		0		
	Shoot		Days	1		0	0	
Car Carrier			Days	1		0	0	
Insert Car (car to car cam platform)			Days	1		0	0	
Water Truck Driver			Days	1		0	0	
Caterer	Shoot		Days	1		0	0	
Caterer Ass't	Shoot		Days	1		0	0	
Additional Drivers			Allow	1		0	0	
22-03 Transportation Equipment Rental								
Minivan (includes CDW)		75	Days	1	150	11,250	11,250	
Crew Cab			Weeks	1		0	0	
Production Van (40' w/ 2 gennies)			Weeks	1		0	0	
Camera Truck			Weeks	1		0	0	
Stakebed			Weeks	1		0	0	
Set Dressing 5 Ton			Weeks	1		0	0	
Add'l Set Dressing 5 Ton			Weeks	1		0	0	
Set Dress Van			Weeks	1		0	0	
Props 5 Ton			Weeks	1		0	0	
Wardrobe/Make-Up			Weeks	1		0	0	
Crew Stake Bed			Weeks	1		0	0	
Prod. Office Trailer			Weeks	1		0	0	
Honeywagon (Portable Toilets)			Days	1		0	0	
Water Truck			Days	1		0	0	
Gas Truck			Days	1		0	0	
15-Passenger Van			Days	1		0	0	
Car Tow Trailer			Days	1		0	0	
Car Trailer			Days	1		0	0	
Camera Car			Days	1		0	0	
22-04 Parking/Tolls/Gas		75	Days	1	100	7,500	7,500	
22-05 Repairs & Maintenance			Allow	1		0	0	
22-06 Honeywagon Pumping			Allow	1		0	0	
22-07 Miscellaneous			Allow	1		0	0	
	Payroll				0	0	0	
					Total for 22-00			**18,750**
23-00 Location Expenses								
23-01 Location Manager			Weeks	1		0	0	
23-02 Location Assistants								
Assistant Location Mgr.			Weeks	1		0	0	
Local Contact Person			Weeks	1		0	0	
23-03 First Aid/Medic			Weeks	1		0	0	
23-04 Fire Officers								

$1 Million Documentary Budget

		Amt.	Units	x	Rate	Sub-Total	Total	
	Shoot		Days	1		0	0	
23-05 Security			Allow	1		0	0	
23-06 Police			Days	1		0	0	
	Additional Police		Allow	1		0	0	
23-07 Permits			Allow	1		0	0	
23-08 Parking			Allow	1		0	0	
23-09 Catering Services								
Crew Meals		28	Days	8	20	4,480	4,480	
Extras			Meals	1		0	0	
Ice/Propane			Weeks	1		0	0	
2nd Meals			Days	1		0	0	
Sales Tax			Allow	1		0	0	
Tent			Allow	1		0	0	
23-11 Location Office Space Rental			Months	1		0	0	
23-12 Location Office Supplies			Allow	1		0	0	
23-13 Location Office Equipment			Allow	1		0	0	
23-14 Location Office Telephone/Fax			Allow	1		0	0	
23-17 Location Site Rental Fees								
	Shoot		Days	1		0	0	
23-18 Location Scout			Allow	1		0	0	
	Photos		Allow	1		0	0	
23-19 Auto Rentals								
Location Manager			Weeks	1		0	0	
Assistants			Weeks	1		0	0	
23-20 Miscellaneous Expenses								
	Mileage/DGA/SAG/Crew		Allow	1		0	0	
	Payroll				0	0	0	
					Total for 23-00			4,480
24-00 Picture Vehicles/Animals								
24-01 Animal Trainers								
Boss Wrangler			Weeks	1		0	0	
Assistant Wrangler			Weeks	1		0	0	
Wranglers			Week	1		0	0	
Riders/Handlers, etc			Day	1		0	0	
24-02 Animals								
	Horses		Allow	1		0	0	
Veterinary Expenses			Allow	1		0	0	
Feed/Shelter			Allow	1		0	0	
Transportation			Allow	1		0	0	
24-03 Picture Cars								
	Car #1		Weeks	1		0	0	
	Car #2		Weeks	1		0	0	
	Car #3		Weeks	1		0	0	
	Background Cars		Allow	1		0	0	
	Payroll				0	0	0	
					Total for 24-00			0
25-00 Media								
25-01 Digital Media-hard drives+back ups		5	Allow	2	300	3,000	3,000	
25-02 Raw Film Stock			Feet	1		0	0	
25-03 Film Lab-Negative Prep & Process			Feet	1		0	0	
25-04 Telecine/Film to Digital transfer			Allow	1		0	0	
25-05 Videotape stock			Each	1		0	0	
					Total for 25-00			3,000
26-00 Travel and Living - Crew								
26-01 Airfares	U.S.	5	Fares	3	600	9,000	9,000	
	International	2	Fares	3	1,600	9,600	9,600	
28-02 Hotels	U.S.	15	Nites	3	300	13,500	13,500	
	International	12	Nites	3	325	11,700	11,700	
28-03 Taxi		1	Allow	1	1,000	1,000	1,000	
28-04 Auto			Days	1		0	0	
28-05 Train			RT	1		0	0	
28-06 Excess Baggage			Allow	1		0	0	
28-08 PerDiem	U.S.	17	Days	3	75	3,825	3,825	

$1 Million Documentary Budget

	Amt.	Units	x	Rate	Sub-Total	Total	
International	14	Days	3	75	3,150	3,150	
28-09 Gratuities		Days	1		0	0	
28-10 Airport Transfers-U.S.	2	RT	3	100	600	600	
Airport Transfers-International	5	RT	3	100	1,500	1,500	
				Total for 26-00			53,875
TOTAL PRODUCTION							369,371
27-00 Editorial							
27-01 Editor - Shoot/Post	27	Weeks	1	3,500	94,500	94,500	
27-02 Assistant Editor - Shoot/Post	29	Weeks	1	1,250	36,250	36,250	
27-04 Post-Production Supervisor	7	Weeks	1	2,500	17,500	17,500	
27-05 Editing Room Rental	27	Weeks	2	500	27,000	27,000	
27-06 Edit System Rental	27	Weeks	1	500	13,500	13,500	
27-08 WIP screening	3	Hours	1	250	750	750	
27-10 On-Line Editing/Conform	1	Allow	1	3,000	3,000	3,000	
Payroll				36,250	7,975	7,975	
				Total for 27-00			200,475
28-00 Music							
28-01 Composer Fee	1	Allow	1	25,000	25,000	25,000	
28-02 Musicians		Allow	1		0	0	
28-03 Music Prep		Allow	1		0	0	
28-04 Studio Costs		Allow	1		0	0	
28-05 Music Scoring Stage		Hours	1		0	0	
28-06 Cartage and Rentals		Allow	1		0	0	
28-07 Music Mix Room		Allow	1		0	0	
28-08 Singers		Allow	1		0	0	
28-09 Payroll Service		Allow	1		0	0	
28-10 Miscellaneous		Allow	1		0	0	
28-11 Music Licensing	1	Allow	1	10,000	10,000	10,000	
28-12 Music Supervisor/Clearance	1	Allow	1	3,000	3,000	3,000	
				Total for 28-00			38,000
29-00 Post-Production Sound							
29-01 Sound Editor	3	Weeks	1	2,000	6,000	6,000	
29-02 Assistant Sound Editor		Weeks	1		0	0	
29-03 Music Editor		Weeks	1		0	0	
29-04 Dialogue Editor	3	Weeks	1	2,000	6,000	6,000	
29-05 Spotting (Music & FX)		Hours	1		0	0	
29-08 ADR (Studio/Editor)		Days	1		0	0	
29-09 Foley Stage/Editor							
Foley Record	16	Hours	1	300	4,800	4,800	
Foley Editor	3	Weeks	1	2,000	6,000	6,000	
29-10 Foley Artists		Days	1		0	0	
29-12 Narration Recording	3	Hours	1	400	1,200	1,200	
29-13 Audio Laydown		Hours	1		0	0	
29-15 Audio Mix							
Final Mix	40	Hours	1	500	20,000	20,000	
M+E Mix	16	Hours	1	400	6,400	6,400	
29-17 Dolby License		Allow	1		0	0	
29-18 Miscellaneous Expenses		Allow	1		0	0	
				Total for 29-00			50,400
30-00 Post-Producton - Digital and Film							
30-01 Stock Footage	90	Secs	1	50	4,500	4,500	
30-02 Archive Film/Television Clips		Allow	1		0	0	
30-04 Archival Researcher		Weeks	1		0	0	
30-06 Clearance Supervisor		Weeks	1		0	0	
30-09 Screeners		Allow	1		0	0	
30-11 Film Prints		Allow	1		0	0	
30-12 Miscellaneous Expenses		Allow	1		0	0	
				Total for 30-00			4,500
31-00 Digital Intermediate							

$1 Million Documentary Budget

		Amt.	Units	x	Rate	Sub-Total	Total	
31-01 Digital Intermediate			Allow	1		0	0	
31-02 Hard Drive Purchases		4	Allow	1	400	1,600	1,600	
31-03 Color Grading								
	P3 Color Space	46	Hours	1	500	23,000	23,000	
	Rec 709 Trim Pass	10	Hours	1	300	3,000	3,000	
					Total for 31-00			27,600
32-00 Titling and Graphics								
32-01 Titling							0	
	Opening title-design	1	Allow	1	2,500	2,500	2,500	
	End crawl	1	Allow	1	500	500	500	
32-02 Graphic Designer			Allow	1		0	0	
32-05 Special Graphic Effects			Allow	1		0	0	
32-06 Motion Control			Allow	1		0	0	
32-08 Closed Captioning			Allow	1		0	0	
32-09 Subtitling			Allow	1		0	0	
					Total for 32-00			3,000
33-00 Deliverables								
33-01 Masters/Clones								
	Pan&Scan	8	Hours	1	350	2,800	2,800	
	HDCamSR Master (incl Stock)	1	Allow	1	1,500	1,500	1,500	
	Quality Control	1	Allow	1	1,500	1,500	1,500	
	HD Cam Master 1.78	1	Allow	1	1,500	1,500	1,500	
	HD Cam Clone	1	Allow	1	1,100	1,100	1,100	
	HD Cam Master 1.33	1	Allow	1	1,500	1,500	1,500	
	DVD Master (watermarked)	1	Allow	1	300	300	300	
	DVD Master (clean)	1	Allow	1	300	300	300	
	File deliverables	1	Allow	1	750	750	750	
	Archive deliverables	6	Reels	1	350	2,100	2,100	
	NTSC DBeta 4:3 Full Frame	1	Allow	1	600	600	600	
	PAL DBeta 4:3 Full Frame	1	Allow	1	600	600	600	
	NTSC DBeta 16x9	1	Allow	1	600	600	600	
	PAL DBeta 16x9	1	Allow	1	600	600	600	
	DCP	1	Allow	1	450	450	450	
	DVD copies	10	Allow	1	10	100	100	
33-03 Transfers and Dubs			Allow	1		0	0	
33-05 Screening Copies			Allow	1		0	0	
33-06 Continuity Script		1	Allow	1	1,375	1,375	1,375	
33-07 LTO Archiving								
	LTO Archiving of ProRes Raw	5000	GB	1	0	1,250	1,250	
	LTO Archiving DPX (finished film)	1500	GB	1	0	375	375	
					Total for 33-00			19,300
34-00 Digital Visual Effects/Animation								
34-01 VFX			Allow	1		0	0	
34-07 Animation			Allow	1		0	0	
					Total for 34-00			0
POST-PRODUCTION TOTAL								343,275
35-00 Insurance								
35-01 Producers Entertainment Pckg.								
including workers comp.		1	Allow	1	12,000	12,000	12,000	
Faulty Stock			Allow	1		0	0	
Equipment			Allow	1		0	0	
Props/Sets			Allow	1		0	0	
Extra Expense			Allow	1		0	0	
3rd Party Property Damage			Allow	1		0	0	
Office Contents			Allow	1		0	0	
35-02 General Liability			Allow	1		0	0	
35-03 Hired Auto			Allow	1		0	0	
35-04 Cast Insurance			Allow	1		0	0	
35-05 Workers Compensation			Allow	1		0	0	
35-06 Errors & Omissions		1	Allow	1	5,000	5,000	5,000	
					Total for 35-00			17,000
36-00 General & Administrative Expenses								

$1 Million Documentary Budget

		Amt.	Units	x	Rate	Sub-Total	Total	
36-01 Business License/Taxes		1	Allow	2	850	1,700	1,700	
36-02 Legal		1	Allow	1	17,500	17,500	17,500	
36-03 Accounting fees		1	Allow	2	500	1,000	1,000	
36-05 Telephone/Fax			Allow	1		0	0	
36-06 Copying/Scanning			Allow	1		0	0	
36-07 Postage & Freight			Allow	1		0	0	
36-08 Office Space Rental			Allow	1		0	0	
36-09 Office Furniture			Allow	1		0	0	
36-10 Office Equipment & Supplies		1	Allow	1	750	750	750	
36-11 Computer Rental								
	Line Producer		Weeks	1		0	0	
	First AD		Weeks	1		0	0	
	Prod. Coordinator		Weeks	1		0	0	
	Prod. Accountant		Weeks	1		0	0	
	Office		Months	1		0	0	
	Printers		Months	1		0	0	
36-12 Software/Apps/FTP			Allow	1		0	0	
36-13 Transcription		12	Hours	1	110	1,320	1,320	
36-14 Messenger/Overnight Shipping		12	Allow	1	160	1,920	1,920	
36-15 Parking			Allow	1		0	0	
36-16 Storage			Allow	1		0	0	
36-17 Bank charges		12	Allow	1	50	600	600	
36-18 Publicity			Allow	1		0	0	
	Website Creation	1	Allow	1	2,500	2,500	2,500	
	Social Media Manager	1	Allow	1	3,000	3,000	3,000	
	Trailer production/editing	1	Allow	1	5,000	5,000	5,000	
36-19 Wrap Party			Allow	1		0	0	
36-20 Working Meals		1	Allow	1	1,000	1,000	1,000	
36-21 Overhead (Production fee)			Allow	1		0	0	
36-22 Completion Bond			Allow	1		0	0	
					Total for 36-00			36,290
37-00 Publicity and Marketing								
37-01 Publicity			Allow	1		0	0	
	Film Festival travel costs	1	Allow	1	3,500	3,500	3,500	
37-02 Marketing			Allow	1		0	0	
					Total for 37-00			3,500
Total Above-the-Line								140,000
Total Below-the-Line								769,436
Total Above and Below-the-Line								909,436
Contingency								90,944
	GRAND TOTAL							$1,000,380

02–02 Producer

This is a flat fee for the entire life of the project. She anticipates that the production and post-production for the film will take 2 to 3 years.

03–01 Director

This is a flat fee for the entire life of the project. He is in accord with the Producer and expects to spend 2 to 3 years on the production.

08–01 Field Producer

This person will monitor the budget, hire crew, and coordinate all aspects of production.

08–03 International Fixer

The director anticipates two international shoots — one in the UK and one in Japan. This is money to hire a local person for each country — two weeks prep/wrap and seven days for each shoot.

08–06 Production Accountant

This person will do a cost report monthly and put together the documents for the tax filing.

08–08 Production Assistants

For any shoot days and pickup/returns for other days.

13–06 Grip Rentals

For the days with two cameras, this will allow for rentals for grip equipment.

13–07 Expendables

For gaffers tape, gels, clothespins, etc.

13–10 Craft Service

Snacks for crew on shoot days.

19–01 Gaffer

For the days with two cameras, this is to pay for a gaffer to help light the scenes.

19–06 Lighting Package Rental
For the two-camera days, this is for lighting rentals.

19–10 Kit Rentals
For the Gaffer's Kit Rental.

20–01 Director of Photography
Money is budgeted for a separate cinematographer. If the budget gets tight or if the director wants to shoot more cinema-vérité days, he can shoot the A camera.

20–02 B Camera Operator
Two cameras are planned for 18 of the 28 days. This person will shoot the B camera.

20–05 Digital Imaging Technician (DIT)
For a DIT for all planned shoot days.

20–06 Still Photographer
For a still photographer to take production stills for two days on set. To be used for the press kit.

20–07 Camera Package Rental
This is for the B camera and some lenses for the 18 shoot days. It will be the same type as the A camera so they match. The director wants to do super slo-mo for one day so they have budgeted for a Phantom camera which can do the very high-speed shooting that is necessary to produce a good quality slo-mo image.

20–10 DIT Rental
For the DIT equipment necessary for the shoot days.

20–17 Loss & Damage
For any possible loss or damage to equipment.

20–19 Expendables
For miscellaneous camera expenses like gaffers tape and sharpies.

21–01 Sound Mixer
The director plans to travel the sound recordist for all shoot days — they have worked together on five previous films.

21–02 2nd Mixer
For the 18 days with two cameras.

21–04 Sound Package
For the sound equipment rentals for all shoot days with one or two cameras.

22–03 Minivan Rental
For transport of crew and equipment on shoot days. The director will drive his SUV to set when shooting in the greater New York area.

22–04 Parking/Tolls/Gas
For the transportation expenses.

23–09 Catering Services
For crew lunches for all shoot days. For such a small crew it probably makes sense to go to a local restaurant for lunch depending on the location each day.

25–01 Digital Media
Because it is cinema-vérité, the shooting ratio will be a lot higher than on a narrative feature and they will need to purchase more hard drives and backup hard drives. Shooting ratio corresponds to the proportion of film shot to the amount of film ultimately used in the final master.

26–01 Airfares
This section is for airfare for Director, Sound Recordist, and one other person — either the field producer or the B camera operator. The plan is to fly to five US cities and two cities in the UK and Japan.

26–02 Hotels
Same configuration as above.

26–03 Taxi
For various taxi cab rides.

26–08 Per Diem
Per diem for the crew when on location.

26–10 Airport Transfers
For transfers to and from the airports.

27–01 Editor
For a top documentary editor to edit the film. The director would like to edit for two 5-week periods during production and then a final long edit period to lock picture. That way the edit can inform the direction of the film and allow the director to adjust his decisions as he goes.

27–02 Assistant Editor
There will be a lot of material to "break down" and track. They also plan to use a little bit of stock footage for the final film.

27–04 Post-Production Supervisor
A Post-Production Supervisor will come on just before they lock picture and oversee the post-production finishing and deliverables for the US television network.

27–05 Editing Room Rental
The editor will work from her home edit room.

27–06 Edit System Rental
The editor will rent her computer editing system to the production.

27–08 WIP screening
The producer and director plan to have one work-in-progress screening for trusted colleagues prior to locking picture. This will cover the rental of a screening room with projectionist.

27–10 On-Line Editing/Conform
The editor will do as much as possible of the on-line editing in her system before having it conformed at the Post House.

28–01 Composer Fee

For a composer to create and record the music (including composer fee, musicians' fees, instrument rentals, music editor, and recording costs).

28–11 Music Licensing

This fee is for a few pieces of music for sync and master use licenses.

28–12 Music Supervisor/Clearance

The person will clear the music in the film.

29–01 Sound Editor

The person will edit the multiple audio tracks and oversee the Audio Mix.

29–09 Foley Stage/Editor

For replacement sounds for various audio tracks.

29–15 Audio Mix

To mix the film at an Audio Post facility. They plan to get a flat deal. The M&E mix is part of the deliverables — music and effects separated out on one channel.

30–01 Stock Footage

They plan to use up to 2 minutes of stock footage for one section of the film. This will cover licensing for all territories in perpetuity.

31–02 Hard Drive Purchases

For additional hard drives during post-production.

31–03 Color Grading

For color grading in both P3 and Rec 709 color spaces.

32–01 Titling

The director plans for a very simple opening title sequence plus an end crawl — white letters on black screen are most cost-effective.

33–01 Masters/Clones
For the television sale, they were given a list of deliverables and have bid it out at the Post facility.

33–06 Continuity Script
To hire someone to create the continuity script after picture is locked.

33–07 LTO Archiving
They plan to archive materials and the final master after finishing is complete.

35–01 Production Insurance
The production insurance will cover general liability, auto, and other necessary insurance for the year.

35–06 Errors & Omissions
Because of the US television sale they need to purchase E&O insurance as part of the deliverables to the network.

36–01 Business License/Taxes
The director has an S Corporation already. He'll need to file tax returns.

36–02 Legal
This is a flat deal with an entertainment attorney. The production is fairly straightforward. The license agreements for music and stock footage will need to be negotiated.

36–03 Accounting Fees
To file the tax return.

36–10 Office Equipment & Supplies
For miscellaneous charges.

36–13 Transcription
Most of the film will be cinema-vérité but they plan to do a few sit-down interviews and will get them transcribed.

36–14 Messenger/Overnight Shipping

For messengers and overnight shipping costs.

36–17 Bank Charges

For monthly bank fees, wire transfer fees, and any other fees from the production's bank account.

36–18 Publicity

They plan to create a website, trailer, and hire a social media manager during production to generate interest about the film over the year of production.

36-20 Working Meals

To pay for some meals for key meetings.

37–01 Publicity

This is for Film Festival travel costs and creation of a press kit.

Contingency

The contingency is 10% for this project.

$625K NARRATIVE FEATURE FILM BUDGET TEMPLATE

- Go to *www.mwp.com.*
- Click on "MW Film School."
- Open the item "Sample Budgets/Forms."
- Download the corresponding free Excel Budget Template.
- Save it to your computer.
- Last, this budget is a sample template. Make sure to create your budget with figures based on your research on current rates and prices available to you.

Budget Assumptions

This is a low-budget narrative film shot in the greater New York area for 18 days. The budget is very tight so they will shoot 6-day weeks and use the SAG-AFTRA Modified Low-Budget agreement. They will shoot Digital HD and deliver a DCP and a digital file. The crew is non-union and all have agreed to a very low rate for a 12-hr. day. If they go over 12 hrs. the crew will be paid overtime at 1.5× for the next two hours.

The budget was raised by a crowdfunding campaign, family and friends' money, and a $50,000 grant because the script storyline highlights a social justice theme that is important to this particular foundation. Once they get to a strong cut of the film they can apply for more money from the foundation and there are a few other film-making post-production grants they will be eligible for. The plan is to sell the film after premiering at a prestigious film festival.

$625K Narrative Feature Budget

		SUMMARY BUDGET			
Fringe assumptions:		Production:	$625K Narrative Budget		
Payroll Tax	0.00%	Shoot Days:	18 (6-day weeks)		
WGA	0.00%	Location:	New York, NY		
DGA	0.00%	Unions:	SAG-AFTRA Modified Low Budget		
SAG-AFTRA	17.30%	Shooting Format: Digital HD			
Overtime	10%	Delivery format: DCP and digital file			
Contingency	10%				
01-00 Story & Rights				$15,000	
02-00 Producers Unit				$40,000	
03-00 Direction				$40,000	
04-00 Cast				$60,631	
05-00 Travel & Living – Producers/Director				$0	
06-00 Travel & Living- Cast				$0	
07-00 Residuals				$0	
	TOTAL ABOVE-THE-LINE				$155,631
08-00 Production Staff				$37,055	
09-00 Background Actors/Extras				$5,500	
10-00 Sound Stage				$0	
11-00 Production Design				$12,625	
12-00 Set Construction				$4,400	
13-00 Set Operations				$25,718	
14-00 Special Effects				$0	
15-00 Set Dressing				$17,616	
16-00 Property				$8,188	
17-00 Wardrobe				$14,306	
18-00 Make-Up and Hair				$7,850	
19-00 Electrical				$19,830	
20-00 Camera				$18,865	
21-00 Production Sound				$5,675	
22-00 Transportation				$16,350	
23-00 Location Expenses				$64,925	
24-00 Picture Vehicle/Animals				$1,800	
25-00 Media				$2,000	
26-00 Travel and Living-Crew				$0	
	TOTAL PRODUCTION				$262,703
27-00 Editorial				$26,000	
28-00 Music				$22,500	
29-00 Post-Production Sound				$34,500	
30-00 Post-Production - Digital and Film				$0	
31-00 Digital Intermediate				$1,500	
32-00 Titling and Graphics				$12,000	
33-00 Deliverables				$2,600	
34-00 Digital Visual Effects/Animation				$0	
	TOTAL POST-PRODUCTION				$99,100
35-00 Insurance				$18,000	
36-00 General & Administrative Expenses				$24,350	
37-00 Publicity and Marketing				$9,000	
	TOTAL GENERAL				$51,350
Total Above-the-Line					$155,631
Total Below-the-Line					$413,153
Total Above and Below-the-Line					$568,784
Contingency					$56,878
	GRAND TOTAL				$625,662

$625K Narrative Feature Budget

ABOVE-THE-LINE								
		Amt.	*Units*	*x*	*Rate*	*Sub-Total*	*Total*	
01-00 Story & Rights								
01-01 Rights Purchases			Allow	1		0	0	
01-02 Options			Allow	1		0	0	
01-03 Writer Salaries/Screenplay Purchase		1	Allow	1	15,000	15,000	15,000	
01-04 Research/Clearances			Allow	1		0	0	
01-05 Title Registration			Allow	1		0	0	
01-06 Script Timing			Allow	1		0	0	
01-07 Storyboards/Pre-Viz			Allow	1		0	0	
01-08 WGA Publication fee			Allow	1		0	0	
01-10 Development			Allow	1		0	0	
	Payroll					15,000	0	
	WGA					15,000	0	
					Total for 01-00			**15,000**
02-00 Producers Unit								
02-01 Executive Producer		1	Allow	1	10,000	10,000	10,000	
02-02 Producer		1	Allow	1	30,000	30,000	30,000	
02-03 Associate Producer			Allow	1		0	0	
02-04 Assistant to Producer(s)			Week(s)	1		0	0	
02-06 Consultants			Allow	1		0	0	
02-07 Miscellaneous Expenses			Allow	1		0	0	
	Payroll					40,000	0	
					Total for 02-00			**40,000**
03-00 Direction								
03-01 Director		1	Allow	1	40,000	40,000	40,000	
03-02 Assistant to Director		1	Weeks	1		0	0	
	Payroll					40,000	0	
	DGA					40,000	0	
					Total for 03-00			**40,000**
04-00 Cast								
04-01 Lead Actors								
	Actor #1-Rehearsal	3	Days	1	268	804		
	Actor #1-Shoot	3	Weeks	1	1,201	3,603		
	Actor #2-Rehearsal	3	Days	1	268	804		
	Actor #2-Shoot	3	Weeks	1	1,201	3,603		
	Actor #3-Rehearsal	3	Days	1	268	804		
	Actor #3-Shoot	3	Weeks	1	1,201	3,603		
Overtime Allowance (+30%)			Allow	1	13,221	3,966	17,187	
04-02 Supporting Cast								
	Actor #4-Rehearsal	2	Days	1	268	536		
	Actor #4-Shoot	10	Days	1	268	2,680		
	Actor #5-Rehearsal	1	Day	1	268	268		
	Actor #5-Shoot	5	Days	1	268	1,340		
Overtime Allowance (+30%)			Allow	1	4,824	1,447	6,271	
04-03 Day Players								
	Actor #6	5	Day(s)	1	268	1,340		
	Actor #7	4	Day(s)	1	268	1,072		
	Actor #8	3	Day(s)	1	268	804		
	Actor #9	3	Day(s)	1	268	804		
	Actor #10	2	Day(s)	1	268	536		
	Actor #11	2	Day(s)	1	268	536		
	Actor #12	1	Day(s)	1	268	268		
	Actor #13	2	Day(s)	1	268	536		
	Actor #14	3	Day(s)	1	268	804		
	Actor #15	1	Day(s)	1	268	268		
Overtime Allowance (+30%)			Allow	1	6,968	2,090	9,058	
04-04 Casting Director/Staff		1	Allow	1	7,500	7,500	7,500	
04-05 Casting Expenses			Allow	1		0	0	
04-06 Choreographer			Weeks	1		0	0	

$625K Narrative Feature Budget

		Amt.	Units	x	Rate	Sub-Total	Total	
04-07 Assistant(s) to Choreographer			Weeks	1		0	0	
04-08 Dialect Coach			Weeks	1		0	0	
04-09 Narrator/Voiceover Artist			Weeks	1		0	0	
04-10 Stunt Coordinator		1	Flat	1	859	859	859	
04-11 Stunt Players		1	Day	2	268	536	536	
04-12 Stunt Costs/Adjustments			Allow	1		0	0	
04-13 Stunt Equipment		1	Allow	1	500	500	500	
04-14 ADR (Actors' fees)		5	Days	1	268	1,340	1,340	
	Payroll (SAG-AFTRA only)					35,252	7,755	
	SAG-AFTRA					35,252	6,099	
	Agency fees (10%)						3,525	
					Total for 04-00			60,631
05-00 Travel & Living – Producers/Director								
05-01 Airfares			RT	1		0	0	
05-02 Hotel			Nights	1		0	0	
05-03 Taxi/Limo			Allow	1		0	0	
05-04 Auto			Allow	1		0	0	
05-05 Train			Allow	1		0	0	
05-06 Excess Baggage			Allow	1		0	0	
05-07 Phone			Allow	1		0	0	
05-08 Gratuities			Allow	1		0	0	
05-09 Per Diem			Days	1		0	0	
					Total for 05-00			0
06-00 Travel & Living- Cast								
06-01 Airfares			RT	1		0	0	
06-02 Hotels			Nights	1		0	0	
06-03 Taxi/Limo			Allow	1		0	0	
06-04 Auto			Allow	1		0	0	
06-05 Train			Allow	1		0	0	
06-06 Excess Baggage			Allow	1		0	0	
06-07 Phone			Allow	1		0	0	
06-08 Gratuities			Allow	1		0	0	
06-09 Per Diem			Days	1		0	0	
					Total for 06-00			0
07-00 Residuals			Allow	1		0	0	
					Total for 07-00			0
TOTAL ABOVE-THE -LINE								155,631

$625K Narrative Feature Budget

		Amt.	Units	x	Rate	Sub-Total	Total	
BELOW-THE-LINE								
08-00 Production Staff								
08-01 Unit Production Manager								
	Prep/Travel	8	Weeks	1	750	6,000		
	Shoot	3	Weeks	1	750	2,250		
	Wrap	2	Weeks	1	750	1,500		
	Severance		Allow	1		0	9,750	
08-02 Assistant Directors								
1st AD								
	Prep/Travel	2	Weeks	1	750	1,500		
	Shoot	3	Weeks	1	750	2,250		
	Prod. Fee (shoot days)		Days	1		0		
	Severance		Allow	1		0		
	Overtime Allow		Days	1		0	3,750	
2nd AD								
	Prep/Travel	3	Days	1	125	375		
	Shoot	3	Weeks	1	625	1,875		
	Prod. Fee		Days	1		0		
	Severance		Allow	1		0		
	Overtime Allow		Days	1		0	2,250	
08-03 Stage Manager								
	Prep/Travel		Weeks	1		0		
	Shoot		Weeks	1		0		
	Prod. Fee		Days	1		0		
	Severance		Allow	1		0		
	Overtime Allow		Days	1		0	0	
08-04 Production Coordinator								
	Prep/Travel	8	Weeks	1	625	5,000		
	Shoot	3	Weeks	1	625	1,875		
	Wrap	1	Weeks	1	625	625	7,500	
Ass't Coord.								
	Prep		Weeks	1		0		
	Shoot		Weeks	1		0		
	Wrap		Weeks	1		0	0	
08-05 Script Supervisor								
	Prep	1	Days	1	150	150		
	Shoot	3	Weeks	1	750	2,250		
	Saturdays Worked		Days	1		0		
	Wrap	1	Days	1	150	150		
	2nd Camera Days		Days	1		0		
	Overtime		Allow		2,550	255	2,805	
08-06 Production Accountant/Auditor								
	Prep/Travel		Weeks	1		0		
	Shoot		Weeks	1		0		
	Wrap		Weeks	1		0		
	Post-Production		Weeks	1		0	0	
Assistant Accountant								
	Prep/Travel		Weeks	1		0		
	Shoot		Weeks	1		0		
	Wrap		Weeks	1		0	0	
08-07 Technical Advisors			Flat	1		0	0	
08-08 Production Assistants								
Office Prod. Assistant(s)								
	Prep	1	Week	1	500	500		
	Shoot	3	Weeks	1	500	1,500		
	Wrap	2	Days	1	100	200		
Set Prod. Assistant(s)								
	Prep/Wrap	1.4	Weeks	4	500	2,800		
	Shoot	3	Weeks	4	500	6,000	11,000	
08-09 Studio Teacher/Tutor			Weeks	1		0	0	
	Payroll					37,055	0	
	DGA					15,750	0	
					Total for 08-00			37,055

$625K Narrative Feature Budget

		Amt.	*Units*	*x*	*Rate*	*Sub-Total*	*Total*	
09-00 Background Actors/Extras								
09-01 Stand-ins			Days	1		0	0	
09-02 Extras	(non-union)	50	Extras	1	100	5,000	5,000	
09-05 Extras Casting Fee @ 10%			Allow	1	5,000	500	500	
09-10 Extras Transportation			Allow	1		0	0	
	Payroll					5,000	0	
	P&H					5,000	0	
					Total for 09-00			5,500
10-00 Sound Stage								
10-01 Stage Rental			Allow	1		0	0	
	Prep		Allow	1		0	0	
	Pre-Light		Allow	1		0	0	
	Shoot		Allow	1		0	0	
	Wrap		Allow	1		0	0	
	Overtime		Allow	1		0	0	
10-02 Stage Lighting Rental			Allow	1		0	0	
10-03 Stage Grip Rental			Allow	1		0	0	
10-04 Phones/ Internet			Allow	1		0	0	
10-05 Garbage removal			Allow	1		0	0	
10-06 Green Room			Allow	1		0	0	
10-07 Make Up Room			Allow	1		0	0	
10-08 Office Rental			Allow	1		0	0	
10-09 Parking			Allow	1		0	0	
					Total for 10-00			0
11-00 Production Design								
11-01 Production Designer								
	Prep/Travel	5	Weeks	1	750	3,750		
	Shoot	3	Weeks	1	750	2,250		
	Wrap	1	Weeks	1	750	750	6,750	
11-02 Art Director								
	Prep/Wrap	4	Weeks	1	625	2,500		
	Shoot	3	Weeks	1	625	1,875	4,375	
11-03 Art Assistants								
	Prep/Travel		Days	1		0		
	Shoot		Days	1		0	0	
11-04 Set Designer								
	Prep/Travel		Weeks	1		0		
	Shoot		Weeks	1		0	0	
11-05 Model Makers/Miniatures			Allow	1		0	0	
11-06 Draftsperson			Allow	1		0	0	
11-08 Research/Materials		1	Allow	1	500	500	500	
11-09 Vehicle Expenses			Weeks	1		0	0	
11-10 Purchases/Rentals		1	Allow	1	1,000	1,000	1,000	
	Payroll					11,125	0	
					Total for 11-00			12,625
12-00 Set Construction								
12-01 Construction Coordinator								
	Prep		Days	1		0		
	Shoot		Days	1		0		
	Overtime		Allow	1	0	0	0	
12-02 Foreman								
	Prep	5	Days	1	150	750		
	Shoot		Days	1		0		
	Overtime		Allow	1	750	75	825	
Carpenters		5	Allow	2	125	1,250	1,250	
12-03 Scenic Painters								
Lead Scenic Painter								
	Prep	5	Days	1	150	750		
	Shoot		Days	1		0		
	Overtime		Allow	1	750	75	825	
Painters			Allow	1		0	0	

$625K Narrative Feature Budget

		Amt.	Units	x	Rate	Sub-Total	Total	
12-05 Greensmen			Allow	1		0	0	
12-06 Construction materials - Purchases		1	Allow	1	500	500	500	
12-07 Construction materials - Rentals		1	Allow	1	1,000	1,000	1,000	
12-08 Construction Equipment			Allow	1		0	0	
12-09 Set Strike			Allow	1		0	0	
	Payroll					2,900	0	
					Total for 12-00			4,400
13-00 Set Operations								
13-01 Key Grip								
	Prep/Scout	2	Days	1	150	300		
	Shoot	3	Weeks	1	750	2,250		
	Wrap		Days	1		0		
	Overtime		Allow	1	2,550	255	2,805	
13-02 Best Boy Grip								
	Prep		Days	1		0		
	Shoot	3	Weeks	1	625	1,875		
	Wrap		Days	1		0		
	Overtime		Allow	1	1,875	188	2,063	
13-03 Grips								
3rd Grip								
	Prep		Days	1		0		
	Shoot	2	Weeks	1	625	1,250		
	Wrap		Days	1		0		
	Overtime		Allow	1	1,250	125	1,375	
4th Grip								
	Prep		Days	1		0		
	Shoot		Days	1		0		
	Wrap		Days	1		0		
	Overtime		Allow	1	0	0	0	
Additional Grips			Days	1		0		
	Overtime		Allow	1		0	0	
13-04 Dolly Grip								
	Prep		Days	1		0		
	Shoot	3	Weeks	1	750	2,250		
	Overtime		Allow	1	2,250	225	2,475	
13-06 Grip Rentals								
	Package	3	Weeks	1	3,000	9,000		
	Dollies	3	Weeks	1	1,200	3,600		
	Cranes (incl. Driver)		Days	1		0		
	Add'l Equip.		Allow	1		0	12,600	
13-07 Expendables		1	Allow	1	500	500	500	
13-08 Kit Rentals								
	Key Grip		Weeks	1		0	0	
	Craft Service		Weeks	1		0	0	
13-10 Craft Service								
	Prep		Days	1		0		
	Shoot		Days	1		0		
	Wrap		Days	1		0		
	Overtime		Allow	1	0	0	0	
Purchases		18	Days	1	175	3,150	3,150	
Rentals - Tables & Chairs		3	Weeks	1	250	750	750	
13-15 Air Conditioning/Heating			Days	1		0	0	
	Payroll					8,718	0	
					Total for 13-00			25,718
14-00 Special Effects								
14-01 Special Effects Person								
	Prep/Travel		Days	1		0		
	Shoot		Days	1		0		
	Overtime		Allow	1	0	0	0	
14-02 SFX Assistant(s)								
	Shoot		Days	1		0		
	Overtime		Allow	1	0	0	0	

$625K Narrative Feature Budget

		Amt.	Units	x	Rate	Sub-Total	Total	
14-03 Additional Labor								
	Shoot		Days	1		0		
	Overtime		Allow	1	0	0	0	
14-06 Manufacturing Labor			Allow	1		0	0	
14-07 Fabrication			Allow	1		0	0	
14-09 Rentals			Allow	1		0	0	
	Payroll				0	0	0	
					Total for 14-00			0
15-00 Set Dressing								
15-01 Set Decorator								
	Prep/Travel	4	Weeks	1	625	2,500		
	Shoot	3	Weeks	1	625	1,875		
	Wrap	0.5	Weeks	1	625	313		
	Overtime				4,688	469	5,156	
15-02 Lead Person								
	Prep/Travel		Days	1		0		
	Shoot		Days	1		0		
	Wrap		Days	1		0		
	Overtime				0	0	0	
15-03 Set Dressers								
Set Dresser #1								
	Prep	3	Days	1	100	300		
	Shoot	3	Weeks	1	500	1,500		
	Wrap		Days	1		0		
	Overtime				1,800	180	1,980	
Set Dresser #2								
	Prep		Days	1		0		
	Shoot		Days	1		0		
	Wrap		Days	1		0		
	Overtime				0	0	0	
Set Dresser #3								
	Prep		Days	1		0		
	Shoot		Days	1		0		
	Wrap		Days	1		0		
	Overtime				0	0	0	
15-04 Additional Labor								
On-Set Dresser (Shoot)		18	Days	1	100	1,800		
	Overtime				1,800	180	1,980	
15-05 Expendables		1	Allow	1	500	500	500	
15-06 Purchases		1	Allow	1	4,000	4,000	4,000	
15-07 Rentals		1	Allow	1	4,000	4,000	4,000	
15-08 Loss & Damage			Allow	1		0	0	
15-09 Kit Rentals						0	0	
	Set Decorator		Weeks	1		0	0	
	Lead Person		Weeks	1		0	0	
15-10 Vehicle Expenses								
	Set Decorator		Weeks	1		0	0	
	Lead Person		Weeks	1		0	0	
	Payroll				9,116	0	0	
					Total for 15-00			17,616
16-00 Property								
16-01 Property Master								
	Prep/Travel	4	Weeks	1	750	3,000		
	Shoot	3	Weeks	1	750	2,250		
	Wrap	0.5	Weeks	1	750	375		
	Overtime				5,625	563	6,188	
16-02 Prop Assistant								
	Prep		Days	1		0		
	Shoot		Days	1		0		
	Wrap		Days	1		0		
	Overtime				0	0	0	

$625K Narrative Feature Budget

		Amt.	Units	x	Rate	Sub-Total	Total	
16-03 Purchases		1	Allow	1	1,000	1,000	1,000	
16-04 Rentals		1	Allow	1	1,000	1,000	1,000	
16-05 Loss & Damage			Allow	1		0	0	
16-06 Kit Rentals								
	Prop Master		Weeks			0	0	
16-07 Vehicle Expenses								
	Prop Master		Weeks	1		0	0	
	Assistant		Weeks	1		0	0	
	Payroll				6,188	0	0	
					Total for 16-00			8,188
17-00 Wardrobe								
17-01 Costume Designer								
	Prep/Travel	4	Weeks	1	750	3,000		
	Shoot	3	Weeks	1	750	2,250		
	Wrap		Week	1		0	5,250	
17-02 Costumer								
	Prep/Travel		Days	1		0		
	Shoot		Days	1		0		
	Wrap		Days	1		0		
	Overtime		Allow	1	0	0	0	
17-03 Additional Costumer(s)								
	Prep		Days	1		0		
	Shoot	3	Weeks	1	625	1,875		
	Wrap	0.5	Weeks	1	625	313		
	Overtime		Allow	1	2,188	219	2,406	
17-04 Expendables			Allow	1		0	0	
17-05 Purchases		1	Allow	1	2,000	2,000	2,000	
17-06 Rentals		1	Allow	1	2,000	2,000	2,000	
17-07 Alteration & Repairs		1	Allow	1	1,250	1,250	1,250	
17-08 Cleaning & Dyeing		1	Allow	1	1,250	1,250	1,250	
17-09 Loss & Damage			Allow	1		0	0	
17-10 Kit Rentals								
	Costume Designer	3	Weeks	1	50	150	150	
17-11 Vehicle Expenses								
	Costume Designer		Weeks	1		0	0	
	Payroll				7,656	0	0	
					Total for 17-00			14,306
18-00 Make-Up and Hair								
18-01 Key Make-Up Artist								
	Prep	0.5	Weeks	1	750	375		
	Shoot	3	Weeks	1	750	2,250		
	Wrap		Days	1		0		
	Overtime		Allow	1	2,625	263	2,888	
18-02 Additional Make-Up Artist(s)			Days	1		0		
	Shoot	10	Days	1	125	1,250		
	Overtime		Allow	1	1,250	125	1,375	
18-03 Key Hair Stylist								
	Prep/Travel	0.5	Weeks	1	750	375		
	Shoot	3	Weeks	1	750	2,250		
	Wrap		Days	1		0		
	Overtime		Allow	1	2,625	263	2,888	
18-04 Additional Hair Stylist(s)			Days	1		0		
	Shoot		Days	1		0		
	Overtime		Allow	1	0	0	0	
18-05 Special Effects Makeup Effects			Allow	1		0	0	
18-06 Purchases			Allow	1		0	0	
18-07 Rentals			Weeks	1		0	0	
18-08 Kit Rentals								
	Key Make-Up	3	Weeks	1	100	300	300	
	Add'l Make-Up	10	Days	1	10	100	100	
	Hair Stylist	3	Weeks	1	100	300	300	
	Add'l Hair		Days	1		0	0	
	Payroll				7,150	0	0	

$625K Narrative Feature Budget

		Amt.	Units	x	Rate	Sub-Total	Total	
					Total for 18-00			7,850
19-00 Electrical								
19-01 Gaffer								
	Prep/Scout	2	Days	1	150	300		
	Shoot	3	Weeks	1	750	2,250		
	Wrap/Travel		Days	1		0		
	Overtime		Allow	1	2,550	255	2,805	
19-02 Best Boy Electric								
	Prep	1	Days	1	125	125		
	Shoot	3	Weeks	1	625	1,875		
	Wrap		Days	1		0		
	Overtime		Allow	1	2,000	200	2,200	
19-03 Electrics								
3rd Electric								
	Prep		Days	1		0		
	Shoot		Days	1		0		
	Wrap		Days	1		0		
	Overtime		Allow	1	0	0	0	
4th Electric								
	Prep		Days	1		0		
	Shoot		Days	1		0		
	Wrap		Days	1		0		
	Overtime		Allow	1	0	0	0	
19-04 Additional Labor								
	Shoot	10	Days	1	125	1,250		
	Overtime		Allow	1	1,250	125	1,375	
19-05 Equipment Purchases			Allow	1		0	0	
19-06 Lighting Package Rental		3	Weeks	1	2,900	8,700	8,700	
	Add'l Equip.		Allow	1		0	0	
	Condors		Allow	1		0	0	
	Additional Generator		Days	1		0	0	
19-07 Additional Rentals			Allow	1		0	0	
19-08 Electrical Generator + Driver		5	Days	1	800	4,000	4,000	
19-09 Loss & Damage		1	Allow	1	750	750	750	
19-10 Kit Rentals								
	Gaffer		Weeks	1		0	0	
	Payroll				6,380	0	0	
					Total for 19-00			19,830
20-00 Camera								
20-01 Director of Photography								
	Prep/Travel	2	Weeks	1	750	1,500		
	Shoot	3	Weeks	1	750	2,250	3,750	
20-02 Camera Operator or B Camera								
	Prep/Travel		Days	1		0		
	Shoot	10	Days	1	125	1,250		
	Overtime		Allow	1	1,250	125	1,375	
20-03 1st Assistant Camera								
	Prep	1	Days	1	150	150		
	Shoot	3	Weeks	1	750	2,250		
	Wrap		Days	1		0		
	Overtime		Allow	1	2,400	240		
	B Cam 1st Ass't		Days	1		0	2,640	
	Overtime		Allow	1	0	0	0	
20-04 2nd Ass't Camera								
	Prep		Days	1		0		
	Shoot		Days	1		0		
	Wrap		Days	1		0		
	Overtime		Allow	1	0	0	0	
	B Cam 2nd Ass't		Days	1		0		
	Overtime		Allow	1	0	0	0	
20-05 Digital Imaging Technician (DIT)		3	Weeks	1	750	2,250	2,250	
20-06 Still Photographer		2	Days	1	150	300	300	

$625K Narrative Feature Budget

		Amt.	Units	x	Rate	Sub-Total	Total	
20-07 Camera Package Rental		3	Weeks	1	2,250	6,750	6,750	
20-10 Camera Package Purchase		1	Allow	1	1,000	1,000	1,000	
20-11 Steadicam Operator & Equip.			Days	1		0	0	
20-12 Teleprompter/Operator			Days	1		0	0	
20-13 Video Assist/Operator			Days	1		0	0	
20-14 Aerial Photography			Days	1		0	0	
20-15 Underwater and Topside Photography			Days	1		0	0	
20-16 Drones/GoPros			Days	1		0	0	
20-17 Maintenance/Loss & Damage		1	Allow	1	500	500	500	
20-18 Motion Control			Allow	1		0	0	
20-19 Expendables			Weeks	1		0	0	
20-20 Video Truck			Weeks	1		0	0	
20-25 Video Truck Crew			Weeks	1		0	0	
20-26 Kit Rentals								
	1st Ass't Cam	3	Weeks	1	100	300	300	
	Payroll				10,315	0	0	
					Total for 20-00			18,865
21-00 Production Sound								
21-01 Mixer								
	Prep		Days	1		0		
	Shoot	3	Weeks	1	750	2,250		
	Wrap/Travel		Days	1		0		
	Overtime		Allow	1	2,250	225	2,475	
21-02 Boom Operator								
	Shoot		Days	1		0		
	Overtime		Allow	1	0	0	0	
21-03 Expendables/Batteries		1	Allow	1	200	200	200	
21-04 Sound Package		3	Weeks	1	750	2,250	2,250	
21-05 Walkie-Talkies		3	Weeks	1	250	750	750	
21-06 Sound Truck			Weeks	1		0	0	
21-08 Misc. / Loss & Damage			Allow	1		0	0	
	Payroll				2,475	0	0	
					Total for 21-00			5,675
22-00 Transportation								
22-01 Transportation Coordinator								
			Weeks	1		0	0	
22-02 Drivers								
Captain								
	Prep		Days	1		0		
	Shoot		Days	1		0		
	Wrap		Days	1		0	0	
Star Trailer Drivers								
Driver #1								
	Prep		Day	1		0		
	Shoot		Days	1		0		
	Wrap		Day	1		0	0	
Driver #2								
	Prep		Day	1		0		
	Shoot		Days	1		0		
	Wrap		Day	1		0	0	
Production Van Driver								
	Prep		Days	1		0		
	Shoot		Days	1		0		
	Wrap		Days	1		0	0	
Camera Truck Driver								
	Prep		Days	1		0		
	Shoot		Days	1		0		
	Wrap		Days	1		0	0	
Stakebed Driver (Construction)								
	Shoot		Days	1		0	0	
Set Dressing Driver								
	Prep		Days	1		0		
	Shoot		Days	1		0		

$625K Narrative Feature Budget

		Amt.	Units	x	Rate	Sub-Total	Total	
	Wrap		Days	1		0	0	
Second Set Dressing 5 Ton			Days	1		0	0	
Props Driver								
	Prep		Days	1		0		
	Shoot		Days	1		0		
	Wrap		Days	1		0	0	
Make-Up/Wardrobe Driver								
	Prep		Days	1		0		
	Shoot		Days	1		0		
	Wrap		Days	1		0	0	
Prod. Office Trailer Driver								
	Prep		Days	1		0		
	Shoot		Days	1		0		
	Wrap		Days	1		0	0	
Honeywagon Driver								
	Shoot		Days	1		0		
	Wrap		Days	1		0	0	
15-Passenger Van #1 Driver								
	Prep		Days	1		0		
	Shoot		Days	1		0	0	
15-Passenger Van #2 Driver								
	Prep		Days	1		0		
	Shoot		Days	1		0	0	
Car Carrier			Days	1		0	0	
Insert Car (car to car-cam platform)			Days	1		0	0	
Water Truck Driver			Days	1		0	0	
Caterer	Shoot		Days	1		0	0	
Caterer Ass't	Shoot		Days	1		0	0	
Additional Drivers			Allow	1		0	0	
22-03 Transportation Vehicle Rental								
Star Dressing Trailers			Weeks	1		0	0	
Crew Cab			Weeks	1		0	0	
Production Van		4	Weeks	1	750	3,000	3,000	
Camera Van		3.4	Weeks	1	750	2,550	2,550	
			Weeks	1		0	0	
Art 5 Ton Truck		4	Weeks	1	750	3,000	3,000	
Add'l Set Dressing 5 Ton			Weeks	1		0	0	
Set Dress Van			Weeks	1		0	0	
Props 5 Ton			Weeks	1		0	0	
Wardrobe/Make-Up			Weeks	1		0	0	
Crew Stake Bed			Weeks	1		0	0	
Prod. Office Trailer			Weeks	1		0	0	
Honeywagon (Portable Toilets)			Days	1		0	0	
Water Truck			Days	1		0	0	
Gas Truck			Days	1		0	0	
15-Passenger Van		2	Weeks	2	750	3,000	3,000	
Car Tow Trailer			Days	1		0	0	
Car Trailer			Days	1		0	0	
Camera Car			Days	1		0	0	
22-04 Parking/Tolls/Gas		24	Allow	1	200	4,800	4,800	
22-05 Repairs & Maintenance			Allow	1		0	0	
22-06 Honeywagon Pumping			Allow	1		0	0	
22-07 Miscellaneous			Allow	1		0	0	
	Payroll				0	0	0	
					Total for 22-00			16,350
23-00 Location Expenses								
23-01 Location Manager								
	Scout	4	Weeks	1	750	3,000	3,000	
	Shoot	3	Weeks	1	750	2,250	2,250	
23-02 Location Assistants								
Assistant Location Mgr.			Weeks	1		0	0	
Local Contact Person			Weeks	1		0	0	
23-03 First Aid/Medic		18	Days	1	150	2,700	2,700	
23-04 Fire Officers								

$625K Narrative Feature Budget

		Amt.	Units	x	Rate	Sub-Total	Total	
	Shoot		Days	1		0	0	
23-05 Security			Allow	1		0	0	
23-06 Police			Days	1		0	0	
	Additional Police		Allow	1		0	0	
23-07 Permits		1	Allow	1	300	300	300	
23-08 Parking		1	Allow	1	1,000	1,000	1,000	
23-09 Catering Services								
Crew Meals		18	Days	35	25	15,750	15,750	
Extras		10	Days	10	15	1,500	1,500	
Ice/Propane			Weeks	1		0	0	
2nd Meals			Days	1		0	0	
Sales Tax			Allow	1		0	0	
Tables & Chairs		3	Weeks	1	400	1,200	1,200	
23-11 Location Office Space Rental			Months	1		0	0	
23-12 Location Supplies		1	Allow	1	350	350	350	
23-13 Location Office Equipment			Allow	1		0	0	
23-14 Location Office Telephone/Fax			Allow	1		0	0	
23-17 Location Site Rental Fees								
	Shoot	18	Days	1	2,000	36,000	36,000	
23-18 Location Scout			Allow	1		0	0	
	Photos		Allow	1		0	0	
23-19 Auto Rentals								
Location Manager-Reimbursement		7	Weeks	1	125	875	875	
Assistants			Weeks	1		0	0	
23-20 Miscellaneous Expenses								
	Mileage/DGA/SAG/Crew		Allow	1		0	0	
	Payroll				7,950	0	0	
					Total for 23-00			64,925
24-00 Picture Vehicles/Animals								
24-01 Animal Trainers								
Boss Wrangler			Weeks	1		0	0	
Assistant Wrangler			Weeks	1		0	0	
Wranglers			Week	1		0	0	
Riders/Handlers, etc			Day	1		0	0	
24-02 Animals								
	Horses		Allow	1		0	0	
Veterinary Expenses			Allow	1		0	0	
Feed/Shelter			Allow	1		0	0	
Transportation			Allow	1		0	0	
24-03 Picture Cars								
	Motorcycle	4	Days	1	300	1,200	1,200	
	Police Car	2	Days	1	300	600	600	
	Car #3		Weeks	1		0	0	
	Background Cars		Days	1		0	0	
	Payroll				0	0	0	
					Total for 24-00			1,800
25-00 Media								
25-01 Digital Media		4	Each	1	500	2,000	2,000	
25-02 Raw Film Stock			Feet	1		0	0	
25-03 Film Lab-Negative Prep & Process			Feet	1		0	0	
25-04 Telecine/Film to Digital transfer			Allow	1		0	0	
25-05 Videotape stock			Each	1		0	0	
					Total for 25-00			2,000
26-00 Travel and Living - Crew								
26-01 Airfares			Fares	1		0	0	
28-02 Hotels			Nites	1		0	0	
28-03 Taxi			Allow	1		0	0	
28-04 Auto			Days	1		0	0	
28-05 Train			RT	1		0	0	
28-06 Excess Baggage			Allow	1		0	0	
28-08 Per Diem			Days	1		0	0	
28-09 Gratuities			Days	1		0	0	
					Total for 26-00			0

$625K Narrative Feature Budget

	Amt.	Units	x	Rate	Sub-Total	Total	
TOTAL PRODUCTION							262,703
27-00 Editorial							
27-01 Editor - Shoot/Post	16	Weeks	1	1,000	16,000	16,000	
27-02 Assistant Editor - Shoot/Post	5	Weeks	1	750	3,750	3,750	
27-04 Post-Production Supervisor	3	Weeks	1	750	2,250	2,250	
27-05 Editing Room Rental-At Home		Weeks	1		0	0	
27-06 Edit System Rental	16	Weeks	1	250	4,000	4,000	
27-10 On-Line Editing/Conform		Days	1		0	0	
Payroll				22,000	0	0	
				Total for 27-00			26,000
28-00 Music							
28-01 Composer Fee	1	Allow	1	12,500	12,500	12,500	
28-02 Musicians		Allow	1		0	0	
28-03 Music Prep		Allow	1		0	0	
28-04 Studio Costs		Allow	1		0	0	
28-05 Music Scoring Stage		Allow	1		0	0	
28-06 Cartage and Rentals		Allow	1		0	0	
28-07 Music Mix Room		Allow	1		0	0	
28-08 Singers		Allow	1		0	0	
28-09 Payroll Service		Allow	1		0	0	
28-10 Miscellaneous		Allow	1		0	0	
28-11 Music Licensing	1	Allow	1	7,500	7,500	7,500	
28-12 Music Supervisor/Clearance	1	Allow	1	2,500	2,500	2,500	
				Total for 28-00			22,500
29-00 Post-Production Sound							
29-01 Sound Editor	2	Weeks	1	2,500	5,000	5,000	
29-02 Assistant Sound Editor	2	Weeks	1	1,500	3,000	3,000	
29-03 Music Editor		Weeks	1		0	0	
29-04 Dialogue Editor		Weeks	1		0	0	
29-05 Spotting (Music & FX)		Hours	1		0	0	
29-08 ADR (Studio/Editor)	2	Days	1	2,500	5,000	5,000	
29-09 Foley Stage/Editor	1	Allow	1	5,500	5,500	5,500	
29-10 Foley Artists		Days	1		0	0	
29-12 Narration Recording		Hours	1		0	0	
29-13 Audio Laydown		Hours	1		0	0	
29-15 Audio Mix	1	Flat	1	16,000	16,000	16,000	
29-17 Dolby License		Allow	1		0	0	
29-18 Miscellaneous Expenses		Allow	1		0	0	
				Total for 29-00			34,500
30-00 Post-Producton - Digital and Film							
30-01 Stock Footage		Reels	1		0	0	
30-02 Archive Film/Television Clips		Allow	1		0	0	
30-04 Archival Researcher		Weeks	1		0	0	
30-06 Clearance Supervisor		Weeks	1		0	0	
30-09 Screeners		Allow	1		0	0	
30-11 Film Prints		Allow	1		0	0	
30-12 Miscellaneous Expenses		Allow	1		0	0	
				Total for 30-00			0
31-00 Digital Intermediate							
31-01 Digital Intermediate		Allow	1		0	0	
31-02 Hard Drive Purchases	1	Allow	1	1,500	1,500	1,500	
				Total for 31-00			1,500
32-00 Titling and Graphics							
32-01 Titling	1	Allow	1	4,000	4,000	4,000	
32-02 Graphic Designer	1	Allow	1	8,000	8,000	8,000	
32-05 Special Graphic Effects		Allow	1		0	0	
32-06 Motion Control		Allow	1		0	0	
32-08 Closed Captioning		Allow	1		0	0	
32-09 Subtitling		Allow	1		0	0	

$625K Narrative Feature Budget

		Amt.	Units	x	Rate	Sub-Total	Total	
					Total for 32-00			12,000
33-00 Deliverables								
33-01 Masters/Clones		1	Allow	1	2,500	2,500	2,500	
33-03 Transfers and Dubs			Allow	1		0	0	
33-05 Screening Copies		1	Allow	1	100	100	100	
					Total for 33-00			2,600
34-00 Digital Visual Effects/Animation								
34-01 VFX			Allow	1		0	0	
34-07 Animation			Allow	1		0	0	
					Total for 34-00			0
POST-PRODUCTION TOTAL								99,100
35-00 Insurance								
35-01 Producers Entertainment Pckg.								
Media/Negative			Allow	1		0	0	
Faulty Stock			Allow	1		0	0	
Equipment			Allow	1		0	0	
Props/Sets			Allow	1		0	0	
Extra Expense			Allow	1		0	0	
3rd Party Property Damage			Allow	1		0	0	
Office Contents			Allow	1		0	0	
35-02 General Liability		1	Allow	1	11,000	11,000	11,000	
35-03 Hired Auto		1	Allow	1	2,000	2,000	2,000	
35-04 Cast Insurance			Allow	1		0	0	
35-05 Workers Compensation		1	Allow	1	1,000	1,000	1,000	
35-06 Errors & Omissions		1	Allow	1	4,000	4,000	4,000	
					Total for 35-00			18,000
36-00 General & Administrative Expenses								
36-01 Business License/Taxes		1	Allow	1	1,000	1,000	1,000	
36-02 Legal		1	Allow	1	7,500	7,500	7,500	
36-03 Accounting Fees		1	Allow	1	2,000	2,000	2,000	
36-05 Telephone/Fax			Allow	1		0	0	
36-06 Copying/Scanning		1	Allow	1	1,000	1,000	1,000	
36-07 Postage & Freight			Allow	1		0	0	
36-08 Office Space Rental		2	Months	1	2,500	5,000	5,000	
36-09 Office Furniture		2	Months	1	1,500	3,000	3,000	
36-10 Office Equipment & Supplies		2	Months	1	700	1,400	1,400	
36-11 Computer Rental								
	Line Producer		Weeks	1		0	0	
	First AD		Weeks	1		0	0	
	Prod. Coordinator		Weeks	1		0	0	
	Prod. Accountant		Weeks	1		0	0	
	Office		Months	1		0	0	
	Printers		Months	1		0	0	
36-12 Software/Apps/FTP		1	Allow	1	500	500	500	
36-13 Transcription			Hours	1		0	0	
36-14 Messenger/Overnight Shipping		1	Allow	1	1,200	1,200	1,200	
36-15 Parking			Allow	1		0	0	
36-16 Storage		1	Allow	1	750	750	750	
36-18 Publicity			Allow	1		0	0	
36-19 Wrap Party			Allow	1		0	0	
36-20 Working Meals		1	Allow	1	1,000	1,000	1,000	
36-21 Overhead (Production fee)			Allow	1		0	0	
36-22 Completion Bond			Allow	1		0	0	
					Total for 36-00			24,350
37-00 Publicity and Marketing								
37-01 Publicity		1	Allow	1	9,000	9,000	9,000	
37-02 Marketing			Allow	1		0	0	
					Total for 37-00			9,000
Total Above-the-Line								$155,631
Total Below-the-Line								$413,153
Total Above and Below-the-Line								$568,784
		Amt.	Units	x	Rate	Sub-Total	Total	
Contingency								$56,878
	GRAND TOTAL							$625,662

01–03 Screenplay Purchase
The two non-WGA co-writers will split this nominal fee for the script.

02–01 Executive Producer
This fee is for the Executive Producer who raised 50% of the budget. She really loved the script and wants to make sure that the film gets produced.

02–02 Producer
This is a flat fee for the producer who will work as Line Producer as well.

03–01 Director
This is the director's first film. He'll take a flat fee through the entire project till the end of post-production.

04–01 thru 04–03 Lead Actors, Supporting Cast, and Day Players
These rates are scale for rehearsal, shoot, and overtime under the Modified Low-Budget SAG-AFTRA agreement.

04–04 Casting Director
This is a low rate for the Casting Director. She has been an assistant to a major NYC Casting Director for three years and has started her own business. This will be her first feature.

04–10 and 4–11 Stunt Coordinator and Stunt Players
There is a motorcycle crash that will be shot in one day on a closed down road in Harlem. This is for the SAG-AFTRA scale rates for the stunt.

04–13 Stunt Equipment
They will need to rent some safety equipment.

04–14 ADR (Actors' fees)
For a few actors to record ADR in post-production.

08–01 Unit Production Manager

This fee will cover prep, shoot, and wrap for the film. The non-union crew rates are quite low. It's MFN (most favored nations) so everyone is getting the same low rate depending if they are the Key Department Head, Second or Third in any given department.

08–02 1st and 2nd Directors

For prep and shoot on the film.

08–04 Production Coordinator

For prep, shoot, and wrap time for the film.

08–05 Script Supervisor

The Scriptie will have one day to prep and will be on for each shoot day.

08–08 Production Assistants

There will be one Office Production Assistant and four Set PAs. They will probably have one or two Production Interns from a local film school work on the film for their course credit.

09–02 Extras

There are only a few scenes that require Background Actors and they can be non-union under this SAG-AFTRA agreement. The Production Coordinator will hire the Extras.

09–03 Extras Casting Fee

The 10% fee for the actors' agents.

11–01 Production Designer

For prep, shoot, and wrap for the film. This is a contemporary film so no "period" sets, props, or dressing.

11–02 Art Director

For prep, shoot, and wrap for the film.

11–08 Research/Materials

Miscellaneous expenses for the Art Department.

11–10 Purchases/Rentals
For minimal Art Department purchases and rentals.

12–02 and 12–03 Foreman, Carpenters, and Scenic Painters
One location will require that a wall be constructed to create an office and a receptionist area. This covers their time to build and install the set.

12–06 and 12–07 Construction Materials
For the purchase or rental of items like lumber, flats, and other construction materials.

13–01 thru 13–04 Key Grip, Best Boy Grip, Grips, and Dolly Grip
For the Grip Department crew for tech scout, prep, and shoot.

13–06 Grip Rentals
For the grip equipment rentals for the production including a dolly rental.

13–07 Expendables
For gaffers tape, gels, clothespins, etc.

13–10 Craft Service
For food purchases and table and chair rentals.

15–01 and 15–03 Set Decorator and Set Dressers
To hire a Set Decorator and Dresser for prep and shoot.

15–04 Additional Labor
To hire an additional Set Dresser.

15–05 thru 15–07 Expendables, Purchases, and Rentals
Because they are shooting on-location for the entire film, Set Dressing will be key in making the locations work as the film's sets.

16–01 Property Master
For prep, shoot, and wrap for the Property Master.

16–03 and 16–04 Purchases and Rentals

Luckily, there are not too many expensive props that need to be purchased or rented outside of what is available at most of the locations. They will make purchases from eBay to help keep the budget down.

17–01 thru 17–03 Costume Designer, Costumer, and Additional Costumer

For prep, shoot, and wrap for the film.

17–05 thru 17–08 Purchases, Rentals, Alterations & Repairs, Cleaning & Dyeing

For Costumes and repairing, etc., for the actors' clothing.

17–10 Kit Rentals — Costume Designer

For the shoot weeks to reimburse for the Kit usage.

18–01 thru 18–03 Key Makeup Artist, Additional Makeup Artists, and Key Hair Stylist

For prep and shoot for the Makeup and Hair Departments

18–08 Kit Rentals

For replenishing all the makeup and hair used on the actors.

19–01 and 19–02 Gaffer and Best Boy Electric

For the Lighting Department crew for tech scout, prep, and shoot.

19–04 Additional Labor

For additional Electric labor for about half of the shoot days.

19–06 Lighting Package Rental

None of their locations are too large and they don't have any night filming so they were able to get a great rate for a 3-week rental on the lighting equipment.

19–08 Electrical Generator + Driver

For five days they will be at locations that don't have any electrical power, so they will bring their own genny and driver.

19–09 Loss & Damage
For any damage to the lighting equipment.

20–01 Director of Photography
The DP will be paid the same rate as all the other Key Department Heads.

20–02 B Camera
They plan to have a second camera for over half the shoot days.

20–03 1st Assistant Camera
The 1st AC will be paid for a checkout day and the entire shooting period.

20–05 Digital Imaging Technician (DIT)
For the DIT for the entire shooting period.

20–06 Still Photographer
For two days to have a Still Photographer take set photos.

20–07 and 20–10 Camera Package Rental and Purchase
For the camera rental and some money to buy a few things for the camera.

20–17 Loss & Damage
For any damage to the camera equipment.

20-26 Kit Rentals
To reimburse the 1st AC for gaffers tape, sharpies, etc.

21–01 Mixer
To hire a Mixer for the sound during the shooting period.

21–03 Expendables/Batteries
For any batteries or sound expenses.

21–04 Sound Package
To rent the Mixer's sound equipment for the shooting period.

21–05 Walkie-Talkies
To rent Walkie-Talkies for the shooting period.

22–03 Transportation Vehicle Rental
The production will rent a Production Van, a Camera Van, a 5-Ton Art Truck, and a 15-Passenger Van.

22–04 Parking/Tolls/Gas
To keep the vehicles overnight in a secure parking lot and for tolls and gas.

23–01 Location Manager
For scouting all locations and managing on the shoot days. No studio shooting so everything will be shot in real locations.

23–03 First Aid/Medic
For all days in the shooting period.

23–07 Permits
The Mayor's Office of Film, Theatre and Broadcasting charges a one-time fee of $300 for a permit for the shooting days in NYC.

23–08 Parking
For parking on location for the production vehicles. In New York the parking permits are free but Production Assistants need to clear the street the night before if they want the street empty for their production trucks and vehicles to be parked for the shoot day.

23–09 Catering Services
This is a catered meal once a day for cast and crew plus some additional money for Extras' meals on the days that they are on set. Included is money to rent tables and chairs for the shooting period.

23–12 Location Supplies
For miscellaneous costs.

23–17 Location Site Rental Fees
This is an average fee for each day of shooting. Some locations will be free and some may cost a bit more but this will have to cover all Site Rental Fees.

23–19 Auto Rentals
The Location Manager will charge a weekly fee for the use of his car.

24–03 Picture Cars
The motorcycle and police car are the two picture vehicles that will be rented for this film.

25–01 Digital Media
For enough hard drive space for all media and a backup.

27–01 Editor — Shoot/Post
For editing during the shoot and through to finishing of the film. This is the Editor's first feature; she has been an Assistant Editor for three years and wants to move up now.

27–02 Assistant Editor — Shoot/Post
The Assistant Editor will work for the final weeks to prep the film for finishing.

27–04 Post-Production Supervisor
The Post-Production Supervisor will come in for the final weeks to finish and create the deliverables.

27–06 Edit System Rental
The Editor will edit out of her house and charge the production a low rental fee for her system.

28–01 Composer Fee
For the composer and the recording of the music.

28–11 Music Licensing
For two or three songs that won't cost too much, which means avoiding Top Forty hits, chartbusters, and other widely popular tunes.

28–12 Music Supervisor/Clearance
For the person to clear the songs and obtain the licenses.

29–01 Sound Editor

The Editor will plan to do as much Sound work as possible to make the Sound Editor's time most productive.

29–02 Assistant Sound Editor

The Assistant will work with the Sound Editor on all the audio tracks.

29–08 ADR

For the recording of the Automatic Dialogue Replacement for a few of the actors in the film.

29–09 Foley Stage/Editor

To create sounds that can't be acquired from an online catalog.

29–15 Audio Mix

A flat deal to mix the film at the Audio Post facility.

31–02 Hard Drive Purchases

For additional hard drives during the post-production phase.

32–01 Titling

They will do a very simple graphic treatment for the opening title sequence and the end crawl.

32–02 Graphic Designer

There are a few graphic elements that must be created to explain some important information that needs to be diagrammed.

33–01 Masters/Clones

The film hasn't been sold yet so they will create a DCP and a digital file master for film festival projection.

33–05 Screening Copies

For a few DVD copies.

35–02 General Liability Insurance

To purchase an annual production and general liability insurance policy.

35–03 Hired Auto
They need an additional insurance rider to cover the motorcycle stunt.

35–05 Workers' Compensation
For an annual policy to cover cast and crew.

35–06 Errors & Omissions
For an E&O policy to cover this film after it is sold to a distributor.

36–01 Business License/Taxes
For the creation of an LLC and filing of the annual tax return.

36–02 Legal
A friend from college has been practicing entertainment law for several years and wants to help out by doing the legal work for a low flat deal.

36–03 Accounting Fees
The Producer will do most of the accounting work with a software program. This fee will be to pay a CPA to file the tax return.

36–06 Copying/Scanning
For various copying charges.

36–08 Office Space Rental
To rent an office space for prep, production, and wrap.

36–09 Office Furniture
To rent furniture for the office.

36–10 Office Equipment & Supplies
For miscellaneous office expenses.

36–12 Software/Apps/FTP
To upload cuts to an FTP site and other tech needs during the filming and post-production.

36–14 Messenger/Overnight Shipping
For any messenger or overnight shipping costs.

36–16 Storage

The office and Art Department will need to store some equipment and purchases for a few months.

36-20 Working Meals

To pay for meals while fundraising for the film during the development and prep for the film.

37–01 Publicity

To hire a publicist for their premiere at a prestigious film festival and to pay for film fest application fees and travel costs.

Contingency

The contingency fee is 10%.

$350K DOCUMENTARY FEATURE FILM BUDGET

- Go to *www.mwp.com*.
- Click on "MW Film School."
- Open the item "Sample Budgets/Forms."
- Download the corresponding free Excel Budget Template.
- Save it to your computer.
- Last, this budget is a sample template. Make sure to create your budget with figures based on your research on current rates and prices available to you.

Budget Assumptions

This film will be produced and edited over the course of a year. There is a Director/Producer and two other Producers who will make the film together. Although they have budgeted for a Director of Photography and a Sound Recordist, the Director can shoot and one of the Producers can record sound if they need to save money. Basing the budget on a 35-day shoot schedule, the crew will be a total of three to five people for each day of shooting cinema-vérité style and for some sit-down interviews. They would like to shoot a few "art directed" scenes or elements or have a clever graphic treatment throughout the film. They could decide to produce some "re-creation" scenes instead of the graphics and use that line item to pay for the re-created elements.

Basing themselves out of a small office in Los Angeles, CA, they plan to take a few trips in the US to film various scenes for the film. This budget assumes that each new person will be a freelance contractor with a loan-out company and there will be no payroll fringes. They will finish to an HD master digital file and DCP for film festivals where they plan to hire a publicist and expect to sell the film.

As first-time documentary feature filmmakers, they will raise money from family and friends and then apply for finishing/post-production grants once they have a rough cut for applications.

$350K Documentary Feature Budget

	SUMMARY BUDGET		
Fringe assumptions:	Production:	$350K Documentary Feature	
Payroll Tax 0.00%	Shoot Days:	35 Days	
WGA 0.00%	Location:	Los Angeles, CA	
DGA 0.00%	Unions:	No	
SAG 0.00%	Shooting Format: Digital HD		
Overtime 0%	Delivery Format: DCP		
Contingency 0%			
01-00 Story & Rights		$800	
02-00 Producers Unit		$66,000	
03-00 Direction		$43,000	
04-00 Cast		$0	
05-00 Travel & Living – Producers/Director		$0	
06-00 Travel & Living- Cast		$0	
07-00 Residuals		$0	
	TOTAL ABOVE-THE-LINE		$109,800
08-00 Production Staff		$20,550	
09-00 Background Actors/Extras		$0	
10-00 Sound Stage		$0	
11-00 Production Design		$6,250	
12-00 Set Construction		$0	
13-00 Set Operations		$0	
14-00 Special Effects		$0	
15-00 Set Dressing		$0	
16-00 Property		$0	
17-00 Wardrobe		$0	
18-00 Make-Up and Hair		$0	
19-00 Electrical		$11,250	
20-00 Camera		$33,750	
21-00 Production Sound		$16,350	
22-00 Transportation		$3,275	
23-00 Location Expenses		$0	
24-00 Picture Vehicle/Animals		$0	
25-00 Media		$2,250	
26-00 Travel and Living-Crew		$19,300	
	TOTAL PRODUCTION		$112,975
27-00 Editorial		$35,000	
28-00 Music		$26,000	
29-00 Post-Production Sound		$16,500	
30-00 Post-Production - Digital and Film		$10,500	
31-00 Digital Intermediate		$0	
32-00 Titling and Graphics		$4,000	
33-00 Deliverables		$2,000	
34-00 Digital Visual Effects/Animation		$8,000	
	TOTAL POST-PRODUCTION		$102,000
35-00 Insurance		$8,000	
36-00 General & Administrative Expenses		$12,800	
37-00 Publicity and Marketing		$5,000	
	TOTAL GENERAL		$25,800
Total Above-the-Line			$109,800
Total Below-the-Line			$240,775
Total Above and Below-the-Line			$350,575
Contingency			$0
GRAND TOTAL			$350,575

$350K Documentary Feature Budget

ABOVE-THE-LINE	Amt.	Units	x	Rate	Sub-Total	Total	
01-00 Story & Rights							
01-01 Rights Purchases		Allow	1		0	0	
01-02 Options		Allow	1		0	0	
01-03 Writer Salaries/Screenplay Purchase		Allow	1		0	0	
01-04 Research/Clearances	1	Allow	1	800	800	800	
01-05 Title Registration		Allow	1		0	0	
01-06 Script Timing		Allow	1		0	0	
01-07 Storyboards/Pre-Viz		Allow	1		0	0	
01-08 WGA Publication fee		Allow	1		0	0	
01-10 Development		Allow	1		0	0	
Payroll					0	0	
WGA					0	0	
				Total for 01-00			800
02-00 Producers Unit							
02-01 Executive Producer		Allow	1		0	0	
02-02 Producers	1	Allow	2	33,000	66,000	66,000	
02-03 Associate Producer		Allow	1		0	0	
02-04 Assistant to Producer(s)		Week(s)	1		0	0	
02-06 Consultants		Allow	1		0	0	
02-07 Miscellaneous Expenses		Allow	1		0	0	
Payroll					66,000	0	
				Total for 02-00			66,000
03-00 Direction							
03-01 Director	1	Allow	1	43,000	43,000	43,000	
03-02 Assistant to Director	1	Weeks	1		0	0	
Payroll					43,000	0	
DGA					43,000	0	
				Total for 03-00			43,000
04-00 Cast							
04-01 Lead Actors							
		Allow	1		0		
		Allow	1		0		
Overtime Allowance		Allow	1		0	0	
04-02 Supporting Cast							
		Week(s)	1		0		
		Week(s)	1		0		
		Week(s)	1		0		
		Week(s)	1		0		
Overtime Allowance		Allow	1		0	0	
04-03 Day Players							
		Day(s)	1		0		
		Day(s)	1		0		
		Day(s)	1		0		
		Day(s)	1		0		
		Day(s)	1		0		
		Day(s)	1		0		
		Day(s)	1		0		
		Day(s)	1		0		
		Day(s)	1		0		
		Day(s)	1		0		
		Day(s)	1		0		
Overtime Allowance		Allow	1		0	0	
04-04 Casting Director/Staff		Allow	1		0	0	
04-05 Casting Expenses		Allow	1		0	0	
04-06 Choreographer		Weeks	1		0	0	
04-07 Assistant(s) to Choreographer		Weeks	1		0	0	
04-08 Dialect Coach		Weeks	1		0	0	
04-09 Narrator/Voiceover Artist		Weeks	1		0	0	

$350K Documentary Feature Budget

		Amt.	Units	x	Rate	Sub-Total	Total	
04-10 Stunt Coordinator			Weeks	1		0	0	
04-11 Stunt Players (6 day weeks)			Weeks	1		0	0	
04-12 Stunt Costs/Adjustments			Allow	1		0	0	
04-13 Stunt Equipment			Allow	1		0	0	
04-14 ADR (Actors' fees)			Allow	1		0	0	
	Payroll					0	0	
	SAG					0	0	
					Total for 04-00			0
05-00 Travel & Living – Producers/Director								
05-01 Airfares			RT	1		0	0	
05-02 Hotel			Nights	1		0	0	
05-03 Taxi/Limo			Allow	1		0	0	
05-04 Auto			Allow	1		0	0	
05-05 Train			Allow	1		0	0	
05-06 Excess Baggage			Allow	1		0	0	
05-07 Phone			Allow	1		0	0	
05-08 Gratuities			Allow	1		0	0	
05-09 Per Diem			Days	1		0	0	
					Total for 05-00			0
06-00 Travel & Living- Cast								
06-01 Airfares			RT	1		0	0	
06-02 Hotels			Nights	1		0	0	
06-03 Taxi/Limo			Allow	1		0	0	
06-04 Auto			Allow	1		0	0	
06-05 Train			Allow	1		0	0	
06-06 Excess Baggage			Allow	1		0	0	
06-07 Phone			Allow	1		0	0	
06-08 Gratuities			Allow	1		0	0	
06-09 Per Diem			Days	1		0	0	
					Total for 06-00			0
07-00 Residuals			Allow	1		0	0	
					Total for 07-00			0
TOTAL ABOVE-THE -LINE								109,800

$350K Documentary Feature Budget

		Amt.	Units	x	Rate	Sub-Total	Total	
BELOW-THE-LINE								
08-00 Production Staff								
08-01 UPM/Line Producer								
	Prep/Travel		Weeks	1		0		
	Shoot		Weeks	1		0		
	Wrap		Weeks	1		0		
	Severance		Allow	1		0	0	
08-02 Assistant Directors								
First AD								
	Prep/Travel		Weeks	1		0		
	Shoot		Weeks	1		0		
	Prod. Fee (shoot days)		Days	1		0		
	Severance		Allow	1		0		
	Overtime Allow		Days	1		0	0	
2nd AD								
	Prep/Travel		Weeks	1		0		
	Shoot		Weeks	1		0		
	Prod. Fee		Days	1		0		
	Severance		Allow	1		0		
	Overtime Allow		Days	1		0	0	
08-03 Stage Manager								
	Prep/Travel		Weeks	1		0		
	Shoot		Weeks	1		0		
	Prod. Fee		Days	1		0		
	Severance		Allow	1		0		
	Overtime Allow		Days	1		0	0	
08-04 Production Coordinator								
	Prep/Travel		Weeks	1		0		
	Shoot		Weeks	1		0		
	Wrap		Weeks	1		0	0	
Ass't Coord.								
	Prep		Weeks	1		0		
	Shoot		Weeks	1		0		
	Wrap		Weeks	1		0	0	
08-05 Script Supervisor								
	Prep		Days	1		0		
	Shoot		Days	1		0		
	Saturdays Worked		Days	1		0		
	Wrap		Days	1		0		
	2nd Camera Days		Days	1		0		
	Overtime		Allow		0	0	0	
08-06 Production Accountant/Auditor								
	Prep/Travel		Weeks	1		0		
	Shoot		Weeks	1		0		
	Wrap		Weeks	1		0		
	Post-Production		Weeks	1		0	0	
Assistant Accountant								
	Prep/Travel		Weeks	1		0		
	Shoot		Weeks	1		0		
	Wrap		Weeks	1		0	0	
08-07 Technical Advisors		1	Allow	2	3,000	6,000	6,000	
08-08 Production Assistants								
Office Prod. Assistant(s)								
	Prep		Days	1		0		
	Shoot		Days	1		0		
	Wrap		Days	1		0		
Set Prod. Assistant(s)								
	Prep	31	Days	2	150	9,300		
	Shoot	35	Days	1	150	5,250	14,550	
08-09 Studio Teacher/Tutor			Weeks	1		0	0	
	Payroll					20,550	0	
	DGA					0	0	
					Total for 08-00			20,550

$350K Documentary Feature Budget

		Amt.	Units	x	Rate	Sub-Total	Total	
09-00 Background Actors/Extras								
09-01 Stand-ins			Days	1		0	0	
09-02 Extras			Extras	1		0	0	
09-05 Extras Casting Fee @ 10%			Allow	1		0	0	
09-10 Extras Transportation			Allow	1		0	0	
	Payroll					0	0	
	P&H					0	0	
					Total for 09-00			0
10-00 Sound Stage								
10-01 Stage Rental			Allow	1		0	0	
	Prep		Allow	1		0	0	
	Pre-Light		Allow	1		0	0	
	Shoot		Allow	1		0	0	
	Wrap		Allow	1		0	0	
	Overtime		Allow	1		0	0	
10-02 Stage Lighting Rental			Allow	1		0	0	
10-03 Stage Grip Rental			Allow	1		0	0	
10-04 Phones/ Internet			Allow	1		0	0	
10-05 Garbage removal			Allow	1		0	0	
10-06 Green Room			Allow	1		0	0	
10-07 Make Up Room			Allow	1		0	0	
10-08 Office Rental			Allow	1		0	0	
10-09 Parking			Allow	1		0	0	
					Total for 10-00			0
11-00 Production Design								
11-01 Production Designer								
	Prep/Travel		Weeks	1		0		
	Shoot		Weeks	1		0	0	
11-02 Art Director								
	Flat Rate	1	Flat	1	3,250	3,250		
	Shoot		Weeks	1		0	3,250	
11-03 Art Assistants								
	Prep/Travel		Days	1		0		
	Shoot		Days	1		0	0	
11-04 Set Designer								
	Prep/Travel		Weeks	1		0		
	Shoot		Weeks	1		0	0	
11-05 Model Makers/Miniatures			Allow	1		0	0	
11-06 Draftsperson			Allow	1		0	0	
11-08 Research/Materials			Allow	1		0	0	
11-09 Vehicle Expenses			Weeks	1		0	0	
11-10 Purchases/Rentals		1	Allow	1	3,000	3,000	3,000	
	Payroll					3,250	0	
					Total for 11-00			6,250
12-00 Set Construction								
12-01 Construction Coordinator								
	Prep		Days	1		0		
	Shoot		Days	1		0		
	Overtime		Allow	1	0	0	0	
12-02 Foreman								
	Prep		Days	1		0		
	Shoot		Days	1		0		
	Overtime		Allow	1	0	0	0	
Carpenters			Allow	1		0	0	
12-03 Scenic Painters								
Lead Scenic Painter								
	Prep		Days	1		0		
	Shoot		Days	1		0		
	Overtime		Allow	1	0	0	0	
Painters			Allow	1		0	0	
12-05 Greensmen			Allow	1		0	0	

$350K Documentary Feature Budget

		Amt.	Units	x	Rate	Sub-Total	Total	
12-06 Construction materials - Purchases			Allow	1		0	0	
12-07 Construction materials - Rentals			Allow	1		0	0	
12-08 Construction Equipment			Allow	1		0	0	
12-09 Set Strike			Allow	1		0	0	
	Payroll					0	0	
					Total for 12-00			0
13-00 Set Operations								
13-01 Key Grip								
	Prep/Travel		Days	1		0		
	Shoot		Days	1		0		
	Wrap		Days	1		0		
	Overtime		Allow	1	0	0	0	
13-02 Best Boy Grip								
	Prep		Days	1		0		
	Shoot		Days	1		0		
	Wrap		Days	1		0		
	Overtime		Allow	1	0	0	0	
13-03 Grips								
3rd Grip								
	Prep		Days	1		0		
	Shoot		Days	1		0		
	Wrap		Days	1		0		
	Overtime		Allow	1	0	0	0	
4th Grip								
	Prep		Days	1		0		
	Shoot		Days	1		0		
	Wrap		Days	1		0		
	Overtime		Allow	1	0	0	0	
Additional Grips			Days	1		0		
	Overtime		Allow	1		0	0	
13-04 Dolly/Crane Grips								
	Prep		Days	1		0		
	Shoot		Days	1		0		
	Overtime		Allow	1	0	0	0	
13-06 Grip Rentals								
	Package		Weeks	1		0		
	Dollies		Weeks	1		0		
	Cranes (incl. Driver)		Days	1		0		
	Add'l Equip.		Allow	1		0	0	
13-07 Expendables			Allow	1		0	0	
13-08 Kit Rentals								
	Key Grip		Weeks	1		0	0	
	Craft Service		Weeks	1		0	0	
13-10 Craft Service								
	Prep		Days	1		0		
	Shoot		Days	1		0		
	Wrap		Days	1		0		
	Overtime		Allow	1	0	0	0	
Purchases			Days	1		0	0	
Rentals			Allow	1		0	0	
13-15 Air Conditioning/Heating			Days	1		0	0	
	Payroll					0	0	
					Total for 13-00			0
14-00 Special Effects								
14-01 Special Effects Person								
	Prep/Travel		Days	1		0		
	Shoot		Days	1		0		
	Overtime		Allow	1	0	0	0	
14-02 SFX Assistant(s)								
	Shoot		Days	1		0		
	Overtime		Allow	1	0	0	0	
14-03 Additional Labor								

$350K Documentary Feature Budget

		Amt.	Units	x	Rate	Sub-Total	Total	
	Shoot		Days	1		0		
	Overtime		Allow	1	0	0	0	
14-06 Manufacturing Labor			Allow	1		0	0	
14-07 Fabrication			Allow	1		0	0	
14-09 Rentals			Allow	1		0	0	
	Payroll				0	0	0	
					Total for 14-00			0
15-00 Set Dressing								
15-01 Set Decorator								
	Prep/Travel		Days	1		0		
	Shoot		Days	1		0		
	Wrap		Days	1		0		
	Overtime				0	0	0	
15-02 Lead Person								
	Prep/Travel		Days	1		0		
	Shoot		Days	1		0		
	Wrap		Days	1		0		
	Overtime				0	0	0	
15-03 Swing Gang/Set Dressers								
Set Dresser #1								
	Prep		Days	1		0		
	Shoot		Days	1		0		
	Wrap		Days	1		0		
	Overtime				0	0	0	
Set Dresser #2								
	Prep		Days	1		0		
	Shoot		Days	1		0		
	Wrap		Days	1		0		
	Overtime				0	0	0	
Set Dresser #3								
	Prep		Days	1		0		
	Shoot		Days	1		0		
	Wrap		Days	1		0		
	Overtime				0	0	0	
15-04 Additional Labor								
On-Set Dresser (Shoot)			Days	1		0		
	Overtime				0	0	0	
15-05 Expendables			Allow	1		0	0	
15-06 Purchases			Allow	1		0	0	
15-07 Rentals			Allow	1		0	0	
15-08 Loss & Damage			Allow	1		0	0	
15-09 Kit Rentals						0	0	
	Set Decorator		Weeks	1		0	0	
	Lead Person		Weeks	1		0	0	
15-10 Vehicle Expenses								
	Set Decorator		Weeks	1		0	0	
	Lead Person		Weeks	1		0	0	
	Payroll				0	0	0	
					Total for 15-00			0
16-00 Property								
16-01 Property Master								
	Prep/Travel		Days	1		0		
	Shoot		Days	1		0		
	Wrap		Days	1		0		
	Overtime				0	0	0	
16-02 Prop Assistant								
	Prep		Days	1		0		
	Shoot		Days	1		0		
	Wrap		Days	1		0		
	Overtime				0	0	0	
16-03 Purchases			Allow	1		0	0	

$350K Documentary Feature Budget

		Amt.	Units	x	Rate	Sub-Total	Total	
16-04 Rentals			Allow	1		0	0	
16-05 Loss & Damage			Allow	1		0	0	
16-06 Kit Rentals								
	Prop Master		Weeks	1		0	0	
16-07 Vehicle Expenses								
	Prop Master		Weeks	1		0	0	
	Assistant		Weeks	1		0	0	
	Payroll				0	0	0	
					Total for 16-00			0
17-00 Wardrobe								
17-01 Costume Designer								
	Prep/Travel		Weeks	1		0		
	Shoot		Weeks	1		0		
	Wrap		Week	1		0	0	
17-02 Costumer								
	Prep/Travel		Days	1		0		
	Shoot		Days	1		0		
	Wrap		Days	1		0		
	Overtime		Allow	1	0	0	0	
17-03 Additional Costumer(s)								
	Prep		Days	1		0		
	Shoot		Days	1		0		
	Wrap		Days	1		0		
	Overtime		Allow	1	0	0	0	
17-04 Expendables			Allow	1		0	0	
17-05 Purchases			Allow	1		0	0	
17-06 Rentals			Allow	1		0	0	
17-07 Alteration & Repairs			Allow	1		0	0	
17-08 Cleaning & Dyeing			Allow	1		0	0	
17-09 Loss & Damage			Allow	1		0	0	
17-10 Kit Rentals								
	Costume Designer		Weeks	1		0	0	
17-11 Vehicle Expenses								
	Costume Designer		Weeks	1		0	0	
	Payroll				0	0	0	
					Total for 17-00			0
18-00 Make-Up and Hair								
18-01 Key Make-Up Artist								
	Prep/Travel		Days	1		0		
	Shoot		Days	1		0		
	Wrap		Days	1		0		
	Overtime		Allow	1	0	0	0	
18-02 Additional Make-Up Artist(s)			Days	1		0		
	Shoot		Days	1		0		
	Overtime		Allow	1	0	0	0	
18-03 Key Hair Stylist								
	Prep/Travel		Days	1		0		
	Shoot		Days	1		0		
	Wrap		Days	1		0		
	Overtime		Allow	1	0	0	0	
18-04 Additional Hair Stylist(s)			Days	1		0		
	Shoot		Days	1		0		
	Overtime		Allow	1	0	0	0	
18-05 Special Effects Makeup Effects			Allow	1		0	0	
18-06 Purchases			Allow	1		0	0	
18-07 Rentals			Weeks	1		0	0	
18-08 Kit Rentals								
	Key Make-Up		Days	1		0	0	
	Add'l Make-Up		Days	1		0	0	
	Hair Stylist		Days	1		0	0	
	Add'l Hair		Days	1		0	0	
	Payroll				0	0	0	
					Total for 18-00			0

$350K Documentary Feature Budget

		Amt.	Units	x	Rate	Sub-Total	Total	
19-00 Electrical								
19-01 Gaffer								
	Prep/Travel		Days	1		0		
	Shoot		Days	1		0		
	Wrap/Travel		Days	1		0		
	Overtime		Allow	1	0	0	0	
19-02 Best Boy Electric								
	Prep		Days	1		0		
	Shoot		Days	1		0		
	Wrap		Days	1		0		
	Overtime		Allow	1	0	0	0	
19-03 Electrics								
3rd Electric								
	Prep		Days	1		0		
	Shoot		Days	1		0		
	Wrap		Days	1		0		
	Overtime		Allow	1	0	0	0	
4th Electric								
	Prep		Days	1		0		
	Shoot		Days	1		0		
	Wrap		Days	1		0		
	Overtime		Allow	1	0	0	0	
19-04 Additional Labor								
	Shoot		Days	1		0		
	Overtime		Allow	1	0	0	0	
19-05 Equipment Purchases			Allow	1		0	0	
19-06 Lighting Package Rental		25	Days	1	450	11,250	11,250	
	Add'l Equip.		Allow	1		0	0	
	Condors		Allow	1		0	0	
	Additional Generator		Allow	1		0	0	
19-07 Additional Rentals			Allow	1		0	0	
19-08 Electrical Generator/Driver			Days	1		0	0	
19-09 Loss & Damage			Allow	1		0	0	
19-10 Kit Rentals								
	Gaffer		Weeks	1		0	0	
	Payroll				0	0	0	
					Total for 19-00			11,250
20-00 Camera								
20-01 Director of Photography								
	Flat Rate	1	Flat	1	20,000	20,000		
	Shoot		Weeks	1		0	20,000	
20-02 Camera Operator or B Camera								
	Prep/Travel		Days	1		0		
	Shoot		Days	1		0		
	Overtime		Allow	1	0	0	0	
20-03 1st Assistant Camera								
	Prep/Travel		Days	1		0		
	Shoot		Days	1		0		
	Wrap		Days	1		0		
	Overtime		Allow	1	0	0		
	B Cam 1st Ass't		Days	1		0	0	
	Overtime		Allow	1	0	0	0	
20-04 2nd Ass't Camera								
	Prep		Days	1		0		
	Shoot		Days	1		0		
	Wrap		Days	1		0		
	Overtime		Allow	1	0	0	0	
	B Cam 2nd Ass't		Days	1		0		
	Overtime		Allow	1	0	0	0	
20-05 Digital Imaging Technician (DIT)			Week	1		0	0	
20-06 Still Photographer			Allow	1		0	0	
20-07 Camera Package Rental		5	Days	1	250	1,250	1,250	

$350K Documentary Feature Budget

		Amt.	Units	x	Rate	Sub-Total	Total	
20-10 Camera Package Purchase		1	Allow	1	12,500	12,500	12,500	
20-11 Steadicam Operator & Equip.			Days	1		0	0	
20-12 Teleprompter/Operator			Days	1		0	0	
20-13 Video Assist/Operator			Days	1		0	0	
20-14 Aerial Photography			Days	1		0	0	
20-15 Underwater and Topside Photography			Days	1		0	0	
20-16 Drones/GoPros			Days	1		0	0	
22-17 Maintenance/Loss & Damage			Allow	1		0	0	
20-18 Motion Control			Allow	1		0	0	
20-19 Expendables			Weeks	1		0	0	
20-20 Video Truck			Weeks	1		0	0	
20-25 Video Truck Crew			Weeks	1		0	0	
20-26 Kit Rentals								
	1st Ass't Cam		Weeks	1		0	0	
	Payroll				20,000	0	0	
					Total for 20-00			33,750
21-00 Production Sound								
21-01 Mixer								
	Prep		Days	1		0		
	Shoot	35	Days	1	350	12,250		
	Wrap/Travel		Days	1		0		
	Overtime		Allow	1	12,250	0	12,250	
21-02 Boom Operator								
	Shoot		Days	1		0		
	Overtime		Allow	1	0	0	0	
21-03 Expendables/Batteries		1	Allow	1	600	600	600	
21-04 Sound Package		35	Days	1	100	3,500	3,500	
21-05 Walkie Talkies			Weeks	1		0	0	
21-06 Sound Truck			Weeks	1		0	0	
21-08 Misc. / Loss & Damage			Allow	1		0	0	
	Payroll				12,250	0	0	
					Total for 21-00			16,350
22-00 Transportation								
22-01 Transportation Coordinator								
			Weeks	1		0	0	
22-02 Drivers								
Captain								
	Prep		Days	1		0		
	Shoot		Days	1		0		
	Wrap		Days	1		0	0	
Star Trailer Drivers								
Driver #1								
	Prep		Day	1		0		
	Shoot		Days	1		0		
	Wrap		Day	1		0	0	
Driver #2								
	Prep		Day	1		0		
	Shoot		Days	1		0		
	Wrap		Day	1		0	0	
Production Van Driver								
	Prep		Days	1		0		
	Shoot		Days	1		0		
	Wrap		Days	1		0	0	
Camera Truck Driver								
	Prep		Days	1		0		
	Shoot		Days	1		0		
	Wrap		Days	1		0	0	
Stakebed Driver (Construction)								
	Shoot		Days	1		0	0	
Set Dressing Driver								
	Prep		Days	1		0		
	Shoot		Days	1		0		
	Wrap		Days	1		0	0	

$350K Documentary Feature Budget

		Amt.	Units	x	Rate	Sub-Total	Total	
Second Set Dressing 5 Ton			Days	1		0	0	
Props Driver								
	Prep		Days	1		0		
	Shoot		Days	1		0		
	Wrap		Days	1		0	0	
Make-Up/Wardrobe Driver								
	Prep		Days	1		0		
	Shoot		Days	1		0		
	Wrap		Days	1		0	0	
Prod. Office Trailer Driver								
	Prep		Days	1		0		
	Shoot		Days	1		0		
	Wrap		Days	1		0	0	
Honeywagon Driver								
	Shoot		Days	1		0		
	Wrap		Days	1		0	0	
15-Passenger Van #1 Driver								
	Prep		Days	1		0		
	Shoot		Days	1		0	0	
15-Passenger Van #2 Driver								
	Prep		Days	1		0		
	Shoot		Days	1		0	0	
Car Carrier			Days	1		0	0	
Insert Car (car to car cam platform)			Days	1		0	0	
Water Truck Driver			Days	1		0	0	
Caterer	Shoot		Days	1		0	0	
Caterer Ass't	Shoot		Days	1		0	0	
Additional Drivers			Allow	1		0	0	
22-03 Transportation Vehicle Rental								
Minivan		25	Days	1	75	1,875	1,875	
Crew Cab			Weeks	1		0	0	
Production Van (40' w/ 2 gennies)			Weeks	1		0	0	
Camera Truck			Weeks	1		0	0	
Stake Bed			Weeks	1		0	0	
Set Dressing 5 Ton			Weeks	1		0	0	
Add'l Set Dressing 5 Ton			Weeks	1		0	0	
Set Dress Van			Weeks	1		0	0	
Props 5 Ton			Weeks	1		0	0	
Wardrobe/Make-Up			Weeks	1		0	0	
Crew Stake Bed			Weeks	1		0	0	
Prod. Office Trailer			Weeks	1		0	0	
Honeywagon (Portable Toilets)			Days	1		0	0	
Water Truck			Days	1		0	0	
Gas Truck			Days	1		0	0	
15-Passenger Van			Days	1		0	0	
Car Tow Trailer			Days	1		0	0	
Car Trailer			Days	1		0	0	
Camera Car			Days	1		0	0	
22-04 Parking/Tolls/Gas		35	Days	1	40	1,400	1,400	
22-05 Repairs & Maintenance			Allow	1		0	0	
22-06 Honeywagon Pumping			Allow	1		0	0	
22-07 Miscellaneous			Allow	1		0	0	
	Payroll				0	0	0	
					Total for 22-00			3,275
23-00 Location Expenses								
23-01 Location Manager			Weeks	1		0	0	
23-02 Location Assistants								
Assistant Location Mgr.			Weeks	1		0	0	
Local Contact Person			Weeks	1		0	0	
23-03 First Aid/Medic			Weeks	1		0	0	
23-04 Fire Officers								
	Shoot		Days	1		0	0	
23-05 Security			Allow	1		0	0	
23-06 Police			Days	1		0	0	

$350K Documentary Feature Budget

		Amt.	Units	x	Rate	Sub-Total	Total	
	Additional Police		Allow	1		0	0	
23-07 Permits			Allow	1		0	0	
23-08 Parking			Allow	1		0	0	
23-09 Catering Services								
Crew Meals			Days	1		0	0	
Extras			Meals	1		0	0	
Ice/Propane			Weeks	1		0	0	
2nd Meals			Days	1		0	0	
Sales Tax			Allow	1		0	0	
Tent			Allow	1		0	0	
23-11 Location Office Space Rental			Months	1		0	0	
23-12 Location Office Supplies			Allow	1		0	0	
23-13 Location Office Equipment			Allow	1		0	0	
23-14 Location Office Telephone/Fax			Allow	1		0	0	
23-17 Location Site Rental Fees								
	Shoot		Days	1		0	0	
23-18 Location Scout			Allow	1		0	0	
	Photos		Allow	1		0	0	
23-19 Auto Rentals								
Location Manager			Weeks	1		0	0	
Assistants			Weeks	1		0	0	
23-20 Miscellaneous Expenses								
	Mileage/DGA/SAG/Crew		Allow	1		0	0	
	Payroll				0	0	0	
					Total for 23-00			0
24-00 Picture Vehicles/Animals								
24-01 Animal Trainers								
Boss Wrangler			Weeks	1		0	0	
Assistant Wrangler			Weeks	1		0	0	
Wranglers			Week	1		0	0	
Riders/Handlers, etc			Day	1		0	0	
24-02 Animals								
	Horses		Allow	1		0	0	
Veterinary Expenses			Allow	1		0	0	
Feed/Shelter			Allow	1		0	0	
Transportation			Allow	1		0	0	
24-03 Picture Cars								
	Car #1		Weeks	1		0	0	
	Car #2		Weeks	1		0	0	
	Car #3		Weeks	1		0	0	
	Background Cars		Allow	1		0	0	
	Payroll				0	0	0	
					Total for 24-00			0
25-00 Media								
25-01 Digital Media		1	Allow	3	750	2,250	2,250	
25-02 Raw Film Stock			Feet	1		0	0	
25-03 Film Lab-Negative Prep & Process			Feet	1		0	0	
25-04 Telecine/Film to Digital transfer			Allow	1		0	0	
25-05 Videotape stock			Each	1		0	0	
					Total for 25-00			2,250
26-00 Travel and Living - Crew								
26-01 Airfares		5	RT	3	400	6,000	6,000	
26-02 Hotels		15	Nites	3	250	11,250	11,250	
26-03 Taxi			Allow	1		0	0	
26-04 Auto			Days	1		0	0	
26-05 Train			RT	1		0	0	
26-06 Excess Baggage			Allow	1		0	0	
26-08 Per Diem		15	Days	3	40	1,800	1,800	
26-09 Gratuities		1	Allow	1	250	250	250	
					Total for 26-00			19,300
TOTAL PRODUCTION								112,975

$350K Documentary Feature Budget

	Amt.	Units	x	Rate	Sub-Total	Total	
27-00 Editorial							
27-01 Editor - Shoot/Post	1	Flat	1	35,000	35,000	35,000	
27-02 Assistant Editor - Shoot/Post		Weeks	1		0	0	
27-04 Post-Production Supervisor		Weeks	1		0	0	
27-05 Editing Room Rental		Weeks	1		0	0	
27-06 Edit System Rental		Weeks	1		0	0	
27-10 On-Line Editing/Conform		Days	1		0	0	
Payroll				35,000	0	0	
				Total for 27-00			**35,000**
28-00 Music							
28-01 Composer Fee	1	Allow	1	10,000	10,000	10,000	
28-02 Musicians		Allow	1		0	0	
28-03 Music Prep		Allow	1		0	0	
28-04 Studio Costs		Allow	1		0	0	
28-05 Music Scoring Stage		Allow	1		0	0	
28-06 Cartage and Rentals		Allow	1		0	0	
28-07 Music Mix Room		Allow	1		0	0	
28-08 Singers		Allow	1		0	0	
28-09 Payroll Service		Allow	1		0	0	
28-10 Miscellaneous		Allow	1		0	0	
28-11 Music Licensing	5	Songs	1	2,000	10,000	10,000	
28-12 Music Supervisor/Clearance	1	Allow	1	6,000	6,000	6,000	
				Total for 28-00			**26,000**
29-00 Post-Production Sound							
29-01 Sound Editor		Weeks	1		0	0	
29-02 Assistant Sound Editor		Weeks	1		0	0	
29-03 Music Editor		Weeks	1		0	0	
29-04 Dialogue Editor		Weeks	1		0	0	
29-05 Spotting (Music & FX)		Hours	1		0	0	
29-08 ADR (Studio/Editor)		Days	1		0	0	
29-09 Foley Stage/Editor		Days	1		0	0	
29-10 Foley Artists		Days	1		0	0	
29-12 Narration Recording		Hours	1		0	0	
29-13 Audio Laydown		Hours	1		0	0	
29-15 Audio Mix	1	Flat	1	16,500	16,500	16,500	
29-17 Dolby License		Allow	1		0	0	
29-18 Miscellaneous Expenses		Allow	1		0	0	
				Total for 29-00			**16,500**
30-00 Post-Producton - Digital and Film							
30-01 Stock Footage	1	Allow	1	10,500	10,500	10,500	
30-02 Archive F Supplies		Allow	1		0	0	
30-04 Archival Researcher		Weeks	1		0	0	
30-06 Clearance Supervisor		Weeks	1		0	0	
30-09 Screeners		Allow	1		0	0	
30-11 Film Prints		Allow	1		0	0	
30-12 Miscellaneous Expenses		Allow	1		0	0	
				Total for 30-00			**10,500**
31-00 Digital Intermediate							
31-01 Digital Intermediate		Allow	1		0	0	
31-02 Hard Drive Purchases		Allow	1		0	0	
				Total for 31-00			**0**
32-00 Titling and Graphics							
32-01 Titling	1	Allow	1	4,000	4,000	4,000	
32-02 Graphic Designer		Allow	1		0	0	
32-05 Special Graphic Effects		Allow	1		0	0	
32-06 Motion Control		Allow	1		0	0	
32-08 Closed Captioning		Allow	1		0	0	
32-09 Subtitling		Allow	1		0	0	
				Total for 32-00			**4,000**
33-00 Deliverables							
33-01 Masters/Clones	1	Allow	1	1,500	1,500	1,500	

$350K Documentary Feature Budget

		Amt.	Units	x	Rate	Sub-Total	Total	
33-03 Transfers and Dubs		1	Allow	1	500	500	500	
33-05 Screening Copies			Allow	1		0	0	
					Total for 33-00			2,000
34-00 Digital Visual Effects/Animation								
34-01 VFX			Allow	1		0	0	
34-07 Animation		1	Allow	1	8,000	8,000	8,000	
					Total for 34-00			8,000
POST-PRODUCTION TOTAL								102,000
35-00 Insurance								
35-01 Producers Entertainment Pckg.								
Media/Negative			Allow	1		0	0	
Faulty Stock			Allow	1		0	0	
Equipment			Allow	1		0	0	
Props/Sets			Allow	1		0	0	
Extra Expense			Allow	1		0	0	
3rd Party Property Damage			Allow	1		0	0	
Office Contents			Allow	1		0	0	
35-02 General Liability		1	Allow	1	7,000	7,000	7,000	
35-03 Hired Auto			Allow	1		0	0	
35-04 Cast Insurance			Allow	1		0	0	
35-05 Workers Compensation		1	Allow	1	1,000	1,000	1,000	
35-06 Errors & Omissions			Allow	1		0	0	
					Total for 35-00			8,000
36-00 General & Administrative Expenses								
36-01 Business License/Taxes		1	Allow	1	2,500	2,500	2,500	
36-02 Legal		1	Allow	1	5,000	5,000	5,000	
36-03 Accounting fees			Allow	1		0	0	
36-05 Telephone/Fax			Allow	1		0	0	
36-06 Copying/Scanning		1	Allow	1	500	500	500	
36-07 Postage & Freight			Allow	1		0	0	
36-08 Office Space Rental		12	Months	1	350	4,200	4,200	
36-09 Office Furniture			Allow	1		0	0	
36-10 Office Equipment & Supplies		12	Months	1	50	600	600	
36-11 Computer Rental								
	Line Producer		Weeks	1		0	0	
	First AD		Weeks	1		0	0	
	Prod. Coordinator		Weeks	1		0	0	
	Prod. Accountant		Weeks	1		0	0	
	Office		Months	1		0	0	
	Printers		Months	1		0	0	
36-12 Software/Apps/FTP			Allow	1		0	0	
36-13 Transcription			Hours	1		0	0	
38-14 Messenger/Overnight			Allow	1		0	0	
36-15 Parking			Allow	1		0	0	
36-16 Storage			Allow	1		0	0	
36-18 Publicity			Allow	1		0	0	
36-19 Wrap Party			Allow	1		0	0	
36-20 Working Meals			Allow	1		0	0	
36-21 Overhead (Production fee)			Allow	1		0	0	
36-22 Completion Bond			Allow	1		0	0	
					Total for 36-00			12,800
37-00 Publicity and Marketing								
37-01 Publicity		1	Allow	1	5,000	5,000	5,000	
37-02 Marketing			Allow	1		0	0	
37-03 Outreach			Allow	1		0	0	
	Web designer	1	Allow	1	1,000	1,000	1,000	
	Web hosting	1	Allow	1	300	300	300	
					Total for 37-00			5,000
Total Above-the-Line								109,800
Total Below-the-Line								240,775
Total Above and Below-the-Line								350,575
		Amt.	Units	x	Rate	Sub-Total	Total	
Contingency								0
	GRAND TOTAL							$350,575

01–04 Research/Clearances
They will need to clear the title of the film with a title search attorney.

02–02 Producers
There are two producers who will help crew the film as well.

03–01 Director
The director can film some of the cinema-vérité scenes if necessary.

08–07 Technical Advisors
The filmmakers need to hire two expert witnesses to interview for the film.

08–08 Production Assistants
To round out the crew and assist in the office.

11–02 Art Director
This fee is to art direct some narrative elements to add to the visual storytelling of the film.

11–10 Purchases/Rentals
Art budget for the narrative elements.

19–06 Lighting Package Rental
Most of the time they will not use any lights. This package will supplement if they need some lighting for a portion of the shoot days.

20–01 Director of Photography
A flat fee for the DP. The Director can shoot if necessary on certain days as well.

20–07 Camera Package Rental
They may want to shoot a few days with a second camera or rent a special lens.

20–10 Camera Package Purchase
They plan to purchase a digital HD camera and sell the camera after they finish shooting.

21–01 Mixer
A low documentary rate for a Sound Recordist who is a friend of one of the producers.

21–03 Expendables/Batteries
For miscellaneous sound expenses and batteries.

21–04 Sound Package
For wireless lavalier microphones, boom microphone, and cables.

22–03 Transportation Vehicle Rental
The filmmakers can use their personal vehicles for some transport and will rent a minivan for a portion of the shoot days.

22–04 Parking/Tolls/Gas
For this production's transportation costs.

25–01 Digital Media
For enough data storage for production materials and a backup hard drive.

26–01 Airfares
They plan to travel for up to five domestic flights.

26–02 Hotels
The hotels for these trips.

26–08 Per Diem
Per diem for three people.

26–09 Gratuities
For tips and other miscellaneous cash.

27–01 Editor
A flat rate for the editor for a 15-week gig — 3 weeks while shooting and 12 weeks after principal photography ends.

28–01 Composer Fee
A flat fee for the composer, recording costs and musicians' fees, instrument rentals, and a music editor.

28–11 Music Licensing
Fees for five songs at a low rate.

28–12 Music Supervisor/Clearance
Fee for a Music Supervisor to clear the music licensing.

29–15 Audio Mix
A flat rate for the sound editor and audio mix.

30–01 Stock Footage
The filmmakers may need to license a short clip from a feature film.

32–01 Titling
For a simple opening title sequence and the end crawl credits.

33–01 Masters/Clones
For an HDCam SR master and a DCP file.

33–03 Transfers/Dubs
For miscellaneous post transfers.

34–07 Animation
The filmmakers plan to include a short graphic animation for one scene in the film.

35–02 General Liability
For the annual production/general liability insurance premium.

35–05 Workers' Compensation
To cover the crew during the production days.

36–01 Business License/Taxes
Fees to create an LLC and file the annual taxes.

36–02 Legal
The director's friend will do the legal work for a low flat fee.

36–06 Copying/Scanning
For miscellaneous office needs.

36–08 Office Space Rental
The producers have an office — this will offset a portion of their rent for one year.

36–10 Office Equipment/Supplies
For miscellaneous office needs.

37–01 Publicity
For creating the materials for press kits and film festival applications. They would like to hire a publicist as well. This is a very low rate.

37–03 Outreach
Fees to hire a web designer and web hosting. They will post information on the website during the prep, production, and post-production phases of the film.

Contingency
This is a very low budget film and there is no contingency. If there are any overages, the producer will need to lower expenses on another line item to cover them.

$145K INDUSTRIAL/SHORT DOCUMENTARY BUDGET

- Go to *www.mwp.com.*
- Click on "MW Film School."
- Open the item "Sample Budgets/Forms."
- Download the corresponding free Excel Budget Template.
- Save it to your computer.
- Last, this budget is a sample template. Make sure to create your budget with figures based on your research on current rates and prices available to you.

Budget Assumptions

This is an 8-minute industrial film for a Fortune 500 company about their new products for the coming year. It will be a 5-day shoot with 2 days locally in New York City and 3 days in Nashville, TN, at corporate headquarters. The director will write the script, prep, shoot, and work with the editor to complete the film for the corporate marketing team. The final master will be shown at seminars throughout the company via a video streaming service in conference rooms and on individual laptops. It will also be uploaded to the company website and used in other marketing initiatives.

$145K Industrial Budget

	SUMMARY BUDGET		
Fringe assumptions:	Production:	$145K Industrial/Short Documentary Budget	
Payroll Tax 0.00%	Shoot Days:	5	
WGA 0.00%	Location:	NYC (Local) & Nashville, TN	
DGA 0.00%	Unions:	No	
SAG 0.00%	Shooting Format:	Digital HD	
Overtime 0%	Delivery format:	HD Cam	
Contingency			

Account	Subtotal	Total
01-00 Story & Rights	$10,000	
02-00 Producers Unit	$20,000	
03-00 Direction	$20,000	
04-00 Cast	$0	
05-00 Travel & Living – Producers/Director	$6,900	
06-00 Travel & Living- Cast	$0	
07-00 Residuals	$0	
TOTAL ABOVE-THE-LINE		$56,900
08-00 Production Staff	$5,200	
09-00 Background Actors/Extras	$0	
10-00 Sound Stage	$0	
11-00 Production Design	$0	
12-00 Set Construction	$0	
13-00 Set Operations	$8,575	
14-00 Special Effects	$0	
15-00 Set Dressing	$0	
16-00 Property	$0	
17-00 Wardrobe	$0	
18-00 Make-Up and Hair	$0	
19-00 Electrical	$7,750	
20-00 Camera	$20,750	
21-00 Production Sound	$4,350	
22-00 Transportation	$2,525	
23-00 Location Expenses	$1,350	
24-00 Picture Vehicle/Animals	$0	
25-00 Media	$600	
26-00 Travel and Living-Crew	$2,195	
TOTAL PRODUCTION		$53,295
27-00 Editorial	$12,000	
28-00 Music	$2,000	
29-00 Post-Production Sound	$0	
30-00 Post-Production - Digital and Film	$0	
31-00 Digital Intermediate	$1,000	
32-00 Titling and Graphics	$0	
33-00 Deliverables	$375	
34-00 Digital Visual Effects/Animation	$0	
TOTAL POST-PRODUCTION		$15,375
35-00 Insurance	$5,600	
36-00 General & Administrative Expenses	$660	
37-00 Publicity and Marketing	$0	
TOTAL GENERAL		$6,260
Total Above-the-Line		$56,900
Total Below-the-Line		$74,930
Total Above and Below-the-Line		$131,830
Contingency		$13,183
GRAND TOTAL		$145,013

$145K Industrial Budget

ABOVE-THE-LINE								
		Amt.	Units	x	Rate	Sub-Total	Total	
01-00 Story & Rights								
01-01 Rights Purchases			Allow	1		0	0	
01-02 Options			Allow	1		0	0	
01-03 Writer Salary		1	Allow	1	5,000	5,000	5,000	
01-04 Research		1	Allow	1	5,000	5,000	5,000	
01-05 Title Registration			Allow	1		0	0	
01-06 Script Timing			Allow	1		0	0	
01-07 Storyboards/Pre-Viz			Allow	1		0	0	
01-08 WGA Publication fee			Allow	1		0	0	
01-10 Development			Allow	1		0	0	
	Payroll					5,000	0	
	WGA					5,000	0	
					Total for 01-00			10,000
02-00 Producers Unit								
02-01 Executive Producer			Allow	1		0	0	
02-02 Producer(including Post-Prod./Delivery		1	Allow	1	20,000	20,000	20,000	
02-03 Associate Producer			Allow	1		0	0	
02-04 Assistant to Producer(s)			Week(s)	1		0	0	
02-06 Consultants			Allow	1		0	0	
02-07 Miscellaneous Expenses			Allow	1		0	0	
	Payroll					20,000	0	
					Total for 02-00			20,000
03-00 Direction								
03-01 Director		1	Allow	1	20,000	20,000	20,000	
03-02 Assistant to Director		1	Weeks	1		0	0	
	Payroll					20,000	0	
	DGA					20,000	0	
					Total for 03-00			20,000
04-00 Cast								
04-01 Lead Actors								
			Allow	1		0		
			Allow	1		0		
Overtime Allowance			Allow	1		0	0	
04-02 Supporting Cast								
			Week(s)	1		0		
			Week(s)	1		0		
			Week(s)	1		0		
			Week(s)	1		0		
Overtime Allowance			Allow	1		0	0	
04-03 Day Players								
			Day(s)	1		0		
			Day(s)	1		0		
			Day(s)	1		0		
			Day(s)	1		0		
			Day(s)	1		0		
			Day(s)	1		0		
			Day(s)	1		0		
			Day(s)	1		0		
			Day(s)	1		0		
			Day(s)	1		0		
			Day(s)	1		0		
Overtime Allowance			Allow	1		0	0	
04-04 Casting Director/Staff			Allow	1		0	0	
04-05 Casting Expenses			Allow	1		0	0	
04-06 Choreographer			Weeks	1		0	0	
04-07 Assistant(s) to Choreographer			Weeks	1		0	0	
04-08 Dialect Coach			Weeks	1		0	0	
04-09 Narrator/Voiceover Artist			Weeks	1		0	0	

$145K Industrial Budget

		Amt.	Units	x	Rate	Sub-Total	Total	
04-10 Stunt Coordinator			Weeks	1		0	0	
04-11 Stunt Players (6 day weeks)			Weeks	1		0	0	
04-12 Stunt Costs/Adjustments			Allow	1		0	0	
04-13 Stunt Equipment			Allow	1		0	0	
04-14 ADR (Actors' fees)			Allow	1		0	0	
	Payroll					0	0	
	SAG					0	0	
					Total for 04-00			0
05-00 Travel & Living – Producers/Director								
05-01 Airfares		2	RT	2	500	2,000	2,000	
05-02 Hotel		6	Nights	2	275	3,300	3,300	
05-03 Taxi		2	Allow	2	120	480	480	
05-04 Auto		8	Allow	1	65	520	520	
05-05 Train			Allow	1		0	0	
05-06 Excess Baggage			Allow	1		0	0	
05-07 Phone			Allow	1		0	0	
05-08 Gratuities			Allow	1		0	0	
05-09 Per Diem		8	Days	1	75	600	600	
					Total for 05-00			6,900
06-00 Travel & Living – Cast								
06-01 Airfares			RT	1		0	0	
06-02 Hotels			Nights	1		0	0	
06-03 Taxi/Limo			Allow	1		0	0	
06-04 Auto			Allow	1		0	0	
06-05 Train			Allow	1		0	0	
06-06 Excess Baggage			Allow	1		0	0	
06-07 Phone			Allow	1		0	0	
06-08 Gratuities			Allow	1		0	0	
06-09 Per Diem			Days	1		0	0	
					Total for 06-00			0
07-00 Residuals			Allow	1		0	0	
					Total for 07-00			0
TOTAL ABOVE-THE-LINE								56,900

$145K Industrial Budget

		Amt.	Units	x	Rate	Sub-Total	Total	
BELOW-THE-LINE								
08-00 Production Staff								
08-01 UPM/Line Producer								
	Prep/Travel		Weeks	1		0		
	Shoot		Weeks	1		0		
	Wrap		Weeks	1		0		
	Severance		Allow	1		0	0	
08-02 Assistant Directors								
First AD								
	Prep/Travel		Weeks	1		0		
	Shoot		Weeks	1		0		
	Prod. Fee (shoot days)		Days	1		0		
	Severance		Allow	1		0		
	Overtime Allow		Days	1		0	0	
2nd AD								
	Prep/Travel		Weeks	1		0		
	Shoot		Weeks	1		0		
	Prod. Fee		Days	1		0		
	Severance		Allow	1		0		
	Overtime Allow		Days	1		0	0	
08-03 Stage Manager								
	Prep/Travel		Weeks	1		0		
	Shoot		Weeks	1		0		
	Prod. Fee		Days	1		0		
	Severance		Allow	1		0		
	Overtime Allow		Days	1		0	0	
08-04 Production Coordinator								
	Prep/Travel		Weeks	1		0		
	Shoot		Days	1		0		
	Wrap		Weeks	1		0	0	
Ass't Coord.								
	Prep		Weeks	1		0		
	Shoot		Weeks	1		0		
	Wrap		Weeks	1		0	0	
08-05 Script Supervisor								
	Prep		Days	1		0		
	Shoot		Days	1		0		
	Saturdays Worked		Days	1		0		
	Wrap		Days	1		0		
	2nd Camera Days		Days	1		0		
	Overtime		Allow		0	0	0	
08-06 Production Accountant/Auditor								
	Prep/Travel		Weeks	1		0		
	Shoot		Weeks	1		0		
	Wrap		Weeks	1		0		
	Post-Production		Weeks	1		0	0	
Assistant Accountant								
	Prep/Travel		Weeks	1		0		
	Shoot		Weeks	1		0		
	Wrap		Weeks	1		0	0	
08-07 Technical Advisors			Flat	1		0	0	
08-08 Production Assistants								
Office Prod. Assistant(s)								
	Prep		Days	1		0		
	Shoot		Days	1		0		
	Wrap		Days	1		0		
Set Prod. Assistant(s)								
	Prep	4	Days	2	200	1,600	1,600	
	Shoot	5	Days	2	200	2,000	3,600	
08-09 Studio Teacher/Tutor			Weeks	1		0	0	
	Payroll					5,200	0	
	DGA					0	0	
					Total for 08-00			5,200

$145K Industrial Budget

		Amt.	Units	x	Rate	Sub-Total	Total	
09-00 Background Actors/Extras								
09-01 Stand-ins			Days	1		0	0	
09-02 Extras			Extras	1		0	0	
09-05 Extras Casting Fee @ 10%			Allow	1		0	0	
09-10 Extras Transportation			Allow	1		0	0	
	Payroll					0	0	
	P&H					0	0	
					Total for 09-00			0
10-00 Sound Stage								
10-01 Stage Rental			Allow	1		0	0	
	Prep		Allow	1		0	0	
	Pre-Light		Allow	1		0	0	
	Shoot		Allow	1		0	0	
	Wrap		Allow	1		0	0	
	Overtime		Allow	1		0	0	
10-02 Stage Lighting Rental			Allow	1		0	0	
10-03 Stage Grip Rental			Allow	1		0	0	
10-04 Phones/ Internet			Allow	1		0	0	
10-05 Garbage removal			Allow	1		0	0	
10-06 Green Room			Allow	1		0	0	
10-07 Make Up Room			Allow	1		0	0	
10-08 Office Rental			Allow	1		0	0	
10-09 Parking			Allow	1		0	0	
					Total for 10-00			0
11-00 Production Design								
11-01 Production Designer								
	Prep/Travel		Weeks	1		0		
	Shoot		Weeks	1		0	0	
11-02 Art Director								
	Prep/Travel		Weeks	1		0		
	Shoot		Weeks	1		0	0	
11-03 Art Assistants								
	Prep/Travel		Days	1		0		
	Shoot		Days	1		0	0	
11-04 Set Designer								
	Prep/Travel		Weeks	1		0		
	Shoot		Weeks	1		0	0	
11-05 Model Makers/Miniatures			Allow	1		0	0	
11-06 Draftsperson			Allow	1		0	0	
11-08 Research/Materials			Allow	1		0	0	
11-09 Vehicle Expenses			Weeks	1		0	0	
11-10 Purchases/Rentals			Allow	1		0	0	
	Payroll					0	0	
					Total for 11-00			0
12-00 Set Construction								
12-01 Construction Coordinator								
	Prep		Days	1		0		
	Shoot		Days	1		0		
	Overtime		Allow	1	0	0	0	
12-02 Foreman								
	Prep		Days	1		0		
	Shoot		Days	1		0		
	Overtime		Allow	1	0	0	0	
Carpenters			Allow	1		0	0	
12-03 Scenic Painters								
Lead Scenic Painter								
	Prep		Days	1		0		
	Shoot		Days	1		0		
	Overtime		Allow	1	0	0	0	
Painters			Allow	1		0	0	
12-05 Greensmen			Allow	1		0	0	

$145K Industrial Budget

		Amt.	Units	x	Rate	Sub-Total	Total	
12-06 Construction materials - Purchases			Allow	1		0	0	
12-07 Construction materials - Rentals			Allow	1		0	0	
12-08 Construction Equipment			Allow	1		0	0	
12-09 Set Strike			Allow	1		0	0	
	Payroll					0	0	
					Total for 12-00			0
13-00 Set Operations								
13-01 Key Grip								
	Prep/Travel		Days	1		0		
	Shoot	5	Days	1	550	2,750		
	Wrap		Days	1		0		
	Overtime		Allow	1	2,750	0	2,750	
13-02 Best Boy Grip								
	Prep		Days	1		0		
	Shoot		Days	1		0		
	Wrap		Days	1		0		
	Overtime		Allow	1	0	0	0	
13-03 Grips								
3rd Grip								
	Prep		Days	1		0		
	Shoot		Days	1		0		
	Wrap		Days	1		0		
	Overtime		Allow	1	0	0	0	
4th Grip								
	Prep		Days	1		0		
	Shoot		Days	1		0		
	Wrap		Days	1		0		
	Overtime		Allow	1	0	0	0	
Additional Grips			Days	1		0		
	Overtime		Allow	1		0	0	
13-04 Dolly/Crane Grips								
	Prep		Days	1		0		
	Shoot		Days	1		0		
	Overtime		Allow	1	0	0	0	
13-06 Grip Rentals								
	Package	5	Days	1	1,000	5,000		
	Dollies		Weeks	1		0		
	Cranes (incl. Driver)		Days	1		0		
	Add'l Equip.		Allow	1		0	5,000	
13-07 Expendables		1	Allow	1	200	200	200	
13-08 Kit Rentals								
	Key Grip		Weeks	1		0	0	
	Craft Service		Weeks	1		0	0	
13-10 Craft Service								
	Prep		Days	1		0		
	Shoot		Days	1		0		
	Wrap		Days	1		0		
	Overtime		Allow	1	0	0	0	
Purchases		5	Days	1	125	625	625	
Rentals			Allow	1		0	0	
13-15 Air Conditioning/Heating			Days	1		0	0	
	Payroll					2,750	0	
					Total for 13-00			8,575
14-00 Special Effects								
14-01 Special Effects Person								
	Prep/Travel		Days	1		0		
	Shoot		Days	1		0		
	Overtime		Allow	1	0	0	0	
14-02 SFX Assistant(s)								
	Shoot		Days	1		0		
	Overtime		Allow	1	0	0	0	
14-03 Additional Labor								

$145K Industrial Budget

		Amt.	*Units*	*x*	*Rate*	*Sub-Total*	*Total*	
	Shoot		Days	1		0		
	Overtime		Allow	1	0	0	0	
14-06 Manufacturing Labor			Allow	1		0	0	
14-07 Fabrication			Allow	1		0	0	
14-09 Rentals			Allow	1		0	0	
	Payroll				0	0	0	
					Total for 14-00			0
15-00 Set Dressing								
15-01 Set Decorator								
	Prep/Travel		Days	1		0		
	Shoot		Days	1		0		
	Wrap		Days	1		0		
	Overtime				0	0	0	
15-02 Lead Person								
	Prep/Travel		Days	1		0		
	Shoot		Days	1		0		
	Wrap		Days	1		0		
	Overtime				0	0	0	
15-03 Swing Gang/Set Dressers								
Set Dresser #1								
	Prep		Days	1		0		
	Shoot		Days	1		0		
	Wrap		Days	1		0		
	Overtime				0	0	0	
Set Dresser #2								
	Prep		Days	1		0		
	Shoot		Days	1		0		
	Wrap		Days	1		0		
	Overtime				0	0	0	
Set Dresser #3								
	Prep		Days	1		0		
	Shoot		Days	1		0		
	Wrap		Days	1		0		
	Overtime				0	0	0	
15-04 Additional Labor								
On-Set Dresser (Shoot)			Days	1		0		
	Overtime				0	0	0	
15-05 Expendables			Allow	1		0	0	
15-06 Purchases			Allow	1		0	0	
15-07 Rentals			Allow	1		0	0	
15-08 Loss & Damage			Allow	1		0	0	
15-09 Kit Rentals						0	0	
	Set Decorator		Weeks	1		0	0	
	Lead Person		Weeks	1		0	0	
15-10 Vehicle Expenses								
	Set Decorator		Weeks	1		0	0	
	Lead Person		Weeks	1		0	0	
	Payroll				0	0	0	
					Total for 15-00			0
16-00 Property								
16-01 Property Master								
	Prep/Travel		Days	1		0		
	Shoot		Days	1		0		
	Wrap		Days	1		0		
	Overtime				0	0	0	
16-02 Prop Assistant								
	Prep		Days	1		0		
	Shoot		Days	1		0		
	Wrap		Days	1		0		
	Overtime				0	0	0	
16-03 Purchases			Allow	1		0	0	

$145K Industrial Budget

		Amt.	Units	x	Rate	Sub-Total	Total	
16-04 Rentals			Allow	1		0	0	
16-05 Loss & Damage			Allow	1		0	0	
16-06 Kit Rentals								
	Prop Master		Weeks	1		0	0	
16-07 Vehicle Expenses								
	Prop Master		Weeks	1		0	0	
	Assistant		Weeks	1		0	0	
	Payroll				0	0	0	
					Total for 16-00			0
17-00 Wardrobe								
17-01 Costume Designer								
	Prep/Travel		Weeks	1		0		
	Shoot		Weeks	1		0		
	Wrap		Week	1		0	0	
17-02 Costumer								
	Prep/Travel		Days	1		0		
	Shoot		Days	1		0		
	Wrap		Days	1		0		
	Overtime		Allow	1	0	0	0	
17-03 Additional Costumer(s)								
	Prep		Days	1		0		
	Shoot		Days	1		0		
	Wrap		Days	1		0		
	Overtime		Allow	1	0	0	0	
17-04 Expendables			Allow	1		0	0	
17-05 Purchases			Allow	1		0	0	
17-06 Rentals			Allow	1		0	0	
17-07 Alteration & Repairs			Allow	1		0	0	
17-08 Cleaning & Dyeing			Allow	1		0	0	
17-09 Loss & Damage			Allow	1		0	0	
17-10 Kit Rentals								
	Costume Designer		Weeks	1		0	0	
17-11 Vehicle Expenses								
	Costume Designer		Weeks	1		0	0	
	Payroll				0	0	0	
					Total for 17-00			0
18-00 Make-Up and Hair								
18-01 Key Make-Up Artist								
	Prep/Travel		Days	1		0		
	Shoot		Days	1		0		
	Wrap		Days	1		0		
	Overtime		Allow	1	0	0	0	
18-02 Additional Make-Up Artist(s)			Days	1		0		
	Shoot		Days	1		0		
	Overtime		Allow	1	0	0	0	
18-03 Key Hair Stylist								
	Prep/Travel		Days	1		0		
	Shoot		Days	1		0		
	Wrap		Days	1		0		
	Overtime		Allow	1	0	0	0	
18-04 Additional Hair Stylist(s)			Days	1		0		
	Shoot		Days	1		0		
	Overtime		Allow	1	0	0	0	
18-05 Special Effects Makeup Effects			Allow	1		0	0	
18-06 Purchases			Allow	1		0	0	
18-07 Rentals			Weeks	1		0	0	
18-08 Kit Rentals								
	Key Make-Up		Days	1		0	0	
	Add'l Make-Up		Days	1		0	0	
	Hair Stylist		Days	1		0	0	
	Add'l Hair		Days	1		0	0	
	Payroll				0	0	0	
					Total for 18-00			0

$145K Industrial Budget

		Amt.	*Units*	*x*	*Rate*	*Sub-Total*	*Total*	
19-00 Electrical								
19-01 Gaffer								
	Prep/Travel		Days	1		0		
	Shoot	5	Days	1	550	2,750		
	Wrap/Travel		Days	1		0		
	Overtime		Allow	1	2,750	0	2,750	
19-02 Best Boy Electric								
	Prep		Days	1		0		
	Shoot		Days	1		0		
	Wrap		Days	1		0		
	Overtime		Allow	1	0	0	0	
19-03 Electrics								
3rd Electric								
	Prep		Days	1		0		
	Shoot		Days	1		0		
	Wrap		Days	1		0		
	Overtime		Allow	1	0	0	0	
4th Electric								
	Prep		Days	1		0		
	Shoot		Days	1		0		
	Wrap		Days	1		0		
	Overtime		Allow	1	0	0	0	
19-04 Additional Labor								
	Shoot		Days	1		0		
	Overtime		Allow	1	0	0	0	
19-05 Equipment Purchases			Days	1		0	0	
19-06 Lighting Package Rental		5	Days	1	1,000	5,000	5,000	
	Add'l Equip.		Allow	1		0	0	
	Condors		Allow	1		0	0	
	Additional Generator		Allow	1		0	0	
19-07 Additional Rentals			Allow	1		0	0	
19-08 Electrical Generator/Driver			Days	1		0	0	
19-09 Loss & Damage			Allow	1		0	0	
19-10 Kit Rentals								
	Gaffer		Weeks	1		0	0	
	Payroll				2,750	0	0	
					Total for 19-00			7,750
20-00 Camera								
20-01 Director of Photography								
	Prep/Travel	2	Days	1	750	1,500		
	Shoot	5	Days	1	1,250	6,250	7,750	
20-02 Camera Operator or B Camera								
	Prep/Travel		Days	1		0		
	Shoot		Days	1		0		
	Overtime		Allow	1	0	0	0	
20-03 1st Assistant Camera								
	Prep/Travel		Days	1		0		
	Shoot		Days	1		0		
	Wrap		Days	1		0		
	Overtime		Allow	1	0	0		
	B Cam 1st Ass't		Days	1		0	0	
	Overtime		Allow	1	0	0	0	
20-04 2nd Ass't Camera								
	Prep		Days	1		0		
	Shoot		Days	1		0		
	Wrap		Days	1		0		
	Overtime		Allow	1	0	0	0	
	B Cam 2nd Ass't		Days	1		0		
	Overtime		Allow	1	0	0	0	
20-05 Digital Imaging Technician (DIT)		5	Days	1	550	2,750	2,750	
	Overtime		Allow	1	2,750	0	2,750	
20-06 Still Photographer			Allow	1		0	0	

$145K Industrial Budget

		Amt.	Units	x	Rate	Sub-Total	Total	
20-07 Camera Package Rental		5	Days	1	1,000	5,000	5,000	
20-10 Camera Package Purchase			Allow	1		0	0	
20-11 Steadicam Operator & Equip.			Days	1		0	0	
20-12 Teleprompter/Operator			Days	1		0	0	
20-13 Video Assist/Operator			Days	1		0	0	
20-14 Aerial Photography			Days	1		0	0	
20-15 Underwater and Topside Photography			Days	1		0	0	
20-16 Drones/GoPros			Days	1		0	0	
22-17 Maintenance/Loss & Damage			Allow	1		0	0	
20-18 Motion Control			Allow	1		0	0	
20-19 Expendables		1	Allow	1	250	250	250	
20-20 Video Truck			Weeks	1		0	0	
20-21 DIT Equipment Rental		5	Days	1	450	2,250	2,250	
20-25 Video Truck Crew			Weeks	1		0	0	
20-26 Kit Rentals								
	1st Ass't Cam		Weeks	1		0	0	
	Payroll				13,250	0	0	
					Total for 20-00			**20,750**
21-00 Production Sound								
21-01 Mixer								
	Prep		Days	1		0		
	Shoot	5	Days	1	550	2,750		
	Wrap/Travel		Days	1		0		
	Overtime		Allow	1	2,750	0	2,750	
21-02 Boom Operator								
	Shoot		Days	1		0		
	Overtime		Allow	1	0	0	0	
21-03 Expendables/Batteries		1	Allow	1	100	100	100	
21-04 Sound Package		5	Days	1	300	1,500	1,500	
21-05 Walkie-Talkies			Weeks	1		0	0	
21-06 Sound Truck			Weeks	1		0	0	
21-08 Misc. / Loss & Damage			Allow	1		0	0	
	Payroll				2,750	0	0	
					Total for 21-00			**4,350**
22-00 Transportation								
22-01 Transportation Coordinator								
			Weeks	1		0	0	
22-02 Drivers								
Captain								
	Prep		Days	1		0		
	Shoot		Days	1		0		
	Wrap		Days	1		0	0	
Star Trailer Drivers								
Driver #1								
	Prep		Day	1		0		
	Shoot		Days	1		0		
	Wrap		Day	1		0	0	
Driver #2								
	Prep		Day	1		0		
	Shoot		Days	1		0		
	Wrap		Day	1		0	0	
Production Van Driver								
	Prep		Days	1		0		
	Shoot		Days	1		0		
	Wrap		Days	1		0	0	
Camera Truck Driver								
	Prep		Days	1		0		
	Shoot		Days	1		0		
	Wrap		Days	1		0	0	
Stakebed Driver (Construction)								
	Shoot		Days	1		0	0	
Set Dressing Driver								
	Prep		Days	1		0		

$145K Industrial Budget

		Amt.	Units	x	Rate	Sub-Total	Total	
	Shoot		Days	1		0		
	Wrap		Days	1		0	0	
Second Set Dressing 5 Ton			Days	1		0	0	
Props Driver								
	Prep		Days	1		0		
	Shoot		Days	1		0		
	Wrap		Days	1		0	0	
Make-Up/Wardrobe Driver								
	Prep		Days	1		0		
	Shoot		Days	1		0		
	Wrap		Days	1		0	0	
Prod. Office Trailer Driver								
	Prep		Days	1		0		
	Shoot		Days	1		0		
	Wrap		Days	1		0	0	
Honeywagon Driver								
	Shoot		Days	1		0		
	Wrap		Days	1		0	0	
15-Passenger Van #1 Driver								
	Prep		Days	1		0		
	Shoot		Days	1		0	0	
15-Passenger Van #2 Driver								
	Prep		Days	1		0		
	Shoot		Days	1		0	0	
Car Carrier			Days	1		0	0	
Insert Car (car to car cam platform)			Days	1		0	0	
Water Truck Driver			Days	1		0	0	
Caterer	Shoot		Days	1		0	0	
Caterer Ass't	Shoot		Days	1		0	0	
Additional Drivers			Allow	1		0	0	
22-03 Transportation Vehicle Rental								
Minivan - Scout		3	Days	1	75	225	225	
Minivan - Prep/Shoot		9	Days	1	75	675	675	
Cargo Van		9	Days	1	125	1,125	1,125	
Production Van (40' w/ 2 gennies)			Weeks	1		0	0	
Camera Truck			Weeks	1		0	0	
Stake Bed			Weeks	1		0	0	
Set Dressing 5 Ton			Weeks	1		0	0	
Add'l Set Dressing 5 Ton			Weeks	1		0	0	
Set Dress Van			Weeks	1		0	0	
Props 5 Ton			Weeks	1		0	0	
Wardrobe/Make-Up			Weeks	1		0	0	
Crew Stake Bed			Weeks	1		0	0	
Prod. Office Trailer			Weeks	1		0	0	
Honeywagon (Portable Toilets)			Days	1		0	0	
Water Truck			Days	1		0	0	
Gas Truck			Days	1		0	0	
15-Passenger Van			Days	1		0	0	
Car Tow Trailer			Days	1		0	0	
Car Trailer			Days	1		0	0	
Camera Car			Days	1		0	0	
22-04 Parking/Tolls/Gas		1	Allow	1	500	500	500	
22-05 Repairs & Maintenance			Allow	1		0	0	
22-06 Honeywagon Pumping			Allow	1		0	0	
22-07 Miscellaneous			Allow	1		0	0	
	Payroll				0	0	0	
					Total for 22-00			2,525
23-00 Location Expenses								
23-01 Location Manager			Weeks	1		0	0	
23-02 Location Assistants								
Assistant Location Mgr.			Weeks	1		0	0	
Local Contact Person			Weeks	1		0	0	
23-03 First Aid/Medic			Weeks	1		0	0	
23-04 Fire Officers								

$145K Industrial Budget

		Amt.	Units	x	Rate	Sub-Total	Total	
	Shoot		Days	1		0	0	
23-05 Security			Allow	1		0	0	
23-06 Police			Days	1		0	0	
	Additional Police		Allow	1		0	0	
23-07 Permits			Allow	1		0	0	
23-08 Parking			Allow	1		0	0	
23-09 Catering Services								
Crew Meals		5	Days	10	25	1,250	1,250	
Extras			Meals	1		0	0	
Ice/Propane			Weeks	1		0	0	
2nd Meals			Days	1		0	0	
Sales Tax			Allow	1		0	0	
Tent			Allow	1		0	0	
23-11 Location Office Space Rental			Months	1		0	0	
23-12 Location Office Supplies		1	Allow	1	100	100	100	
23-13 Location Office Equipment			Allow	1		0	0	
23-14 Location Office Telephone/Fax			Allow	1		0	0	
23-17 Location Site Rental Fees								
	Shoot		Days	1		0	0	
23-18 Location Scout			Allow	1		0	0	
	Photos		Allow	1		0	0	
23-19 Auto Rentals								
Location Manager			Weeks	1		0	0	
Assistants			Weeks	1		0	0	
23-20 Miscellaneous Expenses								
	Mileage/DGA/SAG/Crew		Allow	1		0	0	
	Payroll				0	0	0	
					Total for 23-00			1,350
24-00 Picture Vehicles/Animals								
24-01 Animal Trainers								
Boss Wrangler			Weeks	1		0	0	
Assistant Wrangler			Weeks	1		0	0	
Wranglers			Week	1		0	0	
Riders/Handlers, etc			Day	1		0	0	
24-02 Animals								
	Horses		Allow	1		0	0	
Veterinary Expenses			Allow	1		0	0	
Feed/Shelter			Allow	1		0	0	
Transportation			Allow	1		0	0	
24-03 Picture Cars								
	Car #1		Weeks	1		0	0	
	Car #2		Weeks	1		0	0	
	Car #3		Weeks	1		0	0	
	Background Cars		Allow	1		0	0	
	Payroll				0	0	0	
					Total for 24-00			0
25-00 Media								
25-01 Digital Media		1	Each	2	300	600	600	
25-02 Raw Film Stock			Feet	1		0	0	
25-03 Film Lab-Negative Prep & Process			Feet	1		0	0	
25-04 Telecine/Film to Digital transfer			Allow	1		0	0	
25-05 Videotape stock			Each	1		0	0	
					Total for 25-00			600
26-00 Travel and Living - Crew								
26-01 Airfares		1	RT	1	500	500	500	
28-02 Hotels		4	Nites	1	275	1,100	1,100	
28-03 Taxi		1	Trip	1	120	120	120	
28-04 Auto			Days	1		0	0	
28-05 Train			RT	1		0	0	
28-06 Excess Baggage			Allow	1		0	0	
28-08 Per Diem		5	Days	1	75	375	375	
28-09 Gratuities		1	Allow	1	100	100	100	
					Total for 26-00			2,195

$145K Industrial Budget

	Amt.	Units	x	Rate	Sub-Total	Total	
TOTAL PRODUCTION							**$53,295**
27-00 Editorial							
27-01 Editor - Shoot/Post	4	Weeks	1	2,500	10,000	10,000	
27-02 Assistant Editor - Shoot/Post		Weeks	1		0	0	
27-04 Post-Production Supervisor		Weeks	1		0	0	
27-05 Editing Room Rental-At Home		Weeks	1		0	0	
27-06 Edit System Rental	4	Weeks	1	500	2,000	2,000	
27-10 On-Line Editing/Conform		Days	1		0	0	
Payroll				10,000	0	0	
				Total for 27-00			**12,000**
28-00 Music							
28-01 Composer Fee		Allow	1		0	0	
28-02 Musicians		Allow	1		0	0	
28-03 Music Prep		Allow	1		0	0	
28-04 Studio Costs		Allow	1		0	0	
28-05 Music Scoring Stage		Allow	1		0	0	
28-06 Cartage and Rentals		Allow	1		0	0	
28-07 Music Mix Room		Allow	1		0	0	
28-08 Singers		Allow	1		0	0	
28-09 Payroll Service		Allow	1		0	0	
28-10 Miscellaneous		Allow	1		0	0	
28-11 Music Licensing	1	Allow	1	2,000	2,000	2,000	
28-12 Music Supervisor/Clearance		Allow	1		0	0	
				Total for 28-00			**2,000**
29-00 Post-Production Sound							
29-01 Sound Editor		Weeks	1		0	0	
29-02 Assistant Sound Editor		Weeks	1		0	0	
29-03 Music Editor		Weeks	1		0	0	
29-04 Dialogue Editor		Weeks	1		0	0	
29-05 Spotting (Music & FX)		Hours	1		0	0	
29-08 ADR (Studio/Editor)		Days	1		0	0	
29-09 Foley Stage/Editor		Days	1		0	0	
29-10 Foley Artists		Days	1		0	0	
29-12 Narration Recording		Hours	1		0	0	
29-13 Audio Laydown		Hours	1		0	0	
29-15 Audio Mix		Hours	1		0	0	
29-17 Dolby License		Allow	1		0	0	
29-18 Miscellaneous Expenses		Allow	1		0	0	
				Total for 29-00			**0**
30-00 Post-Producton - Digital and Film							
30-01 Stock Footage		Reels	1		0	0	
30-02 Archive F Supplies		Allow	1		0	0	
30-04 Archival Researcher		Weeks	1		0	0	
30-06 Clearance Supervisor		Weeks	1		0	0	
30-09 Screeners		Allow	1		0	0	
30-11 Film Prints		Allow	1		0	0	
30-12 Miscellaneous Expenses		Allow	1		0	0	
				Total for 30-00			**0**
31-00 Digital Intermediate							
31-01 Digital Intermediate		Allow	1		0	0	
31-02 Hard Drive Purchases	1	Allow	1	1,000	1,000	1,000	
31-03 Color Grading		Hours	1		0	0	
				Total for 31-00			**1,000**
32-00 Titling and Graphics							
32-01 Titling		Allow	1		0	0	
32-02 Graphic Designer		Allow	1		0	0	
32-05 Special Graphic Effects		Allow	1		0	0	
32-06 Motion Control		Allow	1		0	0	
32-08 Closed Captioning		Allow	1		0	0	

$145K Industrial Budget

		Amt.	Units	x	Rate	Sub-Total	Total	
32-09 Subtitling			Allow	1		0	0	
					Total for 32-00			0
33-00 Deliverables								
33-01 Masters/Clones		3	Allow	1	125	375	375	
3303 Transfers and Dubs			Allow	1		0	0	
33-05 Screening Copies			Allow	1		0	0	
					Total for 33-00			375
34-00 Digital Visual Effects/Animation								
34-01 VFX			Allow	1		0	0	
34-07 Animation			Allow	1		0	0	
					Total for 34-00			0
POST-PRODUCTION TOTAL								**$15,375**
35-00 Insurance								
35-01 Producers Entertainment Pckg.								
Media/Negative			Allow	1		0	0	
Faulty Stock			Allow	1		0	0	
Equipment			Allow	1		0	0	
Props/Sets			Allow	1		0	0	
Extra Expense			Allow	1		0	0	
3rd Party Property Damage			Allow	1		0	0	
Office Contents			Allow	1		0	0	
35-02 General Liability		1	Allow	1	5,000	5,000	5,000	
35-03 Hired Auto			Allow	1		0	0	
35-04 Cast Insurance			Allow	1		0	0	
35-05 Workers Compensation		1	Allow	1	600	600	600	
35-06 Errors & Omissions			Allow	1		0	0	
					Total for 35-00			5,600
36-00 General & Administrative Expenses								
36-01 Business License/Taxes			Allow	1		0	0	
36-02 Legal			Allow	1		0	0	
36-03 Accounting fees			Allow	1		0	0	
36-05 Telephone/Fax			Allow	1		0	0	
36-06 Copying/Scanning			Allow	1		0	0	
36-07 Postage & Freight			Allow	1		0	0	
36-08 Office Space Rental			Allow	1		0	0	
36-09 Office Furniture			Allow	1		0	0	
36-10 Office Equipment & Supplies			Allow	1		0	0	
36-11 Computer Rental								
	Line Producer		Weeks	1		0	0	
	First AD		Weeks	1		0	0	
	Prod. Coordinator		Weeks	1		0	0	
	Prod. Accountant		Weeks	1		0	0	
	Office		Months	1		0	0	
	Printers		Months	1		0	0	
36-12 Software/Apps/FTP			Allow	1		0	0	
36-13 Transcription			Hours	1		0	0	
36-14 Messenger/Overnight Shipping		1	Allow	1	500	500	500	
36-15 Parking			Allow	1		0	0	
36-16 Storage			Allow	1		0	0	
36-18 Publicity			Allow	1		0	0	
36-19 Wrap Party			Allow	1		0	0	
36-20 Working Meals		1	Allow	1	160	160	160	
36-21 Overhead			Allow	1		0	0	
36-22 Completion Bond			Allow	1		0	0	
					Total for 36-00			660
37-00 Publicity and Marketing								
37-01 Publicity			Allow	1		0	0	
37-02 Marketing			Allow	1		0	0	
					Total for 37-00			0
Total Above-the-Line								56,900
Total Below-the-Line								74,930
Total Above and Below-the-Line								131,830
Production Fee (10%)								13,183
	GRAND TOTAL							**$145,013**

01–03 and 01–04 Writer Salary and Research
The writer has to pre-interview many of the people she will be interviewing for the project. Then she will need to write a script, get company feedback, and do a polish.

02–02 Producer
The producer will coordinate meetings/calls with the client, scout locations, hire crew, create the schedule and budget, produce the shoot days, organize post-production, oversee the approval process, and deliver the master according to pre-approved tech specs.

03–01 Director
The director (who is the also the writer) will research, write, and revise the script. Create the interview questions, scout locations, approve crew hires, consult on schedule and budget, direct all filming, create a paper cut edit, work directly with the editor, oversee all creative editorial decisions (including music) with client consultation, and deliver the final master according to the schedule.

05–01 Airfares
The producer and director will fly to Nashville for a location scout/client meetings once before they fly in for the three shoot days.

05–02 Hotel
For the two trips to Nashville for scout and shoot.

05–03 Taxi
For round-trip taxi to and from the airport in NYC.

05–04 Auto
For car rental when in Nashville.

05–09 Per Diem
For the days away from NYC.

08–08 Production Assistants
Will need to hire two Production Assistants for pickup days, shoot days, and returns days. They will be local to NYC or Nashville.

13–01 Key Grip
The Key Grip will be a local NYC or Nashville hire for a 10-hr. day with lunch "off the clock" — the crew person isn't paid for the meal period.

13–06 Grip Rentals
Grip equipment will be rented locally in NYC or Nashville.

13–07 Expendables
For gaffers tape, gels, clothespins, etc.

13–10 Craft Service
For snacks for a small crew.

19–01 Gaffer
Same as above for Key Grip.

19–06 Lighting Package Rental
Same as above for Grip Rentals.

20–00 Director of Photography
The DP will shoot in NYC and Nashville. He will look at location scout photos and work with local crew in Nashville that he knows from a shoot he did there three years ago.

20–05 Digital Imaging Technician (DIT)
Local hire in NYC and Nashville.

20–07 Camera Package Rental
If they shoot 5 days straight—going from NYC to Nashville and back again—it might be cheaper to rent the camera for a weekly rate in NYC and pay the excess baggage fees on the airplane. If the shoot dates are separated by a period of time, they will rent the same camera in Nashville.

20–19 Expendables
Same as above Grip Expendables.

20-21 DIT Equipment Rental
The DIT will rent his equipment based on the equipment list the producer gives him.

21–01 Mixer
Local hire in NYC or Nashville.

21–03 Expendables/Batteries
For batteries and miscellaneous sound expenses.

21–04 Sound Package
The Sound Recordist will rent her equipment based on the equipment list the producer gives her.

22–03 Transportation Vehicle Rentals
They need to rent a minivan and cargo van to transport crew and equipment. The Production Assistants will do pickups and returns in the cargo van.

22–04 Parking/Tolls/Gas
For the costs in both cities. They need to put the cargo van in a secure garage at night because all the equipment will be inside.

23–09 Catering Services
For a small crew and some clients on shoot days.

23–12 Location Office Supplies
For various supplies.

25–01 Digital Media
For two hard drives (one is the backup).

26–01 Airfares
For the DP to fly to Nashville.

26–02 Hotels
For the DP during production in Nashville.

26–03 Taxi
For the DP's round-trip to the NYC airport.

26–08 Per Diem
For DP when away in Nashville.

26–09 Gratuities
For tips to valets, concierges, etc.

27–01 Editor
The Editor will work with the director to get to fine cut. Then the clients will give notes. Another final cut will be revised and sent to client. The client will give a final round of comments and then the cut is locked. The Editor will do the audio mix and a simple color grading in his own Avid system.

27–06 Edit System Rental
The Editor will rent his system to the production.

28–11 Music Licensing
The director uses an online music service to license music pieces for corporate and Internet usage.

31–02 Hard Drive Purchases
For additional hard drives to send the master to the client.

33–01 Masters/Clones
For various miscellaneous costs.

35–02 General Liability Insurance
The producer maintains an annual policy and will charge this project 3.5% of the budget to use the production company's policy.

35–05 Workers' Compensation
Same as above — a certain fee is charged to this project.

36–14 Messenger/Overnight Shipping
For costs to send out cuts to the clients or will be used for an FTP service to send cuts online.

36-20 Working Meals
For client meals and post-production meals.

Production Fee
This production company is small and the producer works out of her home office. Thus she can keep her production fee at the lower rate of 10%.

$125K NARRATIVE FEATURE FILM BUDGET

- Go to *www.mwp.com*.
- Click on "MW Film School."
- Open the item "Sample Budgets/Forms."
- Download the corresponding free Excel Budget Template.
- Save it to your computer.
- Last, this budget is a sample template. Make sure to create your budget with figures based on your research on current rates and prices available to you.

Budget Assumptions

This is a very low-budget/micro-budget film shot on location in Connecticut near where the director lives. The schedule is four 6-day weeks for 24 days of shooting on a digital HD/DSLR type camera. Everyone on the crew (from Key Department Heads to Production Assistants) will be paid $100 flat per day. It's a most favored nations (MFN) deal and the plan is to not work longer than 12-hr. days. The budget qualifies for the SAG-AFTRA Ultra Low-Budget Agreement and the crew will be non-union. Depending on the Connecticut tax incentive laws at the time of shooting, the production may qualify for a rebate on salaries and production costs spent in the state. These rules usually change every few years so they will need to research and find out if their production qualifies. If so, they could definitely use that money during post-production.

$125K Narrative Feature Film

		SUMMARY BUDGET
Fringe assumptions:		Production: $125K Narrative
Payroll Tax	0.00%	Shoot Days: 24 (4 - 6 day weeks)
WGA	0.00%	Location: Connecticut (crew from NYC & Boston)
DGA	0.00%	Unions: SAG-AFTRA Ultra Low Budget
SAG	17.30%	Shooting format: DSLR HD
Overtime	0%	Delivery format: HDCam SR
Contingency	5%	

01-00 Story & Rights		$0	
02-00 Producers Unit		$2,400	
03-00 Direction		$2,400	
04-00 Cast		$20,602	
05-00 Travel & Living – Producers/Director		$0	
06-00 Travel & Living- Cast		$4,000	
07-00 Residuals		$0	
	TOTAL ABOVE-THE-LINE		$29,403
08-00 Production Staff		$12,000	
09-00 Background Actors/Extras		$200	
10-00 Sound Stage		$0	
11-00 Production Design		$2,400	
12-00 Set Construction		$500	
13-00 Set Operations		$6,070	
14-00 Special Effects		$0	
15-00 Set Dressing		$3,400	
16-00 Property		$2,900	
17-00 Wardrobe		$3,400	
18-00 Make-Up and Hair		$2,540	
19-00 Electrical		$6,100	
20-00 Camera		$9,590	
21-00 Production Sound		$3,200	
22-00 Transportation		$7,750	
23-00 Location Expenses		$5,994	
24-00 Picture Vehicle/Animals		$0	
25-00 Media		$750	
26-00 Travel and Living-Crew		$10,300	
	TOTAL PRODUCTION		$77,094
27-00 Editorial		$5,500	
28-00 Music		$500	
29-00 Post-Production Sound		$1,000	
30-00 Post-Production - Digital and Film		$0	
31-00 Digital Intermediate		$1,000	
32-00 Titling and Graphics		$0	
33-00 Deliverables		$750	
34-00 Digital Visual Effects/Animation		$0	
	TOTAL POST-PRODUCTION		$8,750
35-00 Insurance		$0	
36-00 General & Administrative Expenses		$4,700	
37-00 Publicity and Marketing		$0	
	TOTAL GENERAL		$4,700
Total Above-the-Line			$29,403
Total Below-the-Line			$90,544
Total Above and Below-the-Line			$119,947
Contingency			$5,997
GRAND TOTAL			$125,944

$125K Narrative Feature Film

ABOVE-THE-LINE		Amt.	Units	x	Rate	Sub-Total	Total	
01-00 Story & Rights								
01-01 Rights Purchases			Allow	1		0	0	
01-02 Options			Allow	1		0	0	
01-03 Writer Salaries/Screenplay Purchase			Allow	1		0	0	
01-04 Research/Clearances			Allow	1		0	0	
01-05 Title Registration			Allow	1		0	0	
01-06 Script Timing			Allow	1		0	0	
01-07 Storyboards/Pre-Viz			Allow	1		0	0	
01-08 WGA Publication fee			Allow	1		0	0	
01-10 Development			Allow	1		0	0	
	Payroll					0	0	
	WGA					0	0	
					Total for 01-00			0
02-00 Producers Unit								
02-01 Executive Producer			Allow	1		0	0	
02-02 Producer		24	Days	1	100	2,400	2,400	
02-03 Associate Producer			Allow	1		0	0	
02-04 Assistant to Producer(s)			Week(s)	1		0	0	
02-06 Consultants			Allow	1		0	0	
02-07 Miscellaneous Expenses			Allow	1		0	0	
	Payroll					2,400	0	
					Total for 02-00			2,400
03-00 Direction								
03-01 Director		24	Days	1	100	2,400	2,400	
03-02 Assistant to Director		1	Weeks	1		0	0	
	Payroll					2,400	0	
	DGA					2,400	0	
					Total for 03-00			2,400
04-00 Cast								
04-01 Lead Actors								
	Actor #1-Prep	3	Days	1	125	375		
	Actor #1-Shoot	24	Days	1	125	3,000		
	Actor #2-Prep	3	Days	1	125	375		
	Actor #2-Shoot	12	Days	1	125	1,500		
Overtime Allowance (10%)		1	Allow	1	5,250	525	5,775	
04-02 Supporting Cast								
	Actor #3-Prep/Shoot	9	Days	1	125	1,125		
	Actor #4-Prep/Shoot	4	Days	1	125	500		
	Actor #5-Prep/Shoot	9	Days	1	125	1,125		
	Actor #6-Prep/Shoot	8	Days	1	125	1,000		
	Actor #7-Prep/Shoot	4	Days	1	125	500		
	Actor #8-Prep/Shoot	4	Days	1	125	500		
Overtime Allowance (10%)		1	Allow	1	4,750	475	5,225	
04-03 Day Players								
	Actor #10	3	Day(s)	1	125	375		
	Actor #11	4	Day(s)	1	125	500		
	Actor #12	2	Day(s)	1	125	250		
	Actor #13	1	Day(s)	1	125	125		
	Actor #14	3	Day(s)	1	125	375		
	Actor #15	2	Day(s)	1	125	250		
Overtime Allowance (10%)		1	Allow	1	1,875	188	2,063	
04-04 Casting Director/Staff		1	Allow	1	1,000	1,000	1,000	
04-05 Casting Expenses		1	Allow	1	100	100	100	
04-06 Choreographer			Weeks	1		0	0	
04-07 Assistant(s) to Choreographer			Weeks	1		0	0	
04-08 Dialect Coach			Weeks	1		0	0	
04-09 Narrator/Voiceover Artist			Weeks	1		0	0	
04-10 Stunt Coordinator			Weeks	1		0	0	

$125K Narrative Feature Film

		Amt.	Units	x	Rate	Sub-Total	Total	
04-11 Stunt Players (6 day weeks)			Weeks	1		0	0	
04-12 Stunt Costs/Adjustments			Allow	1		0	0	
04-13 Stunt Equipment			Allow	1		0	0	
04-14 ADR (Actors' fees)			Allow	1		0	0	
	Payroll - SAG only					13,063	2,874	
	Talent Agency fee (10%)					13,063	1,306	
	SAG P&H					13,063	2,260	
					Total for 04-00			**20,603**
05-00 Travel & Living – Producers/Director								
05-01 Airfares			RT	1		0	0	
05-02 Hotel			Nights	1		0	0	
05-03 Taxi/Limo			Allow	1		0	0	
05-04 Auto			Allow	1		0	0	
05-05 Train			Allow	1		0	0	
05-06 Excess Baggage			Allow	1		0	0	
05-07 Phone			Allow	1		0	0	
05-08 Gratuities			Allow	1		0	0	
05-09 Per Diem			Days	1		0	0	
					Total for 05-00			0
06-00 Travel & Living- Cast								
06-01 Airfares		1	RT	1	500	500	500	
06-02 Hotels		25	Nights	2	60	3,000	3,000	
06-03 Taxi/Limo			Allow	1		0	0	
06-04 Auto			Allow	1		0	0	
06-05 Train		1	Allow	1	500	500	500	
06-06 Excess Baggage			Allow	1		0	0	
06-07 Phone			Allow	1		0	0	
06-08 Gratuities			Allow	1		0	0	
06-09 Per Diem			Days	1		0	0	
					Total for 06-00			**4,000**
07-00 Residuals			Allow	1		0	0	
					Total for 07-00			0
TOTAL ABOVE-THE -LINE								29,403

$125K Narrative Feature Film

		Amt.	*Units*	*x*	*Rate*	*Sub-Total*	*Total*	
BELOW-THE-LINE								
08-00 Production Staff								
08-01 Unit Production Manager								
	Prep/Travel		Weeks	1		0		
	Shoot	24	Days	1	100	2,400		
	Wrap		Weeks	1		0		
	Severance		Allow	1		0	2,400	
08-02 Assistant Directors								
1st AD								
	Prep/Travel		Weeks	1		0		
	Shoot	24	Days	1	100	2,400		
	Prod. Fee (shoot days)		Days	1		0		
	Severance		Allow	1		0		
	Overtime Allow		Days	1		0	2,400	
2nd AD								
	Prep/Travel		Weeks	1		0		
	Shoot	24	Days	1	100	2,400		
	Prod. Fee		Days	1		0		
	Severance		Allow	1		0		
	Overtime Allow		Days	1		0	2,400	
08-03 Stage Manager								
	Prep/Travel		Weeks	1		0		
	Shoot		Weeks	1		0		
	Prod. Fee		Days	1		0		
	Severance		Allow	1		0		
	Overtime Allow		Days	1		0	0	
08-04 Production Coordinator								
	Prep/Travel		Weeks	1		0		
	Shoot	24	Days	1	100	2,400		
	Wrap		Weeks	1		0	2,400	
Ass't Coord.								
	Prep		Weeks	1		0		
	Shoot		Weeks	1		0		
	Wrap		Weeks	1		0	0	
08-05 Script Supervisor								
	Prep		Days	1		0		
	Shoot	24	Days	1	100	2,400		
	Saturdays Worked		Days	1		0		
	Wrap		Days	1		0		
	2nd Camera Days		Days	1		0		
	Overtime		Allow		2,400	0	2,400	
08-06 Production Accountant/Auditor								
	Prep/Travel		Weeks	1		0		
	Shoot		Weeks	1		0		
	Wrap		Weeks	1		0		
	Post-Production		Weeks	1		0	0	
Assistant Accountant								
	Prep/Travel		Weeks	1		0		
	Shoot		Weeks	1		0		
	Wrap		Weeks	1		0	0	
08-07 Technical Advisors			Flat	1		0	0	
08-08 Production Assistants								
Office Prod. Assistant(s)								
	Prep		Days	1		0		
	Shoot		Days	1		0		
	Wrap		Days	1		0		
Set Prod. Assistant(s)								
	Prep		Days	1		0		
	Shoot		Days	1		0	0	
08-09 Studio Teacher/Tutor			Weeks	1		0	0	
	Payroll					12,000	0	
	DGA					7,200	0	
					Total for 08-00			12,000

$125K Narrative Feature Film

		Amt.	Units	x	Rate	Sub-Total	Total	
09-00 Background Actors/Extras								
09-01 Stand-ins			Days	1		0	0	
09-02 Extras			Extras	1		0	0	
09-05 Extras Casting Fee @ 10%			Allow	1		0	0	
09-10 Extras Transportation		20	Allow	1	10	200	200	
	Payroll					0	0	
	P&H					0	0	
					Total for 09-00			200
10-00 Sound Stage								
10-01 Stage Rental			Allow	1		0	0	
	Prep		Allow	1		0	0	
	Pre-Light		Allow	1		0	0	
	Shoot		Allow	1		0	0	
	Wrap		Allow	1		0	0	
	Overtime		Allow	1		0	0	
10-02 Stage Lighting Rental			Allow	1		0	0	
10-03 Stage Grip Rental			Allow	1		0	0	
10-04 Phones/ Internet			Allow	1		0	0	
10-05 Garbage removal			Allow	1		0	0	
10-06 Green Room			Allow	1		0	0	
10-07 Make Up Room			Allow	1		0	0	
10-08 Office Rental			Allow	1		0	0	
10-09 Parking			Allow	1		0	0	
					Total for 10-00			0
11-00 Production Design								
11-01 Production Designer								
	Prep/Travel		Weeks	1		0		
	Shoot	24	Weeks	1	100	2,400	2,400	
11-02 Art Director								
	Prep/Travel		Weeks	1		0		
	Shoot		Weeks	1		0	0	
11-03 Art Assistants								
	Prep/Travel		Days	1		0		
	Shoot		Days	1		0	0	
11-04 Set Designer								
	Prep/Travel		Weeks	1		0		
	Shoot		Weeks	1		0	0	
11-05 Model Makers/Miniatures			Allow	1		0	0	
11-06 Draftsperson			Allow	1		0	0	
11-08 Research/Materials			Allow	1		0	0	
11-09 Vehicle Expenses			Weeks	1		0	0	
11-10 Purchases/Rentals			Allow	1		0	0	
	Payroll					2,400	0	
					Total for 11-00			2,400
12-00 Set Construction								
12-01 Construction Coordinator								
	Prep		Days	1		0		
	Shoot		Days	1		0		
	Overtime		Allow	1	0	0	0	
12-02 Foreman								
	Prep		Days	1		0		
	Shoot		Days	1		0		
	Overtime		Allow	1	0	0	0	
Carpenters			Allow	1		0	0	
12-03 Scenic Painters								
Lead Scenic Painter								
	Prep		Days	1		0		
	Shoot		Days	1		0		
	Overtime		Allow	1	0	0	0	
Painters			Allow	1		0	0	
12-05 Greensmen			Allow	1		0	0	

$125K Narrative Feature Film

		Amt.	Units	x	Rate	Sub-Total	Total	
12-06 Construction materials - Purchases		1	Allow	1	250	250	250	
12-07 Construction materials - Rentals		1	Allow	1	250	250	250	
12-08 Construction Equipment			Allow	1		0	0	
12-09 Set Strike			Allow	1		0	0	
	Payroll					0	0	
					Total for 12-00			500
13-00 Set Operations								
13-01 Key Grip								
	Prep/Travel		Days	1		0		
	Shoot	24	Days	1	100	2,400		
	Wrap		Days	1		0		
	Overtime		Allow	1	2,400	0	2,400	
13-02 Best Boy Grip								
	Prep		Days	1		0		
	Shoot		Days	1		0		
	Wrap		Days	1		0		
	Overtime		Allow	1	0	0	0	
13-03 Grips								
3rd Grip								
	Prep		Days	1		0		
	Shoot		Days	1		0		
	Wrap		Days	1		0		
	Overtime		Allow	1	0	0	0	
4th Grip								
	Prep		Days	1		0		
	Shoot		Days	1		0		
	Wrap		Days	1		0		
	Overtime		Allow	1	0	0	0	
Additional Grips			Days	1		0		
	Overtime		Allow	1		0	0	
13-04 Dolly/Crane Grips								
	Prep		Days	1		0		
	Shoot		Days	1		0		
	Overtime		Allow	1	0	0	0	
13-06 Grip Rentals								
	Package	1	Allow	1	1,500	1,500		
	Dollies		Weeks	1		0		
	Cranes (incl. Driver)		Days	1		0		
	Add'l Equip.		Allow	1		0	1,500	
13-07 Expendables		1	Allow	1	250	250	250	
13-08 Kit Rentals								
	Key Grip		Weeks	1		0	0	
	Craft Service		Weeks	1		0	0	
13-10 Craft Service								
	Prep		Days	1		0		
	Shoot		Days	1		0		
	Wrap		Days	1		0		
	Overtime		Allow	1	0	0	0	
Purchases		24	Days	1	80	1,920	1,920	
Rentals			Allow	1		0	0	
13-15 Air Conditioning/Heating			Days	1		0	0	
	Payroll					2,400	0	
					Total for 13-00			6,070
14-00 Special Effects								
14-01 Special Effects Person								
	Prep/Travel		Days	1		0		
	Shoot		Days	1		0		
	Overtime		Allow	1	0	0	0	
14-02 SFX Assistant(s)								
	Shoot		Days	1		0		
	Overtime		Allow	1	0	0	0	
14-03 Additional Labor								

$125K Narrative Feature Film

		Amt.	Units	x	Rate	Sub-Total	Total	
	Shoot		Days	1		0		
	Overtime		Allow	1	0	0	0	
14-06 Manufacturing Labor			Allow	1		0	0	
14-07 Fabrication			Allow	1		0	0	
14-09 Rentals			Allow	1		0	0	
	Payroll				0	0	0	
					Total for 14-00			**0**
15-00 Set Dressing								
15-01 Set Decorator								
	Prep/Travel		Days	1		0		
	Shoot	24	Days	1	100	2,400		
	Wrap		Days	1		0		
	Overtime				2,400	0	2,400	
15-02 Lead Person								
	Prep/Travel		Days	1		0		
	Shoot		Days	1		0		
	Wrap		Days	1		0		
	Overtime				0	0	0	
15-03 Swing Gang/Set Dressers								
Set Dresser #1								
	Prep		Days	1		0		
	Shoot		Days	1		0		
	Wrap		Days	1		0		
	Overtime				0	0	0	
Set Dresser #2								
	Prep		Days	1		0		
	Shoot		Days	1		0		
	Wrap		Days	1		0		
	Overtime				0	0	0	
Set Dresser #3								
	Prep		Days	1		0		
	Shoot		Days	1		0		
	Wrap		Days	1		0		
	Overtime				0	0	0	
15-04 Additional Labor								
On-Set Dresser (Shoot)			Days	1		0		
	Overtime				0	0	0	
15-05 Expendables			Allow	1		0	0	
15-06 Purchases		1	Allow	1	500	500	500	
15-07 Rentals		1	Allow	1	500	500	500	
15-08 Loss & Damage			Allow	1		0	0	
15-09 Kit Rentals						0	0	
	Set Decorator		Weeks	1		0	0	
	Lead Person		Weeks	1		0	0	
15-10 Vehicle Expenses								
	Set Decorator		Weeks	1		0	0	
	Lead Person		Weeks	1		0	0	
	Payroll				2,400	0	0	
					Total for 15-00			**3,400**
16-00 Property								
16-01 Property Master								
	Prep/Travel		Days	1		0		
	Shoot	24	Days	1	100	2,400		
	Wrap		Days	1		0		
	Overtime				2,400	0	2,400	
16-02 Prop Assistant								
	Prep		Days	1		0		
	Shoot		Days	1		0		
	Wrap		Days	1		0		
	Overtime				0	0	0	
16-03 Purchases		1	Allow	1	250	250	250	

$125K Narrative Feature Film

		Amt.	Units	x	Rate	Sub-Total	Total	
16-04 Rentals		1	Allow	1	250	250	250	
16-05 Loss & Damage			Allow	1		0	0	
16-06 Kit Rentals								
	Prop Master		Weeks	1		0	0	
16-07 Vehicle Expenses								
	Prop Master		Weeks	1		0	0	
	Assistant		Weeks	1		0	0	
	Payroll				2,400	0	0	
					Total for 16-00			2,900
17-00 Wardrobe								
17-01 Costume Designer								
	Prep/Travel		Weeks	1		0		
	Shoot	24	Days	1	100	2,400		
	Wrap		Week	1		0	2,400	
17-02 Costumer								
	Prep/Travel		Days	1		0		
	Shoot		Days	1		0		
	Wrap		Days	1		0		
	Overtime		Allow	1	0	0	0	
17-03 Additional Costumer(s)								
	Prep		Days	1		0		
	Shoot		Days	1		0		
	Wrap		Days	1		0		
	Overtime		Allow	1	0	0	0	
17-04 Expendables			Allow	1		0	0	
17-05 Purchases		1	Allow	1	250	250	250	
17-06 Rentals		1	Allow	1	250	250	250	
17-07 Alteration & Repairs			Allow	1		0	0	
17-08 Cleaning & Dyeing		1	Allow	1	500	500	500	
17-09 Loss & Damage			Allow	1		0	0	
17-10 Kit Rentals								
	Costume Designer		Weeks	1		0	0	
17-11 Vehicle Expenses								
	Costume Designer		Weeks	1		0	0	
	Payroll				2,400	0	0	
					Total for 17-00			3,400
18-00 Make-Up and Hair								
18-01 Key Hair & Make-Up Artist								
	Prep/Travel		Days	1		0		
	Shoot	24	Days	1	100	2,400		
	Wrap		Days	1		0		
	Overtime		Allow	1	2,400	0	2,400	
18-02 Additional Make-Up Artist(s)			Days	1		0		
	Shoot		Days	1		0		
	Overtime		Allow	1	0	0	0	
18-03 Key Hair Stylist								
	Prep/Travel		Days	1		0		
	Shoot		Days	1		0		
	Wrap		Days	1		0		
	Overtime		Allow	1	0	0	0	
18-04 Additional Hair Stylist(s)			Days	1		0		
	Shoot		Days	1		0		
	Overtime		Allow	1	0	0	0	
18-05 Special Effects Makeup Effects			Allow	1		0	0	
18-06 Purchases			Allow	1		0	0	
18-07 Rentals			Weeks	1		0	0	
18-08 Kit Rentals								
	Key Make-Up	4	Weeks	1	35	140	140	
	Add'l Make-Up		Days	1		0	0	
	Hair Stylist		Days	1		0	0	
	Add'l Hair		Days	1		0	0	
	Payroll				2,400	0	0	
					Total for 18-00			2,540

$125K Narrative Feature Film

		Amt.	Units	x	Rate	Sub-Total	Total	
19-00 Electrical								
19-01 Gaffer								
	Prep/Travel		Days	1		0		
	Shoot	24	Days	1	100	2,400		
	Wrap/Travel		Days	1		0		
	Overtime		Allow	1	2,400	0	2,400	
19-02 Best Boy Electric								
	Prep		Days	1		0		
	Shoot	24	Days	1	100	2,400		
	Wrap		Days	1		0		
	Overtime		Allow	1	2,400	0	2,400	
19-03 Electrics								
3rd Electric								
	Prep		Days	1		0		
	Shoot		Days	1		0		
	Wrap		Days	1		0		
	Overtime		Allow	1	0	0	0	
4th Electric								
	Prep		Days	1		0		
	Shoot		Days	1		0		
	Wrap		Days	1		0		
	Overtime		Allow	1	0	0	0	
19-04 Additional Labor								
	Shoot		Days	1		0		
	Overtime		Allow	1	0	0	0	
19-05 Equipment Purchases			Allow	1		0	0	
19-06 Lighting Package Rental		1	Allow	1	1,000	1,000	1,000	
	Add'l Equip.		Allow	1		0	0	
	Condors		Allow	1		0	0	
	Additional Generator		Allow	1		0	0	
19-07 Additional Rentals			Allow	1		0	0	
19-08 Electrical Generator/Driver			Days	1		0	0	
19-09 Loss & Damage		1	Allow	1	300	300	300	
19-10 Kit Rentals								
	Gaffer		Weeks	1		0	0	
	Payroll				4,800	0	0	
					Total for 19-00			6,100
20-00 Camera								
20-01 Director of Photography								
	Prep/Travel		Days	1		0		
	Shoot	24	Days	1	100	2,400	2,400	
20-02 Camera Operator or B Camera								
	Prep/Travel		Days	1		0		
	Shoot	24	Days	1	100	2,400		
	Overtime		Allow	1	2,400	0	2,400	
20-03 1st Assistant Camera/DIT								
	Prep/Travel		Days	1		0		
	Shoot	24	Days	1	100	2,400		
	Wrap		Days	1		0		
	Overtime		Allow	1	2,400	0		
	B Cam 1st Ass't		Days	1		0	2,400	
	Overtime		Allow	1	0	0	0	
20-04 2nd Ass't Camera								
	Prep		Days	1		0		
	Shoot		Days	1		0		
	Wrap		Days	1		0		
	Overtime		Allow	1	0	0	0	
	B Cam 2nd Ass't		Days	1		0		
	Overtime		Allow	1	0	0	0	
20-05 Digital Imaging Technician (DIT)			Week	1		0	0	
20-06 Still Photographer			Allow	1		0	0	
20-07 Camera Package Rental		1	Allow	1	2,000	2,000	2,000	

$125K Narrative Feature Film

		Amt.	Units	x	Rate	Sub-Total	Total	
20-10 Camera Package Purchase			Allow	1		0	0	
20-11 Steadicam Operator & Equip.			Days	1		0	0	
20-12 Teleprompter/Operator			Days	1		0	0	
20-13 Video Assist/Operator			Days	1		0	0	
20-14 Aerial Photography			Days	1		0	0	
20-15 Underwater and Topside Photography			Days	1		0	0	
20-16 Drones/GoPros			Days	1		0	0	
22-17 Maintenance/Loss & Damage			Allow	1		0	0	
20-18 Motion Control			Allow	1		0	0	
20-19 Expendables		1	Allow	1	250	250	250	
20-20 Video Truck			Weeks	1		0	0	
20-25 Video Truck Crew			Weeks	1		0	0	
20-26 Kit Rentals								
	1st Ass't Cam	4	Weeks	1	35	140	140	
	Payroll				7,200	0	0	
					Total for 20-00			9,590
21-00 Production Sound								
21-01 Mixer								
	Prep		Days	1		0		
	Shoot	24	Days	1	100	2,400		
	Wrap/Travel		Days	1		0		
	Overtime		Allow	1	2,400	0	2,400	
21-02 Boom Operator								
	Shoot		Days	1		0		
	Overtime		Allow	1	0	0	0	
21-03 Expendables/Batteries			Allow	1		0	0	
21-04 Sound Package			Weeks	1		0	0	
21-05 Walkie-Talkies		4	Weeks	1	200	800	800	
21-06 Sound Truck			Weeks	1		0	0	
21-08 Misc. / Loss & Damage			Allow	1		0	0	
	Payroll				2,400	0	0	
					Total for 21-00			3,200
22-00 Transportation								
22-01 Transportation Coordinator								
			Weeks	1		0	0	
22-02 Drivers								
Captain								
	Prep		Days	1		0		
	Shoot		Days	1		0		
	Wrap		Days	1		0	0	
Star Trailer Drivers								
Driver #1								
	Prep		Day	1		0		
	Shoot		Days	1		0		
	Wrap		Day	1		0	0	
Driver #2								
	Prep		Day	1		0		
	Shoot		Days	1		0		
	Wrap		Day	1		0	0	
Production Van Driver								
	Prep		Days	1		0		
	Shoot		Days	1		0		
	Wrap		Days	1		0	0	
Camera Truck Driver								
	Prep		Days	1		0		
	Shoot		Days	1		0		
	Wrap		Days	1		0	0	
Stakebed Driver (Construction)								
	Shoot		Days	1		0	0	
Set Dressing Driver								
	Prep		Days	1		0		
	Shoot		Days	1		0		
	Wrap		Days	1		0	0	

$125K Narrative Feature Film

		Amt.	Units	x	Rate	Sub-Total	Total	
Second Set Dressing 5 Ton			Days	1		0	0	
Props Driver								
	Prep		Days	1		0		
	Shoot		Days	1		0		
	Wrap		Days	1		0	0	
Make-Up/Wardrobe Driver								
	Prep		Days	1		0		
	Shoot		Days	1		0		
	Wrap		Days	1		0	0	
Prod. Office Trailer Driver								
	Prep		Days	1		0		
	Shoot		Days	1		0		
	Wrap		Days	1		0	0	
Honeywagon Driver								
	Shoot		Days	1		0		
	Wrap		Days	1		0	0	
15-Passenger Van #1 Driver								
	Prep		Days	1		0		
	Shoot		Days	1		0	0	
15-Passenger Van #2 Driver								
	Prep		Days	1		0		
	Shoot		Days	1		0	0	
Car Carrier			Days	1		0	0	
Insert Car (car to car cam platform)			Days	1		0	0	
Water Truck Driver			Days	1		0	0	
Caterer	Shoot		Days	1		0	0	
Caterer Ass't	Shoot		Days	1		0	0	
Additional Drivers			Allow	1		0	0	
22-03 Transportation Vehicle Rental								
Production Truck - 14 ft.		5	Weeks	1	400	2,000	2,000	
Production Van		5	Weeks	1	500	2,500	2,500	
Production Car		5	Weeks	1	250	1,250	1,250	
Camera Truck			Weeks	1		0	0	
Stakebed			Weeks	1		0	0	
Set Dressing 5 Ton			Weeks	1		0	0	
Add'l Set Dressing 5 Ton			Weeks	1		0	0	
Set Dress Van			Weeks	1		0	0	
Props 5 Ton			Weeks	1		0	0	
Wardrobe/Make-Up			Weeks	1		0	0	
Crew Stake Bed			Weeks	1		0	0	
Prod. Office Trailer			Weeks	1		0	0	
Honeywagon (Portable Toilets)			Days	1		0	0	
Water Truck			Days	1		0	0	
Gas Truck			Days	1		0	0	
15-Passenger Van			Days	1		0	0	
Car Tow Trailer			Days	1		0	0	
Car Trailer			Days	1		0	0	
Camera Car			Days	1		0	0	
22-04 Parking/Tolls/Gas		1	Allow	1	2,000	2,000	2,000	
22-05 Repairs & Maintenance			Allow	1		0	0	
22-06 Honeywagon Pumping			Allow	1		0	0	
22-07 Miscellaneous			Allow	1		0	0	
	Payroll				0	0	0	
					Total for 22-00			7,750
23-00 Location Expenses								
23-01 Location Manager			Weeks	1		0	0	
23-02 Location Assistants								
Assistant Location Mgr.			Weeks	1		0	0	
Local Contact Person			Weeks	1		0	0	
23-03 First Aid/Medic			Weeks	1		0	0	
23-04 Fire Officers								
	Shoot		Days	1		0	0	
23-05 Security			Allow	1		0	0	
23-06 Police			Days	1		0	0	

$125K Narrative Feature Film

		Amt.	*Units*	*x*	*Rate*	*Sub-Total*	*Total*	
	Additional Police		Allow	1		0	0	
23-07 Permits		1	Allow	1	250	250	250	
23-08 Parking			Allow	1		0	0	
23-09 Catering Services								
Crew Meals		24	Days	26	6	3,744	3,744	
Extras			Meals	1		0	0	
Ice/Propane			Weeks	1		0	0	
2nd Meals			Days	1		0	0	
Sales Tax			Allow	1		0	0	
Tent			Allow	1		0	0	
23-11 Location Office Space Rental			Months	1		0	0	
23-12 Location Office Supplies			Allow	1		0	0	
23-13 Location Office Equipment			Allow	1		0	0	
23-14 Location Office Telephone/Fax			Allow	1		0	0	
23-17 Location Site Rental Fees								
	Shoot	1	Allow	1	1,000	1,000	1,000	
23-18 Location Scout			Allow	1		0	0	
	Photos		Allow	1		0	0	
23-19 Auto Rentals								
Scouting		1	Allow	1	500	500	500	
Assistants			Weeks	1		0	0	
23-20 Miscellaneous Expenses								
	Mileage	1	Allow	1	500	500	500	
	Payroll				0	0	0	
					Total for 23-00			5,994
24-00 Picture Vehicles/Animals								
24-01 Animal Trainers								
Boss Wrangler			Weeks	1		0	0	
Assistant Wrangler			Weeks	1		0	0	
Wranglers			Week	1		0	0	
Riders/Handlers, etc			Day	1		0	0	
24-02 Animals								
	Horses		Allow	1		0	0	
Veterinary Expenses			Allow	1		0	0	
Feed/Shelter			Allow	1		0	0	
Transportation			Allow	1		0	0	
24-03 Picture Cars								
	Car #1		Weeks	1		0	0	
	Car #2		Weeks	1		0	0	
	Car #3		Weeks	1		0	0	
	Background Cars		Allow	1		0	0	
	Payroll				0	0	0	
					Total for 24-00			0
25-00 Media								
25-01 Digital Media		1	Allow	1	750	750	750	
25-02 Raw Film Stock			Feet	1		0	0	
25-03 Film Lab-Negative Prep & Process			Feet	1		0	0	
25-04 Telecine/Film to Digital transfer			Allow	1		0	0	
25-05 Videotape stock			Each	1		0	0	
					Total for 25-00			750
26-00 Travel and Living - Crew								
26-01 Airfares			Fares	1		0	0	
26-02 Hotels		1	Allow	2	700	1,400	1,400	
26-03 Taxi		1	Allow	1	500	500	500	
26-04 Auto			Days	1		0	0	
26-05 Train		1	Allow	1	1,200	1,200	1,200	
26-06 Excess Baggage			Allow	1		0	0	
26-08 Per Diem			Days	1		0	0	
	Breakfast-At House	28	Days	1	125	3,500	3,500	
	Dinner-At House	28	Days	1	125	3,500	3,500	
26-09 Gratuities		1	Allow	1	200	200	200	
					Total for 26-00			10,300
TOTAL PRODUCTION								$77,095

$125K Narrative Feature Film

		Amt.	Units	x	Rate	Sub-Total	Total	
27-00 Editorial								
27-01 Editor - Shoot/Post		1	Flat	1	5,500	5,500	5,500	
27-02 Assistant Editor - Shoot/Post			Weeks	1		0	0	
27-04 Post-Production Supervisor			Weeks	1		0	0	
27-05 Editing Room Rental			Weeks	1		0	0	
27-06 Edit System Rental			Weeks	1		0	0	
27-10 On-Line Editing/Conform			Days	1		0	0	
	Payroll				5,500	0	0	
					Total for 27-00			5,500
28-00 Music								
28-01 Composer Fee			Allow	1		0	0	
28-02 Musicians			Allow	1		0	0	
28-03 Music Prep			Allow	1		0	0	
28-04 Studio Costs			Allow	1		0	0	
28-05 Music Scoring Stage			Allow	1		0	0	
28-06 Cartage and Rentals			Allow	1		0	0	
28-07 Music Mix Room			Allow	1		0	0	
28-08 Singers			Allow	1		0	0	
28-09 Payroll Service			Allow	1		0	0	
28-10 Miscellaneous			Allow	1		0	0	
28-11 Music Licensing		1	Allow	1	500	500	500	
28-12 Music Supervisor/Clearance			Allow	1		0	0	
					Total for 28-00			500
29-00 Post-Production Sound								
29-01 Sound Editor			Weeks	1		0	0	
29-02 Assistant Sound Editor			Weeks	1		0	0	
29-03 Music Editor			Weeks	1		0	0	
29-04 Dialogue Editor			Weeks	1		0	0	
29-05 Spotting (Music & FX)			Hours	1		0	0	
29-08 ADR (Studio/Editor)			Days	1		0	0	
29-09 Foley Stage/Editor			Days	1		0	0	
29-10 Foley Artists			Days	1		0	0	
29-12 Narration Recording			Hours	1		0	0	
29-13 Audio Laydown			Hours	1		0	0	
29-15 Audio Mix		1	Flat	1	1,000	1,000	1,000	
29-17 Dolby License			Allow	1		0	0	
29-18 Miscellaneous Expenses			Allow	1		0	0	
					Total for 29-00			1,000
30-00 Post-Producton - Digital and Film								
30-01 Stock Footage			Reels	1		0	0	
30-02 Archive F	Supplies		Allow	1		0	0	
30-04 Archival Researcher			Weeks	1		0	0	
30-06 Clearance Supervisor			Weeks	1		0	0	
30-09 Screeners			Allow	1		0	0	
30-11 Film Prints			Allow	1		0	0	
30-12 Miscellaneous Expenses			Allow	1		0	0	
					Total for 30-00			0
31-00 Digital Intermediate								
31-01 Digital Intermediate			Allow	1		0	0	
31-02 Hard Drive Purchases			Allow	1		0	0	
31-03 Color Grading		1	Allow	1	1,000	1,000	1,000	
					Total for 31-00			1,000
32-00 Titling and Graphics								
32-01 Titling			Allow	1		0	0	
32-02 Graphic Designer			Allow	1		0	0	
32-05 Special Graphic Effects			Allow	1		0	0	
32-06 Motion Control			Allow	1		0	0	
32-08 Closed Captioning			Allow	1		0	0	
32-09 Subtitling			Allow	1		0	0	

$125K Narrative Feature Film

		Amt.	Units	x	Rate	Sub-Total	Total	
					Total for 32-00			0
33-00 Deliverables								
33-01 Masters/Clones		1	Allow	1	750	750	750	
3303 Transfers and Dubs			Allow	1		0	0	
33-05 Screening Copies			Allow	1		0	0	
					Total for 33-00			750
34-00 Digital Visual Effects/Animation								
34-01 VFX			Allow	1		0	0	
34-07 Animation			Allow	1		0	0	
					Total for 34-00			0
POST-PRODUCTION TOTAL								8,750
35-00 Insurance								
35-01 Producers Entertainment Pckg.								
Media/Negative			Allow	1		0	0	
Faulty Stock			Allow	1		0	0	
Equipment			Allow	1		0	0	
Props/Sets			Allow	1		0	0	
Extra Expense			Allow	1		0	0	
3rd Party Property Damage			Allow	1		0	0	
Office Contents			Allow	1		0	0	
35-02 General Liability			Allow	1		0	0	
35-03 Hired Auto			Allow	1		0	0	
35-04 Cast Insurance			Allow	1		0	0	
35-05 Workers Compensation			Allow	1		0	0	
35-06 Errors & Omissions			Allow	1		0	0	
					Total for 35-00			0
36-00 General & Administrative Expenses								
36-01 Business License/Taxes		1	Allow	1	500	500	500	
36-02 Legal		1	Allow	1	1,000	1,000	1,000	
36-03 Accounting fees		1	Allow	1	1,100	1,100	1,100	
36-05 Telephone/Fax		1	Allow	1	100	100	100	
36-06 Copying/Scanning			Allow	1		0	0	
36-07 Postage & Freight			Allow	1		0	0	
36-08 Office Space Rental		2	Months	1	500	1,000	1,000	
36-09 Office Furniture			Allow	1		0	0	
36-10 Office Equipment & Supplies			Allow	1		0	0	
36-11 Computer Rental								
	Line Producer		Weeks	1		0	0	
	First AD		Weeks	1		0	0	
	Prod. Coordinator		Weeks	1		0	0	
	Prod. Accountant		Weeks	1		0	0	
	Office		Months	1		0	0	
	Printers		Months	1		0	0	
36-12 Software/Apps/FTP			Allow	1		0	0	
36-13 Transcription			Hours	1		0	0	
36-14 Messenger/Overnight Shipping		1	Allow	1	500	500	500	
36-15 Parking			Allow	1		0	0	
36-16 Storage			Allow	1		0	0	
36-18 Publicity			Allow	1		0	0	
36-19 Wrap Party			Allow	1		0	0	
36-20 Working Meals		1	Allow	1	500	500	500	
36-21 Overhead (Production fee)			Allow	1		0	0	
36-22 Completion Bond			Allow	1		0	0	
					Total for 36-00			4,700
37-00 Publicity and Marketing								
37-01 Publicity			Allow	1		0	0	
37-02 Marketing			Allow	1		0	0	
					Total for 37-00			0
Total Above-the-Line								29,403
Total Below-the-Line								90,544
Total Above and Below-the-Line								119,947
Contingency								5,997
	GRAND TOTAL							$125,944

02–02 Producer
Flat rate for the 24 days of shooting.

03–01 Director
Flat rate for the 24 days of shooting.

04–01 thru 04–03 Lead Actors/Supporting Cast/Day Players
The SAG-AFTRA Ultra Low-Budget agreement requires each actor to be paid $125 per 8-hr. day. The overtime allowance is set at 10%. All SAG-AFTRA actors need to be paid through a payroll service with fringes set at 22% and the Pension & Health at 17.3%.

04–04 Casting Director
The Casting Director is a childhood friend of the Director and is doing this rate as a *big* favor.

04–05 Casting Expenses
For miscellaneous costs.

06–01 Airfares — Cast
One lead actor has to be flown in from Los Angeles, CA.

06–02 Hotels — Cast
The two lead actors will be put up in a modest hotel nearby.

06–05 Train — Cast
Most of the cast will take the train from NYC or Boston to Connecticut.

08–01 Unit Production Manager
Flat rate for the 24 days of shooting.

08–02 1st and 2nd Assistant Directors
Flat rate for the 24 days of shooting.

08–04 Production Coordinator
Flat rate for the 24 days of shooting.

08–05 Script Supervisor
Flat rate for the 24 days of shooting.

09–10 Extras Transportation
This money pays for Extras' gas money.

11–01 Production Designer
Flat rate for the 24 days of shooting.

12–06 and 12–07 Construction Materials — Purchases & Rentals
Most of the filming will be on locations that will be shot "as is" but a few production elements will need to be constructed.

13–01 Key Grip
Flat rate for the 24 days of shooting.

13–06 Grip Rentals
This is for a few Grip rentals during the month.

13–07 Expendables — Grip
This is for gaffers tape, gels, clothespins, etc.

13–10 Craft Service
For snack costs for the month-long shoot.

15–01 Set Decorator
Flat rate for the 24 days of shooting.

15–06 and 15–07 Purchases & Rentals — Set Decorating
For some set decorating elements to add to a few locations.

16–01 Property Master
Flat rate for the 24 days of shooting.

16–03 and 16–04 Purchases & Rentals — Props
For some specific props required in the script that need to be added to a few locations.

17–01 Costume Designer
Flat rate for the 24 days of shooting.

17–05 and 17–06 Purchases & Rentals — Costumes
To save money, most of the costumes will be rented from the actors and purchased from consignment shops.

17–08 Cleaning & Dyeing
For any dry cleaning or other wardrobe costs.

18–01 Key Hair & Makeup Artist
Flat rate for the 24 days of shooting. This person will do hair and makeup.

18–08 Kit Rentals — Key Makeup
To reimburse the Hair/Makeup person for the use of their makeup supplies.

19–01 Gaffer
Flat rate for the 24 days of shooting.

19–02 Best Boy Electric
Flat rate for the 24 days of shooting.

19–06 Lighting Package Rental
For a month's rental on a few lights.

19–09 Loss & Damage
In case there is any loss or damage to the lighting equipment.

20–01 Director of Photography
Flat rate for the 24 days of shooting.

20–02 Camera Operator or B Camera
Flat rate for the 24 days of shooting. If not needed for all 24 days, this money can be allocated elsewhere.

20–03 1st Assistant Camera/DIT
Flat rate for the 24 days of shooting.

20–07 Camera Package Rental
The production will rent a low-cost HD/DSLR digital camera with a few lenses. The DP will loan production a few of his own lenses at no cost.

20–19 Expendables
For camera tape, sharpies, etc.

20-26 Kit Rentals — 1st AC
For the Assistant Camera's Kit Rental.

21–01 Sound Mixer
Flat rate for the 24 days of shooting.

21–05 Walkie-Talkies
This is to rent 12–15 walkie-talkies for a month.

22–03 Transportation Vehicle Rentals
The production will rent a 14-ft. truck for the Art Department and Production equipment. A cargo van will be used by Camera, Grip, and Electric. A minivan will be used to transport crew and actors from out of town to and from set.

22–04 Parking/Tolls/Gas
Luckily, the locations are all nearby and parking is easy in this small Connecticut town.

23–07 Permits
The local town hall requires a one-time $250 filming permit fee.

23–09 Catering Services
The production has budgeted for lunch each day on set for all cast and crew. The director has contacts at local restaurants and anticipates getting at least 10 days' lunches donated during the shooting period. They only need Extras for less than 6 hours on any given day so they won't need to feed them lunch.

23–17 Location Site Rental Fees
The director was born and raised in this small town. Everyone wants to help him succeed on his first feature film so no one is charging him for any of the locations. This money is here in case something comes up and they need to pay for something related to site rentals.

23–19 Auto Rentals — Scouting
The Location Scout will rent out her car for scouting purposes.

23-20 Miscellaneous Expenses — Locations
For any miscellaneous charges.

25–01 Digital Media
For the hard drive and backup hard drive for all camera acquisition materials.

26–02 Hotels — Crew

The out-of-town cast and crew will rent two homes for the month to house everyone. The two lead actors are in a nearby hotel. The director and producer will stay at the director's parents' home.

26–03 Taxi — Crew

For the occasional cab ride.

26–05 Train — Crew

To transport the out-of-town crew from NYC or Boston to Connecticut.

26–08 Per Diem — Crew

The production will send a Production Assistant out to the grocery store every few days and buy foods that the cast/crew request. This is a cost-effective way to feed the crew and allows them to get the kind of foods they like while they are away from home.

26–09 Gratuities

For any tips to people who have been helpful to the film.

27–01 Editor — Shoot/Post

The Editor will begin editing while they are shooting so any re-shoots can be scheduled before the end of principal photography. The Editor is making the jump up from Assistant Editor and is willing to work on a low flat rate for this film. She has her own Avid editing computer system that she will lend the production for the editorial period.

28–11 Music Licensing

The director is a former professional musician and has a lot of friends who will give him a free, non-exclusive license for much of their music recordings.

29–15 Audio Mix

The Editor will do most of the Audio Mix in the Avid system and then take it to a professional audio mixer to do a final pass.

31–03 Color Grading

After the film is picture locked, the DP will do a Color Grade on his color correct system on his home computer for a flat rate.

33–01 Masters/Clones
The film will be finished to HDCamSR tape and a backup will be created.

36–01 Business License/Taxes
The LLC was created in Connecticut and will file corporate paperwork and annual tax filings there.

36–02 Legal
An entertainment lawyer will look over legal documents and advise for a very low rate and will do a deferral for the rest of his fee.

36–03 Accounting Fees
An accountant will need to be hired if the production decides to apply for the tax incentive refund. For all production accounting, the producer will use personal accounting computer software to keep track of payments, checking, and the accounting.

36–05 Telephone/Fax
For incidental office charges.

36–08 Office Space Rental
This is to rent a production office for two months — prep, production, and wrap. Some of the office prep will be done out of the director's parents' house, too.

36–14 Messenger/Overnight Shipping
This is for miscellaneous shipping costs.

36-20 Working Meals
This is for the producer and director to pay for a few meetings with Actors and key creatives while prepping for the film.

Contingency
There is a 5% contingency fee for this budget.

$20K STUDENT SHORT FILM BUDGET

- Go to *www.mwp.com*.
- Click on "MW Film School."
- Open the item "Sample Budgets/Forms."
- Download the corresponding free Excel Budget Template.
- Save it your computer.
- Last, this budget is a sample template. Make sure to create your budget with figures based on your research on current rates and prices available to you.

Budget Assumptions

This film is directed and produced by two film students at a graduate film program in New York. It will be shot in and around New York City for 5 days of location shooting. Their film school will be providing production and general liability insurance coverage, a Digital HD camera with four lenses, a solid Grip and Lighting package, and an Avid editing system. The school will also create a free DCP master from their master digital file. Most of the crew will be fellow students who will work for free. The producer has signed on to the SAG-AFTRA Student Short Film agreement which means the actor fees are deferred until when/if the filmmakers sell the film for distribution.

$20K Student Short Budget

		SUMMARY BUDGET	
Fringe assumptions:		Production:	$20K Student Short Film
Payroll Tax	0.00%	Shoot Days: 5	
WGA	0.00%	Location: Greater NYC area	
DGA	0.00%	Unions: SAG Student Deferred agreement	
SAG	0.00%	Shooting Format: Digital HD-Raw	
Overtime	0%	Delivery format: DCP & Digital file	
Contingency	0%		

01-00 Story & Rights		$0	
02-00 Producers Unit		$0	
03-00 Direction		$0	
04-00 Cast		$750	
05-00 Travel & Living – Producers/Director		$0	
06-00 Travel & Living- Cast		$0	
07-00 Residuals		$0	
	TOTAL ABOVE-THE-LINE		$750
08-00 Production Staff		$0	
09-00 Background Actors/Extras		$0	
10-00 Sound Stage		$0	
11-00 Production Design		$0	
12-00 Set Construction		$0	
13-00 Set Operations		$1,700	
14-00 Special Effects		$0	
15-00 Set Dressing		$300	
16-00 Property		$500	
17-00 Wardrobe		$950	
18-00 Make-Up and Hair		$285	
19-00 Electrical		$1,200	
20-00 Camera		$3,000	
21-00 Production Sound		$1,250	
22-00 Transportation		$1,750	
23-00 Location Expenses		$2,670	
24-00 Picture Vehicle/Animals		$150	
25-00 Media		$1,200	
26-00 Travel and Living-Crew		$0	
	TOTAL PRODUCTION		$14,955
27-00 Editorial		$1,000	
28-00 Music		$500	
29-00 Post-Production Sound		$1,500	
30-00 Post-Production - Digital and Film		$0	
31-00 Digital Intermediate		$1,500	
32-00 Titling and Graphics		$0	
33-00 Deliverables		$0	
34-00 Digital Visual Effects/Animation		$0	
	TOTAL POST-PRODUCTION		$4,500
35-00 Insurance		$310	
36-00 General & Administrative Expenses		$0	
37-00 Publicity and Marketing		$0	
	TOTAL GENERAL		$310
Total Above-the-Line			$750
Total Below-the-Line			$19,765
Total Above and Below-the-Line			$20,515
Contingency			$0
GRAND TOTAL			$20,515

$20K Student Short Budget

ABOVE-THE-LINE								
		Amt.	*Units*	*x*	*Rate*	*Sub-Total*	*Total*	
01-00 Story & Rights								
01-01 Rights Purchases			Allow	1		0	0	
01-02 Options			Allow	1		0	0	
01-03 Writer Salaries/Screenplay Purchase			Allow	1		0	0	
01-04 Research/Clearances			Allow	1		0	0	
01-05 Title Registration			Allow	1		0	0	
01-06 Script Timing			Allow	1		0	0	
01-07 Storyboards/Pre-Viz			Allow	1		0	0	
01-08 WGA Publication fee			Allow	1		0	0	
01-10 Development			Allow	1		0	0	
	Payroll					0	0	
	WGA					0	0	
					Total for 01-00			0
02-00 Producers Unit								
02-01 Executive Producer			Allow	1		0	0	
02-02 Producer			Allow	1		0	0	
02-03 Associate Producer			Allow	1		0	0	
02-04 Assistant to Producer(s)			Week(s)	1		0	0	
02-06 Consultants			Allow	1		0	0	
02-07 Miscellaneous Expenses			Allow	1		0	0	
	Payroll					0	0	
					Total for 02-00			0
03-00 Direction								
03-01 Director		1	Allow	1		0	0	
03-02 Assistant to Director		1	Weeks	1		0	0	
	Payroll					0	0	
	DGA					0	0	
					Total for 03-00			0
04-00 Cast								
04-01 Lead Actors								
			Allow	1		0		
			Allow	1		0		
Overtime Allowance			Allow	1		0	0	
04-02 Supporting Cast								
			Week(s)	1		0		
			Week(s)	1		0		
			Week(s)	1		0		
			Week(s)	1		0		
Overtime Allowance			Allow	1		0	0	
04-03 Day Players								
			Day(s)	1		0		
			Day(s)	1		0		
			Day(s)	1		0		
			Day(s)	1		0		
			Day(s)	1		0		
			Day(s)	1		0		
			Day(s)	1		0		
			Day(s)	1		0		
			Day(s)	1		0		
			Day(s)	1		0		
			Day(s)	1		0		
Overtime Allowance			Allow	1		0	0	
04-04 Casting Director/Staff		1	Allow	1	750	750	750	
04-05 Casting Expenses			Allow	1		0	0	
04-06 Choreographer			Weeks	1		0	0	
04-07 Assistant(s) to Choreographer			Weeks	1		0	0	
04-08 Dialect Coach			Weeks	1		0	0	
04-09 Narrator/Voiceover Artist			Weeks	1		0	0	

$20K Student Short Budget

		Amt.	Units	x	Rate	Sub-Total	Total	
04-10 Stunt Coordinator			Weeks	1		0	0	
04-11 Stunt Players (6 day weeks)			Weeks	1		0	0	
04-12 Stunt Costs/Adjustments			Allow	1		0	0	
04-13 Stunt Equipment			Allow	1		0	0	
04-14 ADR (Actors' fees)			Allow	1		0	0	
	Payroll					750	0	
	SAG					750	0	
					Total for 04-00			750
05-00 Travel & Living – Producers/Director								
05-01 Airfares			RT	1		0	0	
05-02 Hotel			Nights	1		0	0	
05-03 Taxi/Limo			Allow	1		0	0	
05-04 Auto			Allow	1		0	0	
05-05 Train			Allow	1		0	0	
05-06 Excess Baggage			Allow	1		0	0	
05-07 Phone			Allow	1		0	0	
05-08 Gratuities			Allow	1		0	0	
05-09 Per Diem			Days	1		0	0	
					Total for 05-00			0
06-00 Travel & Living- Cast								
06-01 Airfares			RT	1		0	0	
06-02 Hotels			Nights	1		0	0	
06-03 Taxi/Limo			Allow	1		0	0	
06-04 Auto			Allow	1		0	0	
06-05 Train			Allow	1		0	0	
06-06 Excess Baggage			Allow	1		0	0	
06-07 Phone			Allow	1		0	0	
06-08 Gratuities			Allow	1		0	0	
06-09 Per Diem			Days	1		0	0	
					Total for 06-00			0
07-00 Residuals			Allow	1		0	0	
					Total for 07-00			0
TOTAL ABOVE-THE -LINE								750

$20K Student Short Budget

		Amt.	Units	x	Rate	Sub-Total	Total	
BELOW-THE-LINE								
08-00 Production Staff								
08-01 UPM/Line Producer								
	Prep/Travel		Weeks	1		0		
	Shoot		Weeks	1		0		
	Wrap		Weeks	1		0		
	Severance		Allow	1		0	0	
08-02 Assistant Directors								
First AD								
	Prep/Travel		Weeks	1		0		
	Shoot		Weeks	1		0		
	Prod. Fee (shoot days)		Days	1		0		
	Severance		Allow	1		0		
	Overtime Allow		Days	1		0	0	
2nd AD								
	Prep/Travel		Weeks	1		0		
	Shoot		Weeks	1		0		
	Prod. Fee		Days	1		0		
	Severance		Allow	1		0		
	Overtime Allow		Days	1		0	0	
08-03 Stage Manager								
	Prep/Travel		Weeks	1		0		
	Shoot		Weeks	1		0		
	Prod. Fee		Days	1		0		
	Severance		Allow	1		0		
	Overtime Allow		Days	1		0	0	
08-04 Production Coordinator								
	Prep/Travel		Weeks	1		0		
	Shoot		Weeks	1		0		
	Wrap		Weeks	1		0	0	
Ass't Coord.								
	Prep		Weeks	1		0		
	Shoot		Weeks	1		0		
	Wrap		Weeks	1		0	0	
08-05 Script Supervisor								
	Prep		Days	1		0		
	Shoot		Days	1		0		
	Saturdays Worked		Days	1		0		
	Wrap		Days	1		0		
	2nd Camera Days		Days	1		0		
	Overtime		Allow		0	0	0	
08-06 Production Accountant/Auditor								
	Prep/Travel		Weeks	1		0		
	Shoot		Weeks	1		0		
	Wrap		Weeks	1		0		
	Post-Production		Weeks	1		0	0	
Assistant Accountant								
	Prep/Travel		Weeks	1		0		
	Shoot		Weeks	1		0		
	Wrap		Weeks	1		0	0	
08-07 Technical Advisors			Flat	1		0	0	
08-08 Production Assistants								
Office Prod. Assistant(s)								
	Prep		Days	1		0		
	Shoot		Days	1		0		
	Wrap		Days	1		0		
Set Prod. Assistant(s)								
	Prep		Days	1		0		
	Shoot		Days	1		0	0	
08-09 Studio Teacher/Tutor			Weeks	1		0	0	
	Payroll					0	0	
	DGA					0	0	
					Total for 08-00			0

$20K Student Short Budget

		Amt.	Units	x	Rate	Sub-Total	Total	
09-00 Background Actors/Extras								
09-01 Stand-ins			Days	1		0	0	
09-02 Extras			Extras	1		0	0	
09-05 Extras Casting Fee @ 10%			Allow	1		0	0	
09-10 Extras Transportation			Allow	1		0	0	
	Payroll					0	0	
	P&H					0	0	
					Total for 09-00			0
10-00 Sound Stage								
10-01 Stage Rental			Allow	1		0	0	
	Prep		Allow	1		0	0	
	Pre-Light		Allow	1		0	0	
	Shoot		Allow	1		0	0	
	Wrap		Allow	1		0	0	
	Overtime		Allow	1		0	0	
10-02 Stage Lighting Rental			Allow	1		0	0	
10-03 Stage Grip Rental			Allow	1		0	0	
10-04 Phones/ Internet			Allow	1		0	0	
10-05 Garbage removal			Allow	1		0	0	
10-06 Green Room			Allow	1		0	0	
10-07 Make Up Room			Allow	1		0	0	
10-08 Office Rental			Allow	1		0	0	
10-09 Parking			Allow	1		0	0	
					Total for 10-00			0
11-00 Production Design								
11-01 Production Designer								
	Prep/Travel		Weeks	1		0		
	Shoot		Weeks	1		0	0	
11-02 Art Director								
	Prep/Travel		Weeks	1		0		
	Shoot		Weeks	1		0	0	
11-03 Art Assistants								
	Prep/Travel		Days	1		0		
	Shoot		Days	1		0	0	
11-04 Set Designer								
	Prep/Travel		Weeks	1		0		
	Shoot		Weeks	1		0	0	
11-05 Model Makers/Miniatures			Allow	1		0	0	
11-06 Draftsperson			Allow	1		0	0	
11-08 Research/Materials			Allow	1		0	0	
11-09 Vehicle Expenses			Weeks	1		0	0	
11-10 Purchases/Rentals			Allow	1		0	0	
	Payroll					0	0	
					Total for 11-00			0
12-00 Set Construction								
12-01 Construction Coordinator								
	Prep		Days	1		0		
	Shoot		Days	1		0		
	Overtime		Allow	1	0	0	0	
12-02 Foreman								
	Prep		Days	1		0		
	Shoot		Days	1		0		
	Overtime		Allow	1	0	0	0	
Carpenters			Allow	1		0	0	
12-03 Scenic Painters								
Lead Scenic Painter								
	Prep		Days	1		0		
	Shoot		Days	1		0		
	Overtime		Allow	1	0	0	0	
Painters			Allow	1		0	0	
12-05 Greensmen			Allow	1		0	0	

$20K Student Short Budget

		Amt.	Units	x	Rate	Sub-Total	Total	
12-06 Construction materials - Purchases			Allow	1		0	0	
12-07 Construction materials - Rentals			Allow	1		0	0	
12-08 Construction Equipment			Allow	1		0	0	
12-09 Set Strike			Allow	1		0	0	
	Payroll					0	0	
					Total for 12-00			0
13-00 Set Operations								
13-01 Key Grip								
	Prep/Travel		Days	1		0		
	Shoot	5	Days	1	100	500		
	Wrap		Days	1		0		
	Overtime		Allow	1	500	0	500	
13-02 Best Boy Grip								
	Prep		Days	1		0		
	Shoot		Days	1		0		
	Wrap		Days	1		0		
	Overtime		Allow	1	0	0	0	
13-03 Grips								
3rd Grip								
	Prep		Days	1		0		
	Shoot		Days	1		0		
	Wrap		Days	1		0		
	Overtime		Allow	1	0	0	0	
4th Grip								
	Prep		Days	1		0		
	Shoot		Days	1		0		
	Wrap		Days	1		0		
	Overtime		Allow	1	0	0	0	
Additional Grips			Days	1		0		
	Overtime		Allow	1		0	0	
13-04 Dolly/Crane Grips								
	Prep		Days	1		0		
	Shoot		Days	1		0		
	Overtime		Allow	1	0	0	0	
13-06 Grip Rentals								
	Package	1	Allow	1	500	500		
	Dollies		Weeks	1		0		
	Cranes (incl. Driver)		Days	1		0		
	Add'l Equip.		Allow	1		0	500	
13-07 Expendables		1	Allow	1	200	200	200	
13-08 Kit Rentals								
	Key Grip		Weeks	1		0	0	
	Craft Service		Weeks	1		0	0	
13-10 Craft Service								
	Prep		Days	1		0		
	Shoot		Days	1		0		
	Wrap		Days	1		0		
	Overtime		Allow	1	0	0	0	
Purchases		5	Days	1	100	500	500	
Rentals			Allow	1		0	0	
13-15 Air Conditioning/Heating			Days	1		0	0	
	Payroll					500	0	
					Total for 13-00			1,700
14-00 Special Effects								
14-01 Special Effects Person								
	Prep/Travel		Days	1		0		
	Shoot		Days	1		0		
	Overtime		Allow	1	0	0	0	
14-02 SFX Assistant(s)								
	Shoot		Days	1		0		
	Overtime		Allow	1	0	0	0	
14-03 Additional Labor								

$20K Student Short Budget

		Amt.	Units	x	Rate	Sub-Total	Total	
	Shoot		Days	1		0		
	Overtime		Allow	1	0	0	0	
14-06 Manufacturing Labor			Allow	1		0	0	
14-07 Fabrication			Allow	1		0	0	
14-09 Rentals			Allow	1		0	0	
	Payroll				0	0	0	
					Total for 14-00			0
15-00 Set Dressing								
15-01 Set Decorator								
	Prep/Travel		Days	1		0		
	Shoot		Days	1		0		
	Wrap		Days	1		0		
	Overtime				0	0	0	
15-02 Lead Person								
	Prep/Travel		Days	1		0		
	Shoot		Days	1		0		
	Wrap		Days	1		0		
	Overtime				0	0	0	
15-03 Swing Gang/Set Dressers								
Set Dresser #1								
	Prep		Days	1		0		
	Shoot		Days	1		0		
	Wrap		Days	1		0		
	Overtime				0	0	0	
Set Dresser #2								
	Prep		Days	1		0		
	Shoot		Days	1		0		
	Wrap		Days	1		0		
	Overtime				0	0	0	
Set Dresser #3								
	Prep		Days	1		0		
	Shoot		Days	1		0		
	Wrap		Days	1		0		
	Overtime				0	0	0	
15-04 Additional Labor								
On-Set Dresser (Shoot)			Days	1		0		
	Overtime				0	0	0	
15-05 Expendables			Allow	1		0	0	
15-06 Purchases			Allow	1		0	0	
15-07 Rentals		1	Allow	1	300	300	300	
15-08 Loss & Damage			Allow	1		0	0	
15-09 Kit Rentals						0	0	
	Set Decorator		Weeks	1		0	0	
	Lead Person		Weeks	1		0	0	
15-10 Vehicle Expenses								
	Set Decorator		Weeks	1		0	0	
	Lead Person		Weeks	1		0	0	
	Payroll				0	0	0	
					Total for 15-00			300
16-00 Property								
16-01 Property Master								
	Prep/Travel		Days	1		0		
	Shoot		Days	1		0		
	Wrap		Days	1		0		
	Overtime				0	0	0	
16-02 Prop Assistant								
	Prep		Days	1		0		
	Shoot		Days	1		0		
	Wrap		Days	1		0		
	Overtime				0	0	0	
16-03 Purchases		1	Allow	1	250	250	250	

$20K Student Short Budget

		Amt.	Units	x	Rate	Sub-Total	Total	
16-04 Rentals		1	Allow	1	250	250	250	
16-05 Loss & Damage			Allow	1		0	0	
16-06 Kit Rentals								
	Prop Master		Weeks	1		0	0	
16-07 Vehicle Expenses								
	Prop Master		Weeks	1		0	0	
	Assistant		Weeks	1		0	0	
	Payroll				0	0	0	
					Total for 16-00			**500**
17-00 Wardrobe								
17-01 Costume Designer								
	Prep/Travel		Weeks	1		0		
	Shoot	5	Days	1	100	500		
	Wrap		Week	1		0	500	
17-02 Costumer								
	Prep/Travel		Days	1		0		
	Shoot		Days	1		0		
	Wrap		Days	1		0		
	Overtime		Allow	1	0	0	0	
17-03 Additional Costumer(s)								
	Prep		Days	1		0		
	Shoot		Days	1		0		
	Wrap		Days	1		0		
	Overtime		Allow	1	0	0	0	
17-04 Expendables			Allow	1		0	0	
17-05 Purchases		1	Allow	1	150	150	150	
17-06 Rentals		1	Allow	1	150	150	150	
17-07 Alteration & Repairs			Allow	1		0	0	
17-08 Cleaning & Dyeing		1	Allow	1	150	150	150	
17-09 Loss & Damage			Allow	1		0	0	
17-10 Kit Rentals								
	Costume Designer		Weeks	1		0	0	
17-11 Vehicle Expenses								
	Costume Designer		Weeks	1		0	0	
	Payroll				500	0	0	
					Total for 17-00			**950**
18-00 Make-Up and Hair								
18-01 Key Make-Up/Hair								
	Prep/Travel		Days	1		0		
	Shoot	5	Days	1	50	250		
	Wrap		Days	1		0		
	Overtime		Allow	1	250	0	250	
18-02 Additional Make-Up Artist(s)			Days	1		0		
	Shoot		Days	1		0		
	Overtime		Allow	1	0	0	0	
18-03 Key Hair Stylist								
	Prep/Travel		Days	1		0		
	Shoot		Days	1		0		
	Wrap		Days	1		0		
	Overtime		Allow	1	0	0	0	
18-04 Additional Hair Stylist(s)			Days	1		0		
	Shoot		Days	1		0		
	Overtime		Allow	1	0	0	0	
18-05 Special Effects Makeup Effects			Allow	1		0	0	
18-06 Purchases			Allow	1		0	0	
18-07 Rentals			Weeks	1		0	0	
18-08 Kit Rentals								
	Key Make-Up	1	Allow	1	35	35	35	
	Add'l Make-Up		Days	1		0	0	
	Hair Stylist		Days	1		0	0	
	Add'l Hair		Days	1		0	0	
	Payroll				250	0	0	
					Total for 18-00			**285**

$20K Student Short Budget

		Amt.	Units	x	Rate	Sub-Total	Total	
19-00 Electrical								
19-01 Gaffer								
	Prep/Travel		Days	1		0		
	Shoot	5	Days	1	100	500		
	Wrap/Travel		Days	1		0		
	Overtime		Allow	1	500	0	500	
19-02 Best Boy Electric								
	Prep		Days	1		0		
	Shoot		Days	1		0		
	Wrap		Days	1		0		
	Overtime		Allow	1	0	0	0	
19-03 Electrics								
3rd Electric								
	Prep		Days	1		0		
	Shoot		Days	1		0		
	Wrap		Days	1		0		
	Overtime		Allow	1	0	0	0	
4th Electric								
	Prep		Days	1		0		
	Shoot		Days	1		0		
	Wrap		Days	1		0		
	Overtime		Allow	1	0	0	0	
19-04 Additional Labor								
	Shoot		Days	1		0		
	Overtime		Allow	1	0	0	0	
19-05 Equipment Purchases			Allow	1		0	0	
19-06 Lighting Package Rental		1	Weeks	1	500	500	500	
	Add'l Equip.		Allow	1		0	0	
	Condors		Allow	1		0	0	
	Additional Generator		Allow	1		0	0	
19-07 Additional Rentals			Allow	1		0	0	
19-08 Electrical Generator/Driver			Days	1		0	0	
19-09 Loss & Damage		1	Allow	1	200	200	200	
19-10 Kit Rentals								
	Gaffer		Weeks	1		0	0	
	Payroll				500	0	0	
					Total for 19-00			**1,200**
20-00 Camera								
20-01 Director of Photography								
	Prep/Travel		Days	1		0		
	Shoot	1	Fee	1	1,400	1,400	1,400	
20-02 Camera Operator or B Camera								
	Prep/Travel		Days	1		0		
	Shoot		Days	1		0		
	Overtime		Allow	1	0	0	0	
20-03 1st Assistant Camera								
	Prep/Travel		Days	1		0		
	Shoot	5	Days	1	100	500		
	Wrap		Days	1		0		
	Overtime		Allow	1	500	0		
	B Cam 1st Ass't		Days	1		0	500	
	Overtime		Allow	1	0	0	0	
20-04 2nd Ass't Camera								
	Prep		Days	1		0		
	Shoot		Days	1		0		
	Wrap		Days	1		0		
	Overtime		Allow	1	0	0	0	
	B Cam 2nd Ass't		Days	1		0		
	Overtime		Allow	1	0	0	0	
20-05 Digital Imaging Technician (DIT)		5	Days	1	100	500	500	
20-06 Still Photographer			Allow	1		0	0	
20-07 Camera Package Rental			Allow	1	300	300	300	

$20K Student Short Budget

		Amt.	Units	x	Rate	Sub-Total	Total	
20-10 Camera Package Purchase			Allow	1		0	0	
20-11 Steadicam Operator & Equip.			Days	1		0	0	
20-12 Teleprompter/Operator			Days	1		0	0	
20-13 Video Assist/Operator			Days	1		0	0	
20-14 Aerial Photography			Days	1		0	0	
20-15 Underwater and Topside Photography			Days	1		0	0	
20-16 Drones/GoPros			Days	1		0	0	
20-17 Maintenance/Loss & Damage		1	Allow	1	200	200	200	
20-18 Motion Control			Allow	1		0	0	
20-19 Expendables		1	Allow	1	100	100	100	
20-20 Video Truck			Weeks	1		0	0	
20-25 Video Truck Crew			Weeks	1		0	0	
20-26 Kit Rentals								
	1st Ass't Cam		Weeks	1		0	0	
	Payroll				2,400	0	0	
					Total for 20-00			3,000
21-00 Production Sound								
21-01 Mixer								
	Prep		Days	1		0		
	Shoot	5	Days	1	150	750		
	Wrap/Travel		Days	1		0		
	Overtime		Allow	1	750	0	750	
21-02 Boom Operator								
	Shoot		Days	1		0		
	Overtime		Allow	1	0	0	0	
21-03 Expendables/Batteries			Allow	1		0	0	
21-04 Sound Package		5	Days	1	50	250	250	
21-05 Walkie-Talkies		5	Days	1	50	250	250	
21-06 Sound Truck			Weeks	1		0	0	
21-08 Misc. / Loss & Damage			Allow	1		0	0	
	Payroll				750	0	0	
					Total for 21-00			1,250
22-00 Transportation								
22-01 Transportation Coordinator								
			Weeks	1		0	0	
22-02 Drivers								
Captain								
	Prep		Days	1		0		
	Shoot		Days	1		0		
	Wrap		Days	1		0	0	
Star Trailer Drivers								
Driver #1								
	Prep		Day	1		0		
	Shoot		Days	1		0		
	Wrap		Day	1		0	0	
Driver #2								
	Prep		Day	1		0		
	Shoot		Days	1		0		
	Wrap		Day	1		0	0	
Production Van Driver								
	Prep		Days	1		0		
	Shoot		Days	1		0		
	Wrap		Days	1		0	0	
Camera Truck Driver								
	Prep		Days	1		0		
	Shoot		Days	1		0		
	Wrap		Days	1		0	0	
Stakebed Driver (Construction)								
	Shoot		Days	1		0	0	
Set Dressing Driver								
	Prep		Days	1		0		
	Shoot		Days	1		0		
	Wrap		Days	1		0	0	

$20K Student Short Budget

		Amt.	Units	x	Rate	Sub-Total	Total	
Second Set Dressing 5 Ton			Days	1		0	0	
Props Driver								
	Prep		Days	1		0		
	Shoot		Days	1		0		
	Wrap		Days	1		0	0	
Make-Up/Wardrobe Driver								
	Prep		Days	1		0		
	Shoot		Days	1		0		
	Wrap		Days	1		0	0	
Prod. Office Trailer Driver								
	Prep		Days	1		0		
	Shoot		Days	1		0		
	Wrap		Days	1		0	0	
Honeywagon Driver								
	Shoot		Days	1		0		
	Wrap		Days	1		0	0	
15-Passenger Van #1 Driver								
	Prep		Days	1		0		
	Shoot		Days	1		0	0	
15-Passenger Van #2 Driver								
	Prep		Days	1		0		
	Shoot		Days	1		0	0	
Car Carrier			Days	1		0	0	
Insert Car (car to car cam platform)			Days	1		0	0	
Water Truck Driver			Days	1		0	0	
Caterer	Shoot		Days	1		0	0	
Caterer Ass't	Shoot		Days	1		0	0	
Additional Drivers			Allow	1		0	0	
22-03 Transportation Equipment Rental								
Star Dressing Trailers			Weeks	1		0	0	
Crew Cab			Weeks	1		0	0	
Production Van		7	Days	1	150	1,050	1,050	
Camera Truck			Weeks	1		0	0	
Stakebed			Weeks	1		0	0	
Set Dressing 5 Ton			Weeks	1		0	0	
Add'l Set Dressing 5 Ton			Weeks	1		0	0	
Set Dress Van			Weeks	1		0	0	
Props 5 Ton			Weeks	1		0	0	
Wardrobe/Make-Up			Weeks	1		0	0	
Crew Stakebed			Weeks	1		0	0	
Prod. Office Trailer			Weeks	1		0	0	
Honeywagon (Portable Toilets)			Days	1		0	0	
Water Truck			Days	1		0	0	
Gas Truck			Days	1		0	0	
15-Passenger Van		3	Days	1	150	450	450	
Car Tow Trailer			Days	1		0	0	
Car Trailer			Days	1		0	0	
Camera Car			Days	1		0	0	
22-04 Parking/Tolls/Gas		1	Allow	1	250	250	250	
22-05 Repairs & Maintenance			Allow	1		0	0	
22-06 Honeywagon Pumping			Allow	1		0	0	
22-07 Miscellaneous			Allow	1		0	0	
	Payroll				0	0	0	
					Total for 22-00			1,750
23-00 Location Expenses								
23-01 Location Manager			Weeks	1		0	0	
23-02 Location Assistants								
Assistant Location Mgr.			Weeks	1		0	0	
Local Contact Person			Weeks	1		0	0	
23-03 First Aid/Medic			Weeks	1		0	0	
23-04 Fire Officers								
	Shoot		Days	1		0	0	
23-05 Security			Allow	1		0	0	
23-06 Police			Days	1		0	0	

$20K Student Short Budget

		Amt.	Units	x	Rate	Sub-Total	Total	
	Additional Police		Allow	1		0	0	
23-07 Permits		1	Allow	1	300	300	300	
23-08 Parking			Allow	1		0	0	
23-09 Catering Services								
Crew Meals		5	Days	22	12	1,320	1,320	
Extras			Meals	1		0	0	
Ice/Propane			Weeks	1		0	0	
2nd Meals			Days	1		0	0	
Sales Tax			Allow	1		0	0	
Tent			Allow	1		0	0	
23-11 Location Office Space Rental			Months	1		0	0	
23-12 Location Office Supplies			Allow	1		0	0	
23-13 Location Office Equipment			Allow	1		0	0	
23-14 Location Office Telephone/Fax			Allow	1		0	0	
23-17 Location Site Rental Fees								
	Shoot	5	Days	1	200	1,000	1,000	
23-18 Location Scout			Allow	1		0	0	
	Photos		Allow	1		0	0	
23-19 Auto Rentals								
Location Manager			Weeks	1		0	0	
Assistants			Weeks	1		0	0	
23-20 Miscellaneous Expenses								
	Cabs	1	Allow	1	50	50	50	
	Payroll				0	0	0	
					Total for 23-00			2,670
24-00 Picture Vehicles/Animals								
24-01 Animal Trainers								
Boss Wrangler			Weeks	1		0	0	
Assistant Wrangler			Weeks	1		0	0	
Wranglers			Week	1		0	0	
Riders/Handlers, etc			Day	1		0	0	
24-02 Animals								
	Horses		Allow	1		0	0	
Veterinary Expenses			Allow	1		0	0	
Feed/Shelter			Allow	1		0	0	
Transportation			Allow	1		0	0	
24-03 Picture Vehicles								
	Car #1	1	Day	1	150	150	150	
	Car #2		Weeks	1		0	0	
	Car #3		Weeks	1		0	0	
	Background Cars		Allow	1		0	0	
	Payroll				0	0	0	
					Total for 24-00			150
25-00 Media								
25-01 Digital Media-Hard Drive + Back Up		2	Allow	1	600	1,200	1,200	
25-02 Raw Film Stock			Feet	1		0	0	
25-03 Film Lab-Negative Prep & Process			Feet	1		0	0	
25-04 Telecine/Film to Digital transfer			Allow	1		0	0	
25-05 Videotape stock			Each	1		0	0	
					Total for 25-00			1,200
26-00 Travel and Living - Crew								
26-01 Airfares			Fares	1		0	0	
28-02 Hotels			Nites	1		0	0	
28-03 Taxi			Allow	1		0	0	
28-04 Auto			Days	1		0	0	
28-05 Train			RT	1		0	0	
28-06 Excess Baggage			Allow	1		0	0	
28-08 Per Diem			Days	1		0	0	
28-09 Gratuities			Days	1		0	0	
					Total for 26-00			0
TOTAL PRODUCTION								14,955

$20K Student Short Budget

	Amt.	Units	x	Rate	Sub-Total	Total	
27-00 Editorial							
27-01 Editor - Shoot/Post	1	Allow	1	1,000	1,000	1,000	
27-02 Assistant Editor - Shoot/Post		Weeks	1		0	0	
27-04 Post-Production Supervisor		Weeks	1		0	0	
27-05 Editing Room Rental		Weeks	1		0	0	
27-06 Edit System Rental		Weeks	1		0	0	
27-10 On-Line Editing/Conform		Days	1		0	0	
Payroll				1,000	0	0	
				Total for 27-00			1,000
28-00 Music							
28-01 Composer Fee		Allow	1		0	0	
28-02 Musicians		Allow	1		0	0	
28-03 Music Prep		Allow	1		0	0	
28-04 Studio Costs		Allow	1		0	0	
28-05 Music Scoring Stage		Allow	1		0	0	
28-06 Cartage and Rentals		Allow	1		0	0	
28-07 Music Mix Room		Allow	1		0	0	
28-08 Singers		Allow	1		0	0	
28-09 Payroll Service		Allow	1		0	0	
28-10 Miscellaneous		Allow	1		0	0	
28-11 Music Licensing	1	Allow	1	500	500	500	
28-12 Music Supervisor/Clearance		Allow	1		0	0	
				Total for 28-00			500
29-00 Post-Production Sound							
29-01 Sound Editor		Weeks	1		0	0	
29-02 Assistant Sound Editor		Weeks	1		0	0	
29-03 Music Editor		Weeks	1		0	0	
29-04 Dialogue Editor		Weeks	1		0	0	
29-05 Spotting (Music & FX)		Hours	1		0	0	
29-08 ADR (Studio/Editor)		Days	1		0	0	
29-09 Foley Stage/Editor		Days	1		0	0	
29-10 Foley Artists		Days	1		0	0	
29-12 Narration Recording		Hours	1		0	0	
29-13 Audio Laydown		Hours	1		0	0	
29-15 Audio Mix	1	Allow	1	1,500	1,500	1,500	
29-17 Dolby License		Allow	1		0	0	
29-18 Miscellaneous Expenses		Allow	1		0	0	
				Total for 29-00			1,500
30-00 Post-Producton - Digital and Film							
30-01 Stock Footage		Reels	1		0	0	
30-02 Archive F Supplies		Allow	1		0	0	
30-04 Archival Researcher		Weeks	1		0	0	
30-06 Clearance Supervisor		Weeks	1		0	0	
30-09 Screeners		Allow	1		0	0	
30-11 Film Prints		Allow	1		0	0	
30-12 Miscellaneous Expenses		Allow	1		0	0	
				Total for 30-00			0
31-00 Digital Intermediate							
31-01 Digital Intermediate/Color Grading	1	Allow	1	1,500	1,500	1,500	
31-02 Hard Drive Purchases		Allow	1		0	0	
				Total for 31-00			1,500
32-00 Titling and Graphics							
32-01 Titling		Allow	1		0	0	
32-02 Graphic Designer		Allow	1		0	0	
32-05 Special Graphic Effects		Allow	1		0	0	
32-06 Motion Control		Allow	1		0	0	
32-08 Closed Captioning		Allow	1		0	0	
32-09 Subtitling		Allow	1		0	0	
				Total for 32-00			0
33-00 Deliverables							
33-01 Masters/Clones		Allow	1		0	0	

$20K Student Short Budget

	Amt.	Units	x	Rate	Sub-Total	Total	
3303 Transfers and Dubs		Allow	1		0	0	
33-05 Screening Copies		Allow	1		0	0	
				Total for 33-00			0
34-00 Digital Visual Effects/Animation							
34-01 VFX		Allow	1		0	0	
34-07 Animation		Allow	1		0	0	
				Total for 34-00			0
POST-PRODUCTION TOTAL							4,500
35-00 Insurance							
35-01 Producers Entertainment Pckg.							
Media/Negative		Allow	1		0	0	
Faulty Stock		Allow	1		0	0	
Equipment		Allow	1		0	0	
Props/Sets		Allow	1		0	0	
Extra Expense		Allow	1		0	0	
3rd Party Property Damage		Allow	1		0	0	
Office Contents		Allow	1		0	0	
35-02 General Liability	1	Allow	1	150	150	150	
35-03 Hired Auto		Allow	1		0	0	
35-04 Cast Insurance		Allow	1		0	0	
35-05 Workers Compensation	20	Allow	1	8	160	160	
35-06 Errors & Omissions		Allow	1		0	0	
				Total for 35-00			310
36-00 General & Administrative Expenses							
36-01 Business License/Taxes		Allow	1		0	0	
36-02 Legal		Allow	1		0	0	
36-03 Accounting fees		Allow	1		0	0	
36-05 Telephone/Fax		Allow	1		0	0	
36-06 Copying/Scanning		Allow	1		0	0	
36-07 Postage & Freight		Allow	1		0	0	
36-08 Office Space Rental		Allow	1		0	0	
36-09 Office Furniture		Allow	1		0	0	
36-10 Office Equipment & Supplies		Allow	1		0	0	
36-11 Computer Rental							
Line Producer		Weeks	1		0	0	
First AD		Weeks	1		0	0	
Prod. Coordinator		Weeks	1		0	0	
Prod. Accountant		Weeks	1		0	0	
Office		Months	1		0	0	
Printers		Months	1		0	0	
36-12 Software/Apps/FTP		Allow	1		0	0	
36-13 Transcription		Hours	1		0	0	
38-14 Messenger/Overnight		Allow	1		0	0	
36-15 Parking		Allow	1		0	0	
36-16 Storage		Allow	1		0	0	
36-18 Publicity		Allow	1		0	0	
36-19 Wrap Party		Allow	1		0	0	
36-20 Working Meals		Allow	1		0	0	
36-21 Overhead (Production fee)		Allow	1		0	0	
36-22 Completion Bond		Allow	1		0	0	
				Total for 36-00			0
37-00 Publicity and Marketing							
37-01 Publicity		Allow	1		0	0	
37-02 Marketing		Allow	1		0	0	
				Total for 37-00			0
Total Above-the-Line							750
Total Below-the-Line							19,765
Total Above and Below-the-Line							20,515
Contingency							0
GRAND TOTAL							**$20,515**

04–04 Casting Director
There is a local casting director who loves the script and is willing to work for a fraction of her usual rate to help cast the three lead characters.

13–01 Key Grip
They want a professional Key Grip so have budgeted for his services.

13–06 Grip Package Rental
They are getting most of their equipment from school but have allotted some money for additional grip equipment or maybe a dolly.

13–07 Expendables
For various gels, gaffers tape, clothespins, etc.

13–10 Craft Service
Almost everyone is working for free so good food is even more important. This is for craft service for 5 days.

15–07 Set Dressing Rental
This is enough to dress the locations with a few pieces of furniture.

16–03 Props Purchases
This amount is for a few props that are outlined in the budget. They can find most of them cheaply on eBay.

16–04 Props Rental
This will allow them to rent a few key props from a local Prop House.

17–01 Costume Designer
This is another key position that the filmmakers need to pay for. Costumes are very specific for two of the characters and they need a professional.

17–05 Costume Purchases and 17–06 Costume Rentals
The Designer needs some money to get the right wardrobe.

17–08 Cleaning & Dyeing

The Costume Rental House charges a fee for cleaning each rental when it is returned.

18–01 Key Makeup/Hair

This person will do both Makeup and Hair for all the lead characters.

18–08 Makeup Kit Rental

The production will pay this fee for the use of the Makeup person's kit containing lots of supplies and tools.

19–01 Gaffer

Same as the Key Grip.

19–06 Lighting Package Rental

This covers any additional lighting rented from a local vendor, beyond the school's package.

19–09 Loss & Damage

This money is in case equipment is lost or damaged and needs to be repaired.

20–01 Director of Photography

This DP is building her reel and thinks this project will be helpful. This is a flat fee for prep, tech scout, shooting, and overseeing a color grading at the end of post-production.

20–03 1st Assistant Camera

In order to get the DP's usual Assistant Cameraperson, the filmmakers need to pay for each day of shooting. The AC won't charge for a checkout day.

20–05 Digital Imaging Technician (DIT)

The producer doesn't want to take a chance on having any problems with transcoding, downloading, and backing up each day's materials. They decided to hire a separate DIT to make sure everything goes smoothly on set and during editing.

20–17 Loss & Damage

The producers want to make sure they have budgeted for any possible loss or damage to the camera package. If they don't need to pay anything, they can use this money for post-production later.

20–19 Expendables

The camera department needs expendables, too.

21–01 and 21–04 Sound Mixer and Sound Package

This person will come with their own equipment and record sound.

21–05 Walkie-Talkies

They will need to have walkie-talkies for each day of shooting.

22–03 Production Van and 15-passenger Van

They will put all of the equipment, props, and wardrobe in one cargo van for transport each day to set. Two days will require all the cast and crew to be driven to set which is not close to public transportation.

22–04 Parking/Tolls/Gas

This is the estimate for vehicles.

23–07 Permits

They need to pay this fee to the Mayor's Office of Film, Theatre and Broadcasting for the day when they shoot in Central Park. There are no location fees but they need to obtain a permit for the day.

23–09 Catered Meals

They budgeted for 5 days × 22 people × $12 per person.

23–17 Location Site Rental Fees

They are getting a few locations for free. This fee is for any locations they will need to pay for.

23-20 Cabs

For a few taxis that are necessary.

24–03 Picture Vehicles

They need to rent from a rental company that will extend them auto insurance for an additional cost because the school insurance doesn't cover picture vehicles.

25–01 Media

They are shooting RAW so they will need a very large hard drive and a backup to store all of their acquired materials.

27–01 Editor

The director would like to hire a professional editor to fine cut the film after he does his first rough cut edit.

28–11 Music Licensing

They have budgeted some money to license a song for the film. They may only get film festival rights for this amount.

29–15 Audio Mix

This fee is to cover a professional discounted mix for their 12-minute film.

31–01 Digital Intermediate/Color Grading

This fee is to cover a professional discounted color grading for their 12-minute film.

35–02 General Liability Insurance

Their film school extends its insurance coverage to this production but they have to pay an administrative fee to use it and request certificates.

35–05 Workers' Compensation

They need to pay $8 per person for any cast or crew member who is not a currently enrolled student at their school.

Contingency

There is no contingency added to this budget.

APPENDIX

COST-SAVING IDEAS

1. Legal Services

There are several good books to recommend. To see what various contracts look like before you put your lawyer on the clock, check out *Contracts for the Film and Television Industry*, 3rd edition, by Mark Litwak (2012) and *Clearance & Copyright: Everything You Need to Know for Film and Television*, 4th edition, by Michael C. Donaldson (2014). Also see Books below under Legal. There is also an organization called Volunteer Lawyers for the Arts (www.vlany.org) that provides low-cost legal services for arts professionals. There are other organizations like it throughout the country that you can research online.

2. Obtaining Rights

Put together a great pitch to the rights holder as to why you are the best person to make the film based on their material. An option agreement can be as little as $1 or $10!

3. Getting a Writer

When a writer is eager to get his or her property produced or wants to get experience, you can strike a "spec" deal. This means the writer:
a) becomes your partner and gets paid an agreed sum, plus a percentage of the "back end."
b) gets paid an agreed sum at an agreed time but no percentage. Or some combination of the two.
c) If the writer is WGA, there will be a salary fee based on the budget and type of production (television, theatrical, etc.).

4. Getting a Producer

Make the Producer your partner and defer salary to "back end," or some future point. Or pay below rate and defer the balance. This approach can apply to anyone "above-the-line" on your project. It can work for "below-the-line" people as well sometimes.

5. Getting a Director

If the Director really wants to see the project made, or if it's a personal project, salary could be deferred until profits, if any, start rolling in. When you are starting out and producing low-budget projects, you may not be able to pay a Director (even if that's you!).

6. Getting Actors

The SAG-AFTRA Student Film or Short Film agreement is completely deferred. SAG-AFTRA also has many low-budget agreements that keep the day rates lower than their standard agreements. See *www.sagindie.com* for the details.

7. Getting a Dialect Coach

There are many options online including books and audio formats.

8. Getting a Choreographer

Dance schools can be a good resource. It's best to find someone who has experience as a choreographer for film so they know how to get it done quickly and efficiently. Always check references.

9. Getting a Narrator

Narration for experimental films or "cause" projects has a cachet to it. Actors often do it for love and/or recognition. Go to the biggest actor you can think of and ask if he or she will do it for minimum scale. You may be pleasantly surprised.

10. Getting a Production Assistant

Film schools are a good place to find students who want to volunteer or intern on a film so they can get valuable production experience. Some film commissions have training programs and may have graduates who can work on your film for free.

11. Getting Extras

Friends, family, and social media are a way to reach out to people who want to be in a movie and help you out for your project. At the least, you'll need to provide craft services for them and if they work longer than six hours you will need to provide lunch.

12. Getting a Sound Stage

Can't afford a sound stage? You can set up anywhere if all you need is a roof over your heads. Spend a minute standing silently during the time of day when you'll be shooting — what you hear in the background is what you'll likely hear on your show's production soundtrack. Is there an airport nearby? A kennel? A turkey farm? Also, call your local state or city film commission and ask about converted warehouses and other less expensive structures that can be used as sound stages. Make sure to take your audio person as well as your DP on your scout.

13. Getting the Most from Your Department Heads

Negotiate half-day rates for travel if you can. See if your Department Heads (DP, Production Designer, Costume Designer) might be willing to give you a free prep or scout day on a long-term project. It's worth a try.

14. Getting Your Crew Fed

On low-budget shows, if you don't have enough people to warrant hiring a caterer, pass around the menu from a good nearby restaurant and have a PA take orders. If you have connections with certain local restaurants they may willing to donate food.

15. Getting Composers and Musicians

Hire student composers and musicians from music schools. They may well do the job for only a sample reel and a credit, if you cover the hard costs of studios, instrument rental, cartage, tape stock, etc. Yet another way is to ask the composer for any unreleased recordings you can license directly, provided the composer owns 100% of the publishing rights (sync and master rights).

16. Getting Music

If you can't afford to create your score with real musicians, then the composer may be able to record the score with a synthesizer.

17. Getting a Mix

If your "orchestra" is a combo of friends and you can't afford a scoring stage, try packing into a friend's garage recording studio that's rigged for video projection. Remember, if you have not recorded a synthesizer bed already locked to picture, the recording machine needs to be electronically locked to the picture; otherwise music cues may be out of sync. Consult an audio engineer at the audio sound house where you'll do your final mix.

If you did record a synth bed and have transferred the music to a multitrack digital file with timecode, you are already synced to picture, and your combo can play along to the synth track — no picture or picture lock needed.

18. Getting ADR

For bare bones ADR, you need a quiet place, a way to screen the video clips for each scene to be looped, some headphones, decent microphones, a digital recording machine, and the ability to lock your recording machine to your picture.

19. Inexpensive Narrator Recording

Similar to ADR recording, a quiet place with a microphone and digital recording machine is all you need. Make sure to time out each film scene that the narrator will be recording so they know how fast or slow to pace it.

20. Getting a Good Rate on Post

You can try to play one facility against another to get the bids down, but don't make up stories — all these people know each other and word quickly spreads if you're faking low quotes. If the price is still too steep, sit down with the house of your choice and work out what services you can cut to fit your budget. Most houses are willing, and it they really can't do it, they may recommend a lower-end house that can.

21. Getting Inexpensive Titles and Graphics

Film and animation schools are a great place to find students with talent and interest in creating a demo reel. Discuss what you are looking for and have them do a test that you approve before they do the whole sequence.

22. Getting a Graphic Designer for Less

If your graphics budget really is below standard for the kind of show you're producing, go to a Graphic Designer and explain how much you have budgeted for the job. Ask them what they can do for that figure and negotiate from there. They may be able to lower their rate if it's their slow time and have a gap in their work schedule.

RESOURCES

Business Incorporation Websites

www.mycorporation.com and www.myllc.com

Production Guides/Bookstores

Most Film Commissions have online production guides. Check out the state and city film commissions. The *L.A. 411 Production Guide* (www.variety411.com/us/los-angeles), *The Creative Handbook* (www.creativehandbook.com), the *NY 411 Production Guide* (*www.* variety411.com/us/new-york/), and *New York Production Guide*, (*www.nypg.com*) are all helpful.

Larry Edmunds Books

6644 Hollywood Blvd. Hollywood, CA 90028
(323) 463-3273
www.larryedmunds.com
A great resource for books about film, movie posters, and scripts.

The Writers Computer Store

3510 West Magnolia Blvd. Burbank, CA 901505
(800) 272-8972
www.writersstore.com
Books for producers and writers, as well as all kinds of production and scripting software.

DIRECTORIES

IMDb Pro

www.pro-labs.imdb.com
This is the subscription version of the free website www.IMDb.com. It contains lots of industry info, contacts, estimated budgets, and box office numbers.

The Showbiz Labor Guide

The Showbiz Labor Guide contains the most requested rates, rules, and practices of all the major union agreements. If you're doing

union projects, it can save you hours of time and loads of frustration by having this information at your fingertips.
www.showbizsoftware.com

Hollywood Creative Directory
Publishes the directories listed below, plus other industry survival books. Although the name says "Hollywood," the books list companies nationwide.
www.writersstore.com

The Hollywood Creative Directory: Lists all major production companies and studios, their creative executives and story development people, and each company's credits, plus addresses, phones, and fax numbers.

The Hollywood Representation Directory: Lists the agency and management names, addresses and phone numbers for performing, writing, and directing talent.

The Hollywood Distribution Directory: Lists domestic and foreign distribution companies for TV and film, their sales and marketing staff, plus broadcast and cable networks.

The Hollywood Music Industry Directory: Lists composers, lyricists, music production companies, and clearance and licensing people.

The Hollywood Creative Directory also publishes directories listing writers, directors, actors, composers, and below-the-line talent.

TRADE PUBLICATIONS

Advertising Age
Advertising Age
685 Third Avenue
New York, NY 10017
(212) 210–0100
www.AdAge.com

American Cinematographer
The American Society of Cinematographers
1782 N. Orange Drive (the ASC Clubhouse)

Hollywood, CA 90028
(800) 448–0145
www.theasc.com

Billboard
Billboard Subscription
(800) 684–1873
www.billboard.com

Hollywood Reporter
5700 Wilshire Blvd., Suite 500
Los Angeles, CA 90036
(323) 525-2000 Subscriptions: (323) 525-2150
www.hollywoodreporter.com

Millimeter Magazine
5 Penn Plaza, 13th Floor
New York, NY 10001
(212) 613-9700
http:www.millimeter.com

Script
A website with resources for screenwriters and anyone interested in narrative storytelling.
www.scriptmag.com

Variety
11175 Santa Monica Blvd.
Los Angeles, CA 90025
(800) 552-3632
www.variety.com

BOOKS

Your first stop . . .

www.mwp.com

Michael Wiese Productions, the publisher of this book, offers scores of useful books about filmmaking here. Absolutely worth browsing.

General Information
The Filmmaker's Handbook
By Steven Ascher and Edward Pincus
Plume (The Penguin Group), 2008

Cinematography
Cinematography — Theory and Practice
By Blain Brown
Focal Press, 2011

The American Society of Cinematographers Manual
A portable compendium of technical information about shooting on film, digital intermediates, etc. It costs in the $100 range, but it's fully loaded. *www.ascmag.com*

Independent Film Producing
Producer to Producer: A Step-by-Step Guide to Low Budget Independent Film Producing
By Maureen A. Ryan
Michael Wiese Productions, 2010

Production Management
Film Production Management 101, 2nd edition
By Deborah S. Patz
Michael Wiese Productions, 2011

Legal
Clearance & Copyright:
Everything You Need to Know for Film and Television
4th edition
by Michael C. Donaldson
Silman-James Press, 2014

Dealmaking in the Film & Television Industry:
From Negotiations to Final Contracts, 3rd edition
By Mark Litwak
Silman-James Press, 2012

SOFTWARE

Movie Magic Budgeting and Scheduling
Entertainment Partners
2255 N. Ontario Street
Burbank, CA 91504
www.entertainmentpartners.com
(818) 955-6399

Showbiz Budgeting and Scheduling Media Services
30 West 22nd Street #5W
New York, NY 10010
www.media-services.com
(212) 366-9390

MISCELLANEOUS RESOURCES

Thomson Reuters, a copyright search firm. (800) 692-8833
www.trademarks.thomsonreuters.com

Breakdown Services, Ltd., for casting actors. Los Angeles (310) 276-9166, New York (212) 869-2003, Vancouver (604) 943-7100
www.breakdownservices.com

Crowdfunding websites
www.IndieGoGo.com
www.KickStarter.com
www.SeedAndSpark.com

TRADE ASSOCIATIONS

Academy of Motion Picture Arts and Sciences
8949 Wilshire Blvd.
Beverly Hills, CA 90211
(310) 247-3000
www.oscars.org
The organization is involved in a wide array of education, outreach, preservation, and research activities. Besides the annual Oscars telecast, the academy has a library, educational programs, public programming, and outreach activities.

Academy of Television Arts and Sciences
5220 Lankershim Blvd.
North Hollywood, CA 91601
(818) 754-2800
www.emmys.com
Television Academy is primarily a professional membership and awards organization (the Emmy).

American Federation of Musicians (AFM)
www.afm.org
The largest organization in the world representing the interests of professional musicians.

American Society of Cinematographers (ASC)
1782 North Orange Drive
Hollywood, CA 90028
(800) 448–0145
www.theasc.com

American Society of Composers, Authors & Publishers (ASCAP)
7920 Sunset Blvd., 3rd Floor
Los Angeles, CA 90046
(323) 883–1000
For other offices see *www.ascap.com.*

Association of Independent Commercial Editors (AICE)
3 West 18th Street, 5th floor
New York, NY 10011
(212) 665-2679
www.aice.org

Association of Independent Commercial Producers (AICP East)
3 West 18th St. 5th Floor
NY, NY 10011
(212) 929-3000
www.aicp.com

(AICP West)
650 North Bronson Ave. #223B
Los Angeles, CA 90004
(323) 960-4763
www.aicp.com

Broadcast Music, Inc. (BMI)
7 World Trade Center
250 Greenwich Street
New York, NY 10007
(212) 220-3000
See *www.bmi.com* for other offices

Directors Guild of America, Inc. (DGA)
7920 Sunset Blvd.
Los Angeles, CA 90046
(310) 289-2000
See *www.dga.org* for information and other offices.

International Alliance of Theatrical Stage Employees (IATSE)
IATSE represents many different types of craftspeople and technicians spread across more than thirty unions. Since rates vary by geographical location, type of project, media, etc., I recommend contacting a reputable payroll service in your area that handles union personnel.
IATSE General Office
207 West 25th Street, 4th fl.
New York, NY 10001
(212) 730–1770
www.iatse.net

International Documentary Association (IDA)
3470 Wilshire Blvd. Suite 980
Los Angeles, CA 90010
(213) 232–1660
www.documentary.org
The mission of the IDA is to promote nonfiction film and video through programming, education, awards, and a magazine.

SAG-AFTRA
5757 Wilshire Blvd.
Los Angeles, CA 90036
(323) 954–1600
For other offices — *www.sag.org*

Women In Film
6100 Wilshire Blvd. Suite 710
Los Angeles, CA 90048
(323) 935-2211
For other chapters — *www.wif.org.*
Women In Film's purpose is to empower, promote, and mentor women in the entertainment and media industries.

Writers Guild of America-West (WGA)
7000 West Third Street
Los Angeles, CA 90048
(323) 951-4000
www.wga.org

Writers Guild of America-East (WGA)
250 Hudson Street, Suite 700
New York, NY 10013
(212) 767-7800
www.wgaeast.org

BUDGETS FOR GRANTS AND DONATIONS
The Top Ten Do's and Don'ts

By Morrie Warshawski

Funders of noncommercial grant-supported films and videos have a very different mind-set than investors. A savvy funder will read your budget like a book, hoping to find a romance novel and not a mystery nor a comedy. Keep in mind that most funders only rarely review film budgets. Their time is spent primarily on budgets from other types of endeavors in the arts and social services — ballet concerts, capital campaigns, programs for the elderly, etc. Begin with your generic production budget and then go through carefully to adjust for the following before submitting a grant proposal.

1. YOUR SALARY. Be sure to include some payment for yourself. Funders are suspicious when you either do not pay yourself or underpay yourself. To compute your fee (and those of all other participants), use an amount that is fair and comparable for: a) the role you will play in the film; b) your level of expertise in that role; c) your region of the country.

2. CONTINGENCY. Most funders do not understand the concept of "contingency." Only include contingency with funders who have had extensive experience with film, or who specifically put contingency as a line item in their budget formats. Otherwise, just build in a fair contingency amount throughout your budget in all the line items.

3. TALENT. Do not use this word in a grant proposal. Funders equate talent with high-budget Hollywood movies. List all people under a "PERSONNEL" heading and then specifically label the roles they fulfill (e.g., "actors," "director," etc.).

4. DISTRIBUTION. For a noncommercial project you must include at least some start-up costs to get distribution launched. I recommend allocating funds for: package design and production, DVD screening copies, press kits, production stills, and festival entry fees.

5. IN-KIND. This term refers to any goods or services that are donated to your project and for which you will not have to pay cash. Reflect these items in your budget to give funders a sense of the community support you have engendered. These items can include: free lunches for your crew, a 50% discount on editing rates, etc. Again, use the concepts of "fair and comparable" to decide how much these items are worth.

6. EQUIPMENT PURCHASE. Never! It is the rare funder that will let money go toward the purchase of equipment. Always show your equipment as being leased or rented — even if it costs more in the long run than outright purchase.

7. RED FLAG NOTES. Because many funders are unfamiliar with films, it is doubly important that you go through your budget item-by-item and look for anything that might call undue attention to itself. Some examples could include: a higher than normal shooting ratio, extensive travel costs, transfer from digital to film if there is no theatrical distribution in your narrative, etc. Mark each and every questionable budget item with a number or asterisk, and then explain them fully in a BUDGET NOTES section at the end of the budget.

8. STUDY GUIDES. Any program intended for non-theatrical educational distribution should build in a fee for creating at least a modest study guide.

9. FISCAL SPONSOR FEES. Noncommercial projects must use the non-profit status of a fiscal sponsor in order to receive tax-deductible grants and donations (unless the filmmaker has obtained his or her own non-profit status). Be sure to include at the end of your budget the fee that your fiscal sponsor charges. Currently, anything under 10% is considered a fair fee. Anything higher than that should get an explanatory note.

10. INCOME. Since most funders will provide only partial funding for your project, you must demonstrate how the rest of your budget will be raised. Create an "INCOME" section divided between these two categories: "Actual To-Date" and "Projected."

Within these categories you can list the actual and potential sources for funding your project (e.g., foundations, corporations, individuals, special events, etc.). If you have given money out of your pocket to produce the film, then do not list yourself as a donor. Instead, lump your money under "Miscellaneous Individual Donations."

Morrie Warshawski is a consultant and writer whose clients include film and video producers, arts organizations, and foundations. He is the author of *Shaking the Money Tree: How to Get Grants and Donations for Film and Video. www.warshawski.com*

ABOUT THE AUTHOR

Maureen A. Ryan, co-producer of the Academy Award™–winning film *Man on Wire*, is an independent producer based in New York concentrating on narrative feature films and documentaries. Her past work includes television, industrials, short films, and music videos. Ryan's credits include *Project Nim, Bomber, The Gates,* and *Wisconsin Death Trip.* Her projects have received numerous awards including a Peabody, regional Emmy, plus numerous awards from BAFTA, AICP, the Academy of Country Music (ACM), and the Country Music Association (CMA). She is an associate professor at Columbia University's Graduate Film program and author of *Producer to Producer: A Step-by-Step Guide to Low-Budget Independent Film Producing (www.ProducerToProducer.com).*

FILM PRODUCTION MANAGEMENT 2ND EDITION

MANAGEMENT AND COORDINATION IN A DIGITAL AGE

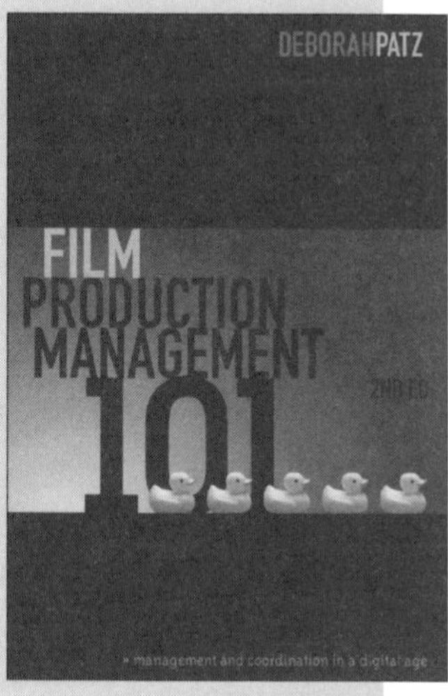

DEBORAH S. PATZ

Known as "the Swiss Army knife of production management," *Film Production Management 101* is actually two books in one – the essential open-on-the-desk guide for both production managers and coordinators. Patz takes you on a journey from development and pre-visualization to postproduction and audit, covering everything with detailed insights, humorous production stories and the inside scoop on working in film and television production.

Film Production Management 101 and Patz' previous *Surviving Production* were quickly adopted as "the" essential road map to the business and logistics of on-the-job film & television production since 1997. Originally developed from practical tools Patz created for her film and television production career, this new edition has undergone a comprehensive update to address the shifting balance between digital and film technologies and to pave the way as we progress further into the digital age. The book includes everything from budgeting, to managing the production office, to script revisions, to cost reporting, to copyright, to publicity, and much, much more. With Patz' penchant for sharing knowledge and her knack for communicating concepts, *Film Production Management 101* continues to be the book you have to have open on your desk for every prep, shoot, and wrap day. The more than 50 useful forms and checklists which are included (and downloadable) will save you time, money, and headaches, working like a pro right from day one.

"At last the complex relationship between the creation of a film and the day-to-day production management and coordination of that film is spelled out in clear, readable, and accurate detail. Deborah has written a wonderful book which should be extremely helpful to novice low-budget independent filmmakers and seasoned professionals alike."

– Sharon McGowan, Independent Producer and Assistant Professor
University of British Columbia Film Program

"An invaluable and comprehensive guide. Deborah Patz has drawn on her own experience and has written a thoroughly researched and helpful book."

– Norman Jewison, Producer/Director, *The Hurricane*, *Moonstruck*, *Fiddler on the Roof*

DEBORAH PATZ has been a filmmaker on award-winning productions since the mid-1980s, primarily as a production manager and coordinator, and then as production executive. She has worked with Lucasfilm, IMAX, MCA/Universal, Alliance/Atlantis, Nelvana, BBC, CBC, the Disney Channel, and the list goes on.

$39.95 · 500 PAGES · ORDER NUMBER 147RLS · ISBN: 9781932907773

24 HOURS | 1.800.833.5738 | WWW.MWP.COM

THE MYTH OF MWP

In a dark time, a light bringer came along, leading the curious and the frustrated to clarity and empowerment. It took the well-guarded secrets out of the hands of the few and made them available to all. It spread a spirit of openness and creative freedom, and built a storehouse of knowledge dedicated to the betterment of the arts.

The essence of the Michael Wiese Productions (MWP) is empowering people who have the burning desire to express themselves creatively. We help them realize their dreams by putting the tools in their hands. We demystify the sometimes secretive worlds of screenwriting, directing, acting, producing, film financing, and other media crafts.

By doing so, we hope to bring forth a realization of 'conscious media' which we define as being positively charged, emphasizing hope and affirming positive values like trust, cooperation, self-empowerment, freedom, and love. Grounded in the deep roots of myth, it aims to be healing both for those who make the art and those who encounter it. It hopes to be transformative for people, opening doors to new possibilities and pulling back veils to reveal hidden worlds.

MWP has built a storehouse of knowledge unequaled in the world, for no other publisher has so many titles on the media arts. Please visit www.mwp.com where you will find many free resources and a 25% discount on our books. Sign up and become part of the wider creative community!

Onward and upward,

Michael Wiese
Publisher/Filmmaker

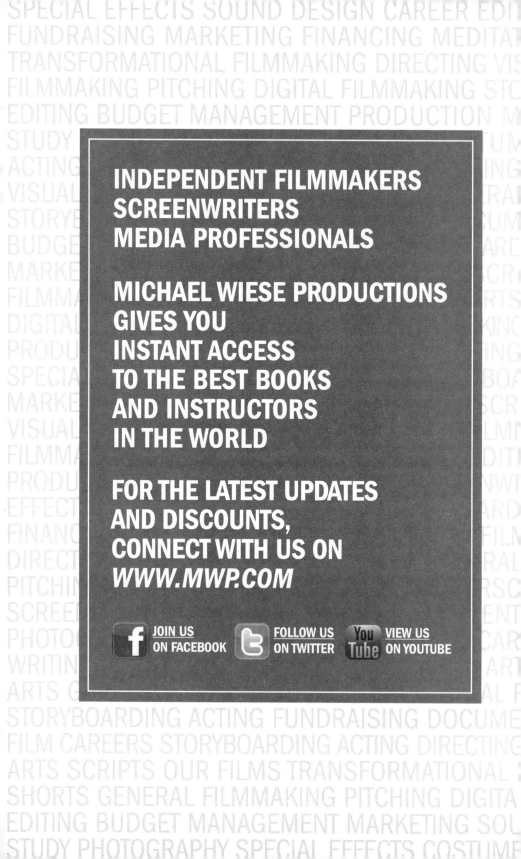